ISBN 978-1-332-91349-7
PIBN 10437245

THE WORKS

OF THE CELEBRATED

Mrs. CENTLIVRE.

IN THREE VOLUMES.

CONTAINING,

PERJUR'D HUSBAND.
BEAUX'S DUEL.
GAMESTER.
BASSET TABLE.
LOVE AT A VENTURE.
LOVE'S CONTRIVANCE.
BUSY BODY.
MARPLOT IN LISBON.
PLATONIC LADY.
PERPLEX'D LOVERS.
CRUEL GIFT.
WONDER, A WOMAN KEEPS A SECRET.
MAN'S BEWITCH'D.
GOTHAM ELECTION.
WIFE WELL MANAGED.
A BICKERSTAFF'S BURY-ING.
BOLD STROKE FOR A WIFE.
ARTIFICE.
STOLEN HEIRESS.

With a NEW ACCOUNT of her LIFE.

LONDON:

Printed for J. KNAPTON, C. HITCH and L. HAWES, J. and R. TONSON, S. CROWDER and Co. W. BATHOE, T. LOWNDS, T. CASLON, and G. KEARSLY.

M.DCC.LXI.

THE

WORKS

OF THE CELEBRATED

Mrs. CENTLIVRE.

IN THREE VOLUMES.

VOLUME THE FIRST.

CONTAINING,

The LIFE of the AUTHOR.
PERJUR'D HUSBAND.
BEAUX'S DUEL.
GAMESTER.
BASSET TABLE.
LOVE AT A VENTURE.
STOLEN HEIRESS.

LONDON:

Printed for J. KNAPTON, C. HITCH and L. HAWES, J. and R. TONSON, S. CROWDER and Co. W. BATHOE, T. LOWNDS, T. CASLON, and G. KEARSLY.

M.DCC.LXI.

TO THE

WORLD.

BE it known that the Person with Pen in Hand is no other than a Woman, not a little piqued to find that neither the Nobility nor Commonalty of the Year 1722, had Spirit enough to erect in *Westminster-Abbey*, a Monument justly due to the Manes of the never to be forgotten Mrs. *Centlivre*, whose Works are full of lively Incidents, genteel Language, and humourous Descriptions of real Life, and deserved to have been recorded by a Pen equal to that which celebrated the * Life of *Pythagoras*. Some Authors have had a *Shandeian* Knack of ushering in their own Praises, sounding their own Trumpet, calling Absurdity Wit, and boasting when they ought to blush; but our Poetess had Modesty, the general Attendant of Merit. She was even asham'd to proclaim her own great Genius, probably because the Custom of the Times discountenanced poetical Excellence in a Female. The Gentlemen of the Quill published it not, perhaps envying her superior Talents; and her Bookseller, complying with national Prejudices, put a fictious Name to her *Love's Contrivance*, thro' Fear that the Work shou'd be condemned, if known to be Feminine. With modest

* Madam *Dacier*.

Diffi-

THE

W O R L D

improve their Minds, furnish them with a more general Knowlege, and of course better fit them for Conversation, and the Management of Business. Have not Women Hearts largely filled with Humanity, and other social Virtues, Parts equally bright, a Discernment of Right and Wrong equally acute with those of Men? and of our Oratory, I call to Witness both *Europe* and *America* which have heard Mrs. DRUMMOND, with her *New Light*, leading Mankind from Darkness. We are allowed to have more native Modesty, that everlasting Charm, than the Sex that lords it over us, and I have oft observed, that the most ignorant amongst the Men are the most impudent, and from thence conclude that if our Sex had a better Education, it would decorate and add Charms to that Modesty. We have been depressed and taught to entertain an humble Idea of our Genius, which not being exerted, we lose the Influence we might have over our present Masters. Oft have I seen, in private Life, an illiterate churlish Fool of a Husband tyrannize over the Will, and with barbarous Insult, compel the Reason and good Sense of his Wife, to give Place to his Folly, and this on no better Foundation than Custom, established by Laws, the Handyworks only of Men.

Our Employment is chiefly in Retirement, and private Life, where our Actions, not being conspicuous, are little regarded; but the *present Days* have seen a Genius employed in translating, and illustrating, *Epictetus*, and the Empress of *Germany* convinces the World that she is a Politician fearless even of the Horrors of War.

A pleasing Prospect I've lately had, *viz.* the Work of the ingenious Lord *Corke*, and the not less ingenious Mr. *Samuel Johnson*, who have took Pains to translate a large Part of Father *Brumoy*'s *Greek* Theatre, and were not ashamed that their Labours should be joined to those of Mrs. *Lenox*. This convinces me that not only that barbarous Custom of denying Women to have Souls, begins to be rejected as foolish and absurd, but also that bold Assertion, that Female Minds are not capable of producing literary Works, equal even to those of *Pope*, now loses Ground, and probably the next Age may be taught by our Pens that our Geniuses have been hitherto cramped and smothered, but not extinguished, and that the Sovereignty which the male Part of the Creation have, until now, usurped over us, is unreasonably arbitrary:. And further, that our natural Abilities entitle us to a larger Share, not only in Literary Decisions, but that, with the present Directors, we are equally intitled to Power both in Church and State. To reform the first, was our Author's latest Employ, and she shewed herself Mistress of the Subject in her Treatise which discloses and confutes the Errors of the *Church of Rome*.

In her early Days she was inclined to be very gay, being left an Orphan before she was twelve Years of Age, her Father, Mr. *Freeman*, of *Holbeach*, in *Lincolnshire*, having at that Time been dead, nine Years; thus was the Princess of Dramatic Poets left without a Guide, but her native Wit soon brought her into Fame. The Spirit of Poetry was born with her, for before she was seven Years old she wrote a very pretty Song, and adapted it to a sprightly Tune, which became a distinguished Country-Dance.

Her Education was such as the Place of her Nativity afforded; where tho' she had but small Instruction, yet by Application to Books, she soon became Mistress of the *Latin*, *Italian*, *Spanish*, and *French* Tongues. Before she attained the Age of fifteen she was married to the Nephew of Sir *Stephen Fox*, who left her a young Widow of sixteen, which State she was soon persuaded to change, in Favour of Captain *Carrol*, who was killed in a Duel about a Year and a half after his Nuptials. Soon after, *viz.* in the twentieth Year of her Age, she wrote her Play of the *Perjured Husband*, and in a short Time gained some Eminence in the literary World. Her Wit procured her the Intimacy of the facetious Mr. *Farquhar*, and her theatrical Knowlege was the Cause of her great Intimacy with Mr. *Wilkes*, and Mrs. *Oldfield*; the latter distinguished our Poetess by speaking the Prologue to her first Play, and generally those great Actors filled the principal Characters in her Comic Performances.

At

At this Time an Intimacy was kept up betwixt her and the moſt eſteemed Writers of the Time. Sir *Richard Steele*, ſpeaking to the Public in his Tatler, thus mentions her *Buſy Body*; "The Plot and Inci-"dents of the Play are laid with that Subtlety and "Spirit which is peculiar to Females of Wit, and is "very ſeldom well performed by thoſe of the other "Sex, in whom Craft in Love is an Act of Inven-"tion, and not as with Women, the Effect of Nature and Inſtinct." Mr. *Rowe* favour'd her with his Friendſhip, aſſiſted her in compoſing the Tragedy called the *Cruel Gift*, and wrote the Prologue to her *Gameſter*.

After a Widowhood of about ten Years, Mrs. *Carrol* again ventured on the Marriage State with Mr. *Centlivre*, a *French* Gentleman, with whom ſhe lived comfortably for many Years, rich in Fame and poſſeſſed of Plenty, which annually aroſe from her Poetical Skill; and at her Death, which happened in 1722, when ſhe was near forty-five Years old, ſhe left many and valuable Ornaments of Gold and Jewels, preſented to her by the Royal Family, Prince *Eugene*, and Perſons of Diſtinction, but theſe Treaſures her Huſband did not long enjoy, for about a Year after he died, and was put into the ſame Grave, in the Pariſh Church of *St. Martin's in the Fields*. Thus drop'd ſhe, RARA AVIS IN TERRIS, after having by her own Works erected a Monument more laſting than that of Marble.

THE

The Perjur'd Husband:

OR, THE

Adventures of VENICE.

A

TRAGEDY.

PREFACE.

I SHOULD *not trouble my Reader with a Preface, if Mr.* Collier *had taught Manners to* Masks, *Sense to* Beaus, *and Good-nature to* Criticks, *as well as Morality to the Stage; the first are sure to envy what they can't equal, and condemn what they don't understand; the* Beaus *usually take a greater Liberty with our Sex than they wou'd with their own, because there's no Fear of drawing a Duel upon their Hands: the latter are a Sort of rude splenatick Men, that seldom commend any thing but what they have had a Hand in. These snarling Sparks were pleased to carp at one or two Expressions, which are spoken in 'em Aside by one of the inferior Characters in the Drama; and without considering the Reputation of the Persons in whose Mouths the Language is put, condemn it strait for loose and obscure: Now (with Submission to better Judges) I cannot believe that a Prayer-Book should be put into the Hands of a Woman, whose innate Virtue won't secure her Reputation; nor is it reasonable to expect a Person, whose Inclinations are always forming Projects to the Dishonour of her Husband, should deliver her Commands to her Confident in the Words of a Psalm. I heartily wish that those that find Fault with the Liberty of my Stile, wou'd be pleased to set a Pattern to the Town, by retrenching some of their Debaucheries, for Modesty thrives best by Example. Modest Language from the truly Virtuous is expected; I mean such as will neither act ill, nor suffer ill to be acted: It is not enough that* Lucy *says she's honest, in having denied the Brutal Part; whoever thinks Virtue centers in that, has a wrong Notion of it; no, Virtue is a tender Plant, which cannot live in tainted*

Ground; Virtue is what the Air of Flattery cannot blast, nor the vile sordid Dress of Gain poison; and she that can withstand these two Shocks, may be stil'd truly Virtuous. I ask my Reader's Pardon for my Bluntness, but I hope none of my Sex so qualified will condemn me for exposing the Vices of the seeming Religious.

I fear there are but too many hit by the Character of Signora Pizalta; *I wish, for the sake of the reverse Party, there were fewer, or they better known, since the malicious World are so apt to judge of Peoples Inclinations by the Company they keep; which is sometimes authentic, but not always an infallible Rule. I shall say little in Justification of the Play, only desire the Reader to judge impartially, and not condemn it by the Shortness of its Life, since the Season of the Year never promised much better Success. It went off with general Applause; and it is the Opinion of some of our best Judges, that it only wanted the Addition of good Actors, and a full Town, to have brought m ea Sixth Night, there having been worse Plays, within this Twelve-month, approv'd of.*

THE

PROLOGUE.

By a GENTLEMAN.

Spoken by Mrs. OLDFIELD.

SUCH dreadful Laws of late 'gainſt Wit are made,
It dares not in the City ſhow its Head.
No Place is ſafe; each Cuckold turns Informer,
If we make merry—it muſt be in a Corner.
And here's To-night, what doubly makes it ſweet,
A private Table, and a Lady's Treat:
At her Reflections none can be uneaſy,
When the kind Creature does her beſt to pleaſe ye.
Humbly ſhe ſues, and 'tis not for your Glory
T'inſult a Lady—when ſhe falls before ye.
But ſince no human Wit can ſtand the Teſt,
With Gorman! *and the* Champion of the Weſt!
She'll fill the Liſts, and then you cannot ſlight her,
(With Honour ſafe) for ſhe's a fair Inviter.
Expects no Favour, but at Honour's Call,
Defies the boldeſt Briton *of you all;*
Whate'er's her Fate, ſhe's ſure to gain the Field,
For Women always conquer, when they yield.

Dramatis Personæ.

MEN.

Count Bassino, *a* Savoyard, *married to* Placentia, *and in Love with* Aurelia,	*Mr.* Mills.
Armando, Bassino's *Friend*,	*Mr.* Simpson.
Alonzo, *a* Venetian *Gentleman, betrothed to* Aurelia,	*Mr.* Thomas.
Pizalto, *a Noble* Venetian,	*Mr.* Norris.
Ludovico, *a* Frenchman,	*Mr.* Fairbank.

WOMEN.

Placentia, Bassino's *Wife*,	*Mrs.* Kent.
Aurelia, *a young* Venetian *Lady, betrothed to* Alonzo, *but in Love with* Bassino,	*Mrs.* Oldfield.
Forella, *her Woman*,	*Mrs.* Baker.
Lady Pizalta, Pizalto's *Wife*,	*Mrs.* Moore.
Lucy, *her Woman*,	*Mrs.* Lucas.

Masters, Dancers, Singers, and Attendants.

SCENE, VENICE, in Carnival-Time.

THE

THE PERJUR'D HUSBAND.

ACT I. SCENE I.

The Curtains fly up, and discover a Mask in Pizalto's *House.* Pizalto, *Lady* Pizalta, Lucy; Ludovico *talking to Lady* Pizalta; Bassino *and* Aurelia *talking together*; Florella *and other Maskers.*

A Spanish *Entry.*

While the Dance is performing, enter Armando, *and gives* Bassino *two Letters, which he opens and reads.*
Lady Pizalta *and* Lucy *advance to the Front of the Stage.*

Lady Pizalta.

OH! *Lucy*, I'm undone——
That Stranger there has charm'd my Heart: I feel
The Pow'r of conquering Love; quick, quickly tell me,
What shall I do to ease this racking Passion?

Lucy. Nay, Madam, I fancy your Passion has little Occasion for Lenitives; it blazes so violently at first, 'tis like to be soon extinguish'd.

L. *Piz.* Dear *Lucy*, don't trifle with me; but contrive, imagine, do any thing, to bless thy Love-sick Mistress

 with

with the Sight of that dear Man: And as an Earnest of further Rewards, here, take this———

[*Gives her a Ring.*

Lucy. Madam, I receive your Commands with much Joy, but your Present with more——— [*Aside.*] I'll try what this projecting Brain can do, and if you step into the next Room, I'll soon give you an Account of my Proceedings. [*Exit L.* Pizalta.

Bass. Ye Gods!
What have I done, that you pursue me thus!
Why did you e'er decree that I should wed
A Wife I now must hate? Why did I see
The bright *Aurelia?* Why am I thus torn
'Twixt Love and Duty? Oh! what Pangs, what Torments
My Soul endures! Oh! my *Aurelia!*

[*Exeunt omnes, but* Lucy *&* Ludov.

Lucy *pulling* Ludovico *by the Sleeve.*

Lucy. Sir, Sir, one Word with you.

Lud. Your Business———

Lucy. May one ask you a civil Question, and be resolv'd?

Lud. Hum—A civil Question, sayst thou? What's it, prithee, a Night's Lodging? If so, pull off thy Mask, and I'll resolve thee instantly——But I never strike Bargains in the Dark.

Lucy. I don't know, Sir, but it may tend to that, by way of Proxy, at the long-run: But at present my Commission reaches no further than to know your Lodgings; if any Thing comes on't, I fancy 'twill not displease you.

Lud (Aside.) Hum——This is but a Pettifogger in Intrigues, I find——Egad, I'm like to be pretty well employ'd during the Carnival——Well, considering I am a Stranger here, this Hit may be a lucky one, and the Lady handsome——Egad, I'll fancy her so at least, wer't but for the Pleasure of Expectation.

Lucy. What are you studying, Sir? Are you so long resolving whether you shall accept a Lady's Favour, or no?

Lud. No, faith, Child: I am not over-scrupulous in those Matters———Let her be but Woman, and we shan't disagree——— And so thou mayst tell her——There's a Direction for thee. [*Tears the Superscription of a Letter and gives it her.* [*Exit* Ludovico.

Lucy. Frank and easy, *a la mode de Paris*——Well, these indifferent Sparks charm more than all your cringing Fops——Now for my Business—Let me see——I'll to my Lady, she'll write; I'll carry the Letter, and the Devil will turn Saint, if I don't bring 'em together, and merit a further Recompence

By Coupling many have their Fortunes made;
I only want Preferment, not my Trade.

[*Exit* Lucy.

SCENE II.

The Scene changes to Bassino's *Lodgings, and discovers the Count in his Night-gown, a Table with Lights, and Letters lying on the Table.*

Bass. All Things lie hush'd in peaceful Silence here:
All but *Bassino*'s Mind——Oh! happy he
Who lives secure and free from Love's Alarms.
But happier far, who, Master of himself,
Ranges abroad without that Clog, a Wife.
Oh! rigorous Laws impos'd on Free-born Man!
On Man, by bounteous Nature first design'd
The Sovereign Lord of all the Universe!
Why must his generous Passion thus be starv'd,
And be confin'd to one alone?
The Woman, whom Heaven sent as a Relief,
To ease the Burden of a tedious Life,
And be enjoy'd when summon'd by Desire,
Is now become the Tyrant of our Fates. [*Takes up a Letter.*
But hold, *Bassino!* whither does thy Passion
Hurry thy wandering Reason: Let this Letter
Re-call the Fugitive, and fix thy Senses
On duteous Love————A Wife, so young, so fair,
So excellent, whose Charms not three Months since
Did fire thy Soul; a Wife, who dotes on thee;
A Wife to whom thou sworest eternal Love———
By Heaven, I swear again I will be true.
This Thought again restores my Peace of Mind——
No, charming Wife; no dear *Placentia*, no.
Thou shalt not beg in vain: I will return. [*Kisses the Letter.*
But who comes here—My Friend *Armando?*

Enter Armando.

Arm. Dear Friend, I heard
The Conflict of your Passion, and my Joys
Are now compleat, since Virtue gains the Day.
Bass. Yes, dear *Armando*, the Conflict is o'er,
And I'm resolv'd to fly to my *Placentia*.
Arm. Cherish that Thought: By Heaven your Resolution
Transports my Soul with Joy!
A kind, a virtuous Wife waits your Embraces;
A Wife, who like a Turtle mourns the Absence
Of her dear Mate. Haste then, my Friend, to drive
That Cloud of Sorrow which o'ercasts her Mind,
And, like the Sun, dispel her gloomy Thoughts.
Bass. Thanks for your Counsel———
You like a God support my feeble Virtue.
This very Morning I'll prepare for *Turin*,
Where Time and Absence will deface the Image
Of that bewitching Beauty, which now haunts
My tortur'd Mind—Yet, first I'll take my Leave
Of this fair Charmer———And Heaven grant
That I may see her unconcern'd———
Arm. My Lord, what d'you mean?
Have you well weigh'd the Danger of this Visit?
Bass. What Danger can there be?
Arm. Danger! my Lord—Consider well how feeble
Our Reason is against the Pow'r of Beauty———
Bass. My Resolution's firm; no Charm can shake it.
Arm. If not her Beauty, fear her Syren Tongue;
Fear her endearing Prayers, her fond Reproaches,
Her tender Sighs, her Vows, her trickling Tears.
Nay—if all these prove vain, fear her Despair,
A Woman, an abandon'd Woman's Rage.
Bass. Were there more Dangers, yet I'll stand 'em all;
My Honour bids me pay this parting Visit:
My Heart shall have no Share in what I'll speak.
Trust me this once, and be yourself a Witness,
Bassino can controul unlawful Love.———
Arm. My Lord, 'tis with Regret I see you go,
May Heaven assist you in this dangerous Strife.

SCENE

SCENE III.

Aurelia's *Chamber; she in an Undress with* Florella.

Aur. No more of that—Cease thy ungrateful Suit,
Alonzo is a Man I cannot love;
I own he's witty, generous, and brave;
Has all the Charms that Nature can bestow
To fire a Woman's Heart———Yet I'm insensible,
His very Sight chills all my trembling Spirits;
Therefore, name him no more—I charge thee do not.
Flor. Madam, I've done—Yet shall I be permitted
To ask a Question? Are you then resolved
Ne'er to admit a Passion in your Breast?
Aur. Oh! Dear *Florella*, press not a Confession,
Which but too well my Eyes themselves disclose.
Alas! I love—I love to such Excess,
That tho' I know I'm lov'd again, my Mind
Is still perplex'd with Doubts and jealous Fears.
Flor. You love and are belov'd! Then sure you reach
The Height of human Bliss, and bounteous Heaven
Can scarce give more——But who's the happy Man;
Is it not Count *Bassino*?
Aur. Oh! charming Name; there's Musick in that Sound!
Yes, Count *Bassino* is the Man I love.
Canst thou now blame my Coldness to *Alonzo*?
Flor. Forgive me, Madam, if I dare presume
To speak my Sentiments: I must confess
Bassino is a Man of excellent Virtue;
His Education at the Court of *Savoy*
Has still refin'd what he receiv'd from Nature;
His Person too is charming———
And, what most Women court, he has a Title——
But then consider, you are unacquainted
With his Estate, and tho' his Equipage
Denotes an ample Fortune, yet we see
Many a Stranger here, during the Carnival,
Who makes a Figure by industrious Gaming.
As for *Alonzo*, he was born at *Venice*,

Of noble Parents; his Estate, a large one——
Even from his Youth you had his amorous Wishes,
And as he grew in Years his Love increas'd:
You lov'd him too——Nay, which is more, your Father
Approv'd your mutual Loves, and at his Death
Bequeath'd you to *Alonzo*.

Aur. Oh! my *Florella*, thou hast rouz'd a Thought,
Which will for ever break *Aurelia*'s Rest.
I know my Father's Tenderness to me
Made him confirm *Alonzo*'s Suit, for then
I lov'd *Alonzo*——
But were my gentle Father still alive,
I'm sure he would not cross my Inclinations,
But, Oh! name not my Father; I cannot bear
The sad Remembrance of so great a Loss. [*Weeps.*

Flor. But fear you not t'offend his peaceful Ghost,
By breaking with the Man he destin'd yours?

Aur. 'Tis not my Fault: and just Heaven must forgive
What Heaven decrees——Yes, 'tis my cruel Stars
That made my Heart inconstant to *Alonzo*,
'Tis with Regret I break my plighted Faith;
In vain I strive to check my new-born Love,
cannot, cannot live without *Bassino*.

Flor. Madam, I wish your Passion ne'er prove fatal,
But much I fear this inauspicious Match.

Enter Bassino, Armando.

Aur. May Heaven avert th' unlucky Combination
Of our presaging Thoughts: For, know, I tremble too—
But here's the Man that will dispel my Fears.

Arm. to *Bass.* My Lord, remember
To keep your Resolution.

Bass. to *Arm.* Yes—I will keep it—[To *Aur.*] Madam, you will pardon
A Morning Visit, when you know what Reasons
Press'd me to fix it on this early Hour.——
By Letters from the Court I was last Night
Commanded to return with Speed to *Turin*,
And thence set out for *France*, to represent
My Sovereign Liege in solemn Embassy.

This

This Day I must prepare to take my Journey,
Tho' 'tis with killing Grief I leave my dear,
My fair *Aurelia*——— [To *Arm.*] Now, my *Armando*.

Arm. My Lord, 'tis well: But still be on your Guard,
The dreadful Shock comes on———

Aur. This Day be gone! What means my Lord!
Oh! Heaven,
My boding Fears are come to pass: I see
A Cloud of Woes just ready to o'erwhelm me.
Is't possible! how can that Form divine
Harbour such Treachery! Is then *Bassino* false?
Say, perjur'd Man, how often did you swear
This happy Day should make you mine for ever!
How can you now forget your solemn Vows?
Why have I met with this inhuman Usage?

Bass. Madam, my Prince's Orders
Are absolute: My Honour is concern'd.

Aur. Must a vain Title be preferr'd to Love?
But no—You never lov'd——'twas base Deceit.
Curs'd, curs'd dissembling Men! Their flattering Tongues
Can feign a Passion that will look like Love,
Till by Degrees they get us in their Power;
Then with bold Impudence they draw the Vizor,
And shew the Cheat that mock'd our credulous Hopes.
Faithless *Bassino*,
How oft you swore your Love could ne'er expire:
How oft you swore one Smile of mine had Charms,
Even above the Glories of a Crown.
Those were the Oaths I fondly did believe;
Those Words convey'd a Poison to my Heart,
And even now I feel its mighty Force:
My Head turns giddy, and my trembling Knees
Betray their sinking Burden———
Alas! I faint, I die———

[*She faints*, Bassino *runs and embraces her.*

Bass. Oh! stay, my Love, my Life, my Soul, my all:
The Conflict's past, and I am thine again,
But she is breathless! Oh! ye rigorous Gods,
Give back her Soul, or let my own be plung'd
To dark *Elysium*——Oh! my dear *Aurelia*! [*Hugs her.*

Arm. Is this your Resolution? By Heaven, I blush

To call you Friend. Your Wife, my Lord, remember
Your Wife———

Baſſ. Curſe on that Name———
Urge me no more to follow your Chimera's,
Leſt you oblige me to break off that Friendſhip
You bluſh to own——Oh! my *Aurelia!*

Arm. aſide. How ſweet is treacherous Vice! how ea- [gerly
Fond Man purſues his Ruin!
All Arguments were vain——yet ſtill one Way remains,
Which cannot fail, to ſtop the Progreſs of this impious [Love.
His Wife, by my Direction, comes to *Venice:*
Her Sight will ſoon awake his ſlumbering Virtue,
At leaſt it will retrieve *Aurelia*'s Senſes. [*Exit* Armando.

Aur. recovering. Where am I? Where's my Lord, my falſe *Baſſino?*

Baſſ. Here, here, my Soul, my charming Dear.

Aur. thruſts him off. Hold off—Approach me not—urge not my Rage,
Or with this Dagger I'll revenge my Wrongs
On thy perfidious Heart———But, oh! his Heart's too hard,
Even for temper'd Steel—Therefore I'll ſheath it here.

[*Offers at her Breaſt:* Baſſino *ſnatches the Dagger, and throws himſelf at her Feet in a diſtracted Manner.*

Baſſ. Oh! hold———forbid it Gods!
I am the curſed Cauſe, and I muſt die.
Oh! who could bear my Load of mortal Woe!
Ye heavenly Powers beſtow the Stroke of Grace,
And rack *Baſſino:* Let your vengeful Thunder
Now cruſh my guilty Head———Or thou, Oh! Parent Earth,
Open thy Boſom, and conceal my Crime. [*Tears the Ground.*

Aur. Is he then mine again! [*Falls down.*
Look up, my Lord, my Love, my Life!
My dear *Baſſino*! 'Tis *Aurelia* calls.
Let me for ever fold thee in my Arms,
And beg thou'lt never ſpeak of parting more.
[*Embraces him.*

Both riſe and embrace in an Extaſy.

Baſſ. Oh! never, never———

The

The Poles shall meet, the Sun and Moon invert
Their wonted Motion e're I part from thee.
I fondly try'd how much I was belov'd,
And since you're true, my Bliss is now compleat.

Aur. Was't but a Trial? then my Griefs are vanish'd,
And I am lost in Joy———*Bassino*'s mine;
[*They embrace again.*

Bass. Thine, thine for ever: And this happy Day,
Shall end *Aurelia*'s Fears———Ha———
This Day, said I, but where's *Placentia* then?
My Wife *Placentia!* Little does she think
What Baseness I intend—Oh! racking Thought!
But 'tis resolv'd, I'll change nor think no more:
I'll try to plunge, and reach the blissful Shore;
And if I sink, yet still this Hope's my Friend,
I'll snatch my Treasure e're my Course I end. [*Aside.*

Aur. My Lord, what makes you pause?

Bass. The ravishing Thoughts of mighty Joys to come
Kept me in Extasy and made me dumb;
When on thy snowy Breast dissolv'd I lie,
What Monarch can there be more blest than I?
[Bassino *leads her off with a languishing Air.*

Enter Alonzo.

Alon. Sure, if my Eyes deceive me not, I saw
Aurelia with the Count just parting hence:
Dissolv'd in Love, and languishing they seem'd.
Damnation———
I cannot bear the Thought—I'll after 'em.

Alonzo *going.* *Enter* Florella.

Flor. aside. Ha———*Alonzo* here! I must prevent a Discovery,

Alon. Florella here! she comes opportunely——she may inform me of what I yet but fear———Good-morrow, *Florella*: How fares my Love, my dear *Aurelia?*

Flor. Signior, Good-morrow; you are an early Visitant.

Alon. Not for a Man in Love; but answer me, How does *Aurelia?*

Flor.

Flor. Well in Health——Only she's now and then in a little Fit of Melancholy, such as usually proceeds from timorous Doubts about that dreadful State of Matrimony. You know the Time draws nigh that gives her to your Arms.

Alon. By Heaven! 'Tis an Age, there's six Days yet to come.

Flor. An Age, indeed, if he knew all. [*Aside.*

Alon. But haste, *Florella*; lead me to my Dear,
She only can contract that tedious Age
Of lingring Pain, and sooth it with her Smiles.
Say, is she alone?

Flor. Yes——No——
Oh! Heaven! What shall I say? [*Aside.*
She's, she's a————

Alon. Ha——What means this faultering Answer?
All's not right, and my Suspicion's true.

Flor. Signior, my Lady is not drest, and I shall displease her, in admitting even you, without her Leave.

Alon. Ha——not drest——Take heed you mock me not;
Nor think to blind me with your feign'd Excuse:
For in your guilty Face I read the Truth.
Come, tell me who's with her? is't not *Bassino*?

Flor. aside. Oh! Heaven! What shall I say?

Alon. Nay, nay, no Study: Lying will not do:
I saw 'em part from hence, just now I saw 'em.
Harkee; sweet Mistress, how long have you practis'd
This subtle Trade? I find you're much improv'd.
Hell and Damnation————quickly, tell me
What did *Bassino* give for his Admittance?
I'll double the Reward—but she's not drest for me——
Oh! damn'd, damn'd Sex!

Flor. Signior, what do you mean?

Alon. To see *Aurelia*——see her instantly————
Nay by Heaven! I will: All Opposition's vain:
For by th' avenging Power of Love I swear,
Tho' in *Bassino*'s Arms, I'll drag her thence,
Only to cast her from my Sight for ever:
Nor shall he live to triumph in my Shame.
What tho' the Marriage Rites be not perform'd,

Yet I may call her Wife. Her Father gave her to me:
And her own Vows have fix'd my Heart in her's.
Must then *Alonzo* be deny'd Admittance,
Under that poor Pretence that she's not drest?
Whilst base *Bassino* lies dissolv'd in Pleasures
On her perfidious Breast——Oh! killing Thought!
She makes my Name of Husband infamous,
Even before the Priest has join'd our Hands.
I'll in, and if th' Affront I tamely bear,
May Heaven deny me at my latest Prayer.

[*Exeunt.*

SCENE IV. Ludovico's *Lodgings.*

Ludovico *solus.*

Lud. Who waits?

Enter Mountaine.

Mount. Did you call, Sir?

Lud. *Mountaine*, run to Signiora *Ronquilla*, and tell her I have done with her for ever, if she does not send this Evening the hundred Ducats she promised to lend me——And harkee, as you come back, acquaint Signiora *Cornara* I shall be busy To-morrow, and desire she will put off her Visit till another Day.

[*Knocking at the Door.*

Mount. Sir, there's somebody at the Door.

Lud. See who 'tis.

Mount. Sir, a Gentlewoman desires to speak with you.

Lud. A Gentlewoman! admit her——Well,
'Tis a great Fatigue to oblige the whole Sex.

Enter Lucy.

Oh! what News from your Lady?

Lucy. This will inform you, Sir. [*Gives him a Letter.*

Lud. reads. Hum, hum, a Letter——*Tho' it may seem improper for one of my Sex to make the first Step in an Amour, yet you ought to consider, that the rigorous Confinement*

finement we are under all the Year round, may, in some Measure, excuse the Liberties we take during the Carnival. If you have the Courage to meet me, I shall be at four in the Afternoon in the Piazza d'Espagna, *invisible to all but yourself.*——Well, I believe all Women in *Venice* are wild for Gallants.

Lucy. Sir, what Answer shall I return to my Lady?

Lud. aside. Egad——I am in Doubt whether I shall throw my Time away on this Intrigue or no——Harkee Child, step into the next Chamber, and I'll answer your Message instantly—— [*Exit* Lucy. Let me see—— [*Reads in his Table-Book*] *Monday*, at Two in the Afternoon, I am to meet Signiora *Belleza* at her Nurse's——She's a pretty Rogue, and so I'll go—At Three of the Clock, Signiora *Dorinda*, the Senator's Wife, at the *Indian* House——Pshaw, she's an old Acquaintance,——I shan't go——At half an Hour past Three, the Countess *Wrinkle*, who presented me with a Gold-hilted Sword——Silly Fool! does she think I'll bestow one of my Visits on an old shrivelled Piece of Antiquity, for a trifling Present, not worth above threescore Pistoles——At a Quarter past Four, my Semstress *Dorothy Steenkirk*, who supplies me with Linen,—Oh! this Visit may be put off for a new Intrigue—And so I'll acquaint the Messenger. [*Exit* Ludovico.

The End of the First Act.

ACT II. SCENE I.

A Chamber in Signior Pizalto's *House.*

Enter Lady Pizalta, Lucy.

Lady *Piz.* DID you deliver my Letter to *Ludovico*, *Lucy*?

Lucy. Madam, I did; I found him in his Study, reading the Lover's Watch, which he swears does not at all

agree

agree with his Conſtitution. He hates Injunctions of Love, like thoſe of Penance: For the one, ſays he, is no more pleaſurable to the Body, than the other beneficial to the Soul.

L. *Piz.* What a fine Gallant I'm like to have with theſe Principles! Well——what did he ſay to a Summons from a Woman of my Quality? Did it not make him wiſh the Time of Aſſignation were ſooner than the Appointment in the Letter?

Lucy. He firſt hum'd over your Billet; and pauſing a while, he deſired me to ſtay for an Anſwer in a next Room; then coming to me, he aſk'd me what Countrywoman you were? For, ſaid he, if ſhe ſhould prove an old Acquaintance, I would uſe her damnably—But when I had aſſured him you never ſaw the Outſide of theſe Walls, he began to have that Deſire which all Men have to a new Face.

L. *Piz.* Very well; and what then?

Luc. He ſtrait enquir'd whether you were black, brown, fair, old, young, Maid, Wife or Widow? I told him you was a wretched Wife to an old, impotent, rich, covetous, noble *Venetian*; beautiful, young, generous, and of a fair Complexion. He hugg'd me at theſe Words, ſeem'd tranſported with the News, and ſwore that in Intrigues a Wife was moſt ſuitable to his Temper; for, ſaid he, there's neither Children to father, nor Honour to repair: And where his Pocket and Liberty are ſafe, he is contented to venture his Body and Soul.

L. *Piz.* Excellent Maxims!

Lucy. In ſhort, Madam, he ſays he has had ſeveral Bills of this Nature drawn upon him of late, and how much his Stock may be exhauſted, he knows not; but however he'll meet you, and if he cannot anſwer your Expectation, he'll give you Earneſt.

L. *Piz.* You talk merrily, Girl; I hope you did not tell my Name. I ſhould be loath to truſt a Man of his Character with my Reputation at firſt Daſh.

Luc. No, Madam, I only told your Quality.

L. *Piz.* That's well: Oh! Reputation, what ſeveral Sorts of Slavery do we undergo to preſerve thee! for to

be

be thought virtuous, we are forced to be constantly railing against Vice, tho' our Tongues and Maxims seldom agree.

Lucy. Alas! Madam, that Pretence is grown too common: For the Men now take it for granted, that a Lady is very near surrendering, when once she holds out that Flag of Defiance.

L. *Piz.* Well—Men use us very barbarously: They will neither suffer us to be honest, nor allow us to be thought so———Here, take this Key, and secure every thing that concerns my Reputation: And if my Husband wakes ere I come back, you may easily find some Excuses to prevent his Enquiries: for the Carnival allows us more Liberty, than at other times we dare pretend to——— I know thy Honesty, and will rely upon't.

Lucy. Yes, indeed, Madam, I am honest at the Bottom.

L. *Piz.* Well, I'll be gone: 'Tis about the Hour. [*Ex.* L. *Piz.*

Enter Pizalto.

Lucy. Good Luck attend you, Madam———Oh! Heavens! here's my Lord————Madam, Madam, Madam———Oh! Lord, what shall I say, now she's gone?

Piz. Hist, hist, *Lucy:* Don't, don't, don't call your Lady, for I have a Word or two to say to thee in private, and have waited for this lucky Opportunity a great while———

Lucy, aside. Now *Venus* be prais'd, I hope he has found some Business of his own, that may give my Lady an Opportunity to mind her's.

Piz. Well, *Lucy,* well,—canst thou guess my Business now?

Lucy. No, indeed, Sir—But I'm certain, an old Man's Business can't be great. [*Aside.*

Piz. [*Gives her a Looking-glass.*] Here, Child, this will tell thee—Look in't, look in't, I say————Ah! ah! thou hast a pretty pouting Lip, a delicate roguish Eye; such an Ogle, such a Cast——Ah! Rogue—— Faith, thou'rt very pretty: And, in short, if any one

rival

rival thy Lady, it will be thee, *Lucy*————Egad, I have Fire in me, yet,

Lucy, aside. O' my Conſcience, and little too, I believe: Yet I wiſh he has enough to ſerve my Ends. I'll make my Fortune————Lord, Sir, what do you mean? I rival my Lady! Heaven forbid; I would not injure ſo good a Woman for the World————

Piz. Pſhaw, pſhaw—Where's the Injury done to her, Child? Adod, I'll give thee a hundred Crowns.

Lucy. No Injury, ſay you, my Lord? Why, I wonder you ſhould be ſo jealous of my Lady, and preach ſuch religious Maxims to her, when your own Principles are quite oppoſite.

Piz. Look ye, Child, a Man may do that, which would look abominable in a Wife———A Woman's Reputation is a nice Thing——

Lucy. 'Tis ſo———and therefore 'tis but Reaſon I ſhould take Care of mine.

Piz. Prithee, no more of that: Thy Reputation ſhall be ſafe; I'll marry thee to my Gentleman.

Lucy. Gentleman—Valet! Faugh—And what Good will a hundred Crowns do me, when my Virginity is gone? Indeed, if you lov'd me as much as you ſay, and would make my Fortune, (for I ſhould love extreamly to be a Lady) I cannot tell how far you might perſuade me———I know my Reputation would be ſafe in your Hands.

Piz. Make thy Fortune! Why, I've known ſome of our Nobles marry a Wife with leſs than a hundred Crowns———But adod, thou'rt a charming Girl, and therefore I'll make it a hundred Piſtoles—What ſay'ſt thou now, *Lucy?* Ah! adod, I muſt buſs thee; [*Kiſſes her.*] Ah! Rogue, methinks I'm a young, luſty, vigorous Fellow again————Thou ſhalt find I am, Girl.

Lucy, aside. I believe I ſhall fail you, old Gentleman. Well, my Lord, make it up a thouſand Piſtoles, and I am your's, elſe I'll die a Maid, I'm reſolv'd.

Piz. A thouſand Piſtoles, why thou art the moſt unconſcionable Wench in *Italy:* Why, 'tis a Price for a Dutcheſs in ſome Countries. Come, come, prithee be reaſonable, *Lucy?*

Lucy.

Lucy. Reasonable! why you don't ask a reasonable Thing———Look you, you know my Mind, I'll not bate a Penny——I'll warrant my Lady will give me two hundred at least for my Discovery. [*Going.*

Piz. aside. Udslife! she won't tell my Wife, sure, I'm ruin'd if she does; I'd rather give her two thousand ——— Hold, hold, *Lucy*, sweet *Lucy*, prithee come back ——— Faith, thou'rt so charming, I can deny thee nothing———Come, it shall be what thou wilt——Come now, Rogue, let's retire to thy Chamber———

Lucy. Nay, nay, no entring the Premises, till you have paid the Purchase.———

Piz. Adod, thou'rt a Wag ——— Come in then, and I'll discharge the Debt: Thou art a cunning Gipsy. [*Exit* Pizal.

Lucy. You shall have Reason to say so, e're I have done with you, old Gentleman———For I am resolv'd to shew you a Trick, and preserve my Virtue. [*Aside.*

For did base Men within my Power fall,
T' avenge my injur'd Sex, I'd jilt 'em all.
And would but Women follow my Advice,
They should be glad at last to pay our Price.

[*Exit* Lucy.

SCENE II.

The Piazza d'Espagna *in* Venice.

Enter Lady Pizalta *sola.*

L. *Piz.* Not come yet! ungrateful Man! must a Woman of my Quality wait?
How have we lost our Pow'r since the Creation?
When the whole World had but one single Lord,
Whom every Creature readily obey'd?
Yet he, that mighty he, caught with a Smile,
Flew to th'Embraces of the tempting Fair.
But now each puny Sinner dares to cross
A Woman's Inclinations———

Enter

Enter Ludovico.

Oh! are you come, Signior? I ſuppoſe you have
Some other Aſſignation, that made you miſs
My Hour——Purſue it pray——I'll not interrupt you—
Your Servant——— [*Going.*
I hope he'll not take me at my Word. [*Aſide.*

Lud. Nay, nay, Signiora, why this Paſſion? [*Stops her.*
You ſent me a Challenge, and I, like a Man of Courage, am come to anſwer it———Pray don't let a Quarter of an Hour break Squares——I own it was a Fault to make a Lady wait; but Friends, Madam, Friends and good Wine are the Devil———Come I'll make you amends.

L. *Piz.* Friends and good Wine! I ſuppoſe thoſe Friends were Female ones———

Lud. No, Faith: You ſhall judge of that———But ſuppoſe they were——Why ſhould you be angry that I did not fly with the deſired Haſte, as long as I am come time enough to give you Satisfaction——Beſides, I han't ſeen your Face yet, and for aught I know, it mayn't reward my Complement in coming now——Prithee, Child, unmaſk, and then I'll tell thee more of my Mind.

L. *Piz.* The Devil take this Fellow——and yet methinks I love him for his Indifferency——[*Aſide.*] You talk as if you were unſkill'd in the Art of Love: Don't you know that Expectation feeds more than twenty taſted Pleaſures?

Lud. Hum——ſome Sort of Fops it may: But I'm none of thoſe——I never give my Opinion of a Diſh till I've taſted; neither do I care to dine often on one Sort of Meat without changing the Sauce——But when that Cloud's withdrawn, how long I ſhall keep my Reſolution I know not.

L. *Piz.* Say you ſo! Why then the only Way to preſerve your Appetite is to feed you ſlenderly; or only let you ſee the food, but not to taſte.

Lud. Faith, Madam, I'm no Camelion, but Fleſh and Blood———Therefore theſe Preſcriptions are of no

Uſe

Use——One Sight of that dear charming Face of your's, would be more obliging to your humble Servant.

L. *Piz. unmasks.* Well, Sir, what think you? Is there any thing in this Face worth your Regard?

Lud. Ah! by Heaven, an Angel——Oh! Madam, now blame yourself for my Neglect, for had you sent the Picture of her, in whom all those Beauties center, I had in this Place waited the Coming of my Goddess, or rather flown on the Wings of eager Love, to meet my Fair, tho' in the Arms of ten thousand Dangers——Say, my charming Angel, do you forgive me? But why do I ask? your Eyes assure me you do; at least I'll force a Pardon from these dear, soft, ruby Lips.

[*Kisses her in Extasy.*

L. *Piz.* Hold, hold! been't so lavish——a sparing Gamester is the likeliest to keep in Stock——whilst a profuse Hand at one Cast throws all he has away.

Lud. To fear that, were to doubt your Charms, in which a Lover is sure to find constant Supplies——But we lose Time——Let's retire to my Lodgings, where I'll give thee the best Proofs of my Love I can?

L. *Piz. aside.* Well! He's a charming Fellow——Oh! how happy are Wives in *France* and *England*, where such as he swarm!

Lud. Come, Madam, come——Why, what do you mean by this Delay? Consider I'm a Man, a mortal, wishing, amorous Man——

L. *Piz.* And consider I'm a Woman——

Lud. aside. Ay, ay: That I know: At least I hope to find you such —— or I would not be in such Haste——

L. *Piz.* And have a Reputation to preserve.

Lud. Oh! Lord, what a damn'd Turn's here? Reputatron, say you? Egad, I find all Women make Pretence to that mysterious Word. [*Aside.*] What! Are not you married, Madam?

L. *Piz.* Yes, what then?

Lud. Why then you have a Reputation to preserve——that's all.

L. *Piz.* All, Sir, yes, and all in all to me——Do you consider what Country you're in, Sir?

Lud.

Lud. Yes, Faith, Madam; and what Conſtitution I am of too. I know Murder is as venial a Sin here, as Adultery is in ſome Countries; And I am too apprehenſive of my mortal Part not to avoid Danger——Therefore, Madam, you have an infallible Security——if I ſhould betray you, I bring myſelf into Jeopardy, and of all Pleaſures, Self-Preſervation is the deareſt.

L. *Piz.* A very open Speaker, I vow.

Lud. Ay, Madam, that's beſt——Hang your creeping, cringing, whining, ſighing, dying, lying Lovers—— Pugh! Their Flames are not more durable than mine, tho' they make more Noiſe in the Blaze.

Sings:

Hang the whining Way of Wooing,
Loving was deſign'd a Sport.

L. *Piz. aſide.* The Duce take me if this Fellow has not charm'd me ſtrangely——Well, the Carnival is almoſt over, and then muſt I be ſhut up like a Nun again ——— Hey! Hoa! This Time will be ſo ſhort———

Lud. Let's make the better Uſe on't then, my Dear. We will conſider when we have nothing elſe to do, but at preſent there's a Matter of the greateſt Moment, which I muſt impart to you ——— Therefore, come dear Rogue, come———

L. *Piz.* [*Looking on her Watch.*] Hold —— I have outſtaid my Time, and muſt return Home inſtantly, to prevent Diſcoveries.

Lud. Faith, Madam, this is not fair——to raiſe a Man's Expectation, and then diſappoint him! Would you be ſerv'd ſo yourſelf now?

L. *Piz.* I'll endeavour to diſengage myſelf from my jealous Huſband, and contrive another Meeting.

Lud. But will you be ſure to meet me again?

L. *Piz.* I give you my Hand as a Pledge——

Lud. Kiſſes it. And I this Kiſs in Return——Adieu, my Charmer.

L. *Piz.* Signior, farewel. [*Exeunt ſeverally.*

Enter Baſſino, Alonzo.

Baſſ. Well, Sir, your Buſineſs———

Alon. It is to tell you———
You are a Villain.

Baſſ. Ha———

Alon. And that as ſuch
I ought to have treated you before the Face
Of falſe *Aurelia*——But I ſcorn to follow
The barbarous Cuſtom of my native Country.
I ſeek with Honour to revenge my Wrongs;
Therefore, Sir, draw———

Baſſ. This Action ſpeaks you noble—be likewiſe juſt,
And let me know the Cauſe that moves your Anger.
By Heaven I'd rather call you ſtill my Friend,
Than be your Enemy———Yet, if I wrong'd you,
I'll give you Satisfaction———

Alon. Trifler, away———Too well thou know'ſt the Cauſe;
And now would'ſt ſooth my Wrongs with Flattery.
But my Reſolve is fix'd as Heaven's Decrees:
And one of us muſt fall——Let the Survivor
Diſpoſe of that baſe, falſe, perjur'd *Aurelia*,
As both his Love and Honour ſhall direct.
If my propitious Stars defend my Life,
You ſhall not die alone——Th' adulterous Fair
Shall bear you Company——Now draw.

Baſſ. Oh! hold.
One Moment hold, I muſt unfold this Riddle:
Adulterous Fair, ſay you?

Alon, Yes: She's my Wife.

Baſſ. Ha———your Wife!
Sure there's a Curſe entail'd upon that Name. [*Aſide.*
What! your real Wife?

Alon. If the Command of an expiring Father,
And her own Vows can make her mine, ſhe's ſo:
Indeed the Marriage Rites are yet to come,
Which ſlily ſhe delay'd theſe two Months paſt,
On ſlight Pretence of finiſhing the Time
Of mourning for her Father———But 'tis plain,
I was a Property to your baſe Love,

And

And only design'd to fill up your Place,
When surfeited you should return to *Turin*.
Hell——Furies! Draw, or in my just Revenge,
I'll pin you to the Earth——

Bass. Oh! Woman! Woman! [*Aside.*
Yes, I will draw——But ere the fatal Stroke
Is past Recal, I swear *Aurelia*'s Virtue
Is clear and spotless, like *Diana*'s self:
Nor was I prompted on this early Visit,
But with Design to take my last Farewel,
Having last Night receiv'd my Prince's Orders
To haste to *Turin*——Therefore if I fall,
I hope she'll meet with Mercy——Now come on.

Alon. Hold, hold, my Lord; Oh! could I credit this,
I would ask Pardon, and entreat your Friendship.

Bass. 'Tis true, upon my Honour——
But if you doubt my Words, I'm ready——
Tho' I have Reason to decline this Combat,
At least at present——Oh! *Placentia!* [*Aside.*
Oh! my *Placentia!* why should I abuse thee?

Alon. My Lord, you seem disturb'd——

Bass. Oh! *Alonzo! Alonzo!*
Should I acquaint you with my wretched Fate,
You'd find that Life itself is grown a Burden,
I cannot bear, since I can ne'er be happy.
But 'tis a Story that must ne'er be told,
Let it suffice, to settle your Repose,
That *Turin* holds the Cause of my Misfortunes.

Alon. Then I am happy: [*Aside.*
My Lord, I wish 'twere in my Power to serve you,
I'd do it as a Friend——

Bass. Generous Sir, I thank you;
As far as I am capable, I am *Alonzo*'s. [*Exit* Alonzo.
Oh! Force of treacherous Love! to gain my End,
I wrong a Wife, a Mistress, and a Friend.
[*Exit* Bassino.

The End of the SECOND ACT.

ACT III. SCENE I.

Aurelia's *Lodgings.*

Enter Aurelia, Florella.

Aur. OH! how I tremble for my dear *Baſſino!*
Haſte, fly, *Florella*, bring me News he lives,
Or elſe expect to ſee thy Miſtreſs die.
Flor. Madam, be patient———
Conſult your Reputation, and conſider
That the leaſt Noiſe you make on this Occaſion,
Reflects upon your Virtue———
Aur. Away, away———Talk not of Reputation,
When Love's in t'other Scale—But what can ſhock my Reputation;
Heaven's my Witneſs, I ne'er lodg'd a Thought,
For Count *Baſſino* that could wrong my Virtue.
Perhaps the Gods purſue me with their Hatred,
Becauſe I break my Promiſe to *Alonzo*.
But then, why did they not ſecure me his?
Why muſt weak Mortals be expos'd to Paſſions,
Which are not in our Power to ſubdue,
And yet account for what they prompt us to?
But I will think no more———Almighty Love,
Now hear my laſt Reſolve———if angry Heaven
Refuſed to guard my dear *Baſſino*'s Life,
Aurelia too ſhall fall, and leave his Murderer
Accurſt for ever———

Enter Alonzo.

Flor. Oh! Heaven! where will this end? [*Aſide.*
Aur. Ha———
The Gods have ſent him to decide my Fate,
How now! how dare you meet my angry View?
Or think I'll e'er forgive the baſe Affront
This very Day you offer'd to my Fame?
Alon. Juſt Heaven refuſes not a Penitent,

Therefore I cannot think that fair *Aurelia*,
Whose Charms are all divine, should fail in Goodness.
Oh! let my Love atone for my rash Deed:
The Count and I are Friends, why should *Aurelia* be more severe?

Aur. He lives, blest News!
Do then rash Actions speak your Love to me?
Must I in publick bear with your Insults
Before I'm yours? what must I then expect
When the strict Ties of Marriage shall confirm
Your jealous Passions?
No, you have taught me to avoid the Shelf
I was just running on———know, base *Alonzo*,
That from this Moment I resume my Freedom,
I disengage you from your former Vows,
And will henceforth be Mistress of myself.

Alon. Ha——— [*Aside.*
This sudden Coldness has another Spring
Than my rash Carriage———Oh! my jealous Fears;
But I'm resolv'd to trace her winding Thoughts,
And fetch the Secret forth———
Madam, I hope you do but try my Love:
I cannot think *Aurelia* would be false.
Besides, you can't recal what's register'd in Heaven.

Aur. Then stay till we come there———There you'll have Witness.

Alon. Witness!
Oh! faithless, perjur'd Woman, can'st thou think
Upon thyself, and bid me call my Witness?
Yes, you are mine———By all the Gods you are.
And shall there be a Power on this Side Heaven,
To stop my Bliss? No———by my Love I swear.
I now can guess at your perfidious Meaning,
And tho' that cowardly Villain slily thought
To blind me with a Tale his Guilt had fram'd,
'Tis plain he is your Minion———yet wants Courage
To own his Treachery.

Aur. Detracting, slanderous Villain!
How dare you treat me thus?
Oh! for the Look of a fierce Basilisk,
To punish this audacious Insolence!

Alon. Marry thee! No——by Heavens, I'd rather
Be rack'd to Death————And for thy vile Injuſtice,
None ſhall enjoy thee, while this Sword is mine.
[*Lays hold on his Sword.*
Nor ſhall your Lover 'ſcape, to ſerve your Luſt,
Till he has forc'd a Paſſage thro' this Breaſt.
[*Points to his Breaſt.*
Aur. Oh! my *Baſſino.* [*Aſide.*
Oh! cruel Man! Are not you then contented
To wreak your Spite on poor *Aurelia?*
Why muſt your Rage involve the Innocent?
Oh! let me fall your Paſſion's Sacrifice;
Let my Blood waſh the Stain you fix on me,
But do not blaſt your Name with baſe Revenge.——
Alon. By Heaven! ſhe doats on him! Oh! cunning Woman!
But this Pretence won't ſerve to ſave his Life;
I'll not be caught again——No, *Syren*, no.
Baſſino dies——Nor will I leave to Fortune
The vengeful Stroke, but take a ſafer Way.
Aur. Oh! Heaven! [*Kneels.*
What Words ſhall I invent to ſooth his Rage, [*Aſide.*
And ſave my dear *Baſſino?* Oh! *Alonzo.*
My once-lov'd Dear, will you not hear me ſpeak?
Oh! I conjure you by our plighted Love's,
Whoſe Purity outſhone the Stars above,
Hear me this Time, then uſe me as you pleaſe.
Alon. Oh! Woman, Woman!
Aur. If e'er *Aurelia*
So much as in her Thoughts did wrong *Alonzo*,
May ſudden Death purſue her perjur'd Steps:
Heaven forgive [*Aſide.*
The Perjury, ſince I've no other way
To ſave *Baſſino*'s Life.————
Alon. Aurelia, riſe———— [*Raiſing her.*
Oh! could I credit this, how happy were *Alonzo!*
But ſomething tells me that thou art forſworn;
And yet thou ſeem'ſt as fair as Truth itſelf;
How is it poſſible that Guilt can look
With ſo divine a Face?

Aur. Oh! kill me instantly: kill me, I beg you, kill me;
Let me not linger out an Age in Pain,
For such is every Moment of your Anger;
I cannot bear to live in your Displeasure.

Alon. By Heaven she's true——
Hence frivolous Fears be gone——she's only mine.
Come to my Breast, my bright *Aurelia*, come.

[*Embraces her.*

To that soft Shrine that holds that Sacred Image,
Which triumphs o'er my Soul, and grasps it all,
I knew my boundless Treasure, and the Thought
Of losing thee had rais'd my Love to Madness.
But now I'm calm—No more shall that fierce Passion,
Rude Jealousy, disturb my peaceful Mind.
Do but forgive the Faults my Rage committed,
And you will find our Loves will grow the purer;
Just as the Sky looks brighter when the Storm
Is chas'd away, and *Phœbus* smiles again.

Aur. Since both have been to blame, let it suffice,
We both repent, and will offend no more.

Alon. Oh! never, never,
I'll ne'er suspect you more—Only resolve me this—

Aur. What is it?

Alon. Why was *Bassino*
Admitted to your View, and I denied?

Aur. He came to take his Leave, and 't had been rude
Not to admit a Man of his high Birth
On this Occasion; nor was you denied,
But thro' Woman's Fears of your Suspicions.
She thought you would misconstrue the Count's Visit,
As you have really done——I blam'd her for it,
Indeed, this is the Truth—I hope *Alonzo*
Believes me now——

Alon. Believe Thee! Yes——As willingly as Martyrs
A State of endless Joy.
I will so love, my Dear, that all Mankind
Shall look with Envy on our mutual Bliss.
I'm like a Merchant tost at Sea by Storms,
Who his last Course with Pray'rs and Toil performs;
And the rich Cargo safely brought on Shore,

He hugs it thus, and vows to part no more.
[*Embraces her.*

Aur. So in a flow'ry Mead a Serpent lurks,
And the unwary Traveller surprizes,
Where he suspects least Danger! Cursed Cheat. [*Aside.*
Oh! that I could disclose the fatal Story!
But it must never out———I beg, *Alonzo*,
You'd leave me for a while, and rest secure,
You have my Love———

Alon. Then the bright Sun in all his circling Turn,
Cannot behold a Man more truly happy,
What you command, I readily obey.
Farewel, my Dear. [*Exit* Alonzo.

Aur. Where art thou now, *Aurelia?*
How wilt thou 'scape that dreadful Precipice,
On which thou art hurried on by thy fatal Passion?
With conscious Horror I deceiv'd *Alonzo*;
I hate this base Treachery, but 'twas unavoidable:
The Truth had been more fatal———
More fatal!———No———For I must never wed
My dear *Bassino*, whilst *Alonzo* lives.
Oh! the distracting Thought! what shall I do?
Why! die *Aurelia:* That's the only Way,
To keep thy Vows to both—Ha——die, said I?
But whether then? who knows what Punishment,
Just Heav'n prepares for guilty Souls like mine.
But I must think no more, lest I grow mad with Thought,
If there's a Power that guards us here below,
Oh! look with pitying Eyes on poor *Aurelia:*
Appease the Tumults of my anxious Fear,
And load me with no more than I can bear.
[*Exeunt* Aurelia, Florella.

SCENE II. *Lady* Pizalta's *Lodgings.*

Enter Lady Pizalta, Lucy.

L. *Piz*. Well, thou'rt an admirable Girl! What would half the Ladies in *Venice* give for such a Servant?

Lucy. (*Aside.*) Truly you have Reason to say so, for 'tis not the first Intrigue I have manag'd for you——— Oh! dear Madam, your Ladyship does me too much Honour—

Honour———But how do you like your new Servant, Madam?

L. *Piz.* Oh! above all Men living, *Lucy:* He has the most bewitching Conversation I ever met with——Say, is there no way to contrive a second Meeting? For I'm impatient till I see the dear Man again———The End of the Carnival draws near, which is indeed the End of Life to me: For then must I be coop'd up with Age: Condemn'd to an eternal Coughing, Spitting, Snoring and Ill-nature———Then let me make the best of Life ———since Hell cannot have a worse Plague in Store than I have felt already.

Luc. Indeed, Madam, I pity you: And wish 'twere in my Power to free you from this old wither'd Log, but tho' that's impossible, yet I may do you some little Services to make Life's tedious Journey pleasant———Let me see, I have it————What would you say now, Madam, if I should contrive a Way to have your Lover in your own Chamber?

L. *Piz.* That were worth a King's Revenue———— Speak, quickly, how, how, good *Lucy?*

Luc. Why, thus: He shall put on my Cloaths, and in my Place attend you.

L. *Piz.* Rare Contrivance! but my Husband, *Lucy?*

Luc. Oh! let me alone, Madam, to manage him: He is defective in Sight, you know; and not mistrusting any thing, will not be over curious: But if he should, I have a way to bring you off——My Life on't——This Plot may be of Use to my Design, I'll manage it with Care. [*Aside.*

L. *Piz.* Oh! the Pleasure of hearing my Husband lie coughing and calling me to Bed: And my answering him, I'm coming, Dear; and while he imagines me in the next Room undressing, I'm happy in the Arms of my *Ludovico.* Certainly there's as much Satisfaction in deceiving a dull jealous Husband, as in getting a new Gallant; were it not grown so common—each Tradesman's Wife must have her Gallant too———and sometimes makes a Journeyman of the Apprentice e'er his Indentures be half out———'Tis an insufferable Fault, that Quality can have no Pleasure above the Vulgar, except it be in not paying their Debts. Well, dear *Lucy*, I admire thy Contrivance——About it instantly——

Lucy. (*Aside*) About it instantly! is that all? I must have my t'other Fee first.——I will, Madam; and you may expect your Lover instantly. But, Madam, what's to be done with your brocade Night-Gown you tore last Night? it can ne'er be mended handsomely.

L. *Piz*. Nothing to be done without a Bribe I find, in Love as well as Law——Well, *Lucy*, if you manage this Intrigue with Care and Secresy, the Gown is yours.

Enter Page.

Page. Madam, my Lord desires to speak with you.

Lucy, Madam, I'll go about your Business: Your Ladyship's very humble Servant. [*Exit* Lucy.

L. *Piz*. Tell him I'm coming——[*Exit* Page.] Now by way of Mortification, must I go entertain my old jealous Husband. [*Exit Lady* Pizalta.

SCENE III. *The Piazza.*

Enter Ludovico *singing*.

Give me but Wine, that Liquor of Life,
And a Girl that is wholesome and clean,
Two or three Friends, but the Devil a Wife,
And I'd not change State with a King.

Enter Lucy.

Lucy. What singing, Signior! Well you're a pleasant Gentleman——

Lud. Ah! my little female *Mercury*, what Message bring'st thou? Ha——will thy Lady bless me with another Sight——Ha——How——When? where? I am all in a Flame.

Lucy. Come along with me, Sir, I'll help you to an Extinguisher presently.

Lud. If thou meanest thy Lady, with all my Heart—

But

But I can tell thee, ſhe'll rather prove Oil, than what you ſpeak of——But, ſay, where am I to ſee my lovely Charmer?

Lucy. In her Chamber——

Lud. Good! But how the Devil can that be done?

Lucy. Nay, without the Help of a Conjurer, I aſſure you; if you dare take me for your Pilot, I'll warrant you Succeſs in your Voyage——I'll ſet you ſafe in the Iſland of Love; 'tis your Buſineſs to improve the Soil.

Lud. I warrant thee, Girl; do you but bring me there once, and if I play not my Part, may I never more know the Pleaſure of an Intrigue.

Lucy, Which, if I miſtake not, is the ſtreateſt Curſe can fall on you——Well, you muſt ſuffer a ſmall Metamorphoſis: What think you of perſonating me a little? That is, dreſſing in my Cloaths, and waiting on your Miſtreſs in her Bed-chamber—Ha——

Lud. Egad, I'm afraid I ſhall make but an aukward Chamber-maid, I'm undiſciplin'd in dreſſing a Lady's Head——

Lucy. Oh! Sir, your Commiſſion won't reach ſo high as the Head: I believe my Lady will excuſe little Matters: You can undreſs, I ſuppoſe.

Lud. Oh! the beſt and the quickeſt of any Man in *Venice.* But a Pox on't—Can'ſt find no other way?—— I, I, I,——I like Petticoats in their proper Places, but I don't care to have my Legs in 'em.

Lucy. And ſo you reſolve againſt it? Ha——

Lud. No, not abſolutely reſolve, Child: But—a——

Lucy. But what, Sir!

Lud. Nothing—I will follow thy Directions, whatever comes on't. Now lead the way, for nothing ſuits better with my Humour than a Friend, a Bottle, a new Miſtreſs and a convenient Place. [*Exit* Lucy, Ludovico.

SCENE IV. Pizalto's *Lodgings.*

Enter Pizalto *with a Bond in his Hand.*

Piz. Well—My Wife's a fine Woman! a very fine Woman! But a Pox ſhe's a Wife ſtill, and this young

Jade runs in my Head plaguily: Well——here 'tis under my Hand; a Thousand Pistoles——A great Sum for a Maidenhead, as Maidenheads go now-a-days——Ah, had I been young now.

A Fiddle and a Treat had bore the Prize away,
But when we old Fools doat, they make us pay.

Enter Lucy.

Oh! are you come! Here, here, *Lucy*: Here's a Fortune for thee, worth twenty Maidenheads, adod! I have not so much Money by me at present, but there's Security. [*Gives her the Bond.*

Lucy. Your Lordship's Bond's sufficient——Well, but that I am satisfied my Reputation is safe with your Lordship, or twice the Sum should not have prevail'd——Go to my Chamber, my Lord, I'll but step and see if my Lady wants any thing, and I'll be with you instantly.

Piz. You won't stay, *Lucy*? Ah, Girl, buss thy Lady's Chucky; now, do now——

Lucy. Oh! Lord! not here, we shall be discovered.

Piz. Well, thou art a cunning Sinner: make haste, *Lucy*, dost hear? [*Exit* Pizalto.

Lucy. You're in mighty Haste, old Gentleman! but I shall deceive you,

My End is gain'd; I have my Fortune made,
Man has not me, but I have Man betray'd.

The End of the Third Act.

ACT

ACT IV. SCENE I.

Armando's *Lodgings.*

Enter Armando, Placentia.

Pla. OH! *Armando!*
Thou more than Friend to the distress'd *Placentia!*
Say, how shall I regain my lost *Bassino,*
My false, perfidious Husband? [*Weeps.*
Arm. Dear Madam, moderate your Sorrow:
Reserve those Tears to move *Bassino*'s Heart,
Mine is all Pity: You may rest secure
Of all the Arguments a Friend can use
To bring him back to your endearing Arms.
Virtue's not quite extinguish'd in his Breast,
Therefore I hope the Sight of bright *Placentia*
Will rouze his slumb'ring Reason——
Pla. Oh! *Bassino! Bassino!*
Oh! wretched Woman! Oh! that I had dy'd
E'er I had known him false: Then I were happy:
And tho' contented with his second Choice,
He with a pitying Sigh, perhaps, had grac'd
My Memory——
Oh! all ye Powers that virtuous Love inspire,
Assist me now: Inform my vocal Organs
With angel Eloquence, such as can melt
His Heart of Flint, and move his former Kindness.
(*Aside.*) But if that fail, I will remove the Cause
Of both our Woes——Yes, that happy Charmer,
That Rival of my Love shall surely die.
Arm. Doubt not of the Success; What Heart of Steel
Could ere resist such Beauty dress'd in Tears?

Enter a Servant.

Serv. Sir, Count *Bassino* enquires if you are within.
Pla. Oh! Heavens! how I tremble!

Arm.

Arm. Lucky Opportunity———ſhew him up.
Madam, be pleas'd to ſtep into that Cloſet,
Till I can ſound the utmoſt of his Thoughts,
And ſhew him naked to your ſecret View.
Then when he's in the Height of impious Paſſion,
You like a Bolt from Heav'n ſhall ruſh on him,
And ſtrike his Folly dumb.

Pla. Almighty Powers, whoſe providential Care
Is ever kind to virtuous Innocence,
Oh! help me now in this Extremity. [*Exit* Placentia.

Enter Baſſino.

Baſſ. How does my Friend *Armando?*

Arm. My Lord, *Armando*'s well,
And wiſhes you were ſo.

Baſſ. Doſt thou diſcover ought that gives thee Cauſe
To doubt I am not well? Indeed I think
I am in perfect Health———

Arm. My Lord, I ſhould be glad
To find that Fever of your Mind abated
In which I left you laſt———

Baſſ. (*Aſide.*) I muſt diſſemble now,
Elſe I'll ne'er gain my Ends—my dear *Armando*,
That Fever thou ſpeak'ſt of, is now ſucceeded
By a cold Ague-Fit: The bare Remembrance
Of my unlawful Paſſion ſhakes my Soul.

Arm. Such ſudden Cures have often prov'd pernicious,
And we have Reaſon to ſuſpect a Wound
Too quickly heal'd———

Baſſ. Not when thou know'ſt what Balſam I applied.

Arm. There's ſcarce a Balm for the deep Wounds of Love,
Beſides Poſſeſſion, and I cannot think
You have enjoy'd *Aurelia.*

Baſſ. I ſwear I have not———
But I enjoy my Reaſon, my free Reaſon:
And who poſſeſſes that, can never cheriſh
A Thought againſt himſelf: For ſuch I call
Whatſoever keeps me from my lawful Wife,
My dear *Placentia*, to whoſe Arms I'll fly

With

With all the eager Haste of a fond Bridegroom.
There I shall revel in the virtuous Pleasures
Of a chaste Bed—Oh! my Friend *Armando!*
My dear *Placentia*'s Friend! can'st thou forgive?
Indeed I'm penitent, and will offend no more.

Arm. My Lord, these are the Words you spoke before:
What greater Reason have I now to think
You'll keep your Promise?

Bass. Pride, Honour, Justice are come to my Aid,
And Love too feeble to withstand 'em all,
Has left the Field to my victorious Reason.
Pride, with the Prospect of my future Greatness,
Allures me to return with Speed to *Turin*,
T'obey my Prince's Orders.
Honour and Justice tell me I'm *Placentia*'s,
And that *Aurelia* is *Alonzo*'s Bride.
To him she gave her Virgin Vows: Nay, more,
To him her dying Father did bequeath her;
He loves her too, and shall not be depriv'd:
My Passion is subdu'd, and I'm resolv'd
Myself to give *Aurelia* to *Alonzo*.

Arm. If this be true, then you are my Friend again;
But how came you to learn *Aurelia*'s
Engagement to *Alonzo*?

Bass. I have it from himself, who an Hour since,
With eager Fury sought to 'venge on me
His injur'd Love, and challeng'd me to fight:
I chose with Justice to defend my Life,
And quit *Aurelia*, rather than to vanquish
In such a Cause—*Alonzo* strait embrac'd me,
Call'd me his Friend, and vow'd I should not go,
Till I had seen him join'd in solemn Marriage
With bright *Aurelia*———This I readily granted.
Canst thou believe me true?

Arm, My Lord, I do believe you———
And am o'erjoy'd to hear your Resolution:
By Heaven! there's more Glory in subduing
Our wild Desires, than an embattl'd Foe.
Now do I wish his Wife had never come. [*Aside.*

Bass. *Armando*, thou'rt my Friend, and on that Score
I must desire you to repair to *Turin*,

With all the Speed you can, to bear these Letters
To our great Prince, and beg he will excuse
My stay for three Days more——And here this Letter
Bear to *Placentia*——speak to her the kindest
The softest Things thy Fancy can suggest.
I shall make good thy Promise———
My dear *Placentia!* Oh! that she were here,
Panting and warm within these longing Arms!
'Tis a long Age since I did see her last!
But come, my Friend, you must this Hour set forward.

Arm. With all my Heart: But 'twill not be amiss,
Before I go, to fix the Victory,
Which conquering Virtue in your Breast has gain'd;
And if what you pretend be real Truth,
I have a welcome Present for *Bassino.*
Madam, come forth———

Enter Placentia.

Bass. What do I see! my Wife! This was a lucky Plot: [*Aside.*
Hypocrisy did ne'er befriend me more.
This was not like a Friend—why should *Armando*
Disturb her soft Tranquility of Mind,
And give her ocular Proofs of my Disloyalty?
Oh! my *Placentia!* my beloved Wife! [*Embraces her.*
Oh! that I should e'er think to wrong my Dear!

Pla. My Lord, waste not a Sigh on my Account:
My Joys are infinite, since you are mine,
And what is past I easily forget.
Nay, let me beg for Pardon: For I know
I have offended you in coming hither.
I should have waited this Return of Virtue;
Or, if abandon'd, silently have mourn'd
My Loss, without upbraiding my lov'd Lord.
All this I should have done, but mighty Love,
Too powerful for Duty to withstand,
Guided my Steps to *Venice*———
In hopes my Presence would retrieve your Heart.

Bass. Gods! that this Woman were *Aurelia!* [*Aside.*
Thou Wonder of thy Sex! thou best of Women!

I blush to think that thou hast heard my Folly:
Yet since your Love cancels your just Complaints,
You make me doubly blest: And I'll reward
This excellent Goodness with eternal Fondness.
Oh! that thou hadst been here! Not all the Beauties
That *Venice* holds could have diverted me;
No, not one Moment from my dear *Placentia*.
Long Absence is the Bane of new-born Love,
But Fate shall ne'er have Power to part us more.

Pla. Oh! my dear Lord, your Goodness is too great:
And I'm o'er-paid for all my Sorrows past.
Armando, say, is not he wondrous kind?

Arm. Madam, I told you Virtue
Was struggling in his Breast; and that it might
O'ercome his vicious Love, I thought your Presence
Was requisite——And now, my Lord, I hope
You will forgive me, since all the Endeavours
I us'd before had been in vain. I once
Design'd to let *Aurelia* know your Marriage;
But then perhaps she would not have believ'd me:
Let this plead my Excuse in sending for *Placentia*
Without your Knowledge.

Baff. I must not let him see I am concern'd. [*Aside*.
I know 'twas Friendship all, well-meaning Friendship:
I only am to blame: But I'll retrieve
My Credit in your Heart, and still deserve
The Name of Friend—And thou, the best of Wives,
Shalt ne'er have Cause to doubt my constant Love.

Pla. Oh! my *Baffino!* this Excess of Kindness
Exalts me o'er all Mortals, if you're true,
There's not a Blast within the Power of Fortune
Can shock my Happiness.

Baff. Thou shalt ne'er find me false, I swear thou shalt not.
Oh! that I could engage
She would return to *Turin* with *Armando*; [*Aside*.
For if she stays, I never can enjoy
My bright *Aurelia*, and by Heaven I will,
Altho' ten thousand Lives should pay the Purchase.

Pla. My Lord, you seem disturb'd.

Baff. It troubles me

You can't appear in *Venice* with a Train
That may bespeak the Rank you hold in *Savoy*.

Pla. to *Arm.* Oh! *Armando!*
He is so kind, I wish I ne'er had come!
What if I offer to return with you?

Arm. Madam, you will do well:
For I myself cannot suspect him now.

Pla. My Lord, let not my Presence here disturb you;
I doubt your Love no more, and to convince you,
I will go back before 'tis known I'm here.
Besides, 'tis fit I should prepare all things
To welcome you at home.

Bass. (*aside.*) Blest Opportunity!
Fortune I thank thee: Would my Dear then leave me
So very soon? Alas! 'twill be an Age
E'er I return to *Turin*: Three long Days;
No, my Dear, no; I will not part from thee,
At least this Night, my Love———

Pla. Will then *Armando* stay?

Bass. No, my best Hopes, he instantly departs
With Letters to my Prince.

Pla. Then suffer me to go this very Moment.
Three Days will soon be o'er, and your Return,
Shall make me fully blest———If I should stay
'Twould look like base Distrust, and I can't think
Bassino would be false———

Bass. (*aside.*) Oh! Heaven! that I were not!

Arm. Indeed, my Lord, I think you're truly happy.
Scarce does any Age produce so good a Wife.

Bass. Oh! that I could reward this wondrous Goodness!

Pla. My Lord, what makes you sigh?

Bass. To part from thee: But since 'tis your Desire,
It shall be so. *Armando*, to thy Charge
I here commit the Treasure of my Soul,
Take Care of her, and think that on her Safety
My Life depends.

Arm. My Lord, I hope you do not doubt my Care.

Bass. Dear Friend, I do not——
May Heaven's Blessings still attend my Love,
My dear *Placentia*. [*Embraces, and goes to lead her off.*

Pla.

Pla. As many more guard my *Baffino.*

Baff. (*aside.*) A sudden Horror seizes all my Limbs:
I tremble at the Thought of this base Deed——
[*Pulls out his Handkerchief, and drops a Letter, which* Armando *takes up.*
Ha——Tears uncall'd for bathe my guilty Eyes——
Gods! either give me Virtue to withstand
This impious Love, or Courage to pursue it
Without Remorse; for I'm but half a Villain.
[*Exeunt* Baffino, Placent.

Arm. opens the Letter. A Letter! and to *Aurelia!* now Curiosity prompts me to know the Subject———What's here?

Reads. *I have dispatch'd* Armando *to the Court of* Savoy, *and found Pretence to stay behind*———
False treacherous Man!
This Night I give a Mask at my Lodgings, which, I hope, will divert Alonzo, *till the Priest has joined our Hands; and while all the Company are engaged in Mirth, I'll steal to the dear Arms of my divine* Aurelia.
Oh! Villain, Villain! Monstrous Villain!
Oh! poor *Placentia!* But I will prevent
His Policy, and break his wicked Measures.
[*Exit* Armando.

SCENE II. Pizalto's *Lodgings.*

Enter Pizalto *solus.*

Piz. Why, what makes this young Jade stay so long? Adod, this is to pay before-hand——Ha——methinks I hear a Laughing and Giggling in my Wife's Apartment; I must know whence their Mirth proceeds. Ho! here's *Lucy* coming——Harkee you, pray, why did you make me wait so long? Nay, I'm resolved you shan't escape me now ——*Goes to the Door, and pulls in* Ludovico *in* Lucy's *Cloaths, whose Commode falls off in the Struggle, and discovers his bald Head.*] Oh! Benedicite! What have we here? A Man disguis'd in my Wife's

Wife's Chamber! and I unarm'd! Oh! Curſt Minute! ——Speak, thou wicked Prophet, thou Son of Iniquity, what cameſt thou here for? Ha —— Thou Prieſt of *Baal*, to offer Sacrifices on the Altar of my Wife? Oh! my Head! myHorns weigh it down to the Ground already——Within there, bring me my Sword and Piſtols.

Lud. A Pox on all Petticoats ——What a Devil ſhall I ſay now? Oh! for a Sword! that would be of more Uſe to me now than my Tongue.

Enter Lady Pizalta.

Piz. Oh! thou wicked fallacious Woman!

L. *Piz.* What ails my dear Chucky? Why doſt thou call for Arms, Deary?

Piz. To cut down that vile Creeper which over-runs thy Garden of Virtue——

L. *Piz.* [*aſide.*] Now Impudence aſſiſt me.
Ah! Heavens! What's here? A Man in Diſguiſe? A Thief it muſt be——Raiſe the Servants——Oh! Heaven! we might have had all our Throats cut in our Beds——Now for *Lucy*, for I am at a Loſs to come off. [*Aſide.*

Piz No, no, I warrant, you know he is more gentle in Bed.

Lud. [*aſide.*] Oh! the Devil, what does ſhe mean? Death, Hell and Furies! if I come off now, catch me at this Sport again, and hang me——

Enter Lucy.

L. *Piz.* Oh! are you there, Miſtreſs? How came this Man here in your Cloaths? Ha! Gentlewoman—

Lucy, [*aſide.*] How confidently ſhe aſks the Queſtion, poor Lady! as if ſhe knew nothing of it! Now muſt I bring her off—For Reaſons you muſt not know, Madam.

Piz. Ah! Thou wicked Pair of Bellows to blow the Fire of Iniquity! Why, thou art the very Caſement thro' which thy Miſtreſs ſucks the Air of Abomination—

Tell

Tell me, I say, how he came here, and for what——and be sure it be a substantial Lie, or 'twill not pass.

Lucy. [*aside*.] All my Hopes are in her Impudence.

Lucy to *Pizal*. Harkee, Sir, one Word with you——Do you remember our Agreement To-night?

Piz. Why, what of that? ha——

Lucy. Then imagine what I design'd that Gentleman for: I'm honest, Sir, that's all——

Piz. I'm honest, Sir, that's all—[*Mimicking her Tone.*] Honest! with a Pox——What! and so you honestly provided a Companion for my Wife in my Absence—ha——

Lucy. No, Sir, I design'd him for your Companion in my Absence——This is the Business he was drest for: Therefore no more Words, but believe my Lady honest, or all shall out.

Piz. Oh! the Devil! this shan't pass, Hussy——Do you think I'll be cuckolded, jilted, bubbled, and let it pass for a *Christmas* Gambol. Adod, give me my Bond again, or——or—— [*Holds up his Cane.*

Lucy. No——hold there, Sir: Women and Lawyers ne'er refund a Fee: But 'tis your best Way to be patient now, I'll not take Blows.

L. *Piz*. Why all this Whispering? Why mayn't I know the Business?

Piz. I am mistaken if you have not known too much Business already: But I am right enough serv'd——I had more Ground before than I could manage; I had no Need of my Neighbour's.

Lucy. Right, my Lord; Ground that lies fallow will breed Weeds in Time; but you'rs is clear yet.

Piz. Damn your Jests: I shall expect a better Account, do you hear? I'll find a Servant to see you out of Doors. [*To* Ludovico. [*Exeunt* Pizalto *and Lady.*

Lud. Well, this was an admirable Lift at a Pinch—She has brought me off now——And if e'er they catch me at this Music again, I'll give 'em Leave to make an *Italian* Singer of me——No more Intrigues in Disguise——if it had not been for the Waiting-Woman now, I might have been hang'd for a Thief.

Lucy. What all amort, Signior, no Courage left?

Lud.

Lud. Faith, not much———I think I have lost my Manhood with my Breeches———This Transformation may suit with Gods, but not with Mortals of my Humour———Come, prithee, good Mistress *Lucy*, help me to my proper Shape again; for tho' I have a natural Inclination to Petticoats, I hate 'em upon my own Back. [*A Flourish of Music within.*

Lucy. Hark! I hear Count *Bassino*'s Music: He gives a Mask To-night; you are already drest for Masquerade, won't you stay and take a Dance?

Lud. Egad, I'd rather dance a Jig with thee elsewhere: Faith thou'rt a pretty Girl—and hast a good deal of Wit too———But then, Pox on't, thour't honest, thou sayest, thou cannot swallow a Pill, except 'tis gilded over with Matrimony.

Lucy——And that turns your Stomach, I warrant.

Lud. Why, Ay: Faith my Stomach is damn'd squeemish in these Matters: Yet, egad, if I could find one with half as much Money as thou hast Wit and Beauty, I'd marry, and live honest.

Lucy. That is, you'd marry her Money———

Lud. One with the other, Child: There's no living upon Love thou knowest———Tho' Faith I could live well enough too.

Lucy. Well, suppose I help you to a Lady with a round Sum; you'd keep your Word, and marry her?

Lud. I am a Gentleman, I scorn to break my Word.

Lucy. Well, Sir, come to the Mask, and I'll engage you a Mistress, if you are not over-curious.

Lud. With all my Heart:
I'm now resolv'd to leave this Wenching-Trade:
For no Man's safe upon a Hackney Jade;
Th' Allay of Danger makes the Pleasure Pain,
A Virtuous Wife will always be same.

The End of the Fourth Act.

ACT

ACT V. SCENE I.

A Mask in Baffino's *Lodgings.*

Baffino, Alonzo, Armando, *in a Difguife*; Placentia *in Man's Cloaths, Signior* Pizalto, *Lady* Pizalta, Lucy, &c.

An Entry of three Men, and three Women of feveral Nations.

Baff. I Can't imagine where I dropt my Letter:
Pray Heaven it be where none can ever find it.
Gods! Let me once enjoy her, then call on me
Your Store of Plagues, and I will meet 'em all.

Enter Ludovico, *finging.*

Lud. Ah! Miftrefs *Lucy!* I'm come thou fee'ft——I expect thou fhalt be as good as thy Word, Child——is the Lady here?

Lucy. The Lady is forth-coming, if you are ftill in the fame Mind?

L. *Piz.* My Lover here! Harkee, *Lucy.*

Lucy. By and by, Madam, I am catering for myfelf now———Well, Sir, will two thoufand Piftoles do?

Lud. I muft humour her——[*Afide.*] Ay Child.

Lucy. Why then I take you at your Word, Sir, and can produce the aforefaid Sum——[*To* Piz.] With a little of your Affiftance, my Lord.

Lud. (*afide.*) Hum———A pretty Wife I am like to have————Catch me there if you can———

Piz. Ha————How's that?

Lud. How! Miftrefs *Lucy*, worth two thoufand Piftoles?

Lucy. Ay: And I have a very good Pay-mafter for one Half of it too—Do you know this Hand, my Lord? [*To* Pizalto.] (*Shews the Bond.*)

Piz. (*afide.*) Confound your jilting Sneer.

Lud. Ha, ha, ha————What, a thoufand Piftoles a Difh, my Lord? I hope you don't change often, ha——ha————

Piz.

Piz. Hussy, I'll be reveng'd———'Tis all false, 'tis counterfeit.

Lucy. Ha—ha—But it had been current Coin, if I had suffer'd you to put your Stamp upon't———in my Bed-chamber, my Lord———

L. *Piz.* How, Mistress, have you trick'd my Husband out of a thousand Pistoles, and never told me of it?

Lucy. Nay, Madam, don't frown———Remember you have trick'd him out of something too, which I never told him of—Don't urge me to more Discoveries.

Lud. (*aside.*) So———Here's Trick upon Trick: But, Faith, you shall never trick me out of my Liberty. I'm not so fond of a Wife to marry a Chamber-maid, tho' with ten Times as much Money: And so, sweet Mistress *Abigail*, your humble Servant. [*Exit* Ludovico.

L. *Piz.* (*aside.*) The Jade has me upon the Hip—I must be silent.

She who has her Husband's Bed abus'd,
Can ne'er expect she should be better us'd. [Exit.

Lucy, Ha———What! my Lover gone! With all my Heart: Better now than after; for whilst I have my Fortune in my own Hands, I shall have no Need to sue for a separate Maintenance, and get nothing for it neither.

Arm. to *Pla.* Now, Madam, go: May Heaven be propitious
To your Designs: I'll stay and watch *Bassino*:
And when he goes, will follow with *Alonzo*.

Pla. Oh! my sick Fancy frames a thousand Forms,
Which tell me that our Meeting will prove fatal,
And warn me not to go, what shall I do?
Must I bear calmly my *Bassino*'s Loss?
Why do I tremble thus?
Sure it can't be the Fear of Death———No, for if
I go not I must lose him, and that's more
Than Death to me———and if I go, I can but fall,
And Life without him is the greater Woe,
Therefore I'll on, I'll use the softest Words
That Tongue can frame to sooth her into Pity,

And

And diſſuade her from this impious Marriage.
If I ſucceed I am compleatly happy,
If not, I'd rather die than live with Hate,
But firſt, curſt Rival, thou ſhalt ſhare my Fate.
[*Exit* Placentia.

A Flouriſh of Muſick.

Baſſ. 'Tis now the Time——But whither do I go?
Shall I a Maid, a Wife, a Friend betray?
No matter————
All Arguments are vain, where Love bears Sway.
[*Exit* Baſſino.

A SONG.

When the Winds rage, and the Seas grow high,
They bid Mankind beware,
But when they ſmooth and calm the Sky,
'Tis then they would enſnare.

So the bright Thais *Kindneſs ſhows,*
By frowning on her Lovers,
For Ruin only from her flows,
When ſhe her Charms diſcovers.

Piz. Come now, Gentlemen and Ladies, be pleas'd to walk into the next Room, and take a ſmall Collation —But where's my Lord *Baſſino?* Come, Gentlemen, he's gone before us.

Arm. Where we will quickly follow. *(Aſide.) Alonzo,* a Word with you— [*Exit Omnes.*

SCENE II.

A Chamber in Aurelia's *Houſe.*

Two Arm-Chairs. Aurelia *ſola.*

Aur. I wonder much at my *Baſſino*'s Stay:
Oh! Love! how ſwiftly fly thy Hours away

When we are bleſt! How tedious are thy Minutes
When cruel Abſence parts two longing Lovers!

Enter Florella.

Is my *Baſſino* come? ſpeak———

Flor. No, Madam, a young Stranger deſires to ſpeak with you: He ſays, you are not acquainted with his Name, but will ſoon with his Buſineſs, which is ſomething of great Import, that can be told to none but yourſelf.

Aur. A Stranger Buſineſs with me! I know of none
I have with Strangers—Heaven! what's this?
I feel a ſudden Throbbing in my Heart,
As if 'twas conſcious of ſome fatal News— [*Aſide.*
Womaniſh Fears———Admit him—(*Exit* Florella) it muſt be
One of *Baſſino*'s Friends, whom he intruſts
To be a Witneſs of our Marriage Vows.

Enter Placentia, *in Man's Cloaths.*

Pla. Madam, I was inform'd that Count *Baſſino*
Was to be here—and having Things t'impart
That much concern him, I made bold to come———

Aur. Sir, I expect him ſtraight—if you're his Friend
I will account you mine—Be pleas'd to ſit. [*Both ſit.*

Pla. My Brother, Madam, is extremely happy
In being favour'd by ſo fair a Lady———

Aur. Your Brother, Sir! is then my Lord your brother?

Pla. Madam, he is.

Aur. Then I may call you Brother too;
For all the ſolemn Vows of Love have paſs'd
'Twixt him and me—And bliſsful *Hymen* waits
With lighted Torch to tie the ſacred Knot,
Which ſhall be done this Hour———

Pla. This Hour! ſay you? Oh! Madam, have a Care:
You tread inchanted Ground, and e'er you know
What Path you take, you're hurried to Deſtruction.

Aur.

Aur. Where lies the Danger?

Pla. Oh! 'Tis a fatal Tale, yet you must hear it;
Therefore summon your Courage to your Aid,
For you will need it all, whilst I relate
The fatal Story——

Aur. Ah! how I tremble!
Say, is he dead? has any murderous Villain
Kill'd my *Bassino*?

Pla. No—he is well in Health: but his distemper'd Mind
Is of a wild and feverish Disposition,
Longing to taste, what tasted will undo him.

Aur. Your Speech is all a Riddle: Pray speak plainer:
But yet, e'er you proceed, if Count *Bassino* lives,
I care not what must follow, since he's mine.

Pla. No, he's not yours—Nor ever must.

Aur. 'Tis false——There's not a Pow'r on Earth can part us:
Perhaps,
You think my Blood too base to mix with yours——
But, Sir, your Brother loves me, and in Love
All Ranks are equal——

Pla. No——I wish that were all:
But there's a greater Obstacle——He—is—married—
Oh! Gods! unfortunately married!

Aur. Married!

Pla. Yes,——Married——to my Sister,
To my unfortunate, abandon'd Sister.
Oh! do not you conspire t'undo her quite;
It is enough, she's false *Bassino*'s Wife.

Aur. Gods! Married!
And is it possible! Oh! faithless Men!
Oh! Truth! Oh! Justice! Whither are you fled?
Now all my Fears and Horrors are explain'd.

Pla. I'm glad I reach'd this Place in Time, to hinder
Those Ills that must have waited on your Marriage,
Now it is in your Power, both to be happy,
And, in some Measure, make my Sister so. [*Both rise.*

Aur. A Paradox in Nature——Bid *Aurelia*
Be happy, when you rob her of her Heaven!
Her dear *Bassino*!

Indeed your Sister may be counted happy,
If she's his Wife—Ha—Wife—By Heaven! 'tis false—
No, no—He has no other Wife but me———
He is not married, you bely him basely———
He cannot be so treacherous———

Pla. Madam, I swear, whate'er I said is Truth—
Do but defer this Marriage for a Day,
And if I don't produce convincing Proofs,
May all the Plagues a Woman can invent
Fall on my perjur'd Head———

Aur. Defer our Marriage—No, by Heaven I will not.
I can't suspect him—Neither do I think
You durst maintain this Story to his Face.

Pla. Madam, I dare; nay, which is more, I'll die,
Or vindicate my injur'd Sister's Honour———

Aur. Bold Arrogance!
Oh! That he were but here to answer the Affront!
Perhaps he may have wrong'd your Family:
Debauch'd your Sister; for which you would force him
To marry her?———But, I must tell thee, Boy,
He's mine already: nor would he forsake me
To hold Command o'er all the Universe.

Pla Oh! Heaven! must I bear this!

Aur. Nay, expect more, if he should find you here,
'Tis not your being Brother to his Mistress,
That will secure you from his just Revenge.

Pla. Revenge! Nay, then away with all Disguise,
Pity be gone———And in its Room fell Rage
Take place, that I may dash that haughty Insolence
That dares to treat me thus—Know, Madam,
I am his Wife—his lawful wedded Wife.
With borrow'd Shape I came to try your Virtue,
Which I have found so light that the least Puff
Of wanton Love will blast it———Else my Visit
Had met a better Welcome—Here with Sword in Hand
I'll wait his coming, [*Draws.*
And as he enters, pierce thy haughty Breast.
I know he loves thee, and therefore 'tis brave
Revenge to let him see thy dying Pangs:
Thy parting Sighs will rack him worse than Hell.

Aur. His Wife! Oh! Insolence!

In vain you waste your Breath, it moves not me:
So much I love him, so much I'm belov'd,
That should an Angel from yon Heaven descend,
To tell me he's marry'd, I'd not credit him,
Kill me if you dare—He will revenge my Death:
That pleasing Thought gives Courage to my Soul:
To live without him would be Death indeed!
No—he'll ne'er leave me for a common Thing,
For such I'm sure thou art———

Pla. Common! Proud Wretch——by Heaven that Word gives Wings
To my Revenge—Vile Creature, die— [*Stabs her.*

Aur. Help,—Murder, murder———

Enter Bassino.

Bass. Ha—That to thy Heart——[*Kills* Plac.] Wer't thou a Demi-god
And durst attempt this Shrine, thus should'st thou fall—

Pla. (*Falling.*) Oh! *Bassino*! Oh!

Aur. Oh! hold, my Lord, what has your Rashness done?
I only should have dy'd———I'll not upbraid
Your Treachery—No, 'tis the Hand of Heaven
That guides the Stroke that takes my guilty Life,
For being faithless to *Alonzo*.

Bass. Talk not of Death, my fair, my dear *Aurelia*;
That very Sound does harrow up my Soul.
But who art thou, whose sacrilegious Hand
Durst to profane the Temple of my Love?

Pla. I am your Wife—Your loving Wife *Placentia*.
Oh! pardon this rash Deed; blame jealous Love—
And grace me with a Sigh, that I may die contented.

Bass. My Wife! and kill'd by me!
Under what Load of Miseries I stand!
Oh! Horror! Horror! Infinity of Guilt!
Hurl now your vengeful Bolts, Almighty Powers,
On my devoted Head!
Oh! I have wrong'd you both: Deceiv'd you basely:
Thus prostrate on the Ground, let me beg Pardon:
[*Throws himself on the Ground.*

I do not ask it with Design to live.

Aur. Oh! dear *Bassino* live:
And try to save her, for she's innocent:
We only are in Fault———
I urg'd my wretched Fate with impious Language,
For which I beg Forgiveness: Generous Lady,
Let not my Soul depart with Guilt opprest.

Pla. As I forgive you, so may Heaven me.

Bass. Oh! *Placentia!* Oh! my Wife!

Aur. One thing more, and I'm happy———
Were but *Alonzo* here, that I might ask
Forgiveness for my Falshood! But, alas!
My Spirits faint within my frozen Veins,
And every Thing seems double to my Sight:
Oh! How I dread the uncertain future State!

Bass. Unhappy Maid! Oh! my once dear *Aurelia!*
Curst, Curst *Bassino!* Oh! my Wife! How dare
I stand the View of both these injur'd Women!
Oh! Heaven! Why name I Heaven! Heaven will not hear
A Wretch like me———No, even Hell wants Torment
Proportion'd to my Guilt—Oh! my *Placentia!* Oh!

Pla. Oh! my dear Lord, I cannot see you thus:
Live, live, my Lord; be happy when I'm dead.
Nay, for your Sake, I wish *Aurelia* too
May live to make you happy———

Bass. Oh! hold!
Heap not more Curses on me by your Kindness:
I wish that she might live, but not for me,
Only to clear me from her guilty Blood———
Oh! *Placentia!*

Pla Rise, my Lord, rise: Do not indulge your Woe,
Your Sighs atone for all, and make e'en Death a pleasure———
I see him coming, he will soon be here———

Bass. No, I will never rise: ne'er see the Day.
The Sun would blush to shine on such an impious Wretch.
Here let me lie, and tear with these curst Hands
[*Tears the Ground in a distracted Manner.*
A Passage thro' the Earth, and hide my Face for ever.

Alon.

Alon. (*Within.*) Where where's this Villain? Where's *Bassino?*

Aur. 'Tis *Alonzo*'s Voice.
Oh! fly, my Lord, fly from his just Revenge.

Enter Alonzo *hastily.*

Bass. Fly———
Where shall I fly from Justice? No, Heaven is kind
In sending him to help my Journey forward.

Alon. Where's *Bassino?*

Bass. (*Rising.*) Here Sir, I stand.

Alon. Then there stands a Villain———Ha—what
Do I see!———*Aurelia* murder'd!
Oh! treacherous Maid, thy Love has cost thee dear,
Think on thy broken Vows, and call to Heaven for Mercy.
Thy Death I will revenge, because I lov'd thee once.

Aur. Oh! *Alonzo*, pardon me.

Alon. to *Bass.* Now Villain, now what Story, what Pretence
Canst thou invent to avoid my just Revenge?
Oh! that I ne'er had list'ned to thy Tongue!
Thy base perfidious Tongue! Then all these Murders
Had been prevented, and thou curst in Hell———
Thou monstrous Fiend———

Bass. You talk too much—Let's see what you can do:
Thus I return your Villain———

Alon. Take thy Reward. [*They fight,* Bassino *falls.*

Enter Armando.

Arm. Hold! hold: Oh Gods! I'm come too late,
What has my fatal Friendship done!
Ha———*Placentia* too—curst Letter!

Bass. My Friend *Armando!* Oh! I blush to see thee:
But let me have your Pardon———now I need it.

Arm. Oh! first pardon me———
For I have been the Cause of all this Mischief.
Whilst my officious Friendship strives to save you,
I bring you all to this unhappy End.

Say, can you pardon me?

Baff. I do———

And Oh! my Friend! had Virtue been my Guide,
As it was thine, I ftill were truly happy.

Aur. Where am I?

Why do I hover thus 'twixt Reft and Mifery?
Oh! good *Alonzo*, fay you pardon me,
And let me die in Peace, elfe full of Horror
My guilty Soul muft wander in the Shades
Of gloomy Night, and never, never reft.

Alon. Thou haft my Pardon, and with it this Promife
Never to love again———

Aur. Oh! you're——too———kind—and I want—
Breath to thank——you——Farewel. [*Dies.*

Baff. Oh! *Placentia!* [*Embraces her.*

Thus in thy Arms my Thread of Life fhall break.

Pla. My Lord, my Hufband, Oh! come nearer yet,
That I may take a parting Kifs, to fmooth
My Paffage to the Realms of endlefs Night. [*Kiffing him.*
So—Now—I die————much happier than I lived.
Farewel———— [*Dies.*

Baff. Farewel, fair Excellence! Thou beft of Wives!
But I fhall quickly follow—Yet before I go,
I beg, *Alonzo*, let my Death atone
For all the Injuries my Life has done you.
Oh! fpare my Memory, when I'm no more.

Alon. By Heaven!

I fee fuch Virtue ftruggling in thy Breaft,
As makes me wifh I could prevent the Flight
Of thy departing Soul————

Baff. No, no———I would not live:

Hadft thou not come, my Hand had fet me free,
But now I fell more nobly, and lefs guilty.
My Friend, my dear *Armando*,
Hafte to inform my Prince, *Baffino* refts:
But hide, if poffible, my Shame: And let
One Grave hold both this wretched Corps and mine,
Oh! my *Placentia*———— [*Dies.*

Alon. Unhappy Pair! But far more wretched me!
For I muft live, and live without *Aurelia!*
Tho' I'm convinc'd fhe lov'd me not, I can't

Banifh

Banish her Image from my Love-sick Mind,
Oh! that I ne'er had seen the charming Fair!
Arm. The Gods are just in all their Punishments:
And by this single Act, we plainly see
That Vengeance always treads on Perjury;
And tho' sometimes no Bolts be at us hurl'd,
Whilst we enjoy the Pleasures of this World;
Yet a Day awaits, a Day of general Doom,
When guilty Souls must to an Audit come;
Then that we may not tremble, blush, or fear,
Let our Desires be just; our Lives unsullied here.

[*Exeunt omnes.*

[redacted]

[redacted]

[redacted]

[redacted]

[redacted]

THE

BEAU'S DUEL:

OR, A

Soldier for the Ladies.

A

COMEDY.

THE PROLOGUE.

By a GENTLEMAN.

WHAT Hazards Poets run, in Times like these,
Sure to offend, uncertain whom to please:
If in a well-work'd Story they aspire,
To imitate old Rome's *or* Athen's *Fire,*
It will not do; for strait the Cry shall be,
'Tis a forc'd heavy Piece of Bombastry.
If Comedy's their Theme, 'tis ten to one
It dwindles into Farce, and then 'tis gone.
If Farce their Subject be, this Witty Age
Holds that below the Grandeur of the Stage.
Our F male Author, tho' she sees what Fate
Does the Event of such Attempts still wait;
With a true British *Courage ventures on,*
Thinks nothing Honour, without Danger won.
She fain wou'd shew our great Fore-Fathers Days,
When Virtue, Honour, Courage, wore the Bays;
Fain wou'd she kindle up those fading Fires,
That warm'd their Noble Blood to fierce Desires.
When the Bold Hero, after tedious Wars,
With Bleeding Wounds adorn'd, and Glorious Scars,
From Conquest back return'd with Laurels Crown'd,
Where from the Fair, their just Rewards they found.
She thinks't a Crime in any one to dare,
Or hope to gain a Conquest o'er the Fair,
Who ne'er cou'd boast a Victory in War.
Let but your Arms abroad successful prove,
The Fair at home shall crown your Toils with Love.

THE EPILOGUE.

By the AUTHOR.

YOU see Gallants 't has been our Poet's Care,
To shew what Beaus in their Perfection are,

EPILOGUE.

By Nature Cowards, foolish, useless Tools,
Made Men *by* Taylors, *and by* Women, Fools:
A Fickle, False, *a* Singing, Dancing *Crew*,
Nay now we hear they've Smiling Masters *too;*
Just now a Frenchman *in the Dressing-room,*
From teaching of a Beau to Smile, was come,
He shew'd five Guineas——Wasn't he rarely paid,
Thus all the World by Smiles *are once betray'd;*
The States-man *Smiles on them he wou'd* undo,
The Courtier's Smiles *are very seldom* true,
The Lover's *Smiles too many do believe,*
And Women Smile *on them they wou'd deceive;*
When Tradesmen *Smile, they safely* Cheat *with Ease;*
And smiling Lawyers *never fail of* Fees.——
The Doctor's Look the Patient's Pain beguiles,
The Sick Man lives, *if the* Physician smiles:
Thus Smiles *with Interest Hand in Hand do go,*
He surest strikes, that Smiling gives the Blow;
Poets, with us this Proverb do defy,
We live by Smiles, *for if you* frown *we die.*
To please you then shall be our chief Endeavour,
And all we ask, is but your Smiles for ever. [Going.
Hold——I forgot, the Author bid me say,
She humbly begs Protection for her Play:
'Tis Yours——She Dedicates it to you all,
And sure you're too generous to let it fall;
She hopes the Ladies will her Cause maintain,
Since Virtue here has been her only Aim.
The Beaus, she thinks, won't fail to do her Right,
Since here they're taught with Safety how to fight.
She's sure of Favour from the Men of War,
A Soldier is her darling Character;
To fear the Murmurs then wou'd be absurd,
They only Mutiny when not prefer'd.
But yet, I see she does your Fury dread,
And like a Prisoner, stands with Fear half dead,
While you are Judges, do her Sentence give,
If you're not pleas'd, she says she cannot live.
Let my Petition then for once prevail;
And let your gen'rous Claps her Pardon seal.

Drama-

Dramatis Personæ.

MEN.

Col. Manly, *in Love with* Clarinda.	*Mr.* Cory.
Capt. Bellmein, *his Friend.*	*Mr.* Booth.
Toper, *an Enemy to Matrimony, and a Friend to the Bottle.*	*Mr.* Powell.
Sir William Mode, *a Fop, in Love with* Clarinda, *and countenanced by her Father.*	*Mr.* Bowman.
Ogle, *a Fortune-hunter, a conceited Fellow that fancies every Body is in Love with him.*	*Mr.* Pack,
Carefull, *Father to* Clarinda.	*Mr.* Fieldhouse.

WOMEN.

Clarinda, *in Love with* Manly.	*Mrs.* Prince.
Emilia, *her Cousin, an Heiress, newly come out of the Country.*	*Mrs.* Porter.
Mrs. Plotwell, *formerly a Mistress to* Bellmein.	*Mrs.* Lee.
Maid to Clarinda.	

A Serjeant, Drummers, and Servants.

The SCENE LONDON.

THE

THE
BEAU'S DUEL:
OR, A
Soldier for the Ladies.

ACT I. SCENE I.

SCENE, *The Street.*

Enter Colonel Manly.

Colonel.

HOW do Men labour to fool themselves? What Pains did I spare, or Excuse did I not invent, to persuade my Friends I was going another Way, to get rid of their troublesome Ceremony, that wou'd have waited on me Home; and all this for an Opportunity only of taking a Turn or two before this Window.

Oh Love! How powerful are thy Charms, thus to unman, and send me like a Boy, gaping after imaginary Joys.

Not all the Hazards of a Soldier's Life could so much affect me, as the dreadful Apprehension of displeasing this Girl.

What-

Whatever I do, whether I eat or drink, whether I ſleep or wake, whether I'm at Home alone, or abroad in Company, my Thoughts are ſtill of her: She's always preſent, I can ſee nothing but her; I can hear nothing but her, I can think of nothing but her; and in ſhort, I care for nothing but her.

'Tis Happineſs enough for any Man to love and be beloved by ſuch a Woman; ſhe's ſo Beautiful, ſo Agreeable, and ſo Loving; yet ſo Virtuous, ſo Chaſte, and ſo Conſtant, that if her Father's rigid Oppoſition were remov'd, nothing could add to the Bleſſing which lies in Store for me.

Enter Captain Bellmein, *goes within two or three Yards of the Door, then ſteps ſhort, looks up.*

Capt. Ho, this muſt be the Houſe—But what the Devil am I the better for't, the Doors are lock'd, Windows barr'd, my Miſtreſs aſleep, and I may return like an Aſs as I came, without ſo much as being dream'd of—Can Love, that never fails its Votaries at a pinch, inſpire no Stratagem now? Egad I was never more able to offer him a plentiful Sacrifice; and did my Miſtreſs know with what warm deſires I come, ſhe'd meet me half Way, or ſhe deſerves to die a Maid.

Col. The more I think I ſtill perplex myſelf the more; like a poor Fly in a Spider's Web, by labouring to get looſe, I work myſelf faſter in the Toil.

And why ſhould I ſtruggle any longer with what I can't maſter? or deſire to be without what I'm perſuaded is the greateſt Bleſſing in the World———

I am reſolved I will love on——[*Turns ſhort upon the Captain.*] Ha! a Man, and if I miſtake not, mad *Bellmein*, whom I left at the *Roſe*; he's upon ſome amorous Deſign, but is too open to hide any thing from his Friend. I'll accoſt him.

Good-morrow, Captain, I commend your early Induſtry, you are chuſing ſome fortify'd Piece of Virtue to lay a manly Siege to.

Capt. Ha! Colonel, Good-morrow to you with all my Heart: No Faith, I never ſtay the Formality of a Siege;

Siege, 'tis your honourable Lovers are forced to undergo that Drudgery; whene'er I meet any, as I rarely do, that resist the Shock of my first Assault, I fairly draw off to the next, who are sure to surrender upon more easy Terms.

Col. So you take all by Storm, plunder the Garrison, fire their Quarters, and march off in Triumph.

Capt. What I do can't be comprehended by constant puling Lovers.

They can't bear those strong Joys we suck from our lusty Draughts of Love; like weak-sighted Birds, they fly about in Twilight of Pleasure, not able to bear the Meridional Heat and Pleasure of it.

One kind Glance crowns your Hopes, and raises you to the highest Happiness; but then a Frown, or sour Look, Colonel, throws you down again to Despair. So that——

Col. Have a care Captain, how far you launch out in this Strain, lest you be too like our modern Widows, who exclaim most against a second Husband, when they are just upon the Point of having one.

Capt. So that from my laughing at honourable Lovers as you call them, you would learnedly infer I am one myself.

Col. Nay Railery apart, it has been seriously observ'd that you are——

Capt. What?

Col. Very much alter'd of late.

How! Faith I think myself the same Man, I have the same Appetites, the same Desires, that ever I had.

Col. Ay, but you saunter about in solitary Places, avoid your Acquaintance, and when you can't escape them, are more uneasy than a rich Miser with a borrowing Friend: And here now I find you out of your Way, addressing yourself to senseless Wood and Stone.

Capt. Ay, my Friend, but this senseless Wood includes a more beautiful *Daphne* than e'er the *Delian* God pursued; a Girl so bright, so sparkling, and what recommends her much more to me, so coming, [*Embraces him.*] that had she lived in the Days of *Venus*, she would have rival'd that Goddess and out-done her too in her own Attributes.

Col.

Col. Have a Care you don't misplace your Worship, for to my particular Knowledge no such Person lodges in this House.

Capt. To my more particular Knowledge such a Person does lodge in this House, and in the Room that looks out at that Window too.

Col. Ha! *Clarinda* lodges there, 'tis true; but that she's such as he describes is false——Yet she's a Woman, and where Dissembling grows so much in Use, Perfection must be a Stranger. I'll for a while lay by the implicit Lover for the more inquisitive jealous Man, and try him farther. [*Aside.*] Well, I may be deceived, but how do you know you are so too?

Capt. Why Faith, since I know you to be an honest Fellow, and a Man of Honour, I don't care if I trust you with the Secret, upon Condition your Assistance shan't be wanting upon Occasion.

Col. 'Slife I shall be drawn in to help him away with my Mistress [*Aside*] If she be such as you describe, I believe you will have no great Occasion for help. But to the Purpose.

Capt. Why you must know, that in this House lives a damn'd positive ill-natured old Fellow.

Col. I know it too well, or by this Time his Daughter had been out of your Reach. [*Aside.*

Capt. And that there's a young Lady, his Daughter, Niece, or something.——

Col. Ay, very probable. What then?

Capt. Why, that likes my Person, that's all.

Col. How do you know this?

Capt. Know it? I have infallible Signs of it; she makes Assignations with me, and keeps them; receives my Addresses, Letters and Songs, nay sings them too; and if these ben't Signs she likes me, the Devil's in't.

Col. Well, but her Name—I'll yet believe *Clarinda* innocent, and 'tis some one else he mistakes for her. [*Aside.*

Capt. Nay, now faith, Colonel, you are unreasonable, you know 'tis not fair to tell Names.

Col. Not tell me her Name! then I shall think you trifled with me all this while, and scorn the Friendship I offer,

Capt. I'll rather tell you all I know, but as for her Name, Faith and Troth I know no more hers than she does mine; her desire to be unknown herself, made her the less pressing, I suppose, so that we freely pass among ourselves for *Celadon* and *Cloe*, as you may see by this Song, if you'll be at the Pains of reading it? 'tis the last I sent her, and tho' inconsiderable in itself, receives from her Voice inestimable Value.

Col. O' my Soul, the very Song I heard *Clarinda* sing, 'tis she past all Doubt.

Capt. What, at a stand *Colonel!* Ha! What means all this Concern?

Col. 'Tis for you, my Friend; that Woman you admire I know to be the most cunning, treacherous, and false Dissembler, nay worse, if worse can be, in the World; I would advise you to proceed with Caution; for Husbands, *Captain*, too late repent, when they can't quit the Ill.

Capt. Ho, if it be only my Dangers that disturb you, I'll soon ease you of that Trouble; Marriage is not the Course I steer, we never admit so sour a Thought to turn our more pleasant Conversation.

Col. How, not marry! what then does all this tend to?

Capt. Phoo, that's unreasonable again; why nothing, nothing but a little harmless Mirth or so.

Col. On my Soul he designs to debauch her. [*Aside.*

Capt. Ha! the Colonel in his Dumps again, there's something in't I don't understand. [*Aside.*

Col. Harkee, Captain, I know you have Courage, and always took you for a Man of Honour, therefore think it worth my while to tell you this Woman you have been so free with is one I have a long Time loved, therefore expect you'll give me unquestionable Proofs of what you have said, or meet me with your Sword, and so leave you to prepare yourself for which you think most proper. [*Going.*

Capt. Hey day! Have I been all this while making a Confident of my Rival, and telling my Secrets to the only Man I ought to hide them from? Now I perceive what 'twas made him so testy, but he shan't part thus.

Lookee,

Lookee, Colonel, to ſhew how much I value your Friendſhip, I'll conſent to what you propoſe; and tho' Fighting may be of leſs Trouble, yet for your Eaſe I'll undertake to make out what I've ſaid.

Col. Upon that Condition I'll call you Friend again; but if you ſhould fail, you had beſt look to it.

Capt. Here's ſome Company coming this Way, let's retire till they paſs, then I'll tell you our whole Intrigue, and leave you to judge whether I have Reaſon to think as I do. [*They withdraw.*

Enter Sir William Mode.

Sir *Will.* *Le Reviere.*——[*Laric*] Sir [Sir *Will.*] Bliſter me if you don't ſpeak plain *Engliſh*! I ſhall have the World think I'm ſuch a Sloven as to keep an *Engliſh* Valet: do you hear, if you don't mimick 'em better I ſhall turn you away.

Le Rev. Me vil take al de Care imaginable, Sir.

Sir *Will.* Very well. Is the Muſick all come?

Le Rev. Yes Sire, here be de Fidle, de Hautbois, de Courtel, and Baſe Vial, dey be all deſpoſe for to receive your Command.

Sir *Will.* 'Tis very well d'hear, do you marſhal them in Order before this Window, and ſee they be ready to ſtrike up as ſoon as I give the Word. [*The Colonel and Captain appear.*

Capt. What the Devil's here, another Lover? What think you now, Colonel; your Miſtreſs muſt be more than Woman if ſhe can hold out againſt ſuch a formal Siege.

Col. This Fop I know too well to be jealous of, and know her ſo far from encouraging him, that her Father's Authority which countenances him, can ſcarce procure him common Civilty from her.

Capt. Hiſt, the Thing opens.

Sir *Will.* Well 'tis an unſpeakable Happineſs we Men of Parts enjoy above the reſt of Mankind: By our good Management we make our Acceſs to every Thing we admire, eaſy and certain: How many thick-ſkull'd Fellows are content to dream of their Miſtreſſes, while I take a more ſecure Method, and wake her in the Morning with harmonious Muſic.

I wonder how the Ladies can ſuffer theſe idle Fellows that take no more Pains to pleaſe them; for my own Part, I believe I have ſomething extraordinary in me that makes me ſo acceptable to all the Women I come in Company with.——Well Muſic!

I hope you will all ſhew yourſelves Maſters in your Performance; come ſtrike up: Ah! merciful *Apollo*, what a hideous Noiſe you make; there's a Sound fitter to ſtorm a Breach with, than approach a Lady's Slumbers. Play ſome ſoft Air, a Concert of Flutes would have done well.

[*While the Muſic plays he uſes a great many odd Poſtures; ſeeing the Door open the Muſic ceaſes, and he runs to meet* Clarinda'*s Maid.*]

Col. How, the Door open?

Sir *Will.* Ha! my dear Angel, How does my Goddeſs receive my Morning Sacrifice?

Flo. As ſhe does every thing that comes from the incomparable Sir *William Mode*, with particular Marks of Favour in private, tho' ſhe's oblig'd to lay great Reſtraint on her Carriage in public, to appear cold to him.

Sir *Will.* But, methinks, ſhe need not be reſerv'd, ſince I have her Father's Conſent.

Flo. Ay, 'tis that makes her ſo; for his croſs Humour, ſhou'd ſhe ſhow the Affection ſhe really has for you, wou'd make him run counter to what he ſo eagerly purſues now out of mere Oppoſition: For he never oppos'd Colonel *Manly*, till ſhe expreſs'd ſome liking for him; and now ſhe fears, ſhou'd ſhe own her Love for you, 'twou'd prove as fatal to her Hopes; therefore begs you, by me, to take all Indifference in public for particular Marks of Favour.

Sir *Will.* Well, I'll take your Advice; and ſweet Mrs. *Flora*, let me intreat you to accept of this ſmall Acknowledgment for Favours I have receiv'd by your means.

Flo. Oh! Lord, Sir, I vow I'm aſham'd; but I ſhall be always ready to do you good Offices with my Lady: Sir, your Servant. [*Exit.*

Sir *Will.* Adieu, Angel,——here Muſic, ſtrike up a merry Ramble, and lead to my Lodgings. [*Exit.*

Col. O Woman! Woman! Now Friend, I believe

all

all you said, and a great deal more; yet who cou'd expect with so much Beauty, such ugly Falshood. For thee, or any Man, she might have some Plea; but this sign of a Man! to fall so low argues a very deprav'd Appetite: S'death, I can't bear the Thoughts on't.

Capt. Have a little Patience, and every small Discovery will help you forward to your lost Liberty: Before To-morrow Night I'll lay such convincing Proofs before your Eyes, as shall infallibly complete your Cure.

Col. What's here, another Serenade? More Lovers yet?

Enter Toper, *Singing.*

The Devil a bit care I for a Wife,
So I have but Wine and a Fire;
A Wench when I please my Passion to ease,
The Devil a Wife I desire.

Capt. Ha, ha, drunken *Toper*, reeling home after a Night's Debauch; sure he's no Lover, 'twou'd be impossible for the blind God to find his Heart for the Fumes of Wine; besides, 'tis so indifferent to every Thing else, there's no taking it but with a Bottle.

Col. Ha, *Toper*, thou holdest thy own yet, I see.

Top. *Colonel*, good Morrow, I wish you hold your own, Boy, for I met a thing in the next Street may chance undermine your Foundation, one who says he can do more in one Night, than you in all the Days of the Week.

Col. What do you mean?

Top. Why I met Sir *William Mode* big with Success returning from *Clarinda*, who, he says, encourages his Addresses in private, and only favours you in public, to egg her Father on to Consummation with him; and this he purchas'd with a Serenade.

Col. S'death, does he boast of his Success, and must my Misfortune be the Subject of the Coxcomb's Raillery? Am I publish'd to the World as a Blind for his Designs? Hell and Furies, 'tis not to be borne: I'll after him immediately, and were every Vanity about him a *Hercules*, I'd force my Way thro' them all, to stop that foul Breath of his. [*Going.*

Capt.

Capt. Hold, hold, you will but widen the Sore you design to heal; 'twill be no hard Matter from the Coxcomb's fruitful Impertinence to take another Occasion for Quarrelling, and then pay old Scores; or if it be my Luck first to meet the Opportunity, you may be sure I'll throw in a hearty Thrust for you.

Top. Nay, Sir, you may save yourself the Labour of Quarrelling, for he won't answer Expectation, I assure you.

Capt. A Coward; Nay, then he shall dance a Minuet the length of the Street, while I beat Time on his Back-side.

Col. Hang him, he's not worth our Resentment: Pr'ythee *Toper*, what is he, for I have but barely seen him?

Toper. In the first Place, he's a mere Compound of Powder, Paint, and Affectation, so perfum'd, you may smell him a Mile; he thinks every Woman in Love with him, and will allow no Man to claim a share in ought above a Chamber-maid; or stand Competition with his Parts or Person.

Capt. And yet not fight, say you?

Toper. Fight! no, no, he hates the Sight of a drawn Sword, as much as I do that of an empty Bottle. He will sometimes pretend to Courage, as some Women will to Honour and Honesty, tho' their Inclinations tend to neither, no more than mine to Matrimony. He has 4000*l.* a Year, which he spends in Intrigues, fine Cloaths, and Musick. And he has always as many Fidlers at his Heels, as a General, Officers at his *Levee*.

Col. Whose Attendance is better rewarded, I fancy, no doubt they taste the Fruits of their Labours sweetly.

Toper. I'my Conscience, I believe they deserve it, for who becomes his Favourite, must use as much Flattery as wou'd purchase a Maidenhead, tho' the Woman's design was Marriage. Oh! that Fortune shou'd be so liberal to such a Fool, when so many honest Fellows sit in a Coffee-house all the Evening, for want of Money to go to the Tavern.

Col. Riches are the common Chance of Knaves and Fools, Fortune is rarely favourable to a Man of Sense;

'tis

'tis with Difficulty and Danger they purchaſe a Smile from that fickle Miſtreſs, but Fools are ſtill her Care.

I ſhall take more Notice of this Fellow the next time I ſee him.

Toper. Which may be this Morning if you will, for he juſt now invited me to an Entertainment of Muſic, that is to be perform'd at his Chamber, by ſome of the beſt Maſters; there will be Champagne, Boy.

Capt. Will you go, Colonel?

Col. Not I; the Converſation of Town Ladies, who entertain you with the Opinions of fifty Fools of their Wit and Beauty, and how manag'd by them to their Ruin, wou'd be a thouſand Times more acceptable to me, than the medley Chat of Fops and Fidlers.

Capt. Then you won't go?

Col. No, I'll expect you at my Lodgings. [*Exit.*

Toper. But you will, there's Champagne, Pox o'the Company.

Capt. And Muſic too, if that be good, the Company be hang'd. [*Exit.*

SCENE *changes to* Clarinda's *Lodging in her Father's Houſe.*

Enter Clarinda, *and her Couſin* Emilia, *undreſs'd, as wak'd by the Serenade.*

Clar. Dear *Emilia*, you aſk ſo many Queſtions, pr'thee have ſome Pity, and ſpare me a little.

Em. Dear Couſin, do you pity me, and anſwer me a little.

Clar. I have anſwer'd you, theſe three Days you have been in Town, more Queſtions than all the Aſtrologers and Philomaths in *London* cou'd reſolve in a Month.

Em. And I have as many more to aſk before I can be ſatisfied: I'd fain know the Cauſe of all this Alteration, why ſo much Uneaſineſs, and ſo much Spleen? Never pleas'd but when you are diſpleas'd, nor like your Company; but when you are alone. In ſhort, I have obſerv'd——

Clar.

Clar. What have you obferv'd, Coufin?

Em. Why, that your Father is never well, but when talking of Sir *William*; nor you pleas'd, but when you are thinking of fomebody elfe.

Clar. Oh, How inquifitive are Girls!

Em. Oh, How referv'd are Lovers!

Clar. Pr'ythee, Coufin, learn to be more ferious.

Em. Pr'ythee, Coufin, learn to be more free.

Clar. Then you pofitively believe I am in Love.

Em. Pofitively.

Clar. And with——

Em. Another-guefs Man than your Father defigns for you.

Clar. And nothing——

Em. Will perfuade me to the contrary.

Clar. Why then I am; and fince 'tis in vain to hide it from you, *Emilia*, I'll try you with that Confidence I hitherto thought you too young for.

Em. Alas, fhe little thinks I have as great Intrigues of my own as any fhe can truft me with, tho' I have been but three Days in Town. [*Afide.*

Clar. I am as you fee, Coufin, befieg'd Night and Day, by two as different as Night and Day; one in the Head of innumerable Fopperies and Infolencies attacks me with the Affurance of a Conqueror, before he enters the Field; being fupported by the harfh Authority of a rigid Father. The other, after a thoufand obfequious Demonftrations of Love at refpectful Diftance, courts to be admitted mine, rather than feeks to have me his.

Em. I'my Confcience, were it my Cafe, I fhou'd not be at a Stand which to chufe, there being fuch apparent Difference.

Clar. Nay, there is more yet; for one is Generous and Brave, the other Cowardly and Pitiful; one Judicious, t'other Impertinent; one Conftant, t'other Whimfical; one a Man of Senfe, t'other a Blockhead; one admir'd by all, t'other ridicul'd by all.

Em. One, I fuppofe, is the Gentleman that gave the Serenade, Sir *William*, of whom I have heard fo much fince I came to Town; but t'other, *Clarinda*, I fear is no where to be found, fuch Men appear but as they fay the Phœnix does, not above one in an Age.

Clar. And that ours has one in him, the judicious part of Mankind bears Witneſs.

Em. Lovers, *Clarinda,* like People in Motion, fancy every thing they ſee, moves as they do; and may be from the Knowledge of your own Principles and Reſolutions, you form your Notion of his——Now cou'd I almoſt find in my Heart to diſcover my own Intrigue, if 'twere only to let her ſee, there are Men that equal, if not exceed, hers, but that I'm aſham'd of its Forwardneſs in ſo ſhort a Time. [*Aſide.*] But how comes it, Couſin, that we never ſee this Man?

Clar. Before you come to Town, my Father forbid him the Houſe, with any farther Pretenſions to me, upon Sir *William*'s Account, to whom his Honour was engag'd before he ſaw him, or elſe I believe his Follies wou'd have out-weigh'd his Eſtate; for he, you know——

Em. I know too much of him, for I have ſeen him.

Clar. So you have t'other too, he was one of the two that bow'd to us t'other Night from the Side-box, and of whom you have ſince been ſo inquiſitive, tho' I never let you into the Secret till now.

Em. Of one of thoſe? I know a Secret which I believe you are a Stranger to, and which I wou'd not for the World diſcover, till I know more on't. [*Aſide.*] If that be he, I like him as well as you can; but I think a Gentleman of Sir *William*'s Eſtate ſhou'd not ſeem ſo contemptible.

Clar. O dear Couſin, don't name him, for beſides the particular Averſion I have for him, 'twould beget in the World a very ſlender Opinion of my Senſe, ſhou'd I encourage ſuch a Fop.

Em. O quite contrary: Beſides, Couſin, if you hate him, you can never get it in your Power to torment him, more than by marrying him.

Clar. That would be making myſelf uneaſy, purely to trouble another: No, no, I muſt have ſome Contrivance to expoſe him, and our Neighbour Mrs. *Plotwell* ſhall help me in it.

Em. Does that Lady ſtill continue her Perſecution of Fops?

Clar. With as much Addreſs and Succeſs as ever; and

her

her pleaſant Accounts of her feign'd Intrigues, makes her very entertaining Company; ſhe hates Sir *William Mode*, and I am ſure will aſſiſt in any thing. I never had a ſtronger Temptation to Diſobedience than now; Love and Merit plead on *Manly*'s Side, Reaſon too approves my Choice; the other's an empty Nothing, a mere Talker; we'll ſhew his right Side, expoſe him, ſhall we not, my Dear?

Em. With all my Heart; I love Miſchief ſo well, I can refuſe nothing that farthers that.

The End of the FIRST ACT.

ACT II. SCENE I.

SCENE *Sir* William's *Lodgings.*

Enter Sir William *in a Night-Gown, looking in his Glaſs.*

Sir *Will.* THIS riſing early is the moſt confounded thing on Earth, nothing ſo deſtructive to the Complexion. Bliſter me, how I ſhall look in the Side-Box to Night, wretchedly upon my Soul. [*Looking in the Glaſs all the while.*] Yet it adds ſomething of a languiſhing Air, not altogether unbecoming, and by Candle-light may do Miſchief; but I muſt ſtay at home to recover ſome Colour; and that may be as well laid on too; ſo 'tis reſolv'd I will go. Oh! 'tis unſpeakable Pleaſure to be in the Side-box, or bow'd to from the Stage, and be diſtinguiſh'd by the Beaus of Quality; to have a Lord fly into one's Arms, and kiſs one as amorouſly as a Miſtreſs: Then tell me aloud, that he din'd with his Grace, and that he and the Ladies were ſo fond of me, they talk'd of nothing elſe. Then, ſays I, my Lord, his Grace does me too much Honour——Then, my Lord,——Pox on this Play, 'tis not worth ſeeing; we han't been ſeen at t'other Houſe to Night; and the Ladies will be disappointed, not to receive a Bow from Sir *William*. He, he, he, says I, my Lord, I'll wait upon your Lordship, Then says my Lord, Lead the Way, Sir *William*. Oh, pray my Lord, I beg your Lordship's Pardon——Nay, Sir *William*——Pray my Lord——[*Enter* La Reviere.] Pray Sir *William*——Pray my Lord.

[*As he says this several Times,* La Reviere *enters behind him, but as he designs to pass by him, is still prevented by his turning from one side to t'other, as he acts himself or the Lord.*

La Rev. Hey! What the Devil is he conjuring and talking with invisible Lords? He's in his Airs, some pleasing Imagination hurries him out of his Senses——But I must to my Cue. Hem, hem, Sir, dere be one two Gentlemen below, come to wait upon you dis Morning; sal I show dem up?

Sir *Will*. No, my Lord, by no Means, I know better things.

La Rev. What then am I a Lord? Egad I never knew my Quality before. [*Aside*.

Sir *Will*. Pshaw this Blockhead has rous'd me from the prettiest Entertainment in the World. [*Aside*.] Well, what would you, Sir?

La Rev. I vov'd tell you, Sir, dere be one two Gentlemen wait upon you.

Sir *Will*. And let 'em wait till I have done—I had a thousand fine things to say upon that Occasion, but this rude Fellow has frighten'd 'em all out of my Head. [*Aside*.] Well, since my better Diversion is over shew 'em up.

La Rev. Yes, Sir. [*Exti La* Reviere.

Enter Captain Bellmein, *and* Toper.

Sir *Will*. Gentlemen, I'm your most humble Servant, Mr. *Toper*, I am extremely yours, for the Honour you have done me in bringing your Friend; I lay under severe Apprehensions that nothing could engage you but a drinking Bout.

Top. Faith you were in the Right; for if your Champaign had not more Charms than your Music, your Fidlers might have play'd by themselves for me.

Sir

Sir *Will.* Oh how unpolish'd! how barbarous that is!

Capt. *Bell.* Why do you expect any other from him? He admires no Music like Wine rattling in the Throat of a Flask, with a Chorus of Drawers at coming, Sir.

Sir *Will.* And that to me is the most nauseous thing under the Moon, impair my Vigour.

Top. Impair my Vigour! ha, ha, very pretty, Faith; Pr'ythee where did'st get that Affirmative?

Sir *Will.* 'Tis my own, at the Purchase of some Days Study; for to use another Man's Oath, is, in my Opinion, as indecent as wearing his Cloaths: And to be in the Road of the Vulgar, is beneath a Gentleman, who, in my Judgment, ought to be as much distinguish'd by his Expressions, as by his Coach and Livery.

Capt. *Bell.* Right, Sir; for since every Body that has Money enough, sets up an Equipage, a Gentleman ought to find out some other Way of distinguishing himself.

Sir *Will.* O'my Conscience, they will ape us in that too; for they are so proud of following their Betters, that they even tread upon their Heels; not a formal Cit, or aukward Lawyer's Clerk, that won't court the Cook-wench a Quarter of a Year for Oil and Flower enough to garnish out his Wig for a Day, that he may impudently mimick a Beau; if 'twere not beneath me, I could kick such Animals to a Jelly.

Top. How! kick 'em to a Jelly——Why I have seen of that kind you talk of, brawny Fellows that cou'd kick and cuff too stoutly.

Sir *Will.* Ay, that may be, but 'tis not a Gentleman's Business, that always wears a Sword, and has some half Dozen of Footmen at his Heels, to kick and cuff; nor stand and consider whether the Mechanick be arm'd or not; 'tis enough that he is, or but thinks he is affronted, to atone for the Life of a Scoundrel.

Capt. *Bell.* Now wou'd this Ass, rank Coward as he is, if not curb'd by the Law, kill a hundred Men, honester and stouter than himself, only because they don't wear Swords, or are not so finical. [*Aside*,

Top. I should think, Sir *William*, these honest People that wear no Swords, very harmless, because they carry no Instruments of Mischief about 'em.

Sir *Will.* Inſtruments! their very Hands, their dirty Cloaths, are Inſtruments of Miſchief. Lookee, Sir, I'll make it very plain to you, I may lawfully kill a Man in my own Defence that comes arm'd *in Terrorem*, to rob me of fifty Pounds.

Capt. *Bell.* Right, Sir.

Sir *Will.* You allow that?

Top. We do.

Sir *Will.* Then I'll prove the reſt in an Inſtant; I have a new Suit on that coſt me fifty Pounds, here comes thundering by a dirty Dray-man with his Cart, that puts me in bodily Fear, and ruſhing rudely by, daubs all my Cloaths, ſo that I can't wear them any more; now here's fifty Pounds loſt by this Raſcal's dirty Cloaths, if I don't prevent it by running him thro' the Body.

Capt. *Bell.* How! kill a Man for wearing dirty Cloaths, ha, ha, ha, the Law makes better Proviſion for Mens Lives.

Sir *Will.* The Law ſhou'd make better Proviſions for Mens Cloaths too; for the Inſolence of the Vulgar is inſufferable, and if one or two of them were made Examples, the reſt wou'd be more civil.

One Night after Play, I waited on a Lady from the Box to her Coach, comes a clumſy Cit with a paultry Maſk out of the Gallery, ruſh'd againſt me, threw down the Lady's Page, bruſh'd all the Powder out of my Wig, then cry'd ha, ha, ha, we have ruin'd the Beau; had I been a Lord, I wou'd have run him thro' the Guts; but to be try'd by a *Middleſex* Jury is the Devil.

Top. Ay——these Vulgar, as you call them, have a greater Reſpect for one another than to ſuffer that Man to eſcape that kills one of them. But I ſuppoſe your principal Concern riſes from your Loſs of the Lady's Favour.

Sir *Will.* It had no ſuch Effect on her, I aſſure you, Sir; wherever I get footing in a Lady's Eſteem, I ſtand too firm to be juſtled out by a Cit: As for Inſtance, I'll give you another Adventure of mine. Being engaged by Appointment to meet a Lady at *White*'s, and detain'd by ſome extraordinary Buſineſs, the Lady chanc'd to be there in her Coach, as ſoon as I arrived in mine; ſo that

lighting

lighting out of my Coach to go to hers, a nasty Fellow running just against me, almost beat me backward; and tho' he did it designedly, yet cried, Zounds, can't you see! Your Wig blinds you, does it! So taking one Side, gave it such a Toss over my Shoulder, that, had not the Lady been passionately in Love with my Person, the Disorder I appear'd in might have spoil'd my Amour.

Enter Servant, and whispers.

Capt. *Bell.* Incorrigible Coxcomb! Pox on him, I'm weary of him, there's no Variety in him. Come, shall we go?

Top. No, pr'ythee stay a little till we see what becomes of the Music.

Capt. *Bell.* Of the Champagne you mean, *Toper*, ha, ha, ha.

Sir *Will.* Ah! Gentlemen, I'm the most unfortunate Man this Day alive.

Capt. *Bell.* Why, what's the Matter?

Sir *Will.* A curst Mischance has robb'd me——

Top. Not of your Wine, I hope.

Capt. *Bell.* Nor your Mistress?

Sir *Will.* No, but of Mr. *Quaver*.

Top. Why, is he dead?

Sir *Will.* Not quite dead, but an unlucky Accident has put it out of his Power to oblige us with his incomparable Voice.

Capt. *Bell.* Is he run thro' the Body?

Top. Or drunk before Dinner?

Sir *Will.* No, no, Gentlemen, but he has scalded his Mouth by drinking his Chocolate too hot this Morning, and can't sing.

Top. Ha, ha, ha, a sad Mischance indeed.

Enter Servant and whispers, then goes out and brings in a Letter.

Capt. *Bell.* Pr'ythee, *Toper*, who is this Fellow he laments so much? Some Rascal, that finding his Weakness, imposes on him.

Top. No, 'tis an intimate Friend of his, one as whimsical as himself, and truly fit for no other Company; he made shift in a Month's Time to purchase the Displeasure of most of the Quality in Town, in spite of some Excellence he has in Music; and now is become fit Entertainment for such Fops as this, who, after the strictest Engagement, will be put off with trifling Excuses. [*Aside*.

Sir *Will*. You see, Gentlemen, how I spend my Life, I divide the greatest Part of it between Love and Music: And, to make amends for the Disappointment of one, Fate has sent me some new Discovery in t'other. A new Amour enfeeble me; for, upon my Soul, Gentlemen, I never saw the Hand before; and to convince you of its novelty, I'll open it fairly before you. [*He opens, and* Toper *looks over his Shoulder*.] *Reads*. Sir *William*, I beg the Favour you'd meet me——Ay, as I said, Gentlemen——Pr'ythee *Toper* read out.

[*While he reads, Sir* William *capers about*.

Top. A Billet-doux do you call it? 'Tis the most masculine one I ever saw, and invites to rougher Entertainment than you imagine; 'tis a very pretty Billet-doux truly: Shall I read it out, Sir *William*?

Sir *Will*. Ay, pr'ythee, dear *Toper*.

Top. Sir *William*, I beg the Favour you'd meet me behind *Montague* House, at Six To-morrow Morning, with your Sword in your Hand, in order to answer what shall be alledg'd against you, by yours, as you use me,

Roughly.

Capt. *Bell*. A Billet-doux, do you call it? Why 'tis a Challenge.

Sir *Will*. Ha! [*Taking the Letter, and looking upon it*.] 'Tis so, impair my Vigour; now blister me, if I did not think it as plain a Billet-doux as ever I read in all my Life. Where did the Porter say he brought this Letter from?

Serv. From *Will*'s Coffee-house, Sir.

Sir *Will*. The Devil he did! Why, what have these Men of the Sword encroach'd upon our Privilege there too? What Business can they have amongst us Beaux and Poets——What shall I do? For in short, I won't fight a Man I don't know——and, Gentlemen, I vow I don't remember I ever saw this Mr *Roughly* in my Life.

Top. Oh! he's a damn'd fighting Fellow, your only way is to send him word you'll meet him on *Calais*

Sands:

Sands: Duelling is unsafe in *England* for Men of Estates, he'll hardly be at the Trouble of going over; so that if he will fight you, he must draw upon you whene'er he meets you; if so, you'll have both the Mob and the Law on your Side; and if you kill him, you need not care a Souse.

Sir *Will.* Say you so, Sir, I'll take your Advice, and answer it immediately.

Capt. *Bell.* I think Mr. *Toper* has given you Counsel as nicely, as if you had given five Guineas for a Fee.

Sir *Will.* I'm infinitely oblig'd to him.

Capt. *Bell.* Sir *William*, I kiss your Hand.

Top. Good-by, Knight.

Sir *Will.* Gentlemen, your most obsequious Servant.

[*Exeunt severally.*

SCENE II. Careful's *House*, Ogle *looking up at it.*

Enter on the other Side Bellmein *and* Toper.

Bell. Who the Devil is that Fellow now? I think in my Conscience this Place is become the Parade of Lovers.

Top. What, don't you know him! Why 'tis *Ogle* the Fortune-hunter.

Bell. A Fortune-hunter! I shou'd sooner have taken him for a Sheep-stealer.

Top. He was an Attorney's Clerk, but his Father dying, left him a small Estate; he bought out his Time, and set up for a Fortune: There's scarce a Match-maker in the whole Town, but has had a Fleece at his Purse; nor scarce a great Fortune in Town, but he'll tell you has receiv'd his Addresses. In short, he's a Medley of Fop, Fool, and Coward. Pr'ythee let's speak to him, he may divert us a little.

Bell. With all my Heart.

Top. Mr. *Ogle*, your Servant——

Ogle. Ha! Mr. *Toper*, I kiss your Hand——Sir, I'm yours. [*To Bellmein.*

Top. What makes you sauntering here? In my Conſcience I believe you are in Love with the great Fortune of this Houſe.

Ogle. Why, really Mr. *Toper*, to be ingenuous with you I am, and not without ſome very good Grounds neither, I aſſure you.

Bell. How! this Coxcomb encourag'd too. [*Aſide*.

Top. I was in hopes to have wiſh'd you Joy e'er now; I think the laſt time I ſaw you, you told me you was to be married to my Lady *Rich*.

Ogle. I did ſo; but ſure I am the moſt unlucky Fellow living, the poor Lady died e'er ſhe could have an Opportunity of declaring her Mind to me; and truly I believe I may, without Vanity ſay, ſhe died for Love.

Top. What, did you never ſpeak to her?

Ogle. Never.

Bell. How! never ſpeak to her, ſay you? Why how the Devil did you make Love then?

Ogle. By a third Perſon, Sir.

Bell. I beg Pardon, Sir—Great Perſons, I remember, do court by Proxy.

Ogle. I had ſeveral Letters from her; Mrs. *Couple* was intimately acquainted with her: You know Mrs. *Couple*, Mr. *Toper*?

Top. Oh very well, Match-making is her Buſineſs.

Ogle. I'll ſhew you what ſhe us'd to write to me, [*Pulling out a Letter*.] Here——no, hold, this is from a Baronet's Lady, with whom I had an Intrigue: This is it——no——this is from a Merchant's Wife, a City Animal, that pretends to a nicer Taſte than thoſe of her Level, and wou'd fain have a Child with the Air of a Gentleman; but I begg'd her Pardon, I left her to the Brutes of her own Corporation, for I will have nothing to do with the Body Politic.

Top. Ha, ha, ha.

Bell. Ridiculous Monſter!

Ogle. For if you obſerve, Sir, a Tradeſman is the moſt litigious Cuckold living, he ne'er conſiders the Honour a Gentleman does him, but values himſelf upon his Charter, and moves for Coſts and Damages, when he ought rather to be thankful for the Favour.

Bell. You are very ſevere upon the City, Sir, but where are the Letters you was about to ſhew us?

Ogle. Ha! upon my Life, Gentlemen, I put 'em i my Scrutore this Morning. But, as I was ſaying, M *Couple* had a hundred Guineas of me, for the Mana; ment of that Buſineſs; and if the Lady had not di I'm certain ſhe had been my Wife. Well, I ſhall ne forget what languiſhing Looks ſhe'd caſt at me Church; then put up her Fan to her Face and ſigh, much as to ſay, you are the only Man can make happy.

Bell. Ha, ha, ha, extraordinary Symptoms, fait 'twas very unlucky that you cou'd not come to the Spe of her.

Ogle. 'Twas my ill Fortune, but I am ſo us'd to D appointments, that I bear them the eaſier; what I h met with, wou'd have broke the Heart of ſome Me the Lady *Wealthy* was perfectly forc'd from me by Uncle; elſe I'm convinc'd ſhe had now call'd Huſband.

Top. Why, what Hopes had you of her?

Ogle. Hopes? why the greateſt in the World; prais'd me to every Body ſhe thought knew me; ſaid I had the handſomeſt Foot and Leg ſhe ever the beſt manner of Dreſſing, and the genteeleſt Carri ——She ſaid, ſhe could hardly believe me an *Eng man*, without doing Violence to her Reaſon.

Bell. I ſhou'd be glad that every *Engliſh-born* Bl head wou'd diſclaim his Country. [*Aſide.*] Truly, I'm partly of the Lady's Opinion.

Ogle. Sir, your very humble Servant——

Bell. But, Sir, was you not ſaying, you had Reaſon to walk before this Houſe?

Ogle. I was ſo, Sir.

Bell. Do you know Mr. *Careful*'s Daughter, Sir

Ogle. Oh, very well, Sir; tho' I believe, not ſo as ſhe deſires, and I hope to do, in a little time.

Bell. Say you ſo, Sir?

Top. Then you are very well acquainted, Sir.

Ogle. Yes, very well acquainted, Sir.

Bell. Pray, Sir, can you introduce me?

Ogle. Faith, Sir, not very well; for I never ſp the Lady in my Life.

Bell. How! never ſpoke to her: Why, I underſtood you, that you was well acquainted, Sir, Ha, ha.

Ogle. Why, ſo I am, Sir——Why is it not poſſible to be acquainted without ſpeaking, Gentlemen? Why a Friend of mine lay all Night with a Lady, and never ſaw her Face, nor knows not who ſhe is to this Moment; now I think ſeeing is of greater Conſequence than ſpeaking. But you ſhall hear how far I'm acquainted with this Lady; I lodge at her Milliner's, you muſt know, and I have ſeveral Times paſs'd through the Shop when ſhe has been in't, and as ſoon as my Back has been turn'd, ſhe has always taken an Occaſion to commend me, and ſay ſomething extraordinary in my Praiſe, which my Landlady never fail'd to tell me, but with ſuch an Air, as if ſhe was deſired to tell me. Then if ſhe ſees me walking here——as I generally do every Morning, ſhe ſtrait repairs to the Window———Thus do you ſee——ſtand you there——Now ſuppoſe me the Lady——you look up at my Window, and walk thus, do you ſee?———Then I run to the Window thus——clap my Arms a-croſs thus——and hang my Head thus—turn my Eyes languiſhing thus———as who ſhou'd ſay, if it were the Cuſtom for Women to make the firſt Addreſſes, I wou'd now beckon you up.

Bell. And is this all the Hopes you have?

Ogle. Why, is this nothing, Gentlemen?

Top. Nothing at all; and Six to Four the Lady never thinks on you.

Ogle Not think on me——Egad if ſhe don't marry me, ſhe's the arranteſt Jilt in Chriſtendom.

Bell. How, Jilt!

Ogle. Jilt! Ay Jilt: Why what the Devil need ſhe have made any Enquiry after me, prais'd, or look'd at me; if ſhe wou'd not have me, why did ſhe give me Encouragement.

Top. Ha, ha, ha.

Bell. Muſt a Woman be oblig'd to marry every Man ſhe looks at?

Ogle. I am not every Man, Gentlemen——Egad I'm reſolv'd I'll write to her; I'll know what ſhe means by her inſinuating Carriage, I'll to the *Roſe* and write my Letter, if you'll go with me, Gentlemen, you ſhall ſee what Anſwer ſhe'll ſend me.

Top. Egad I'm resolv'd to have good Diversion with this Fellow; pr'ythee, Captain, will you go with us?

Bell. I must pay a Visit to an old Mistress of mine that lodges hard by, but I'll come to you.

Ogle. To be jilted! Egad I can't bear the Thoughts on't; come, Gentlemen.

The SCENE *changes to Mrs.* Plotwell's *Lodgings.*

Mrs. Plotwell *sola.*

Mrs. *Plot.* I grow weary of persecuting these Blockheads; the very Idea of a Gallant is nauseous to me: Oh! That all Women would but treat the Fools as they deserve, would they take my Advice, no Fop, whose Impertinence tended to the Prejudice of Virtue, shou'd 'scape unexpos'd.

Their different Turns of Vice I'd show,
That this censorious Town might know
The greatest Monster in the World's a Beau.

Enter Bellmein.

Bell. The Vanity of Fops you say you'd shew,
That all Intriguing Belles might know,
There's Danger in a noisy Beau.

Mrs. *Plot.* Ha! Who's this that Eccho's my Sound so justly, yet so much inverts the Sense?

Bell. One that omits no Pains to invert as many of your Sex as he can. A true try'd old Friend to Love. [*Embracing her.*

Mrs. *Plot.* Ha! Captain *Bellmein.*

Bell. My charming *Plotwell*, as blooming, young, and fair as ever, as beautiful as Martyrs Visions, and full of Pleasure and Delight as Dreams of longing Boys.

Mrs. *Plot.* Oh Lord! Give me Breath —— let me have a little Air, or I shall die—so—well, where have you been all this while? And how have you spent your Time? Lord I think I have a thousand Questions to ask in one Breath.

Bell.

Bell. And I have as many to ask you, but can't spare Time now; some more pressing private Business wou'd take me wholly up, fitter for the next Room —— Shall we retire? [*Pulling her.*

Mrs. *Plotw.* No, stand off; if we retire, it must be upon Conditions agreed to before hand.

Bell. With all my Heart, Child; I was never better condition'd for a Lady's Service in all my Life, lookee here——here are Conditions, [*Shews a Purse of Gold*] Observe the Conditions, and let's be happy; tho' I never thought you mercenary till now.

Mrs. *Plotw.* I'm not so much displeas'd with your mistaking me, as I should be with any one else; for besides some Allowance for your Humour, your Absence from Town so long, may excuse you from the Knowledge of my present Principles and Designs; and as great a Libertine as you profess yourself, I know the awful Lustre of Virtue has always met with due Respect from you, and that Respect is the only Condition I require you to observe.

Bell. Ha, hy, Why what the Devil is here, my old Mistress setting up for Virtue? For Heaven's sake, what do you mean, Madam?

Mrs *Plotw.* As I say, Sir, that I am no more what you once knew me; since your Abode in *Ireland*, my Uncle, who kept me from my Estate, is dead, thank Heaven, and I am now Mistress of a Fortune sufficient for my Use; and, had I possess'd it sooner, I never had been what I was: But now, I scorn Mankind on Terms like those; all innocent Diversions I freely take; I keep the best Company, pay and receive Visits from the highest Quality. People who are better bred than to examine into past Conduct.

Bell. Hey! I find then that Reputation is never lost but in an empty Pocket; well then thou'rt grown virtuous, and I must never hope for the Blessing again.

Mrs. *Plotw.* Never; but talk as free as you will, do but observe the Rules of Modesty; I like your Company and Conversation as well as ever, I'm not so rigidly virtuous to appear a Saint, I can launch out and laugh with you sometimes, nay, perhaps contribute to your

your Mirth. I'll give you a ſhort Account how I have paſs'd my Time, in expoſing to public View all the Follies of your Sex; that Part of them, I mean, whoſe Vanity brought them under my Laſh, ſuch whoſe tiffany Natures are ſo eaſily impos'd upon, to have the commoneſt Drabs in Town topt upon them for Women of Quality.

Bell. This Town does abound with ſuch as you ſpeak of.

Mrs. *Plot*. Oh! did you but ſee with what Variety 'tis furniſh'd, and how univerſally all Men are infected with an Itch after Quality, you'd be convinced there's not one, from the Gentleman of the Bed-Chamber, down to the Groom in the Stable, but thinks himſelf ſufficiently qualified to deſerve the Favour of any Lady in St. *James*'s. I paſs'd upon one for a Counteſs, upon another for a Dutcheſs, another a Baronet's Lady, and ſo forth—ha, ha, the poor Fools were loſt in a Cloud of Ignorance, rais'd by the Hurry of their own Expectations.

Bell. Why, truly it would ſurprize a Man that never convers'd with ought above a Pit-Maſk, to be invited to a Lady's Bed, ha, ha, ha.

Mrs. *Plot*. Such aukward Addreſs, and the Means every Man finds to recommend himſelf by, one for Secrecy, t'other Wit, a third his Perſon, ſo every Fool finds ſomething to think valuable in himſelf.

Bell. There's your weakly finicking, dancing, ſinging, witty Fop, who values himſelf upon writing Billet-doux.

Mrs. *Plotw.* And thinks his Company ſo very agreeable, that he perſecutes People to Death, before they can get rid of his troubleſome Impertinence.

Bell. His chiefeſt Talent conſiſts in the Repartee of an Intrigue. But then there's your old harden'd Sinner.

Mrs. *Plot.* Ay, he cries up Secrecy and Security, his Years, Wrinkles, and diſtorted Body, are ſufficient Defence againſt a ſlanderous Tongue; he values himſelf more for what he has been, than for what he is, recommending himſelf upon his Knowledge and Experience.

Bell. And his great Judgment in the happy Management of an Intrigue. But the Man of Senſe.

Mrs,

Mrs. *Plot.* Him all Women ought to shun, that fear coming under his Power; he approaches securely.

Bell. Addresses cunningly.

Mrs. *Plot.* Insinuates himself slily into a Lady's Favour.

Bell. Then seizes his Prey at once. [*Embracing her.*

Mrs. *Plot.* Oh Lord, hold off.

Enter Plotwell's *Maid, and whispers her.*

Bell. Pox take her for coming so unluckily, this Denial of her's gives me as much Desire as a new Face that she shou'd grow so unreasonably Virtuous. [*Aside.*] Well, Madam, you have Business I see, I'll take my Leave, some other Time I'll hear it out——

Mrs. *Plot.* My Business, at present, is for the good of your Friend *Manly*, and I don't know but we may have Occasion for your Head to help us out.

Bell. My Head, together with the rest of my Body, is at your Service, Madam, whenever you please to command your humble Servant. [*Exit.*

Mrs. *Plot.* *Clarinda* desires to speak with me at her Father's House, say you?

Maid. Yes, Madam, instantly.

Mrs. *Plot.* I'll wait on her.

SCENE *changes to a Tavern.*

Toper *and* Ogle *sealing a Letter.*

Ogle. Here, Porter, carry this Letter as 'tis directed, and bring me an Answer.

Porter. Yes, Sir. [*Sir* William Mode *within.*]

Sir. *Will.* Here, Drawer, shew a Room, and send your Master to me.

Top. Ha, that's *Mode*'s Voice, a good Hint, I'll have rare Sport with these two Puppies [*Aside.*

Ogle. I think I heard Sir *William Mode*'s Voice, Pry'thee *Toper* desire him to walk in.

Top. Not for the World!

Ogle. No, Why pray?

Top.

Top. I know not, but some Body has told him that you are his Rival, and he swears he'll cut your Throat where-ever he sees you.

Ogle. How, I his Rival? Where, pray you?

Top. In *Clarinda*, I suppose.

Ogle. But is it possible Sir *William Mode* shou'd be my Rival, and never tell me on't? But he's such an egregious Coxcomb, that he gives me no Pain.

Top. He call'd you Fop, Blockhead, Baboon——and said he'd make Mince-meat of you.

Ogle. Oh, impossible, Sir, he cou'd not mean me.

Top. Do you think I lye, Sir?

Ogle. Oh, by no means, Sir.

Top. Had any Man said so much of me, I wou'd have made the Sun shone through him; and I think you ought to send him a Challenge.

Ogle. What, challenge my Friend! By no means, Sir: Why, Sir, he's my Friend.

Top. So much the worse; you ought to resent an Affront from him the more for that.

Ogle. Oh, Sir, you don't know us, we never mind what we say of one another: I dare swear he never meant it an Affront.

Top. You Lye, Sir, he did mean it an Affront.

Ogle. Sir, I heartily beg your Pardon; I believe he did, because you say it, Sir, else I should not believe it.

Top. Sir, I say you must fight him, and I'll carry the Challenge.

Ogle. That's a sure Way that I challenge him, but how to come off as sure, hang me if I know: Look you, Mr. *Toper*, I have not the ready Use of both my Legs, for, Dancing at a private Ball t'other Night, I cut something higher than usually, and pitch'd upon a Cherry-stone, which turn'd my Foot so violently, that I vow I have been lame ever since, so that positively I can't fight.

Top. Zounds, I believe you dare not fight him.

Ogle. Pardon me, Sir, I dare fight any Man, that will but give me Time to prepare myself for a Duel; for I think there should be a Diet us'd for fighting, as well as Running.

Top. Ha, ha, ha, well, I find what you hint at; I'll engage to bring you off safe.

Ogle. As how pray?

Top. Why as thus; do you challenge him, and, when you meet, draw your Sword.

Ogle. But suppose he draws again.

Top. Then I'll step in and part you, so you are good Friends; for I don't design you shall fight in Earnest. [*Aside.*

Ogle. A very good Project.

Top. Come, come, write three Words to him upon this Paper.

Ogle. But you'll be sure to part us.

Top. Ay, certainly. [Ogle *writes.*] Now I wish *Bellmein* was here to share the Diversion.

Ogle. There, Sir, there's enough.

Top. Let me see —— Sir, you must resign all Pretensions to *Clarinda*, or fight me immediately, I wait in the next Room for your Answer. *Ogle.*

So, very well; do you stay here, I'll be back in a Minute.

SCENE *changes to another Room in the same House.*

Sir William *and the Tavern-Man.*

Sir *Will.* This Hermetage is not brisk.

Lan. Upon my Word, Sir *William*, there's no better in *London.*

Sir *Will.* It is not so good as the last you sent me.

Lan. It is the very same, Sir.

Sir *Will.* Well, send me in four Dozen.

Lan. And how much Champagne, Sir *William?*

Sir *Will.* Four Dozen of that too, and four of *Burgundy.*

Lan. You shall have it, Sir. [*Exit.*

Enter Toper.

Top. Sir *Will.* I'm your humble Servant.

Sir *Will.*

Sir *Will.* Mr. *Toper*, your Servant: Pray how did you know I was here? I am not uſually found in a Tavern.

Top. I heard your Voice, Sir *William*; juſt as you enter'd. I was engag'd in a Quarrel of yours.

Sir *Will.* Of mine?

Top. Ay: Sir *William*, 'tis a damn'd fooliſh Buſineſs; I wou'd have made it up, but I found it impoſſible; ſo that being your Friend, I undertook to deliver you this. [*Gives him the Letter.*

Sir *Will.* How's this! A Challenge from *Ogle*? Certainly the Fellow's drunk, or he'd never do this.

Top. No, that he is not I'll promiſe you, he's ſober enough, but in a damn'd Paſſion; he ſays you're a Fop, Fool, nay Coward; if I might adviſe you, you ſhou'd fight him inſtantly; 'Zdeath, were I in your Place, Sir *William*, ſuch a Dog ſhou'd not dare to look, nay, think of a Woman I deſign'd to marry.

Sir *Will.* I hate fighting, but dare not tell this bluſtering Fellow ſo, [*Aſide.*] Nay, I know he's a Blockhead, and a Coward too, but what Courage Love may have infus'd into him, I know not—Why what the Devil he ſaid not a Word of his Paſſion to me Yeſterday, he din'd with me.

Top. He did not know it then, but now he ſwears he'll ſpoil your handſome Face.

Sir *Will.* Oh Lord! I had rather be run through the Body, enfeeble me; O' my Soul I wonder what makes Men ſo ſtout!

Top. I'll tell you Sir *William*, Courage is nothing, nothing at all; now if you look big, talk loud, and be very angry, you'll frighten a Man that can't do ſo as well as you, ſo you are reckon'd a ſtout Man; and he that can do it better, is a ſtouter Man than you, that's all.

Sir *Will.* Is that all? Why then I'm reſolv'd to be ſtout, enfeeble me: But ſuppoſe he ſhould draw?

Top. Why then I'll ſtep in and part you.

Sir *Will.* A very good Piece of Contrivance, impair my Vigour.

Top. Be ſure you get the firſt Word, for there's Advantage in having the firſt Word.

Enter

Enter Drawer.

Drawer. Did you call, Gentlemen?

Top. Ay: Is Mr. *Ogle* below?

Drawer. Yes, Sir.

Top. Hold, I'll fetch him myſelf. [*Ex.*

Sir *Will.* Now am I confoundedly afraid, left this Fellow ſhould let us fight in earneſt.

Re-enter Toper *and* Ogle, *to whom he ſpeaks at entering.*

Top. Be ſure you ſpeak angrily, as if you wou'd not hear what I ſay.

Ogle. Be ſure you part us then——Sir, I ſay I will hear of no Reconciliation, except he reſign *Clarinda.*

[Toper *runs to Sir* William.

Top. He's in a damn'd Paſſion, your Hand to your Sword quickly, Sir *William*, fear nothing, I'll ſtand by you.

[*As ſoon as they ſee one another, they run and embrace.*]

Sir *Will.* Mr. Ogle!

Ogle. Sir *William!*

Sir *Will.* Dear Mr. *Ogle*, I'm glad to ſee you.

Top. Zounds have I taken all this Pains for this——Harkee, Sir *William*, Damn you, draw upon him, or I'll draw upon you; do you hear, no Reply, but draw, do you hear.

Sir *Will.* Oh Heaven! I muſt draw in my own Defence; and I'm ſure there's leſs Danger in *Ogle*, than in this Fellow [*Draws.*] I think, Mr. *Ogle*, you ſent me a Challenge juſt now by Mr. *Toper*, and having paid the Ceremony due to Friends and Acquaintance, you muſt draw, Sir, and return my Compliment. I'll be ſure to have ſomebody to part us tho'. [*Aſide.*

[*Runs and knocks at the Door with his Foot.*

Top. Harkee, *Ogle*, you have ruin'd yourſelf by letting him get the Advantage; draw, draw Sir.

Ogle. Draw, Sir; why, Sir, my Paſſion was over upon my Faith. Ho, here's Folks enow, I'm reſolv'd to draw now. [*Draws.*

Enter two Drawers, one runs to Sir William, *t'other to* Ogle, *and holds 'em.*

Sir *Will.* Ah, ſtand off, I had rather be run thro' the

Guts

Guts than you ſhould touch me with your dirty Apron, 'twill daub all my Cloaths; off Scoundrel.

[Toper *holds* Ogle.

Ogle. Let him come, let him come, one Thruſt will decide our Diſpute.

Sir *Will.* Pray give us Way, 'twill ſoon be ended.

Enter Bellmein.

Bell. Hey-day, what's here, Swords drawn? Nay, then I'll make one in the Number. [*Draws.*] Why, what the Devil do you hold the Gentlemen for? Let 'em go, and give one another Satisfaction. Z'death, I'll fight that Man that ſhall but offer to hold 'em. [*Takes off the Drawers and* Toper.] Why don't you fight now, Gentlemen?

Sir *Will.* A Pox take him for his brutiſh Civility, [*When they are at Liberty they ſtand and look at one another.*] Harkee, Mr. *Ogle*, do you come along with me, and we'll contrive ſome way to make theſe Fellows believe we dare fight. [*He goes to* Ogle, *and ſpeaks in a low Voice.*]

Ogle. Agreed.

Sir *Will.* Come, Mr. *Ogle*, you ſhall go along with me, we'll find a more convenient Place to decide this Buſineſs in, where Friends ſhall not interrupt; you ſhall hear of a Duel, Gentlemen, tho' it is not proper to ſee it. Your humble Servant. [*Exit.*

Ogle. With all my Heart, I dare fight you any where——

Top. That's a Lye: pr'ythee order thy Footman to watch 'em, I fancy they'll have ſome comical Stratagem to deceive us. Ha, ha, ha.

Bell. With all my Heart; d'ye hear, be ſure you take Notice where they go, and bring me Word. Pr'ythee, how did'ſt work 'em up to this? [*Exit Servant.*

Top. With a World of Pains and Difficulty, I aſſure you; but there is no fear of their doing one another any Harm in a fighting Way. Is not that Colonel *Manly* yonder?

Bell.

Bell. 'Tis, and I have ſome Buſineſs with him: Will you walk?

Top. My Buſineſs, at preſent lies another way; elſe I'd be glad to drink a Bottle with him.

For tho' we roar and rake, and Broils commence,
Yet give me for a Friend, a Man of Senſe.

The End of the SECOND ACT.

ACT III. SCENE I.

SCENE *Careful's* Houſe.

Careful *ſolus, with* Ogle's *Letter.*

Caref. VERY fine, I ſee my Daughter is reſolv'd to have Strings enow to her Bow; Death, to give Encouragement to a Dog that has neither Wit nor Money to recommend him; good Mr. *Ogle*, if I catch you ogling there, I'll hamſtring you, I can tell you that for your Comfort; I'm glad I got the Letter before her; my Spark's very familiar, methinks; [*Reads.*] *Madam, I'm inform'd you entertain Sir* William Mode; *if ſo, I deſire to know the Reaſon why you encourage me. I am not to be fool'd*——(who the Devil is this Coxcomb) *if you clear not this Imputation, I ſhall believe you deſign to jilt me.*— Very complaiſant, truly———*anſwer per Bearer, as you value your Admirer, Ogle.* Yes, I have anſwer'd *per Bearer* with a broken Pate, and I wiſh yours had been in his Place. Lord, Lord, who would be plagu'd with Children? I'm reſolv'd ſhe ſhall marry Sir *William* To-morrow; why, ſhe'll have as many Fellows at her Heels, as her Colonel has Soldiers waiting for their Pay, why, what a Medley of Suitors has ſhe? Fighters, Fools, and Fops. Well, ſince you are ſo fickle, Miſtreſs, I'll fix you preſently, or marry myſelf. Mr. *Toper* was wiſhing me to a Couſin of his, who will be in Town To-day;

adod,

adod, if this perverſe Baggage make one Scruple of obeying my Will, I'll have her, and try if a Mother-in-Law won't hamper her; but I'll in, and ſend for Sir *William* immediately. [*Exit.*

The SCENE *changes to another Room in the ſame Houſe,* Clarinda *and* Emilia *dreſſing in Boy's Cloaths, Mrs.* Plotwell *with them.*

Clar. Here, here, on with your Manhood quickly.

Emil. I fear, *Clarinda,* this Maſquerade will not be reputable for Women of nice Honour.

Plot. Oh, don't fear that, ſince you only wear it to do yourſelves Juſtice; for Juſtice can never be diſhonourable.

Clar. You are not inſenſible, Couſin, how reſolutely my cruel Father perſecutes me with this Fop; therefore, ſince poor *Clarinda* is in all this Danger, I, my own Knight Errant, and thou my truſty 'Squire, will march *En cavalier,* and deliver the diſtreſs'd Damſel, by beating the Giant into a Pigmy; then be our own Heralds, and proclaim our Victory to my Father, and hollow the Coward ſo loud in his Ears, that we will ſhame him out of all Thoughts of this Fool.

Plot. If that don't do, my Plot ſhall; *Toper* has broke it to him, as I told you.

Clar. I readily ſubmit to any Propoſal of yours, and will rely on your Contrivance.

Plot. You may command me,——but be quick and dreſs; who told you of this Duel?

Clar. Sir *William*'s Valet makes love to my Woman, thro' him we diſcover'd the Time and Place, but I know not the Grounds of this Quarrel.

Plot. That, I ſuppoſe, is your Ladyſhip; for Mr. *Ogle* publickly declares you are in Love with him.

Clar. Ogle! who is he?

Plot. A fooliſh Fellow about Town, he lodges at Mrs. *Commode*'s, your Milliner.

Clar. Oh Heavens! I believe I have ſeen him paſs thro' the Shop, but never had Curioſity enough to aſk his

his Name. In Love with him! I should as soon be in Love with a Weasel, Ha, ha, ha, why, is he Sir *William*'s Antagonist? I fancy we shall have rare Sport.

Plot. They are as like two Peas in every Thing but Estate, and in that Sir *William* out-does him,

Clar. He is the very Quintessence of Foppery; his Name and Nature suits exactly, for he's a nice Observer of the Modes; his Valet is forc'd to counterfeit a *Frenchman*, or he would turn him away.

Emil. Ha, ha, ha, Ridiculous enough; well, thus drest, now what are we to do?

Clar. Why, when we are sated with their sordid Foppery, we'll kick 'em into better Manners.

Emil. How, kick, *Clarinda*? if they should return our Compliment, I shall quickly discover my Manhood to be counterfeit.

Plot. Never fear it, they won't fight with a Mouse, I dare swear, if it were out of a Trap.

Clar. I know Sir *William*'s a Coward, I had been often told so, and to prove it, I sent him a Challenge, as from one Mr. *Roughly*; his Man said it put him into such a Consternation he shou'd never forget him, he sent me word that he'd meet me on *Calais* Sands, and give me Satisfaction, Ha, ha, ha.

Plot. Ha, ha, ha, a good Excuse———Indeed, he's fit for nothing, but to set upon one's Cabinet, to watch one's China. Well, I wish you good Sport, and am your humble Servant. [*Exit* Plot.

Clar. I'm resolv'd, ere I'll be forc'd into the Arms of a Person I loathe and despise, the Passion I have for Colonel *Manly* will tempt me to make him my Sanctuary.

Emil. I must tell her of his Falshood, the Thoughts of which have turn'd all the foolish Passion I had conceiv'd. [*Aside*.] Take Care, *Clarinda*, you ben't deceiv'd in him.

Clar. What mean you, *Emilia*?

Emil. That he is false.

Clar. False! Impossible, how know you this?

Emil. I have the best Proof in the World of it, ocular Demonstration. He makes Love to me; nay, don't start; had I not been too much your Friend, *Clarinda*, I had

had not let you into the Secret; for, upon my Word, I don't think him disagreeable.

Clar. Oh Heavens! she's in Love with him! and therefore would slily persuade me into an ill Opinion of him. [*Aside.*] How know you 'tis he, Cousin?

Emil. I am sure that Gentleman that bow'd to us in the Side-box, the first Night I came to Town, has ever-since pursued me with most violent Love; and I must confess I lik'd his Humour so well, that I could not be displeas'd with his playing the Fool.

Clar. Where did you see him next? How got he an Opportunity?

Emil. You know the next Night I went out with only my Woman.

Clar. I remember.

Emil. Why then I went to the Play in a Mask, on purpose for a little Diversion, and 'twas my Fortune to sit next him in the Pit, where during the Play-time, he entertain'd me with the prettiest Discourse in the World, and when 'twas done he wou'd not part with me till I had promis'd to write to him, and I could not help keeping my Word, if I was to be hang'd,——But finding him false to you, I hate him; this Letter I have writ to upbraid him. [*Shews a Letter.*

Clar. How's this, For Mr. *Celadon*?

Emil, Ay, we pass upon one another for *Celadon*, and *Chloe*; for my Part I did not enquire his Name because he shou'd not ask mine.

Clar. Did he never ask your Name, nor tell you his?

Emil. No, and I suppose that was his Policy to prevent a Discovery to you.

Enter Clarinda's *Maid, giving her a Letter.*

Clar. Ha! 'Tis from *Manly*——What's this, [*Reads.*] *The private Encouragement you give that Fop Sir* William, *is not so closely managed to escape a jealous Lover's Eye that sees you every where; to be deceiv'd touches my tenderest Part, especially from one I thought my own; but we are subject to Mistakes, I find; that I am so in you, my Eyes, my Ears, are all Witnesses. I shall take what Care I can, not to be troublesome to you, since I find you no longer value the Peace of* Manly.

Oh! monstrous, perfidious Mankind! Oh, I perceive your Drift, he charges me with this Fool, on Purpose to find Pretence for his own Falshood——It is a poor Excuse,——but what won't Men fall into, when they quit their Honour; Oh that I had but an Opportunity of upbraiding him to his Face.

Emil. That you shall; he knows not yet of the Discovery, I'll write to him to come here, I have no Reason to suspect his disobeying the Summons, no more now, than formerly.

Clar. Did he use to meet you then?

Emil. Most punctually——But I'll in and write to him, and be here in a Minute. [*Exit*.

Clar. Well, it is impossible to dive into the Heart of Man, for sure he has the Face of Truth, nay, I can hardly believe he's false yet, so deep an Impression did his seeming Honesty stamp upon my Soul.

Re-enter Emilia.

Emil. I have sent it away, and I doubt not but to convince you of the Truth of what I say; but come don't think on't now, but let's begone, methinks I long to bully these Cowards, pray Heaven they prove so——

Clar. Duce on't, this will destroy half the Satisfaction I promis'd myself from this Frolick; but come.

If we succeed in Proteus' *artful School,*
The World shall say, a very Beau's a Fool. [Exeunt.

SCENE *Hyde-Park*.

Enter Sir William *and* Ogle, *with Files, Pumps, and Night-caps.*

Sir *Will*. Here's a Weapon, Mr. *Ogle*, will decide the Quarrel as well as e'er a Sharp in Christendom, and without Danger.

Ogle. An admirable Contrivance, Sir *William*; for now they'll hear of a Duel, and we reckon'd such skilful Artists, that neither cou'd o'ercome.

Sir *Will*. Right, I think a Gentleman ought to wear

a Sharp, for a Terror to the Vulgar, and becauſe 'tis the Faſhion; but he ſhou'd never uſe it but as an Ornament, and Part of his Dreſs. I hope to ſee it as much a Faſhion to fight with Files, as 'tis to fence with them. If I was a Member of Parliament, I'd bring in a Bill againſt Duelling; I'm ſure the Clauſe would paſs, for there's a Majority in the Houſe of my Conſtitution. Come, approach, Sa, ſa.

Enter Clarinda *and* Emilia *with their Swords drawn.*

Clar. Hold, Gentlemen, I'm bound in Honour to part you; ha, what's this?

Emil. Files, upon my Honour, ha, ha, ha.

Sir *Will.* Why do you laugh, Gentlemen? I think this the niceſt way of deciding a Quarrel, the other is fit for none but Bullies and Soldiers, that get their Bread by't; 'tis eaſily ſeen this way who has the moſt Skill; and pray, what is got by the other more rude Method, but a ſcandalous Character, or a ſhameful Death.

Ogle. And by my Conſent, he that draws a Sword out of the immediate Service of the King, ſhould be hang'd.

Clar. Say you ſo, Sir! Now hear my Sentiments, he that would not draw a Sword upon any juſt Account, ſhould be kick'd thus, and thus, Sir. [*Kicks him.*

Sir *Will.* What do you mean, Gentlemen?

Emil. Only to rub your Courage a little.

Ogle. What's that, Sir?

Emil. You don't hear well, Sir, I'll lengthen your Ears a little. [*Pulls him by the Ears.*

Sir *Will.* I wonder that you, who look ſo like a Gentleman, ſhou'd be guilty of ſuch ill-bred Actions; Fye! kick and cuff! Exerciſes for Footmen; Pray learn better Carriage of us.

Clar. I'd as ſoon learn Manners of a *Muſcovite.*

Sir *Will.* Pray Sir, who are you? And what Affairs led you hither?

Clar. I'm a Servant to *Clarinda,* and conſequently a Rival of yours.

Ogle. O Lord! a Rival of mine too. [*Aſide.*

Clar. I came hither to kick you, and expoſe you when I had done, the firſt, you are ſenſible I have perform'd,

 and

and from that Instance of my Honesty, you may take my Word for the rest.

Sir *Will.* I'm undone, blister me, if the very shadow of a Duel be not unfortunate. [*Aside.*

Enter Colonel Manly, *and Captain* Bellmein.

Man. Why how now, young Gentlemen, are you breathing yourselves, or giving Lessons in the Stoic Philosophy to those patient Disciples.

Bell. Or have you a Journey to ride, that you are getting your Backside harden'd for it.

Sir *Will. Manly* here! I'd compound for half my Estate, blister me! [*Aside.*

Emil. Ha! *Manly* here! We must retire, Cousin, lest it spoils our Plot, as doubtless it will, if he knows us.

Clar. Methinks, I could even here reproach him.

[*Exit* Clar. *and* Emil.

Bell. This is hearing of a Duel, indeed,——— Files! Ha, ha, ha, you was resolv'd to prevent Murder; you need never fear the Exaltation of the Gallows, for your Courage reaches but to a chance Medley, at most.

Man. Pr'ythee, who were those Gentlemen, Sir *William*; methinks, they us'd you very familiarly.

Sir *Will.* Men of no Honour you may conclude, Colonel, else they would not have affronted Gentlemen, when they found them defenceless.

Man. Right, but why wou'd you be defenceless? Faith, Sir *William*, if this News reaches your Mistress's Ears, it will ruin you in her Favour. Take this for a Rule, the less Regard you have for your Honour, the more you sink in Esteem with your Mistress; for all Women hate a Coward; you ought to be forbid the Habits of Men, who can be guilty of Effeminacy, that even Women would blush at.

Sir *Will.* Why, Gentlemen, I think passive Valour fits well enough upon Men that have Estates, and have a Mind to live and enjoy them.

Man. Damn him for a cowardly Blockhead; pr'ythee let's go, I'm sick of their Folly; besides you said you would convince me of *Clarinda*'s Falshood.

Enter

Enter Bellmein's *Man, and gives him a Letter.*

Serv. I have run, Sir, all the Way; for the Porter told me it muſt be given you that Moment.

Bell. Ha! there's a lucky Hit, Colonel; ſhe invites me to come to her Lodging, and her Servant ſhould be ready to convey me into her Apartment. Here, read it, Man, now you may convince yourſelf.————Egad if I were not a damn'd honeſt Fellow to my Friend, now cou'd I paſs three Hours the moſt agreeably in the World. Pox on me for a prating Coxcomb, could not I have held my Tongue. Well, what think you of it Colonel?

Man. It is not her Hand, but that's nothing, ſhe might diſguiſe that to conceal it from me. I know not what to think, but I'm reſolv'd to go, and if I find her falſe, 'twill cure me effectually.

Bell. Come on then. [*Exeunt.*

Ogle. I have been conſidering all this while upon what the Colonel ſaid, and I am reſolv'd to be valiant; for if Ladies don't like a Coward————I ſhall never get a Fortune; for ought I know, I may fight as well as any Body, I'm reſolv'd to try. Harkee, Sir *William*, our Servants are here by, let's ſend for our Swords, and fight in earneſt.

Sir *Will.* Not I, Mr. *Ogle*, I declare againſt fighting poſitively.

Ogle. But I declare for fighting, and ſo ſhall you, or reſign all Pretenſions to *Clarinda*; for I deſign to marry her myſelf, therefore don't think of her, do you hear.

Sir *Will.* You marry her, ha, ha, ha.

Ogle. 'Zound, Sir, dare you laugh at a Gentleman, yet dare not fight? Take that, Sir, [*Strikes up his Heels.*] and the next time I hear you ſpeak a Word more of her I'll cut your Throat, and ſo good by.————So this is one Step towards Courage; I am reſolv'd to challenge every Man that pretends to a Fortune, 'till I have got one myſelf; and now my Hand's in, I'll challenge this Colonel the next Time I ſee him, tho' at the Head of his Regiment. [*Exit.*

Sir *Will.* Rat this Blockhead, what a Metamorphoſis is here; 'tis well I fell upon my Cloak, or I had daub'd all my Cloaths, blister me. Well, to sing, dance, or court a Lady, or any such Gentleman-like Employments I'll turn my Back to none; but for this slovenly Exercise of fighting, I shall never be brought to endure it, impair my Vigour. [*Exit.*

SCENE Careful's *House.*

Careful *pulling in* Emillia *in Boy's Cloaths.*

Caref. Who the Devil have we here? Nay, nay, Sir, I must see your Face; another Gallant of my Daughter's, I warrant; Who are you, Sir, from whence come you, what Business have you in my House, ha?

Emil. Oh Lord, what shall I say to this old Fellow? he'll certainly know me.

Caref. What are you studying for a Lie, Sir? Adod I shall make you find your Tongue, speak quickly, or I'll cut your Throat, you Dog you. [*Draws.*

Emil. Ah! Oh Lord a Sword! For Heaven's Sake, Sir, Oh Lord, Sir, don't you know me?

Caref. Know you, Sir? Who the Pox are you, Sir, ha? *Emilia,* Why what Masquerade's this? Where's my Daughter?

Enter Clarinda.

Ho Sir, your humble servant; Why what a Pox, are you going into the Service? You are two pretty Volunteers, faith.

Clar. Ha! my Father, what shall I say?——I'll e'en face it out, since he has catch'd me. We have done a Friend of yours some Service, Sir.

Caref. A Friend of mine! As how, pray forsooth?

Clar. Why you must know, Sir, I was inform'd of a Duel between Sir *William Mode,* and a Brother Beau of his; the Concern I knew you had for Sir *William*'s Safety engag'd my Care for the Prevention; I was unwilling to expose him, by sending any Body else; so that my Cousin and I, by the help of this Disguise, parted them: But we should not need to have made such Haste, for the Puppies were trying their Valour safely, with a Couple of Files, ha, ha.

Caref.

Caref. Ha, ha, ha; and this was the Occasion of your being in Breeches, ha?

Emil. And I think it a good Project too, Uncle.

Caref. You do,———Well, Daughter, pray let's have you in your feminine Capacity again; for tho' you bully in Breeches, I hope you'll marry in Petticoats.

Clar. Marry, Sir!

Caref. Yes forsooth, I have sent for Sir *William*, in order to have the Settlement completed To-night, and To-morrow your Honour shall rise with the Sun; that is to say, you shall be my Lady *Mode*.

Clar. Honour, Sir, Where's the Honour of such a Husband? I hope, Sir, you will not marry me to a Coward; why there's not a needy Bully about Town but will beat a Maintenance out of him; and where is the Reputation of such a Marriage?

Caref. But he'll make a swinging Jointure; and if you don't like him when you have him, you may live apart———

Clar. O Heaven, what shall I say?———Sir, I beg you'll but delay your Purpose for a Month.

Caref. Not for a Day.———

Clar. Sir, I have sworn not to marry this Month.

Caref. Have you so; pray who have you sworn to, Mistress, to Mr. *Ogle*, ha?

Clar. *Ogle!* Who is he, pray Sir?———Heaven, has my Father got this Story too!

Caref. You don't know such a Person, I'll warrant you, as Mr. *Ogle*?

Clar. I have seen such a Fellow, Sir, but never spoke to him.

Caref. No———look in my Face———You never spoke to him, that is, encourag'd his Love?

Clar. No———Upon my Honour.

Caref. ——You lye, you have no Honour, read that [*Throws the Letter.*] and do you hear, resolve to marry Sir *William* To-morrow by Six, or I'll marry myself before Twelve; so take your Choice. I'll *Ogle* you, and Soldier you, with a Pox to you. [*Exit.*

Clar. Oh Impudence from *Ogle!* I'll have the Rascal tost in a Blanket; see *Emilia* what an audacious Letter

 'tis,

'tis, bless me, I have no Patience; I encourage such a Rascal———

Emil. He is very familiar, methinks——hang him, the Fool's below your Anger, never think on't; Come pr'ythee think which Way to turn yourself if the Colonel be false, as I dare swear he is. What think you of marrying Sir *William*, he is Master of a fair Estate, which you may make subservient to your Pleasures, to make Life's rugged Journey pass the smoother. If he be true, as you have but little Reason to think he is, you may yet find some Way to accomplish your Desires. Come, the Time draws on, in which you'll be convinc'd of his Truth or Falshood.

Come what will, resolve to be content,
And trust to Fortune for the wish'd Event. [Exit.

Enter Careful, Toper, *and Mrs.* Plotwell, *drest like a Quaker.*

Caref. Mr. *Toper*, your Cousin is welcome, my House is at your Service, Madam.

Plot. I thank thee, but pray'thee do not Madam me, my Name is *Anne*.

Caref. A very handsome Woman, and very modestly drest.

Top. I have us'd all the Arguments in my Power to convert her from this Formality, but in vain, she's as averse to the Fashions, as other Women are fond of 'em; but I hope your Niece and Daughter will work a Reformation in her.

Caref. I rather hope she'll work one in them, I'll assure you I'll recommend her as a Pattern. Is this the Woman you would recommend to me for a Wife, Mr. *Toper*?

Top. The same, Sir.

Caref. I protest I like her exceedingly, she seems cut out on purpose for me; her plain Way of Living will improve my Estate, and her Morals will hamper my Daughter, I like a religious Woman.

Top. You can't be better match'd, if she has not too much; Yesterday I carried her to wait on a Relation of

ours

ours that has a Parrot, and whilſt I was diſcourſing about ſome private Buſineſs, ſhe converted the Bird, and now it talks of nothing but the Light of the Spirit, and the inward Man. Ha, ha.

Caref. Good lack, Good lack.

Plot. Well, well, thee wilt never leave thy ridiculous Jeſts; I ſay that Mankind were not made for Foppery and Pride, but to do good in their Generation,——— Pr'ythee ſhew me one Text of Scripture for the Faſhions, or where Jewels are commanded, or what Holy Matron ever had a Valet to dreſs 'em, as they ſay the *French* Ladies have, Oh monſtrous Faſhion!———No, no, our devouteſt Women wore coarſe Linen, or rather none at all.

Top. Ay, ſuch Saints as wore their Congregations without-ſide, and ſwarm'd with Chriſtian Vermin, it muſt be them, ha, ha, ha; but you hold every handſome Garment a Sin.

Plot. Handſome Garment! Verily I believe, if we are puniſh'd with Taxes again to carry on another War, 'twill be a juſt Judgment upon this ſinful Land for their long Wigs, hoop'd Coats, Furbelows, falſe Teeth, and Patches.

Caref. Truly I'm of her Opinion, ſhe ſpeaks like an Oracle; for the Devil was never ſo proud as our Women are now a-days, [*Aſide.*] I am reſolv'd, if my Daughter ſhew the leaſt Reluctance to my Will, to marry her out of hand. I'll motion it to her, and try how ſhe likes me———[*Aſide.*] What think you of a Huſband forſooth; for to be plain with you, your extraordinary Qualities have rais'd a great Deſire in me of becoming ſuch?

Plot. I doubt, Friend; thou'lt expect a larger Fortune than I am Dame of.

Caref. I proteſt I don't care if you have not a Groat, your Virtue's a wealthy Dowry to me; ſay you'll but have me and 'tis enough.

Plot. But it may be thou'lt be againſt my Courſe of Life; I love Retirement, muſt have Time for my Devotion in my own Way; I'm not us'd to the Ceremony of Viſits, and hate Tea-Table Vanity, and Card-Play, as they call it.

Top. Our Plot takes rarely.

Caref. This makes me love you the more.

Plot. One Thing more; thou hast a Daughter they say, a topping Gallant, which I desire to see, and try if good Admonitions, together with Example, won't reform her; for plainly, I don't care to come under the Roof where Children are, if they be not dutiful; so I must see her first e'er I can give thee my Answer.

Caref. That you shall presently——Here, carry this Gentlewoman to my Daughter, and tell her, she must entertain her as her Mother that is to be, tell her so from me, d'ye hear. [*Ex. Mrs.* Plot. *and Servant.*

Really Mr. *Toper,* your Cousin is a profound Christian; if my Daughter refuse to marry Sir *William*—I'll jointure her in my whole Estate.

Toper. For aught I know, you can't do better than marry; for who would be plagu'd with a disobedient Child?

Caref. Especially when they depend upon us for their Fortunes; the Devil a young Fellow would care a Souce for their Persons, did not our Purse-strings draw. Here forsooth my Daughter is running mad after a Soldier, a Fellow whose Fortune depends upon his Sword, and here we are going to Wars again, and six to four but a Cannon Bullet takes his Head off, and then the Wife is turn'd Home to her Father again, and in such Cases a Father has never disposed of his Children entirely, and all the Jointure she'll bring, will consist of Housings, Holster-Caps, Pistols, Swords, and so forth.

Enter Servant.

Serv. Here's Sir *William Mode* below, Sir.

Caref. Tell him I'll wait on him presently. Come, Mr. *Toper,* you shall be Witness of our Agreement; I sent for him to compleat the Business, Sign, Seal to Night, and To-morrow we'll have a Dance. [*Exit.*

Toper. I fancy we shall drive Dancing out of your Head, old Gentleman. [*Exit.*

The End of the Third Act.

ACT IV. SCENE I.

Enter Clarinda, Emilia, *and Mrs.* Plotwell.

Clar. WELL in my Conſcience, the firſt Sight of you frighted me horribly, though I knew your Plot. I vow you make a ſanctified Figure.

Plotw. Might I paſs upon the Brethren, think you?

Em. Ay, and hold forth too, I'll warrant you, without being diſcover'd. But is my Uncle ſo hot upon Matrimony, ſay you?

Plotw. As a Hound upon the Scent, tho' he'll ſhare no more of the Pleaſure, than the Dog of the Game he runs down, ha, ha,

Clar. I vow I can't help laughing to think what a Trick we ſhall put upon him, —— but the duce on't I cannot be heartily merry till I ſee the Event of this Meeting; I long till the Colonel comes.

Em. So do I as much as you, to upbraid him with his Treachery.

Enter Maid and whiſpers them.

In my Conſcience he's here, —— ſhow him into my Chamber, tell him I'll wait on him preſently,——Now, *Clarinda*, you ſhall go in my Place.

Clar. Heavens! How I tremble. Oh, the perfidious Wretch, ſure he's quite loſt to Virtue, that he dares thus impudently venture into the very Houſe. Oh give me Patience, Heaven, and Power to back my Reſolution, and Scorn enough to ſhew my deep Reſentment. [*Ex. Clar.*

Plotw. I'll to the old Man, and keep him in Diſcourſe, that he mayn't interrupt you. [*Exit.*

Em. Do ſo, —— I muſt liſten a little to hear what Reception ſhe gives him. [*Exit.*

Enter Colonel Manly, *ſolus.*

Manl. This Love makes Men the greateſt Aſſes in the World; what bluſtering *Mars* with all his ſteely Garniture of War cou'd never do, this blind Boy does with a feather'd Reed. Oh my Soul, I think I'm grown a Coward, and begin to fear, my Heart beats faster than a raw Soldier's in his first Engagement, or a longing Maid in the Arms of a Man she likes when Opportunity creates her Fears. Sure it cannot be *Clarinda.*

Enter Clarinda.

Ha! By Heaven the very Crocodile. [*Aside.*

Clar. By all my Hopes of Happiness the very Monster. [*Aside.*

Manl. Madam, you are surpriz'd I believe, not to meet the Man you expected; I beg your Pardon for this Disappointment.

Clar. Oh Indignation! No, Sir, I have met the Man I expected, tho' you are disappointed in your Woman.

Manl. What does she mean! ——— Have you a Stratagem, Madam, to bring you off, —— come, I'll help you; say, you happened into this Room by Chance; and had no Knowledge of the Plot, expected no Gallant,

Clar. Oh unheard of Impudence! A Gallant! No thou Monster of Ingratitude; have I refus'd all Mankind for thee? Nay, broke in upon the Rules of my Obedience, that I might keep my Faith inviolate, and am I thus rewarded? Is it not enough that you are false, and that I see you so, but you must add to your Barbarity, and throw a Scandal on my Fame, to hide your base Proceeding. Marry thee, No! From this Moment I resolve to hate, and to put it out of thy Power ever to deceive me a second Time, I'll marry instantly [Bellmein *peeping.*

Bellm. I must hear how the Colonel succeeds in my Place.

Manl. It is enough I know thee guilty of that very Crime thou would'st impose on me; know that you writ to my Friend to come here, with whom you have had many private Conferences, tho' I, Heaven knows, would not believe it, till my Eyes convinced me; but now thy Crimes are obvious to my Sight, and I take thee at thy Word, and from this Moment I'll never see you more: Confusion on your Sex. [*Exit.*

Clar.

Clar. Ha, his Friend! What can he mean,——ſure there's ſome Miſtake in this, yet I cannot call him back.

Enter Emilia *pulling in* Bellmein.

Em. What have we Eaves-droppers;——Oh Heavens! Why, was not you with my Couſin?

Bellm. Hey day! Why was not you with the Colonel?

Emil. Why, are not you the Colonel?

Bellm. No faith, and now I begin to ſuſpect you are not *Clarinda.*

Em. You are in the Right indeed, I am not.

Clar. Oh Heavens, I'm undone, *Manly*'s innocent.

Bellm. No, no, Madam, I'll call my Friend back immediately, he ſhall beg Pardon upon the Spot.—— Why, what a damn'd Miſtake is here; faith he's gone, but here's an old Gentleman coming up.

[*Goes to the Door, and returns quickly.*

Clar. Oh Lord, my Father, I'm undone if he finds a Man here; what ſhall I do? This was your Project *Emilia.*

Bellm. Ha! 'Zdeath, Madam, where ſhall I run? For, methinks, I would not do any more Miſchief; what ſhall I do Ladies?

Em. Ha, a lucky Thought comes into my Head; here, here, here, lie down upon this Mat.

Bellm. With all my Heart: Pox on't, to be thus put to't for nothing. If I had but got a Maidenhead, or made a Cuckold, it would not have vex'd me.

[*Lies down, and they rowl him up.*

Enter Careful, *and tumbles over the Mat.*

Emil. There, there, lie ſtill.

Caref. A Pox on your Pride, we muſt have Matts with a Vengeance, but I'll turn over a new Leaf with this Houſe, I'll warrant you; I'll have no Mats, but ſuch as lie under the Feather-Beds: Here I might have broke my Neck,

Enter Toby.

Sirrah, remove that Mat, and do you hear, throw it into

into the Horſe-Pond; I'll have no more Mats in my Houſe.

Toby. Mat, 'tis damn'd heavy; come out here, I believe the Dog is got into it.

Clar. Oh Lord, what ſhall I do? [*Aſide*.

[*The Man goes to take up the Mat, and finds it heavy, ſhakes it, and out drops* Bellmein.

Bell. The Horſe-Pond! Nay then, 'tis time to ſhift for myſelf.

Emil. Here, here, There's a Guinea for you, *Toby*; bring him off ſome Way or other. [*Runs to* Toby.

Caref. Ha, what was that?

Toby. Bark, Sir, bark; only the great Dog, Sir, was crept in the Mat.

Bell. Wough, wough, wough, wough.

[*Creeps off quick*.

Emil. Rarely done; expect a better Reward for this, *Toby*.

Caref. The Dog was it? I proteſt I thought it had been a Thief.

Toby. No Sir, nothing elſe. [*Exit with the Mat*.

Caref. Why, how now? Methinks, you are mightily prink'd up. Mercy upon me, what a Buſh of Hair is there furz'd out; in my Conſcience, I believe you have got the Fore-top of ſome Beau's Wig.

Emil. That's the Faſhion Uncle, you wou'd not have us dreſs like my Quaking Aunt that is to be Ha, ha, ha.

Caref. How now, Sauce-box; your Quaking Aunt, quotha.

Clar. Sir, I hope you don't deſign to marry that Thing.

Caref. Thing do you call her? I cod you ſhall marry Sir *William* immediately, or call that Thing Mother, I can tell you that.

Clar. Oh Heavens, what ſhall I do?

Enter Sir William *and Mrs*. Plotwell.

Caref. Here, Sir *William*, I give her to your Arms; I'll have my Coach harneſs'd, and to Church this Moment.

Sir

Sir *Will.* Madam, tho' I don't pretend to be a Beau, yet I hope the World will distinguish the Difference between a rough, unhewn Soldier, and a polish'd Gentleman; I don't, in the least, hint at *Manly*.

Clar. Insipid Coxcomb. [*Aside.*

Emil. to *Plot.* For Heaven's Sake invent some Way to give her an Hour's Time to consider, or she's undone.

Mrs. *Plot.* Friend, shall I speak one Word with thee?

Caref. Twenty, if you please.

Plot. Let me advise thee, do not be so passionate with thy Daughter; the little Discourse I had with her, shew'd her to be tractable; if thou think'st fit, I'll read her t'other Lesson upon her Duty, and I don't doubt but she'll comply.

Caref. With all my Heart; for whatever thou say'st, must be for her good, I'm convinc'd. Sir *William*, we'll go take a Glass in the next Room till the Bride be ready, and then——

Sir *Will.* And then, Madam, I shall be the happiest Man alive; if I would change Conditions with the Czar of *Muscovy*, may I be condemn'd to the Smoak of Tobacco, and never know the Pleasure of taking Snuff. [*Exit.*

Emil. A very Courtly Wish indeed.

Plot. Come don't trifle away the Time I have given you, but write to *Manly*, and beg him to protect you, and rescue you from the Arms of this Fool.

Clar. Oh, how can I write to him whom I have abus'd?

Plot. And did he not pay you in the same Coin! Come, come, this little Mistake rather serves to increase his Love than diminish it, when he finds you true, as no doubt but *Bellmein* has told him e'er this, he'll be glad to accept the Conditions. Come, come, write to him, *Toper* is within, and he shall carry it.

Clar. Well, it being my last Shift, I'll follow your Advice. [*Exit.*

Plot. Ay, ay, do so, I'll warrant you a Fortune, and the old Man's Consent before I have done with him.

A Drum beating up for Volunteers. Bellmein *crosses the Stage, and a Serjeant after him.*

Serj. Captain, Captain.

Bell. Ha, Serjeant.

Serj. I have got the finest Volunteer, a Beau, Captain.

Bell. A Beau! Nay, if the Beaus begin to list, let the *French* look to't. Where is he, Serjeant?

Serj. He's coming, Sir.

Bell. I can't stay now, but I'll be here in a Moment, and I'll bring the Colonel with me.

Serj. I'll wait on you here, Sir. [*Exit.*

Enter Ogle.

The Captain will be here in a Moment, Sir; but pray Sir, why will you go for a Soldier, methinks, you might get a Commission?

Ogle Because I dreamt, Sir, I should be a General,—— and I have a Mind to rise gradually, I hate jumping into Honour at once.

Serj. Sir, I honour you; no Doubt but your Dream will come true.

Ogle. Sir, I dreamt last Night that I saw two Armies join Battle; and, methought, in the Scuffle, my Brains were knock'd out, and when I wak'd, I wonder'd to find myself with all my Limbs; I straight felt for my other Leg, and suspected my Eyes when they inform'd me I had both Hands.

Serj. A very good Dream, and signifies your Advancement.

Ogle. Nay, after that, I had the strangest Dream, my Man found me scaling my Curtains for a Fort, killing my Pillow, and entering Duel with my Breeches. Methought, all the *Trojan* Faces in the Hangings were turn'd *Frenchmen*, and a Famine raging amongst 'em they resolv'd to eat me; so casting Dice what Part of me to devour first, the Lot fell upon my Head. Now, Sir, all these Dreams I interpret quite contrary, I know I shall be a great Man.

Serj. No doubt on't, Sir——I'm afraid all this Fellow's Courage lies in his Sleep. I'm resolv'd to sound him a little. [*Aside.*

Ogle.

Ogle. Pry'thee, *Serjeant*, tell me, what Sort of a Thing a Camp is?

Serj. Why truly, Sir, a Camp would be a pleaſant Place, did the Fields produce Feather-Beds; or if the Streams like thoſe of the Golden Age, did run pure Wine; or if Camp Meals wou'd every Twelve and Seven obſerve due Hours!——But, Sir, to be half ſtarv'd on ſcarce freſh green Sod, juſt ſo much Earth, to Earth; and then to live the Life of Nature; or as ſome do call it, The Life of the hardy; to quench one's Thirſt at the next Spring, coffin up one's ſelf each Night in Turff, and thence come forth, like one of *Cadmus*'s Soldiers, ſown with Serpents Teeth, and ſtart forth arm'd from a Furrow, is a Courſe of Life, I fear will never ſuit with your Conſtitution.

Ogle, 'Tis ſomething hard, truly, but no Matter, I'm reſolv'd.

Serj. Oh! This is nothing, Sir; here comes on a Troop, and your Honour can't but loſe an Eye; an Engine there goes off, and you will ſhew yourſelf a Coward, unleſs you loſe an Arm——Here you are ſurrounded, and then 'twere baſe to bring more than one Shoulder off.

Ogle. [*Rubbing his Shoulder.*] Ha! I don't like it. [*Aſide.*

Serj. Nay, Sir, conſider e'er you go.——For 'tis a damn'd Diſcredit to have a Noſe after a Battle, or to walk the Streets upon your own Legs.

Ogle. Humph?——I feel myſelf already partly compos'd of Fleſh, partly of Wood. Methinks I hang between two Crutches, like a Man in Chains, toſt by the Wind, I don't like this ſlicing into Reputation.

Enter Bellmein *and Colonel* Manly.

Ogle. But theſe Men that you raiſe, Serjeant, are they to go againſt the *French* or *Spaniards*?

Serj. Why do you aſk, Sir?

Ogle. Becauſe I cannot in Honour draw my Sword againſt the *French*.

Serj. How ſo, pray? You're no *Jacobite*, I hope.

Ogle. Oh? Sir, my Scruples are not founded upon Religion; but I'll tell you, the laſt long Vacation I made the

the Tour of *France* and *Lorrain*, where I receiv'd such extraordinary Marks of Civility, particularly from the Duke of *Berry*, the Duke of *Burgundy*, and the Chevalier de St. *George*, and from the Governor of *Calais*, such extravagant Obligations; But above all from the Governor's Daughter——That upon my Soul, I cannot descend so far from the Punctilio's of Honour, to go against 'em; but against *Spain*, I——Ha? the Colonel, I'm resolv'd to fight him however, Death, Hell and Furies: Draw, Sir?

Col. Draw, Sir, For what, Sir?

Ogle. Sir, I say Draw Sir, or else resign all Pretensions to *Clarinda.*

Bell. Why what a Metamorphosis is here? Is this your Voluntier, Serjeant?

Serj. Yes, Sir; but if you had not come as you did, he had been gone; for I found his Courage began to sink.

Col. [*To* Clarinda!] How dares such a Coxcomb as you name *Clarinda*? [*Draws and Disarms him.*] Now learn more Wit, or get more Courage.

Ogle. Courage, Sir, Z'death, Sir, I'll box with you [*Pulling off his Neckcloth.*] you have got my Sword, but no Matter for that, I'll fight it out at Fists; lose a Fortune for Want of fighting, No!

Col. I'll Box you, you Dog; give me the Cane, [*To the Serjeant.*] Sirrah, I ll make Mummy of your Bones; I'll make you forswear sauntering after Fortunes, nay you shall not dare to look towards the House where they live, or so much as think of them. [*Beats him all this Time.*

Ogle. Oh Lord, Sir, for Heaven's Sake! Sir, I'll observe the Conditions.

Bell. Nay now, you are too rigid, I dare promise for Mr. *Ogle.*

Ogle. I will indeed Sir, only let me think of them; for who can help thinking, Sir?

Col. No; here Serjeant, take this Fellow, and let him run the Gantelope, I'll think you, Sirrah.

Ogle. Oh Lord, Sir! spare that, and I will not think of 'em, upon my Faith, Sir.

Col.

Col. Nay, one Thing more you must promise, which is, to resume your wonted Cowardice, and betake you to your Desk again. Go, take Money of the Men you mean to cozen; talk little, except when you are paid for't, 'tis an Antidote against Beating; keep your Hand from your Sword, and your Laundress's Petticoats, and you'll live at Peace.

Ogle. I will, Colonel —— Give me Wisdom that is beaten into a Man; for that sticks to him, Egad. I'm wiser than a Justice of Peace; your Precepts are very learned. Sir, I'm your humble Servant —— Farewell Sword, and welcome Tongue again. Now can't I positively tell, whether 'tis best to be courageous, or to have no Courage at all; Beaten, if I Fight, and Beaten if I do not——Now I think I know something of the Law, and yet if the Question was put to me I cou'd not resolve it?

But for my own Part, I'll lay Courage down,
As all Men do, when they take up the Gown;
Cloak'd with the Law, I may securely baul,
And who affronts me then, shall pay for all. [*Exit.*

Bell. Ha! ha! ha!

Enter Toper, *and gives the Colonel a Letter.*

Toper. Ha! Colonel, opportunely met; I bring an Express from the Queen of Beauty, her Orders are in that Paper.

Col. Ha! 'Tis *Clarinda*'s Hand—[*Reads.*] I hope by this Time, you are satisfied of my Innocence, as I'm of yours; if not, I beg you, by all the Tyes of Honour, to rescue me from this foolish Knight, to whom I am this Moment to be married, by the rigid Command of my barbarous Father; and if I don't clear your Censures, use me as you please. Yours, *Clarinda.*——Rescue thee, yes, the Fool shall quit all Pretensions to thee, unless this Arm deceive me.

Bell. If it does, Boy, here's another at thy Service.—

Toper. You may seize her at the End of the Street as she passes; be sure you marry her as soon as you have got her; let me alone to bring her Fortune; the Captain must

must help our Plot forward, as soon as he has help'd you away with her.——

Bell. With all my Heart, I love Mischief; I have a plaguy hankering Mind after this Cousin tho', e'er since *Manly* told me she has Ten Thousand Pounds.

Toper. The Yoke shou'd be well lin'd, or 'twill be very uneasy at best.——

Bell. Ay, there must be Gold poportionable to the Alloy, or 'twou'd not be current Coin, Ha, ha.

Toper. Ha, ha, Well, I'm a good-natur'd Fellow now, to spend my Time in your Business when I have an Assignation with one of the prettiest Girls about Town, Faith.

Bell. Some old o'erworn Drab, I'll warrant, cast off by all the Beaus in Town, and now is become a new Face to the Drunkards.

Toper. No Faith, she's a kept Mistress, she costs me not a Souce.

Col. Thou art still labouring between two Tides, Wine and Women: Wilt thou never take up till thou art confin'd by a Doctor to dry Diet?

Toper. Dry Diet? You don't mean a Wife, I hope; catch me at that Meat and choke me with it, that's just as a Confinement to Sea-Bisquit at Land; tho' I'd do you all the Service I can, Colonel, in helping you to your Mistress, yet I can't help lamenting the Loss of a Friend.

Col. Why, will Matrimony lose me to my Friends? I shall love them as well as ever, I assure you.

Toper. Ay, but your Friends won't care that for you. [*Snapping his Fingers.*] for e'er the second Bottle, you'll be calling What's to pay? Your Wife won't go to Bed till you come Home; this makes Company uneasy, and what makes us uneasy decreases our Value for't; For my Part, I had rather be confin'd to Sea-Men in a Storm, or the malicious Conversation of a *Jacobite* Club, than the Company of a married Man; for at every Mouse stirring I shou'd think the Comforts of Matrimony were coming, with all their commanding Retinue: A Wife! Egad, I'd rather want Wine, the only Support of the Body.——

Col. Well, you declare for a Bottle, I for a Wife, which I think the greater Pleasure far.

Toper. Where ſhall we find you? [*Exit.*

Col. At the *Roſe.*

Toper. Adieu; *Bellmein* ſhall come to you there.

Let Fools be fetter'd to that Clog, a Wife,
Whilſt free, I reap the Pleaſure of my Life;
And Heaven grant I may no longer live,
Than I can taſte the Joys which Wine does give. [Exit.

[*A Claſh of Swords, Sir* William *cries Murder, Colonel and* Clarinda, Bellmein *and* Emilia *croſs the Stage.*

Col. Haſte, my Faireſt, and let us tye that Knot, which nought but Death can looſe. [*Exit.*

Enter Careful.

Caref. Certainly, I heard Sir *William*'s Voice cry Murder.

Enter Sir William.

What's the Matter, Sir *William?* Where's my Daughter?

Sir *Will.* Enfeeble me, if I know; you had beſt ſend after her immediately, or ſhe'll be married to *Manly*, who drew upon me; and if I had not quitted her, he had run me quite thro' the Body, impair my Vigour.

Caref. This was her Project of going on Foot, ſhe wou'd not have the Coach under Pretence of Notice being taken, forſooth; and your Perſuaſion made me go before to get the Parſon ready. Ods-fleſh, had I been there, this had not happen'd; old as I am, they ſhou'd not have eſcap'd ſo eaſily. Z'death! Let a Man take your Miſtreſs from you! In my Conſcience, young Fellows are ſo rotten now-a-days, they are afraid of every Scuffle, leſt they drop in Pieces. Zounds, I cou'd curſe the Minute I got this Baſtard, to think what a Fortune ſhe has loſt. *Aſide.*

Sir *Will.* Do you take my Breeding to have been at a Bear-Garden, Sir, or in Bedlam, to endanger my Life for your Daughter? No, let her go, I'd marry an Actreſs ſooner, and have more Hopes of her Virtue.

Caref. Say you so, Mr. Dirty Crown? Adod, I cou'd find in my Heart to dash the Powder out of your Whore's Hair for you.

Sir *Will.* Your Age protects you, Sir. [*Exit.*

Caref. Well, if I don't fit the Baggage, I'm mistaken, Egad. I'll marry *Toper's* Niece immediately.

Enter Toper.

Mr. *Toper*, you came luckily; I am resolv'd to marry your Cousin this Moment. Nay, I'll settle all I have upon her, I'll hamper my Daughter, I'll warrant her.

Top. I came to inform you, Sir, that I saw Colonel *Manly* and your Daughter enter the Church; the Parson met them at the Door, and I'm much afraid they will be married before you can get to 'em.

Caref. Let her marry and be pox't; I'll not give her a Farthing, I'm resolv'd. Let her go a Soldiering with her Husband, and carry his Knap-sack, like a Trull as she is. If there be any Favour or Interest to be had in an *English* Parliament, I'll have the Parson turn'd out of his Place, for a Jacobite, that coupled them.

Top. I have a Friend of mine at the *Rose*, just come from *Oxford*; if you please, Mr. *Careful*, I'll fetch him, and you may be marry'd in your own House.

[*Exit* Toper.

Caref. With all my Heart. Adod, methinks I'm brisk and young again. This audacious Wench——

My Blood boils high, and all my Spirits move,
Revenge gives Strength to Age as much as Love. [Exit.

The End of the FOURTH ACT.

ACT V. SCENE I.

SCENE Careful's *House*.

Careful *leading in* Mrs. Plotwell.

Caref. WELL, my dearest *Anne*, I think myself the happiest Man alive since I espous'd thee: I have settled my whole Estate upon thee, which, with this Kiss, I do confirm to thee again.

[*Offers to kiss her.*

Plot. Pray forbear, Sir——

Caref. How Wife! refuse to kiss me?

Plot. Yes, except a sweeter Air came from you—— Faugh, you've turn'd my Stomach; I wonder you can ask me, knowing your Lungs are perish'd.

Caref. Mercy upon me! Why what have I marry'd?—

Plot. Here, Where are my Servants?

Enter a Maid.

Run to the *Exchange*, fetch me a *French* Night-gown, and *French* Head, set my Dressing-Table in order, Do you hear? Let my Paint, Powder and Patches be ready.

Caref. Oh Lord! Oh Lord! Paint, Powder and Patches; Why harkee, Mistress, are you not a Quaker?

Plot. No, Sir, I only made use of that Disguise to catch you in, but you have Money enough to equip me after the Fashion, and that was the only Motive of my Sanctity.

Caref. Oh! undone, undone!

Plot. Look you, Sir, I shall never endure your Conversation, I must have two Beds, two Chambers, and two Tables, it was an Article of our Agreement, you know, that I shou'd live retir'd———That is, apart, Sir.

Caref. A Curse on that Agreement———but harkee Wife, you are not in earnest sure?

Plot. In earnest? Why, do you think I jest with Age?

Caref. And you won't Bed with me?

Plot.

Plot. Did ever Man of your Hairs ask such Questions? I vow I blush at your Unreasonableness.

Caref. O monstrous!

Plot. Is it fit I shou'd be bury'd? For to bed with you were a direct Emblem of my going to my Grave!

Caref. Mercy upon me! Where is this Rogue, this *Toper?* What damn'd *Succubus* has he topt upon me?

Plot. I'll have your Picture set in my Wedding-Ring; to put me in Mind of Mortality; Do you think I'll come within your Winding Sheets? For what?

Caref. I am married!

Plot. Pray why did you marry? In my Conscience, you're as youthful as a Coffin, and as hot as the sultry Winter that froze over the *Thames*; they say, the hard Time did begin from you. Ha, ha, ha.

Caref. Oh Heavens! I am made the Curse of all Mankind! O Patience! Patience!——Harkee, Mistress, you that have a Fever and Dog-Days in your Blood; if you knew this, why did you marry me?

Plot. That your experienc'd Achs, that have felt Springs and Falls these forty Years, shou'd ask such a Question; as if I could not find Friends to supply your cold Defects: Do you think a young Woman high in her Blood——

Caref. And hot as Goats and Marmosets. [*Aside.*

Plot. Apt to take Flame at any Temptation.——

Caref. And kindle at the Picture of a Man. [*Aside.*

Plot. Wou'd wed Dust and Ashes, unless she were—

Caref. Crack'd, try'd, or broken up, ha!

Plot. Right, Sir; or lack'd a Cloak.

Caref. Mischief and Hell: Was there none to make your Cloak but me?

Plot. Not so well lin'd, Sir, Ha, ha.

Caref. Oh! You staid for a wealthy Cuckold, did you?

Plot. Your tame Beasts should have gilded Horns!— Besides, Sir, I thought your Age wou'd wink at stolen Helps, if I took Comfort from abroad.

Caref. Yes, yes, You shall have Comfort——I'll deliver Letters for you, or hold the Door!——

Plot. No, Sir, I'll not give you that Trouble, I'll have a Maid shall do that—— [*Making a Curtesy.*

Caref. Oh Impudence! unheard of Impudence!

Plot. But, Sir, I look your Coffers ſhou'd maintain me at my Rate.

Caref. How's that, pray?

Plot. Why, like a Lady: I muſt have you knighted, for I don't like Miſtreſs———My Lady, wou'd ſound better.

Caref. Yes—I ſhall riſe to Honour. [*Aſide.*

Plot. I muſt have ſix Horſes in my Coach, four are fit for thoſe that have a Charge of Children, you and I ſhall never have any.

Caref. If we have, all *Middleſex* will be their Fathers—

Plot. I'll have four Footmen, and this Houſe clear'd of all this old Lumber, and new wainſcotted, and lin'd with Looking-Glaſs, have Cabinets, Scrutores, and China.

Caref. Mercy upon me—Harkye, Miſtreſs, you told me you lov'd Retirement, hated Viſits, and bargain'd for Hours of Devotion.

Plot Right, Sir, but what Woman ſpeaks Truth before ſhe's married?

Caref. Politickly anſwer'd, and like one perfect in the ſinning Trade.

Plot. Well, Sir, don't diſcompoſe yourſelf, 'twill ſignify nothing; I'll in and examine your Jewels, chuſe ſome for every Day, and ſome for Maſks and Balls. [*Exit.*

Caref. The Devil go with you: Oh that I had my Daughter again! Two Days more of this, and I ſhall grow mad, or to redeem myſelf, daſh out my Brains. [*Exit.*

SCENE *changes to* Plotwell's *Lodgings.*

Enter on one Side, the Colonel, Clarinda, *and* Emilia; *on the other* Bellmein *and* Toper.

Top. We have done your Buſineſs, Colonel; *Bellmein* here has tack'd 'em together.

Bell. I canted out the Form of Matrimony as gravely as if I had taken my Degree at *Edinburgh.*

Col. And how does it take?

Top. Oh! admirably well, I liſten'd awhile, and found ſhe manag'd it rarely.

Clar. She'll drive my Father out of his Wits.

Top. Well, Captain, you'll obſerve what I told you; I'll follow you with another Project, I warrant you, will give the old Fellow enough of Matrimony. Colonel, do you be ready when I call to come in, do you hear? I fancy they are in ſuch Confuſion that it would be no hard Matter for all of you to get into the Houſe unſeen.

Clar. We'll endeavour it.

Bell. But harkye, Madam, there's ſomething more to be ſaid before you and I part, Have you the Conſcience to let your Friend launch into the Sea of Matrimony alone?

Emil. To chuſe, Sir; for if the Voyage prove dangerous, one at a Time is enough to be loſt.

Clar. Would you have her ſurrender upon the firſt Summons, Captain? You muſt expect ſome Fatigue in Love, as well as War; the little Diſquiet of Hopes and Fears do but enhance the Value of a Miſtreſs, when gain'd! Soldiers and Knight-Errants ſhou'd court Danger, and deſpiſe an Enterprize that had no Difficulty in it.

Bell. Ay, Madam, if I had but the Hopes of a Carnaval after this Lent, 'twould be a ſufficient Recompence; but Expectation and Uncertainty is the worſt Food in the World for a Fellow of my Conſtitution.

Col. Come, Madam, be generous; you cannot have an honeſter Fellow, I'll ſay that for him.

Bell. Lookye there, Madam, he'll vouch for me, if you don't think my own Word ſufficient.

Emil. I ſhall truſt no Body's Judgment but my own, and that tells me you are too much a Libertine for a Huſband; why, you have not the leaſt Reſemblance of a Lover.

Bell. No Reſemblance! Why I'm a perfect Skeleton, do but ſee how pale and wan I look! my Taylor ſhall ſwear I am fall'n away ſix Inches in the Waiſt, ſince this Day Sevennight; and if theſe be no Signs of being in Love, the Devil's in't.

Omnes.

Omnes, Ha, ha, ha, ha.

Emil. Very violent Symptoms, truly.———Have you any more of them, Sir?

Bell. A Thousand; do but feel here the Palpitation of my Heart, the Irregularity of my Pulse, the Emotion of my Brain———In short, my whole Frame's disorder'd; and without immediate Help, I'm a dead Man—I'm quite out of Breath, I hope she won't put me to the Expence of any more Lyes; for certainly I have told enow to deserve any one Woman in *Christendom*. [*Aside.*

Emil. Poor Gentleman; Well! if your Distemper continues, I'll consult my Pillow for a Remedy.

Bell. Take me with you to that Study, Madam, the Sight of me there will very much improve your Understanding. [*Embracing her.*

Col. Come, I hope to see thee blest as I am———And now, my Fairest, my whole study shall be to make you happy. [*To* Clarinda.

Bell. Well, Madam, you had as good give me my Answer.

Emil. Not till I see the Event of your Plot upon my Uncle. [*Exit.*

Top. Come, come, she's thine, Boy.

For tho' at first the Sex our Suit deny,
Press 'em but Home and they will all comply.

SCENE, Careful's *House.*

Careful *solus.*

Caref. Mercy upon me! What shall I do?——Well, thou'rt right enough serv'd, old Boy——Eh——Pox of thy old doating Head. [*Beats his Head.*] Thou must marry for Revenge, must thou———I am reveng'd with a Witness.———

Enter Bellmein.

Bell. Sir, your Servant, I come, Sir, to do you a Piece of Service, if it be not too late; I heard just now, that

that one *Toper* had lodg'd a Woman, under Pretence of a Cousin, in your House.

Caref. Oh Heaven! I'm become the Town-Talk already——Well, Sir, and what then?

Bell. She's a common Strumpet, Sir.

Caref. How, Sir? Have a Care what you say.

Bell. I'll prove it, Sir; she's of known Practice, the Cloaths she wears are but her Quarters Sins——She has no Lining but what she first offends for.

Caref. Oh! I sweat, I sweat.

Bell. Sir, she has known Men of all Nations, and lain by two Parts of the Map, *Africa*, and *America*.

Caref. Oh, oh, oh, oh.

Bell. What ails you, Sir; are you not well?

Caref. Oh undone, undone, I am married, Sir!

Bell. Nay then, Heaven help you—Why wou'd you trust *Toper*, the debauchedest Fellow in Town; she was once his Mistress; Money falling short, I suppose, he has topt her upon you, and is to be maintain'd out of your Bags.

Caref. Oh, I have settled all I have in the World upon her! That damn'd Rascal. Oh, that I could see him stretch'd upon a Rack now, I'd give a thousand Pounds for every Stretch that shou'd but show him Hell, and then recal his fleeting Soul, and give him Strength to endure his Torment often. I'd have him as long a dying as a chop'd Eel.

Enter two Footmen bearing in a Frame of a Picture with a Curtain before it.

What have we here?

Footm. My Lady has sent your Wife a Present, Sir.

Caref. Who is your Lady?

Footm. My Lady *Manlove*.

Caref. Pray what is it?

Footm. A Picture for her Bed-chamber, Sir.

Caref. For her Bed-chamber? There are but one Sort of Pictures will please my Wife there——Pray draw back the Curtain.

Footm. My Lady charg'd that none shou'd see it but your Wife, Sir.

Caref.

Caref. Say you ſo, Sir; but I will ſee it. [*Draws the Curtain and* Toper *comes out of the Frame.*] Hell! and Damnation! Are you there, Bawd, Pander, Sirrah? I'll cut your Ears off. [*Draws*, Bellmein *holds him.*

Bell. Hold, Sir, I muſt prevent your running into further Miſchief; if you kill him the Law purſues you.

Caref. The Law? who wou'd ſcruple hanging to be reveng'd on ſuch a Dog——Sirrah, you are a Villain.—

Top. Sir, you are rude, and ſhou'd be beaten; can't a Man come in private, on Buſineſs to your Wife, but you muſt be inquiſitive————

Enter Mrs. Plotwell.

Caref. Why this is beyond Example; Why do you hold me, Sir? Z'death, I ſhall be cuckolded before my Face.

Top. Ho! Are you come? I thought your Huſband, to keep you chaſte, had ſet a Guard of Eunuchs over you, or ſhut you up in a Room, where no male Beaſt is pictur'd; for I find he is as jealous already as an *Italian.*

Plot. I wonder, Sir, who licens'd you to pry, or ſpy out my Friends that come to me in private; it wou'd be more to your Reputation to truſt to my Management, than to be peeping; but it ſhows your unbred Curioſity, which I ſhall correct.

Caref. Zounds! This is beyond the Suffering of a Saint; let me go and I'll ſlit her Noſe——Thou Woman double ſtampt.

Plot. You'll dare to break up Letters ſhortly, and examine my Taylor when he brings home my Gown, leſt there be a Man in't. I'll have you to know, Sir, I'll have whom I pleaſe, and in what Diſguiſe I pleaſe, and not have your Eyes, ſo ſaucy, to peep, as if by Prevention, you meant to kill a Baſiliſk

Caref. Mercy on me! I ſhall loſe my Underſtanding.

Plot. Couſin *Toper*, I'll fetch you the hundred Pound immediately. [*Exit.*

Caref. A hundred Pound! Oh, oh, oh.

Bell. I vow, Sir, I am very much concern'd at your

Misfortune; if I was in your Place, I'd take my Daughter Home; the Colonel is a Man of Honour, and will at least secure you from such Affronts as these.

Caref. Ah poor Girl! But I have not a Farthing to give her——This damn'd Woman has got all.

Bell. Suppose, I contrive a Way to null your Marriage, wou'd you forgive your Daughter?

Caref. With all my Soul.

Toper. What wou'd you give for such a Project, ha?

Caref. As much as I'd give to see you hang'd——Which is all I am worth——

Toper. Ha, ha, ha, well, you wou'd forgive me too, wou'd you not?

Caref. Ay, tho' thou hadst murder'd my Father, and debauch'd my Mother.

Toper. Say you so, Sir—Well, I'll be with you in an Instant. [*Exit.*

Caref. But which Way will you do it, Sir?

Bell. Why you have not consummated yet, have you?

Caref. No, thank Heaven.

Bell. Well then, take you no Care; you'll give your Daughter the same Fortune you design'd for the Fop Knight?

Caref. Ay, that I will, and 500 *l.* more.

Bell. Come, in Lovers; the Scene's chang'd.

Enter Colonel, Clarinda, Emilia *and* Toper.

Col. Your Blessing, Sir, [*Kneels.*

Clar. And with it your Pardon.

Caref. You have it, provided I get unmarried again.

Bell. We'll now call for your Lady; Oh, here she comes.

Enter Mrs. Plotwell.

Caref. Zounds, I tremble at the Sight of her.

Plot. You shan't need, Sir; for my Fury is over: I wish you Joy, Madam, and Sir, I here resign you up your Settlement again. [*Gives him Papers.*

Caref. How's this? Ha, pray unfold this Mystery.

Toper. Why, Sir, this is Mrs. *Plotwell*, your Neighbour, who only put on this Disguise to be serviceable to your

your Daughter.——This honeſt Gentleman here, was the Parſon that coupled you.

Bell. Now, Sir, I think, I have kept my Word with you.

Caref. Very well.

Plot. Why, truly, Sir, being loth to ſee this young Lady thrown away upon a Fool, when ſhe had the Proſpect of ſuch a worthy Match as Colonel *Manly*, I undertook to reduce you to your Reaſon, and I don't doubt but you'll own I have done you a Piece of Service, in forcing you to exclude a Blockhead out of your Family, and in his Stead receive a Man of Senſe and Honour.

Col. 'Tis now, Madam, my Turn to pay my Acknowledgments for this unexpected Goodneſs; inſtruct me, pray, which Way I may be grateful.

Plot. If I have done Good, it rewards itſelf; and if Mr. *Careful* pleaſes to pardon the Frolic, I ſhall be over-paid.

Caref. With all my Heart, I' faith, the Frolic was a pretty Frolic——Now 'tis over.

Enter Sir William Mode.

Sir *Will.* I heard you was married, Mr. *Careful*, I wiſh you Joy.

Caref. You are miſtaken, Sir *William*, 'tis my Daughter that is married.

Sir *Will.* Ha, the Colonel married to my Miſtreſs? [*Aſide.*

Clar. Sir *William* I deſire all Quarrels between you and I may be cancel'd.

Col. Pray include me in that Treaty too, Sir *William.*

Caref. Here has been ſtrange juggling, Sir *William*, I have been trick'd out of my Conſent, I hope you'll pardon me too.

Sir *Will.* I'm in ſuch Confuſion, that I know not what to ſay, but I muſt ſhew 'em that my Soul's above an Affront, and that nothing can diſorder the Serenity of my Temper. [*Aſide.*] Ay, we are all Friends, Gentlemen, and I forgive the Lady too, for ſhe has done more honeſtly by me than moſt Women wou'd, ſhe has married the Man ſhe lik'd, tho' 'tis the Faſhion to take the rich Huſband they don't like, and make a Friend of the Man they do.

Om. Ha, ha, ha.

Sir *Will*. One Thing I deſire you'd make clear to me, Madam, which is, why did you give me Encouragement by your Woman?

Clar. I give you Encouragement by my Woman! What do you mean?

Maid. I beg your Pardon, Madam, his Gold prevail'd upon me, and I thought what I ſaid would ſignify nothing; I hope you will forgive me.

Clar. Never: Out of my Doors, I ſuppoſe thro' your Management, *Ogle* was ſo familiar with me too —— Out of my Sight. [*Exit Maid*.

Col. Indeed, my Dear, I cannot intercede in her Behalf, ſince thro' her Means my firſt Suſpicion came, that made us both uneaſy; but as to *Ogle*, I ſufficiently reveng'd your Quarrel; for I'll engage he never ſets up for a Beau again.

Sir *Will*. Confound your whole Sex, you're all not worth a Gentleman's Anger; I'll to my Lodgings, and ſend for the Muſic, and think no more of you nor Matrimony; if I do, I'll give e'm Leave to ram me into an Hautboy and blow me out at the Holes; impair my Vigour. [*Exit*.

Om. Ha, ha, ha.

Bell. Well, Madam, what ſay you? Have you a Mind to ſee me ſwing to *Elizium* in my Garters, and hear me ſung about in a Ballad to a doleful new Tune, call'd, The Gentleman's Farewell to his unkind Lady——Or will you take Pity on me?

Emil. Well, Sir, to prevent ſuch ſad Diſaſters, I don't care if I give you my Hand; and as you deſerve, my Heart ſhall follow.

Bell. Ay, give me but the Body, and I'll warrant you I'll get the reſt.

Caref. Hey Day! What a Wedding chopt up there too! Well, I never ſhall believe common Report again, That all Women are *Jacobites*, ſince I find them ſo ready towards the Soldier's Service to the Nation with their Perſons and Fortunes.

Emil.

Emil. I wish every brave Man was rewarded according to his Merit, I'm certain Captain *Bellmein* deserves more than I can give him.

Bell. Don't compliment your Husband, Madam, you don't know half my Deserts yet.

Caref. Brave Boys, brave Boys.

Enter Servant.

Serv. Sir, here's the Music without come to congratulate your Marriage.

Caref. Bid 'em come in, we'll have a Dance.

[*Here a Dance.*

Toper. Well, Gentlemen, I wish you Joy, if there can be any such Thing in a Wife; but for my Part, it shall always be my Maxim not to part with my Liberty, till I can't help it; What Bird would be confin'd in a Cage, when it can skip from Tree to Tree? Colonel, I'll come and take a Bottle with you by and by. [*Exit.*

Clar. Madam, you deserve our best Thanks for this exemplary Piece of Justice; and, be assured, you have laid an eternal Obligation on me.

Plot. I am pleas'd that I have done you Service, and henceforth shall devote myself to Virtue, and I hope Heaven will pardon the Follies of my past Life.

Col. *Blest in my Love, I envy no Man's Fate,*
Content alone is the true happy State.

Plot. Virtue, thou shining Jewel of my Sex——— Thou precious Thing, that none knows how to value as they ought, while they enjoy it, but like spendthrift Heirs, when they have wasted all their Store, wou'd give the World they cou'd retrieve their lost Estate: Therefore beware, you happy Maids, how you listen to the deluding Tongues of Men, 'tis only they have Power to betray you.

Oh happy she, that can securely say
Folly be gone, I have no Mind to Play.
My Fame is clear, I have not sinn'd to-day.

THE
GAMESTER:
A
COMEDY.

Dramatis Personæ.

MEN.

Sir Thomas Valere, *Father to* Valere *the Gamester*,	*Mr*. Freeman.
Dorante, *his Brother, in Love with* Angelica.	*Mr*. Corey.
Young Valere, *a Gentleman much in Love with* Angelica.	*Mr*. Verbruggen.
Mr. Lovewell, *in Love with Lady* Wealthy.	*Mr*. Betterton.
Marquis of Hazard, *a ſuppoſed* French *Marquis*.	*Mr*. Fieldhouſe.
Hector, *Valet to* Valere.	*Mr*. Pack.
Mr. Galoon, *a Taylor*.	*Mr*. Smeaton.
Count Cogdie, } *Three Gameſters*.	*Mr*. Dickins.
1ſt Gentleman, } *Three Gameſters*.	*Mr*. Weller.
2d Gentleman, } *Three Gameſters*.	*Mr*. Knap.
Box-Keeper.	*Mr*. Francis Lee.

WOMEN.

Lady Wealthy, *a very vain coquettiſh Widow, very rich, Siſter to* Angelica	*Mrs* Barry.
Angelica, *in Love with* Valere.	*Mrs*. Bracegirdle.
Betty, *Woman to the Lady* Wealthy.	*Mrs*. Parſons.
Favourite, *Woman to* Angelica.	*Mrs*. Hunt.
Mrs. Security, *one that lends Money upon Pawns*.	*Mrs*. Wallis.
Mrs. Topknot, *a Milliner*.	*Mrs*. Fieldhouſe.

THE

THE GAMESTER.

ACT I.

The Curtain draws up, and discovers Hector *in an Elbow-Chair, just waking, yawning.*

Hector.

BLESS me! 'Tis broad Day-light; Who the Devil would serve a GAMESTER! 'Tis a cursed Life, this that I lead. O, my dear Bed, how seldom do I visit thee! When shall I be lapt in the Fold of thy Embraces, and snore forth my Thanks? I, that could enjoy thee Four and Twenty Hours together, am grown a perfect Stranger to thy Charms. O! My precious Master! Now, Ten to one, will he come Home with an empty Pocket; and then will he be confoundedly out of Humour: Then shan't I dare ask him for any Dinner. Thus am I robb'd of the *two* chiefest Pleasures of my Life, *Eating* and *Sleeping*.

Enter Mrs. Favourite.

Fav. Good-morrow, Monsieur *Hector*: Where is your sweet Master?

Hect. Asleep.

Fav. I must see him.

Hect. My Master sees no body when he's asleep.

Fav. I must speak with him.

Hect. Indeed, sweet Mrs. *Favourite*, but you cannot.

Fav. P'shaw, I tell you I must, and will speak with him.

Hect. With who Child?

Fav. With who? Why, with *Valere*.

Hect. Heark'e, would you speak with my Master in *propria Persona*, or with his Picture?

Fav. Leave Fooling, for I come not upon so merry a Message as you imagine.

Hect. Why then, to be serious, my Master is not come in: He's a Man of Business, Child, and neglects his Ease to follow that.

Fav. Yes, yes, I guess the Business; he is at shaking his Elbows over a Table, saying his Prayers backwards, courting the Dice like a Mistress, and cursing them when he is disappointed. Between you and I, *Angelica* knows his Extravagance; and finding he breaks all the Oaths he made against Play, resolves to see him no more.

Hect. If he has lost his Money, this News will break his Heart.

Fav. Tell him, that I say he has deceiv'd more Women than he has played Games at Hazard; and——

Hect. You say — Ay, I find *Dorante*, my Master's Uncle, has given you a retaining Fee: What should she do with that old Fellow?

Fav. Oh! He's a Lover ripe with Discretion.

Hect. Ay, but Women generally love green Fruit best: besides, my Master's handsome.

Fav. He handsome! Behold his Picture just as he'll appear this Morning, with Arms a-cross, down-cast Eyes, no Powder in his Perriwig, a Steenkirk tuck'd in to hide the Dirt, Sword-knot untied, no Gloves, and Hands and Face as dirty as a Tinker. This is the very Figure of your beautiful Master.

Hect. The Jade has hit it.

Fav. And Pocket as empty as a *Capuchin*'s.

Hect. Hold, hold, this is Spite, mere Spite and burning Envy.

Fav. Ay, 'tis no Matter for that; I'll take Care he

shan't

ſhan't deceive my Miſtreſs: For ſhe that marries a Gameſter that plays upon the Square, as the Fool your Maſter does, can expect nothing but an Alms-Houſe for a Jointure. Once more I tell you, that *Dorante* has both Reaſon and *Favourite* of his Side.

Hect. And we have Love on our Side; and Love never fails to conquer Reaſon: For your Part, you are Like the *Swiſs*, take any Side for Pay.

Fav. Is not *Valere* aſham'd, the only Son of ſuch a Family, to leave his Father's Houſe, and ſneak up and down in Lodgings.

Hect. You're miſtaken, Mrs. *Favourite*; he did not leave his Father's Houſe: But his Father, who is as obſtinate as the Devil, and as ill-natur'd as a *Dutchman*, turn'd him out.

Fav. He was a dutiful Child in the mean Time. Well, you may take my Word, he will have ſmall Welcome at our Houſe: I ſhall let my Lady know he is a Gaming; ſo ſweet Mr. *Hector*, adieu. [*Exit.*

Hect. Farewel, Mrs. *Fripery*; I am glad I know my Maſter's Enemy however. Ho! Here he comes.

Enter Valere, *in Diſorder.*

Val. Sirrah, what's a Clock?

Hect. It is—in Troth, Sir, I have been up ſo long, I have forgot.

Val. Away, I am weary of your Fooleries. My Night Gown, quick, quick. The Devil, the Devil.

Hect. Ah! I find where about he is, he ſwears between his Teeth.

Val. So hey! What, muſt I wait all Day? My Gown here! [Valere *ſtill walks about, and* Hector *ſtill following him with the Gown.*]

Hect. 'Tis ready, Sir.

Val. What a Dog am I? I know I have no Luck, yet can't forbear playing. Oh, Fortune, Fortune! But why do I exclaim againſt her? I'll be even with her I warrant her, ſhe has made me loſe, but I defy her to make me pay, for the Devil a Souſe have I.

Hect. Sir, Sir, pleaſe to put on your Gown, Sir.

Val.

Val. Get you to Bed, you Dog, and don't trouble me.

Hect. With all my Heart, Sir. [*Exit.*

[Valere *sits down in the Arm'd-Chair.*

Val. I think I am sleepy. Death! 'Tis impossible to sleep: [*Rises.*] For I can no sooner shut my Eyes, but methinks my evil Genius flings Am's Ace before me. Why, *Hector*, Sirrah; that Rogue sleeps happy: Why, *Hector*.

Hect. Sir —— [*From the Bottom of the Stage unbutton'd.*

Val. Sir—you Sot, are you never tir'd with sleeping?

Hect. Tir'd—Why, Sir, I han't had Time to unbutton my Coat yet.

Val. Was any Body here to ask for me?

Hect. Yes, Sir, Here was your Music-Master, and your Dancing-Master.

Val. Ay, they want their Quarteridge, I suppose.

Hect. They'll call again, Sir.

Val. Then I'm not at home, Sir.

Hect. Oh! I know that, Sir. But, Sir, here was a kind of a — kind of a shabby-look'd Fellow — He said his Name was *Cogdie*: He'll call again too.

Val. I know him not. None else?

Hect. Yes, Sir, a Back-Friend of yours. Sir, may I be so bold as to ask you one Question? Do you love the charming *Angelica*?

Val. Love her! I adore her!

Hect. Ah! That's an ill Sign. Now do I know he has not a Penny in his Pocket. Ah, Sir, your Fob, like a Barometer, shews the Temper of your Heart, as that does the Weather.

Val. Don't you imagine, whatever Passion I have for Play, that I have Power to forget that amiable Creature?

Hect. Ah, Sir, but if that amiable Creature should have banish'd you———

Val. Impossible!

Hect. Talk not of Impossibilities, good Sir, for pert Mrs. *Favourite* is just gone; who, I find, hates you, and swears her Lady has declared for your Uncle. Ah, Sir—what she says is not altogether false; [*Shaking his Head*] for notwithstanding you have sworn heartily to

Angelica

Angelica never to play again, you do throw away a merry Main; or ſee, Sir———

Val. Ceaſe your Impertinence; I give you Leave to jeſt upon my Loſſes, but my Miſtreſs touches my Heart, Sirrah.

Hect. [*Aſide.*] Ah! Love's Fever is always higheſt when the Caſh is at an Ebb. But, Sir, be not caſt down, I have heard them ſay, a new Paſſion is the only Thing to cure an old one. There's the charming Widow of my Lord *Wealthy*, her Siſter, richer than *Angelica*—Ah, Sir! Had you but made your Addreſſes there.

Val. There! ſhe is the only Woman I would avoid. She's a Coquet of the firſt Rate; addreſſes all, and cares for none. How did ſhe tyrannize over my Friend *Lovewell* before ſhe married my Lord, tho' he is a Gentleman without Exception? and now ſhe's playing the ſame Game over again; for the good-natur'd Fellow is in Love ſtill.

Hect. Truly, Sir, I believe the *French* Marquis will carry it.

Val. No, he is too much of her Temper. Heark! Who's there?

Hect. A Dun, I warrant.

Val. I am not within, Sirrah.

Hect. Oh, Sir! Your Father.

Val. Ah! That's worſe; now will he rail as heartily againſt *Gaming*, as the *Fanaticks* againſt *Plays*.

Enter Sir Thomas Valere.

Sir *Tho.* What, what are you up? This is not a Gameſter's Hour; or have you not been in Bed all Night? That's moſt likely.

Hect. [*Aſide.*] He's the Devil of a Gueſſer. Indeed my Maſter keeps as early Hours as any Man, I'll ſay that for him.

Sir *Tho.* Hold your Tongue, Sirrah, or I ſhall break your Head; your Freedom will not paſs on me.

Hect. Your moſt humble Servant, Sir; I've done, Sir, I've done.

Sir *Tho.* I am come to make the laſt Trial of you, Sir. Your Courſe of Life is ſo very ſcandalous, that

unleſs

unlefs I fee a fpeedy and fincere Reformation, I have refolv'd to difinherit you; then try if what has ruin'd you, will maintain you: But, do you hear, quit the Name of your Anceftors, who never yet produc'd fuch a Profligate. The Eftate has not been referv'd fo long in the Family to be thrown away at Hazard.

Hect. Short and pithy: We are in a hopeful Way. [*Afide.*

Val. Sir, I have been revolving in my Mind all my Acts of Folly, and am afham'd that I harbour'd them fo long, and now am arm'd with manly Refolutions; forgive my paft Faults, and try my future Conduct.

Sir *Tho.* If I could believe thee real, my Joys would be compleat.

Hect. Ah! I fmoak the Defign; a little Money is wanting. [*Afide.*

Val. My cruel Uncle, who never was a Friend to you, now endeavours to fupplant me in *Angelica*'s Heart: you know I live but in her.

Sir *Tho.* I know your Love, and the only Thing I like in you: She's a virtuous Lady, and her Fortune's large; 'tis bafe, and moft unfit my Brother's Years, to become your Rival.

Hect. Ah, Sir, if my Mafter lofes her, I dare fwear it will break his Heart. In my Confcience, I believe it is Love keeps him awake, and puts Gaming into his Head.

Sir *Tho.* Well, Son, if you obtain her, I'll forgive your Fault, and pay your Debts once more.

Val. Sir, I don't doubt it; but I'm a little out of Money at prefent.

Hect. Humph!

Val. Money, Sir, is an Ingredient abfolutely neceffary in a Lover: A Hundred Guineas would accomplifh my Defign.

Hect. As I guefs'd.

Sir *Tho.* At your old Trick again—No, no; I have been too often cozen'd with your fair Promifes.

Val. Try me this Time; lend me but Fifty.

Sir *Tho.* No.

Val. Twenty.

Sir *Tho.* No.

Val. Ten.

Sir *Tho.* No.

Hect. Hard-hearted *Jew.* [*Aside.*

Val. Five, Sir; for I can't go without ſome Money.

Sir *Tho.* Not a Souſe from me.

Hect. One, Sir; that we may dine; for I am ſure my Maſter has not a Groat, by his Humility.

Sir *Tho.* No; if you are hungry, go fling a merry Main for your Dinner.

Hect. Ah, Sir, I never was ſo well bred: Beſides, I hate truſting to Chance for my Food.

Sir *Tho.* I admire you have liv'd ſo long with your Maſter then. Look ye, *Valere*, get you to *Angelica*; out with your Uncle, and you ſhan't want Money. In the mean Time, Sirrah, do you get me a Liſt of his Debts.

Hect. Yes, Sir—There's ſome Hopes I may come in for my Wages. [*Aside.*

Val. Sir, I obey you in every Thing——and fly to *Angelica*. Hearkye, Raſcal, get me ſome Money, or I will cut your Ears off. [*Aside to* Hector.] [*Exit.*

Hect. Money! Mercy on me; where ſhall I get it? Well, I think I am bewitch'd to him. [*Exit.*

Sir *Tho.* If I can but reclaim my Child, and match him to *Angelica*, I ſhall date the happieſt Part of my Life from this Moment.

Enter Cogdie.

Cog. Sir, your moſt humble Servant; is not your Name *Valere*?

Sir *Tho.* It is, Sir.

Cog. Sir, I come to offer you my beſt Service.

Sir *Tho.* In what, pray Sir?

Cog. Sir I am Maſter of all Sorts of Games, and live by that noble Art. My Name is *Cogdie*, call'd by ſome Count *Cogdie.*

Sir *Tho.* He takes me for my Son! I'll humour it, and hear what the Rogue has to ſay. [*Aside.*] Well, Sir, what then?

Cog. Hearing of your ill Fortune at Play, I came, out of pure Generoſity, to teach you the Management of the Die.

Sir

Sir *Tho.* The Management of the Die; Why, is that to be taught?

Cog. O! Ay, Sir; to learn to cog a Die nicely, requires as good a *Genius* as the *Study* of the Mathematics. Now, Sir, here is your true Dice, a Man seldom gets any Thing by them: Here is your false, Sir, hey, how they run. Now, Sir, those we generally call Doctors.

Sir *Tho.* the *Consumption* rather. Mercy upon me! What is our World come to! [*Aside.*

Cog. Come, throw a Main, Sir, then I'll instruct you how to nick it; he is very dull. I tell you, Sir, in this Age, 'tis necessary that Children learn to play before they learn to read.

Sir *Tho.* I tell you, Sir, that I am amaz'd the Government never preferr'd you to the Pillory for your wonderous Skill.

Cog. I find his ill Fortune has put him horribly out of Humour: I say again, that learning to play is of more Use, than *Fa*, *La*, *Mi*, *Sol*, or cutting a Caper.

Sir *Tho.* I'll *Fa*, *La*, Caper, you Dog; know I am his Father, and hate Gaming, and all such Rascals as you are. But stay, I'll pay you your Wages for the Care you took of my Son.

Cog. Sir, your humble Servant, Sir, not a Penny, Sir.

Sir *Tho.* No, Sir, a Cane.

Cog. Not in the least, Sir: I, I, I would not give you the Trouble by no Means, Sir. What a Sot was I, to mistake the Father for the Son. [*Exit running.*

Enter Hector *running.*

Hect. O, Sir! Undone! Undone! Undone!

Sir *Tho.* Undone! when wert thou otherwise?

Hect. Ah, Sir, but my Master, my Master—

Sir *Tho.* What of him? Surely he was given me for a Curse.

Hect. Ah, Sir! As my Master was just stepping into *Angelica*'s Lodging, so nicely drest; his Wig, I believe, had a Pound of Hair, and two Pound of Powder in it; he look'd so pretty, that had she but seen him, she must have lov'd him, tho' her Heart had been made of Brass: But just as he was stepping in——

Sir *Tho.* She ordered her Footman to ſhut the Door upon him, I ſuppoſe, hearing of his continued Extravagance.

Hect. No, no, Sir, worſe than that; a ſlovenly filthy Fellow whipt his Sword from his Side, whilſt another, as bluff as a Midnight Conſtable, ſlapt him on the Back with an Action of Forty Pounds.

Sir *Tho.* Ha! And did *Angelica* ſee it?

Hect. No, no, Sir, we being cunning, wheedled 'em to the Tavern; and 'tis but giving 'em a luſty Bottle, Sir, and I warrant we get it off for ten Guineas.

Sir *Tho.* How's this, an Action of Forty Pounds got off for Ten Guineas? I ſuſpect a Trick—Come, ſhew me the Way to this Tavern.

Hect. What ſhall I do now? Sir, I, I, I came in ſuch Haſte that I never thought to look up at the Sign.

Sir *Tho.* Then you are likely to carry the Money, Sirrah; Sirrah, this Sham won't take; the next Time, Raſcal, lay your Lies cloſer, Rogue. [*Slaps him.*] [*Exit.*

Hect. Ah *Hector*, *Hector*! Thou art no good Plotter. Well, I draw this Comfort from it, however, I ſhall never dread the Gallows for Plotting.

Enter Valere.

Val. Well, I have over-heard all; I thought what your Projects would come to.

Hect. Why, Sir, the wiſeſt Men ſometimes fail; and you muſt own, that I ſtudy as hard as a ſtarving Poet for your Intereſt: But if my Plots, like their Poetry, miſcarry, 'tis no Fault of mine.

Val. You'll ſtill be witty out of Seaſon; but pr'ythee what's to be done now?

Hect. Oh, Sir! Yonder goes Mrs. *Security*, who lent you once a Hundred Guineas upon your Diamond Ring that you loſt at Play.

Val. I remember I gave her Fifty for the Uſe of it: But, however, call her in this Extremity, and bring up a Bottle of Sack with you. [*Exit* Hector.] Now for the Art of Perſuaſion to ſqueeze this old Spunge of fifty Guineas, that may make me Maſter of a thouſand before Night.

Enter

Enter Hector *and Mrs.* Security.

Val. Mrs. *Security*, good-morrow.

Mrs. *Sec.* Mr. *Valere*, your very humble Servant.

Val. A Chair there, quickly. Mrs. *Security*, let us renew our old Acquaintance, and cement it with a Glaſs of Sack.

Mrs. *Sec.* Oh, dear Mr. *Valere!* I never drink in a Morning.

Val. What, not a Glaſs of Sack? Come, *Hector*, fill. My Service to you.

Mrs. *Sec.* Pray, young Man, give me but a little.

Val. Fill it up, I ſay.

Mrs. *Sec.* Oh! dear Sir! Your Health. [*Drinks half.*

Val. What, my Health by Halves? I'll not bait you a Drop.

Mrs. *Sec.* Well, I profeſs it will be too ſtrong for me.

Val. *Hector*, does not Mrs. *Security* look very handſome?

Hect. Truly, Sir, I think ſhe grows younger and younger.

Mrs. *Sec.* Away, you make me bluſh.

Hect. Ah! She'll have another Huſband, I ſee by thoſe Roguiſh Eyes.

Mrs. *Sec.* Fie, fie, Mr. *Hector*; theſe Eyes have done nothing but wept ſince my good Huſband *Zekiel Security*, died; and the more, becauſe he died ſuddenly. [*Weeps.*

Hect. Suddenly! Good lack! Good lack! It e'en makes me weep to think on't.

Mrs. *Sec.* He died in his Vocation juſt ſealing a Bond.

Val. Ah! Would thou wert with him, ſo I had a little of thy Money. [*Aſide.*] *Hector*, fill t'other Glaſs to Mrs. *Security* to waſh away Sorrow.

Mrs. *Sec.* O, dear Sir, I thank you for your Civility; and you ſhall find me always ready to ſerve you.

Val. I do believe you Mrs. *Security*, and have Occaſion to try your Kindneſs.

Hect, Ay, my Maſter pitch'd upon you.

Sec.

Sec. He knows he may command me.

Val. I would borrow fifty Guineas, Mrs. *Security*, which shall be repaid—

Sec. I don't doubt it, Sir, in the least; for you know my Way—A Pledge—If it be not quite double the Value, I won't stand with a Friend: and it shall be as safe as my Eyes, that I assure you.

Val. Humph!

Hect. Ah, Duce on't, here's the Sack lost.

Sec. You had your Ring again, Mr. *Valere*: And I hope you don't mistrust me now.

Val. Mistrust you? No, no, Madam. *Hector*, fetch Mrs. *Security* a Pledge.

Hect. A Pledge, Sir? Bless me! What does he mean now? A Pen and Ink, Sir?

Val. Ay, ay, Mrs. *Security* shall have my Note.

Hect. As good as any Pledge in *England*.

Sec. It may be so—But I promised good *Zekiel* to be wary of the Money he left me: Yea, and I will be very wary.

Hect. And very wicked—

Val. Refuse my Note! I scorn your Money.

Hect. I'd have you to know, my Master's Note is as good as a Banker's — sometimes, when the Dice run well. [*Aside.*

Sec. Nay, if you are angry for my fair Dealing, good-morrow to you.

Hect. O, Impudence! She calls *Cent per Cent.* fair Dealing—Go thy Ways, but take my Curse along with thee. May some Town-Sharper persuade that sanctify'd Face into Matrimony, and in one Night empty all thy Bags at Hazard.

Sec. Your Wishes hurt not me, ill-manner'd Fellow. I'd have you to know, if I would marry again, I could have a—

Val. Nay, nay, Mistress, if we must have none of your Money, let's have none of your Impertinence.

Hect. Be gone, be gone, Woman, be gone. [*Pushes her off.*

Val. Oh! Deep Reflection—would I could avoid thee: To become the Scoff of mercenary Wretches—And thro' my my own Misſmanagement, reduc'd to baſe Neceſſity. Oh, *Angelica!* I'll caſt a real Penitent beneath thy Feet.

And if once more thy Pardon I obtain,
Love in my Heart ſhall the ſole Monarch reign.

The End of the FIRST ACT.

ACT II.

Enter Angelica *and* Favourite.

Ang. AFTER all his ſolemn Promiſes to quit that ſcandalous Vice, when he can hold my Love upon no other Terms, does he ſtill purſue that certain Ruin to his Fame and Fortune? But I reſolve to baniſh him my Heart, which he has juſtly loſt by his perfidious Dealing. I feel, I feel my Liberty return; and I charge thee, *Favourite*, ſpeak of him no more.

Fav. No, no, Madam, fear not me; I hate him for your Sake, Madam: Was he like his Uncle; there's the Man for my Money.

Ang. Becauſe you have a large Share of his, I ſuppoſe: Old Men muſt bribe high. Name neither to me, I hate Mankind. [*Exit* Favourite.

Enter Lady Wealthy.

L. *Weal.* Well ſaid, Siſter; I hate Mankind too, and yet the Fellows will follow me; but who is the Man that has put you out of Conceit with the whole Sex? *Valere?*

Ang. The ſame; no other had ever Power to ſhock my Quiet——Nor ſhall he; for this Moment I'll 'raze him from my Thoughts.

L. *Weal.* If ſhe holds her Reſolution, I am happy. [*Aſide.*] That Taſk may prove more difficult than you imagine, Siſter. Come, come, this is a Flight of ſudden Paſſion, that would fall upon the Sight of *Valere.*

Ang.

Ang. You miſtake, Siſter, my Reſentment is grounded upon Reaſon.

L. *Weal.* I know he has given you Cauſe enough: But Love is blind; had a Man uſed me ſo, I ſhould have ſuſpected his Reality ſooner.

Ang. Why, do you think he loves me not?

L. *Weal.* It looks with ſuch a Face—

Ang. Why then did he take Pains to be reconcil'd?

L. *Weal.* Gallantry, mere Gallantry; and ſhe that cannot diſtinguiſh, often miſtakes it for a real Amour. Ah, *Angelica!* You are but a Novice yet, and don't underſtand the Beau-Monde. A Woman ſhould always ſpeak more than ſhe thinks, and think more than ſhe writes, or ſhe'll ne'er be upon the Square with Men.

Ang. I ſhall neither write nor ſpeak to any of 'em for the future, I aſſure you.

L. *Weal.* And do you poſitively think you could reſiſt *Valere*, if he ſhould come in this Minute?

Ang. I do, poſitively.

L. *Weal.* What, in his moſt moving Air? For you know he is Maſter of a falſe inſinuating Tongue: Should he, I ſay, throw himſelf at your Feet in a Tone of Tragedy; cry, Forgive me, *Angelica*, or kill me if you pleaſe; I'll not oppoſe the Blow, nor ſtrive to ſave my Life by one poor Word—I love you, and only you: Does not your Soul tell you ſo in my Behalf? Will you not anſwer me? Then riſing from his Knees, Will then, ſays he, Nothing but my Death wipe out my Fault? Give it me then, cruel Fair; for now to live is Pain. If I have loſt you, I have loſt all that's worth my Care. Then offers to draw his Sword; at Sight of which you are melted into Pity, and once again betray'd. Is not this true, *Angelica?* Ha, ha, ha.

Ang. I confeſs I have too often been deceiv'd—but now he ſhall find I am upon my Guard—and were he the only one remaining of his Sex, I would not—if I know my Heart—marry him.

L. *Weal.* I'm pleas'd to hear your Reſolution; and doubly pleas'd to find you Miſtreſs of your Paſſion—'Tis a Point of Wiſdom to caſhier ſuch Follies as blind our Senſe, and make our Judgment err.

Ang. 'Tis very true.

L. *Weal.* Believe me Sister—I had rather see you married to Age, Avarice, or a Fool—than to *Valere,*—for can there be a greater Misfortune than to marry a Gamester?

Ang. I know 'tis the high Road to Beggary.

L. *Weal.* And your Fortune being all ready Money will be thrown off with Expedition—Were it as mine is indeed—But are you sure your Heart is disengaged?

Ang. Why, do you doubt it?

L. *Weal.* I have a Reason, Sister, that when you have satisfy'd me you shall know.

Ang. Then be satisfy'd — I will never see him more —Now the Secret.

L. *Weal.* Why, then know I love him.

Ang. How! You!

L. *Weal.* Yes, I; where's the Wonder?

Ang. You that advis'd against the Gamester.

L. *Weal.* That was for your Good, Sister———Our Circumstances are different—My Estate's intail'd enough to supply his Riots, and why should I not bestow it upon the Man I like?

Ang. What in that Mourning Weed resolv'd on Matrimony, and is your Lord forgot already—Did I take such Pains in rubbing your Temples, whilst *Favourite* apply'd the Harts-horn to your Nose, when the fainting Fits came thicker and thicker, and was it all but Affectation—And does your dead Husband's Picture, that dangles at your Watch there, serve only to put you in Mind of another?

L. *Weal.* And where's the Crime—I lov'd him living as much as any Wife, or rather more; and did what Decency required when he died—But being free, I'm free to chuse.

Ang. Then who so fit as *Lovewell* for your Choice, whose honourable Love has long pursu'd you.

L. *Weal.* You are not to direct my Inclination.

Ang. Nor you mine—*Favourite,* [*Enter* Favourite.] if *Valere* comes, I will see him—That Good you have done, Sister.

Fav. See him, Madam! } *Exeunt* Ang. *and* Fav.
Ang. Yes, Impertinence, }

L. *Weal.* Ay, ſee him, if thou wilt, but to little Purpoſe—I doubt not his Return, when once he finds Encouragement, 'tis his Awe has kept him ſilent, not that I care much for him neither; but it is the greateſt Mortification in Nature to ſee a handſome Fellow make Love to another before one's Face. [*Enter* Footman.

Footm. Madam, the Marquis of *Hazard* to wait on your Honour.

L. *Weal.* Pugh, that Fool. [*Enter* Marquis.

Marq. Hey, let my three Footmen wait with my Chair there—the Raſcals have come ſuch a high Trot—they've jolted me worſe than a Hackney Coach——— and I'm in as much Diſorder — as if I had not been dreſs'd to Day—Pardon me, Madam, I took the Liberty to adjuſt myſelf, e'er I approach'd you.

L. *Weal.* You are the exact Mode of Dreſs — but Monſieur *Marquiſs*, methinks you are grown perfect in our Tongue.

Marq. The Value I have for the *Engliſh* Ladies, made me take particular Pains in the Study——Duce on't, I ſhall be diſcover'd, if I forget my *French* Tone—*Ah, Madam, Vous parlez Francois mieux que je parle l'Anglois.*

L. *Weal.* Ah, *Point de tout Monſieur.*

Marq. But there's no Language like the *Eyes*, Madam—and *Yours* would *ſet the World on Fire.*

L. *Weal.* O, Gallant.

Marquis ſings to the *Widow.*

IN vain You ſable Weeds put on,
Clouds cannot long eclipſe the Sun;
Nature has plac'd you in a Sphere,
To give us Day-light all the Year;
'Tis well for thoſe
Of Cupid's *Foes,*
That your Beauties thus ſhrouded lie;
For when that Night
Puts on the Light,
What Crouds of martyr'd Slaves will die?

SINGS to the *Gamester*, when he has won Money.

FAIR Celia, *she is nice and coy,*
While she hold the lucky Lure;
Her Repartees are Pish and Fie,
And you in vain pursue her.

Stay but till her Hand is out,
And she become your Debtor,
Address her then, and without Doubt,
You'll speed a great deal better.

It is the only Way
When she has lost at Play,
To purchase the courted Favour,
Forgive her the Score,
And offer her more,
I'll lay my Life you have her.

Marq. I had like to have fought last Night, for asserting your Prerogative of Beauty.

L. *Weal.* With whom pray?

Marq. With *Valere*, whose continual Toast was your Sister; I must confess it has given me a passionate Desire of seeing her, that I may hereafter with greater Assurance maintain your Cause.

L. *Weal.* What would the Fellow have me introduce him—My Cause don't want your Sword.

Marq. She's jealous already; if my Footmen observe my Orders, she'll secure me here for Fear of losing the Prize. [*Aside.*

L. *Weal.* This Fool's doubly my Aversion —— now he has nam'd my Sister. Would I were rid of him.

Marq. Has your Ladyship play'd at Court this Winter?

L. *Weal.* in my Weeds?

Marq. I ask your Pardon, Madam, but that Beauty and Gaiety nothing can eclipse. Who can look on you, and mind your Dress?

L. *Weal.* That's well enough exprest — But nothing that he says can please me now.

Enter

Enter Footman, *and gives a Letter.*

Footm. A Footman in Green, Monsieur, waits for an Answer. [*Exit.* Footman.

Marq. Is this a Time? Let him wait at the Chocolate-House at *St. James*'s an Hour hence —— Oh, Madam, did you know how I languish for you!

L. *Weal.* When did I give you Leave to make a Declaration of your Love——Monsieur——pray, read your Letter, and give the Lady an Answer.

Marq. I confess it comes from a Lady——but if——

Enter another Footman.

Footm. My Lady *Gamewell* has sent three Times for you, and will not begin to play till you come.

Marq. *Allez Vous en Coquin*——Let her stay. [*Exit Footman.*

L. *Weal.* Insolence! what does the Fellow mean?

Marq. 'Tis the greatest Fatigue in Nature to hold a Correspondence with Impertinence —— but your Ladyship is the Reverse of—

Enter another Footman.

Footm. Sir, the Lady *Amorous* begs the Honour of your Company this Minute; Sir *Credulous* is just gone out of Town.

Marq. *Le diable t'emporte*—out of my Sight—Am I not engag'd!

L. *Weal.* Engag'd! Upon my Word you are not—What House is the Place you appoint to receive your Assignations in——

Marq. No, upon my Honour, Madam——but I presume they have searched the whole Town——and seeing, my Equipage at your Door, were so audacious to send in their Message——but I'll turn away my Footmen for this Embarrassment.

L. *Weal.* Pray, let not my House be distinguish'd by you, nor your Equipage for the future——I am not to be us'd so, (*angerly.*) Now for a set and grave Face to put me more out of Humour, if possible——

Enter Lovewell.

Love. You ſeem in Diſorder, Madam——

L. *Weal.* Who can be otherwiſe, when People take Liberty beyond the Bounds of good Manners,——

Love. Who dares in my Lady *Wealthy*'s Houſe?

[*Looking angerly at the Marquis.*

Marq. Upon my Soul, Sir, ſhe takes it quite wrong ——Or ſhe's——confoundedly jealous.

Love. Sir, I am poſitive that Lady cannot be in the wrong; and read it in her Looks, your Abſence wou'd pleaſe her——

Marq. Sir——

Love. No Words here, Sir——if you wou'd diſpute it, I'll meet you when, and where you pleaſe——

Marq. Your moſt humble Servant—[*In a low Voice.* You ſhall hear from me——Hey, hey, who's there?—— My Servants——Madam, as your Ladyſhip ſaid, I'm not to be us'd thus—— [*Exit.*

L. *Weal.* Monſieur——He's gone, I wou'd not loſe the Fop neither——

Love. Gone Madam! ſo you would have him, I ſuppoſe.

L. *Weal.* You ſuppoſe! how dare you ſuppoſe my Thoughts——and who gave you this Privilege in my Houſe? Shortly I ſhall be wiſh'd Joy; for this is a Prerogative above a depending Lover.

Love. I plead no Merit; and my long ſucceſsleſs Love aſſures me I have no Power——but I underſtood——

L. *Weal.* You underſtood! Ay, you always underſtand wrong, Mr. *Lovewell.*

Love. I do confeſs I wander in the Mazes——and ſtill purſue a Brightneſs which I cannot fix——To pleaſe you has been my long and only Study; witneſs the many Years of awful Servitude I paid your Virgin-beauty, and the Pains I felt when I beheld you wedded to another: I could not bear the Sight, but in a cruel Baniſhment paſs'd my unlucky Hours, till Fate in pity ſet you free, but all in vain, for ſtill my Portion is Deſpair.

L. *Weal.* Nay, if you are running into that grave

Stuff

Stuff——I muſt leave you, tho' in my own Houſe—for I have got the Spleen intolerably, and cannot endure it.

Love. No, Madam, I'll retire——I love too much to diſobey—— Only when you reflect on your admiring Slaves, think on my Fidelity. [*Exit*.

L. *Weal*. Thou art a poor conſtant Fool, that's the Truth on't——and thou haſt Merit too, I'll ſay that for thee———but we Women don't always mind that—— Here comes the preſent Aſcendant of my Heart———

Enter Valere.

Val. Ha, the Widow here——now could I make her my Friend? Now for a ſerious Face———and an Heroic Stile———Madam———

L. *Weal*. ———Sir———

Val. My Stars ſhed their kindeſt Influence to Day, and bleſt me with the Opportunity of finding you alone —Pity is eſſential to the Fair, and ought to be extended to thoſe that ſink beneath the Rigour of their Chains.—

L. *Weal*. 'Tis the Diverſion of your Sex to complain; I believe Mr. *Valere* finds few barbarous in ours ———

Val. None more unfortunate in Love than I, and tho' my Heart is breaking, I'm forbid to tell my Pain.

L. *Weal*. I hope 'tis to my Wiſh — It may be me he means, elſe why this Addreſs——She muſt be very cruel, that lets you ſigh without Return —— Is it in my Power to aſſiſt you———

Val. Oh, Madam, All, All's in your Power——You rule my Fate———

L. *Weal*. Then you ſhall be happy——— 'tis ſo ——

Val. On my Knees let me receive the Confirmation of your Promiſe———and ſeal it here———

[*Kneels and kiſſes her Hand.*

Enter Angelica.

Ang. Ha! kneeling to my Siſter, faithleſs Man——

Val. There, Madam, there's the angry Brow, that darts Diſtraction to my Peace: Your Aid to clear that Storm is what I ſu'd for———

L. *Weal*. Inſufferable ill Breeding———

Val. Oh, *Angelica!* I caſt me at your Feet.

Ang. No, back to my Sister's, there I found you.

Val. Only to intercede to you——

L. *Weal.* False, by my Honour, he was making violent Love——I'll teize her however.

Val. Making Love; what does she mean?

Ang. And you receiv'd it, I suppose.

L. *Weal.* You interrupted me, e'er I could give my Answer.——

Val. Why, Madam, my Design you know.

L. *Weal.* Yes, yes, Mr. *Valere*, I know your Design——I have not had so many sighing, dying Lovers, but I can guess the Design——

Val. But mine was——

L. *Weal.* Oh, fie, don't declare it here—You know my Sister has a Passion for you——and I wou'd not tyrannize——

Ang. 'Tis not in your Power——

Val. Oh, the Devil——Madam, I own 'tis an Offence to a Lady of your Beauty and Merit, to make a Declaration of Love

L. *Weal.* Not at all, Sir, ——when one likes the Person——I'll——consider on't——but, hark'ee, do not deceive my Sister too far, it may be dangerous.

Ang. 'Tis not in your Power——or his, to deceive me; I see thro' your shallow Artifices, and despise it.

L. *Weal.* Those that rely upon their own Judgment are soonest caught. Sister——Remember, I have given you fair Warning—— [*Exit.*

Val. I'm in amaze——

Ang. You need not——I know my Sister's Design——but that's not my Quarrel to you——Quarrel did I say? No, I am grown to a perfect State of Indifference——Quarrels may be reconciled——but a Man that basely breaks his Word, and forfeits Faith and Honour, is not worth our Anger, but deserves to be despis'd.

Val. I do confess I am a Wretch below your Scorn; I own my Faults and have no Refuge but your Mercy.

Fav. In the old Strain again—— [*Aside.*

Val. If you abandon me, I'm lost for ever——for you, and only you, are Mistress of my Fate.

Ang:

Ang. Your daily Actions contradict your Words—— and ſhews I have no ſuch Power in your Heart—— Did you not promiſe, nay, ſwear you'd never game again—

Val. I did, and for the perjur'd Crime merit your endleſs Hate, but you, in pity, may forgive me——— Oh, *Angelica*, ſee at your Feet an humble Penitent kneel, who, if not by your Goodneſs rais'd———will grow for ever to his native Soil.

Ang. You wou'd be pardon'd only to offend again.

Val. Never, never———Here on this beauteous Hand I ſwear, whoſe Touch runs thrilling thro' my Heart—— and by thoſe lovely Eyes that dart their Fire into my Soul, never to diſoblige you more.

Fav. That Oath hath done the Buſineſs, I ſee by her Looks. [*Aſide*.

Ang. Riſe *Valere* ——— I differ from my Sex in this, I wou'd not change where once I've given my Heart, if poſſible——therefore reſolve to make this laſt Trial— baniſh your Play for Love, and reſt ſecur'd of mine.

Val. Oh, Tranſport! let me kiſs thoſe ſoft forgiving Lips, the Memory of whoſe Sweetneſs ſhall arm me againſt Temptation.

Fav. So———now my old Man may go hang himſelf. [*Aſide*.

Val. Could you but know the anxious Pains I felt, the jealous racking Cares that prey'd upon my Soul——— when I heard my Uncle was allow'd to tell his Suit—— you'd then have found how dear *Valere* had priz'd you.

Ang. What I did was to revenge your Falſhood—— though Love's my Witneſs, *Dorante*'s my Averſion—and let this Preſent ſhew who 'tis that reigns triumphant in my Heart.

Val. Your Picture! Oh, give it me, that in the Abſence of the dear Original—— I may feaſt my Eyes on that.

Ang. But mark, *Valere*, the Injunction I ſhall lay; whilſt you keep ſafe this Picture, my Heart is yours—— but if thro' Avarice, Careleſsneſs, or Falſhood, you ever part with it, you loſe me from that Moment.

[*Gives him the Picture*.

Val. I agree; and when I do, [*Kiſſing it*.] except to

 yourſelf,

yourſelf, may all the Curſes rank'd with your Diſdain, purſue me———This, when I look on't, will correct my Folly, and ſtrike a ſacred Awe upon my Actions—

Fav. 'Tis worth two hundred Pounds, a good Moveable when Caſh runs low. [*Aſide.*

Ang. Well, I am convinc'd, let a Woman make what Reſolutions ſhe will, when alone———the Sight of her Lover will break 'em.

Fav. Madam, Mr. *Dorante* is coming up.

Ang. I'll not be ſeen, Adieu. [*Exit.*

Val. My charming Love, adieu———Take Care to welcome your Benefactor, Mrs. *Favourite*; he's a Lover ripe with Diſcretion, Ha, ha, ha,

Enter Dorante.

Your Servant, Uncle, Ha, ha, ha————

[*Holds up the Picture to his Noſe.*] *Exit.*

Dor. This young Rake's Preſence bodes me no Good, I fear. Mrs. *Favourite*, your Servant——Is your Lady to be ſpoke with?

Fav. I doubt not, Sir.———I don't know what ſhe is——I'm ſure I'm almoſt wild; our Buſineſs is all ſpoil'd——*Valere* is reconcil'd again.

Dor. Ah, that inſinuating young Dog.

Fav. She has juſt now given him her Picture ſet round with Diamonds.

Dor. I thought, indeed, ſomething ſparkled in my Eyes———But what's to be done?

Fav. I know not———He has promis'd her to play no more; if he keeps his Word we have no Hopes; but if he breaks it, as I doubt not but he will, Pride and Revenge may work her to our Ends———You may be certain, Sir, I'll let ſlip no Opportunity to ſerve you.

Dor. I do believe it————and to encourage you to believe me grateful——accept of this Ring.

Fav. Oh, dear Sir, you are too generous——I don't merit it———Pray excuſe me————

Dor. Nay, I will not be deny'd.

Fav. Well, Sir, ſince you will have it ſo——I'll not fail to move your Suit———I'll do my beſt Endeavours, I'll aſſure you; Write, Sir, write, and I'll deliver the Letter———then let me alone to back it.

Dor.

Dor. You must urge the Largeneſs of my Fortune—the Steadineſs of my Temper; and withal tell her, I am not above Two and Forty——I was grey at Thirty.

Fav. I warrant you, Sir———Be ſure you exclaim againſt your Nephew's Gaming.

Dor. Ay, ay, I'll go write it this Moment———and ſend it preſently.

Fav. I'll be in the Way to receive it. [*Exeunt ſeverally.*

SCENE *changes to Sir* Thomas Valere'*s Houſe.*

Enter Sir Thomas *and* Hector, *with Papers.*

Hect. Sir, I have brought you a compleat Account of the Debts of my Maſter—I think I have not forgot one Farthing; for, if I miſtake not, you deſired to know 'em all, Sir———

Sir *Tho.* Ay, ay, come read 'em over.

Hect. That I will, Sir, in two Words——A true Liſt of the Debts of Mr. *James Valere*, which was by him contracted within the City of *London*, and Liberty of *Weſtminſter*, which his Father, Sir *Thomas Valere*, has promiſed to diſcharge.

Sir *Tho.* If I diſcharge them, or not, is not your Buſineſs———Go on——

Hect. 'Tis my Deſign, Sir. In the firſt Place then—*Item*, Due to *Richard Scrape*, Fifty-five Pounds, Nine Shillings and Ten-pence Half-penny——for Five Years Wages——and Money diſburs'd for Neceſſaries.

Sir *Tho.* *Richard Scrape*, who's he?

Hect. Your moſt humble Servant, Sir. [*Bows.*

Sir *Tho.* You, why is not your Name *Hector*?

Hect. Ay, Sir, that is my Name *de Novo*————My Maſter thought *Richard* ſounded too clumſy for a Gentleman's Valet, and a Gameſter——So Sir, he gave me the Name of *Hector* from the Knave of *Diamonds*.

Sir *Tho.* A very pretty Name——I admire he don't call his Miſtreſs *Pallas* from the Queen of *Spades*——But how came you ſo rich, Sirrah, to be able to lend your Maſter Money?

Hect. Why when the Dice has run well, my Maſter would now and then tip me a Guinea, Sir.

Sir *Tho.* And so you supply'd him, when he wanted, with his own Money: Oh, Extravagance!

Hect. 'Tis what many an honest Gentleman is drove to sometimes, Sir.

Sir *Tho.* More Shame for 'em—Go on———

Hect. *Secondly,* Sir, here is due to *Jeremy Aaron,* Usurer by Profession, and Jew by Religion.

Sir *Tho.* Never trouble yourself about that, I shall pay no Usurer's Debts, I assure you.

Hect. Then, Sir, here's two hundred Guineas lost to my Lord *Lovegame,* upon Honour.

Sir *Tho.* That's another Debt I shall not pay.

Hect. How, not pay it, Sir,—Why, Sir, among Gentlemen, that Debt is look'd upon the most just of any: You may cheat Widows, Orphans, Tradesmen, without a Blush——but a Debt of Honour, Sir, must be paid—I could name you some Noblemen that pay no Body——yet a Debt of Honour, Sir, is as sure as their ready Money.

Sir *Tho.* He that makes no Conscience of wronging the Man———Whose Goods have been delivered for his Use, can have no Pretence to Honour———whatever Title he may wear———But to the next.

Hect. Here is the Taylor's Bill———the Milliner's, Hosier's, Shoemaker's, Tavern, and Eating-house, in all 300*l.*

Sir *Tho.* A fine Sum, truly.

Hect. Ah, Sir, I have not nam'd the Barber, Perriwig-maker and Perfumer, which is a 100*l.* more——— Besides, he is in Arrears to Mademoiselle *Margaret de la Plant,* lately arriv'd from *France,* with whom he covenanted for four Guineas a Week.

Sir *Tho.* For four Guineas a Week, for what?

Hect. Oh, Sir, pardon me there, I never betray the Secrets of my Master.

Sir *Tho.* Four Guineas a Week!

Hect. Ay, Sir, and very cheap, considering he made his Bargain in the Winter—and truly I don't know but the Woman lost by it.

Sir *Tho.* You don't————Take that, Sirrah——— You shan't lose by it, however—Go, Rascal, pay your Whores and Debts of Honour out of that.

Hect.

Hect. Ay, Sir, they'll never take this Money of me; if you pleaſe, Sir, I'll ſend 'em to your Levee, and you may pay 'em yourſelf.

Sir *Tho.* Sirrah, I ſhall break your Head——Go get you to the Rake your Maſter; play, hang, or ſtarve together, I care not——Debts, with a Pox; *Gaming, Drinking, Wenching,* rare Debts to bring into a Court of *Chancery*——You, O Lud, O Lud, O Lud—— Bring me ſuch a Bill of Debts, Rogue: Mercy on me, that there can be ſuch Impudence in the World——O, I have much ado to forbear thee——Me ſuch a Bill of Debts—— [*Exit.*

Hect. So, our Affairs go backwards, I find. Honeſt *Richard,* Patience, I ſay; go ſeek thy Maſter out.

Fortune may change, and give a lucky Main:
And what undid us, ſet us up again.

ACT III.

Hector, *ſolus.*

Hect. WHere can my Maſter be now——I ſhould ſuſpect he were at Play——but that I know he has no Money——Sure this old Dad of his will open his Purſe-Strings once more, if he's reconcil'd to *Angelica:* I long to know what Succeſs he meets with.—— O, here he comes——

[*Enter* Valere *with his Hat under his Arm, full of Money, he counting it*——

I waited on your Father, according to Order, Sir, with a Liſt of your Debts——and the generous old Gentleman—I thank him, gave me more than I expected— Hey-day, he minds me not——Ah, I doubt we are all untwiſted——No Hopes of *Angelica*——

Val. Five hundred fifty-ſeven Guineas and a half.

Hect. Ha! What do I ſee! The Plate Fleet's arriv'd——By what Miracle fell theſe Galleons into our Power—I hope, Sir, ſince Fortune has been ſo kind—

Val.

Val. A Curse of ill Luck — [*Stamps*] Had I but held in the last Hand, I should have had 300 Guineas more of my Lord Duke's—besides what I betted.

[*Walks about.*

Hect. I am overjoy'd, Sir, at your good Fortune— But as I was saying, Sir——

Val. But hold, my Lord *Lovegame* owes me 200 upon Honour: Tis pretty well —— I have not made an ill Morning's Work on't.

Hect. There's no speaking to him——

Val. Ah! there's no Music like the Chink of Gold— By *Jove* this Sound is sweeter in my Ear—than all the *Margaretta's* in *Europe*———Ha! *Hector*, where come you from, Sirrah?

Hect. Came, Sir—Why I was here before you — But Fortune's golden Mist conceal'd me from your Sight— Sir, I congratulate your good Success—But how!

Val. Ay, 'tis Success, indeed, if thou knew'st all— Honest *Jack Sharper* lent me *Five* Guineas, to pay him *Ten* if Luck run on my Side. I have discharg'd my Promise and brought off a *Thousand* clear.

Hect. Huzza—Why, you're a made Man!

Val. And we meet again at Five, where I design to win a Thousand more, Boy.

Hect. Ay, but if you should lose all back, Sir.

Val. Impossible. This is a lucky Day—*Angelica* and I are reconcil'd———my Faults forgiven, and all my Wishes crown'd; *Hector*. [*Shewing the Picture.*

Hect. Bless my Eye-sight—A Picture set with Diamonds — Nay then, *Hector*, chear up — for now the bad Times will mend. [*Sings.*] Why now a Fig for your Father's Kindness; you are able to pay your Debts yourself, Sir———

Val. A Pox on thee for naming 'em ——Thou hast given me the Spleen — Pay my Debts, quotha — The bare Word is enough to turn all my Luck.

Hect. Say you so, Sir! Is paying Debts unlucky then?

Val. Ay, certainly; the most unlucky Thing in the World.

Hect. Humph — I now find the Reason why Quality hate to pay their Debts——A duce on't, I wish I had

knowa

known as much this Morning, I would not have paid the Cobler for heel-piecing my Shoes———For aught I know it may be a Guinea out of my Way; for my Master does not use to be so slow————Sir, now you are in Stock, Sir, if you please to put my Wages into my Hands————it shall be very safe in Bank against you want it.

Val. The Devil's in the Fellow—Speak one Word more of paying Debts, Sirrah——and I'll cut your Ears off——I shall have no Occasion to borrow—and my Father will pay your Debt among the rest—

Hect. He won't pay a Souse, Sir——He broke my Head at the very Sight of the List———

Val. Ay, that was in his Passion—There's a Plaister for that Wound— [*Gives him a Guinea.*

Hect. Sir, your most humble Servant——I find we middling People are out of the Quality's Latitude—— Paying Debts are only unlucky to Gentlemen——Sir, pray, Sir, give me Leave to offer one Thing to your serious Consideration.

Val. I bar Debts.———

Hect. Not a Word of that, Sir.

Val. Out with it then.

Hect. That you'd lay by 500 *l.* of that Money against a Rainy Day.

Val. But suppose I should have more set me than I can answer.

Hect. 'Tis but sending for it at worst, Sir.

Val. So baulk my Hand in the mean Time—and lose the winning of a Thousand——No, no; there's nothing like ready Money to nick Fortune.

Hect. Ah, Sir, but you know she has often jilted you; and would it not be better to have a little Pocket-money secure—Put by 200 Sir.

Val. Well I'll consider on't————Ha! see who knocks.

Hect. A Dun, I warrant.

Val. I have not a Farthing of Money, remember that, Sirrah— [*Puts up his Money hastily.*

Hect. Lying is a thriving Vocation.

Enter

Enter Galloon, *a Taylor, and Mrs.* Topknot, *a Milliner.*

Val. Ha! Good-morrow to you——Good-morrow to you Mrs. *Topknot:* Mrs. *Topknot,* you are a great Stranger; why don't you call and ſee me ſometimes?

Mrs. *Topk.* Indeed, Sir, I call very often—tho' I have not had the good Fortune to ſee you—for you was ſtill aſleep, or gone abroad.

Val. I am ſorry it fell out ſo. Well, have you brought your Bill?

Mrs. *Topk.* Yes, Sir. [*Gives him her Bill.*] I hope you lik'd your laſt Linen, Sir.

Val. Very well.

Gal. Sir, I beg the Favour of you—

Hect. I muſt not let two faſten upon him at once—Mr. *Galloon,* a Word with you—You always make my Cloaths, too little for me.

Gal. I am ſorry for that.

Hect. My Breeches are Seam-rent in three or four Places.

Gal. I'll take Care——

Hect. You ſew moſt abominably ſlight.

Mrs. *Topk.* We are about marrying our Daughter.

Val. I hope you have provided a good Match; for ſhe is very handſome, Faith.

Mrs. *Topk.* The Girl is not deſpiſeable—The Man is very well to paſs in the World; but the ſmall Fortune we deſign for her, muſt be paid down upon the Nail—Therefore, Sir, I entreat you to help me to my Money, if poſſible.

Val. If it was poſſible, I would, Mrs. *Topknot;* and am heartily ſorry that it is not in my Power.

Mrs. *Topk.* It is a Debt of a long ſtanding, Mr. *Valere;* and I muſt not be ſaid nay.

Val. I know it is; but upon Honour I can't pay you now.

Mrs. *Topk.* Let me have ſome, if you can't pay me all——Ten Guineas at preſent would do me ſingular Service.

Val. May I ſink if I have ſeen Five theſe Six Months.

Hect. That he has not, to my Knowledge.

Gal.

Gal. Pray, Sir, consider me, if it be never so small; my Wife is ready to lie in, and Coals are very dear, and Journeymen's Wages must be paid.

Hect. Why, the Devil's in the Fellow! Would you have a Man pay what he has not?—What Business had you to get Children, without you had Cabbage enough to maintain 'em?

Val. *Hector*—No Invention? [*Aside to* Hector.

Gal. When will you be pleas'd that I shall call again, Sir.

Val. When you please.

Gal. I'll call To-morrow, Sir.

Val. With all my Heart.

Gal. Do you think, Sir, you can let me have some, if I come?

Val. Not that I know of.

Hect. No, nor I neither—Hark ye, when he has Money, I'll bring you Word.

Mrs. *Topk.* Don't tell me; I won't go out of the House without Money.

Val. With all my Heart—*Hector!* No Stratagem to save me from these Leaches? [*Aside to* Hector

Hect. Then you must e'en lie with my Master or me; for here are no spare Beds— Let me advise you to make no Noise; you'll have your Money sooner than you think for—Your Ear— [*Whispers.*

Mrs. *Topk.* To be married say you?

Gal And to Madam *Angelica*, the great Fortune?

Hect. The same.

Mrs. *Topk.* I wish you Joy, Sir——Pray recommend me to your Lady, for Gloves, Fans, and Ribbons.

Gal. I hope, Sir, I shall have the Honour to make your Wedding Suit.

Val. That you shall, I promise you—The Rogue has hit on't [*Aside.*

Mrs. *Topk.* But will this Match be speedy, Sir?

Val. I hope so.

Gal. To-morrow, Sir?.

Hect. Or next Day—but we must intreat your Absence at present——for my Master expects his Father with the Lady's Trustees, in order to settle the Affair——and if you are seen it may spoil the Business.

Mrs,

Mrs. *Topk.* Well, well, well, I go, I go—— [*Runs a little Way and turns.*] You'll put your Master in mind of me?

Hect. Ay, ay.

Gal. And me too pray.

Hect. I'll do your Business, I'll warrant you: Go, go, go, —— begone, begone, begone, —— [*Pushes 'em out.*] ——There Sir, I have brought you off once more: Here's two or three Days Respite however.

Val. Why then there's two or three Days of Peace — for these are the most disagreeable Companions a Gentleman can meet with———I dine at the *Rummer*, where you'll find me if you want me. I promis'd to visit *Angelica* again to Night, but fear I shall break my Word.

Hect. And will you prefer Play before that charming Lady?

Val. Not before her——but I have given my Parole to some Men of Quality, and I can't in Honour disappoint 'em.

Hect. Ah, What a Juggler's Box is this Word Honour! It is a Kind of Knight of the Post — That will swear on either Side for Interest I find — But, Sir, had you not better make sure Work on't; marry the Lady whilst she's in the Mind, lest Fortune wheel about and throw you back again.

Val. Marry her, say'st thou — I am not resolved if I shall marry or not.

Hect. High-day! Why I thought it had been what you desired above all Things—But I find your Pocket and your Heart runs counter.

Val. No, Sirrah; I love the charming Maid as much as ever: Love her from my Soul——But then I love Liberty.

Hect. And what should hinder you from enjoying it?

Val. Ah, *Hector*, if I marry her, I must forsake my dear Diversion, [*Pulling out a Box and Dice.*] which to me is the very Soul of Living: —— 'tis the genteelest Way of passing one's Time, every Day produces something new ——Who is happier than a Gamester; who more respected, I mean those that make any Figure in the

the World? Who more careſs'd by Lords and Dukes? Or whoſe Converſation more agreeable —— Whoſe Coach finer in the Ring —— Or Finger in the Side Box produces more Luſtre—Who has more Attendance from the Drawers—or better Wine from the Maſter,——or nicer ſerv'd by the Cook? —— In ſhort, there is an Air of Magnificence in't, — a Gameſter's Hand is the Philoſopher's Stone, that turns all it touches into Gold.

Hect. And Gold into Nothing.

Val. A Gentleman that plays is admitted every where ——Women of the ſtricteſt Virtue will converſe with him,——for Gaming is as much in Faſhion here as 'tis in *France*, and our Ladies look upon't as the Height of ill Breeding, not to have a Paſſion for Play: Oh! The charming Company of half a Dozen Ladies, with each a Diſh of Tea, —— to behold their languiſhing Ogles with their Eyes, their raviſhing white Hands, to hear their delicious Scandal which they vent between each Sip, juſt piping hot from Invention's Mint, wherein they ſpare none, from the Stateſman to the Cit—and damn Plays before they are acted, eſpecially if the Author be unknown—This ended, the Cards are call'd for.

Hect. And open War proclaim'd —— and every Cock-boat proves a Privateer.

Val. Our Engagements are not ſo terrible,——with us Revenge reaches no further than the Pocket.

Hect. No more don't a Highwayman —— and yet the World thinks both Lives equally immoral.

Val. None of your Similes, Sirrah, do you hear?—— Where is the Immorality of Gaming——Now I think there can be nothing more moral——It unites Men of all Ranks, the Lord and the Peaſant — the haughty Dutcheſs and the City Dame, —— the Marquis and the Footman, all without Diſtinction play together.

And ſure that Life can ne'er offenſive prove,
That teacheth Men ſuch peaceful Ways of Love.

Hect. The Marquis of *Hazard*, Sir.—

Val. The Marquis of *Hazard*, what wants he!

Enter

Enter the Marquis of Hazard.

Marq. Do you hear; do you wait with my Chair at the Corner of the Street, for I would be *incognito.*

Hect. What does he pretend to?

Marq. I presume, Sir, your Name is *Valere.*

Val. I don't remember I ever had any other, Sir.

Marq. Sir I should take it as an extraordinary Favour, if you'll be pleas'd to command the Absence of your *Valet de Chambre.*

Val. Be gone. [*Exit* Hector.

Marq. Now, Sir, do you know who I am?

Val. I think, Sir, I never had the Honour of your Acquaintance.

Marq. *Allons Courage*, push him home, he seems daunted already; [*Aside.*] Sir, I have made the Tour of *Europe*, and have had the Respect paid to me in all Courts that became my Quality; ——— In *Spain* I kept Company with none but Arch-Dukes, in *France* with Princes of the Blood, ——— and since I have been here, I have had the Honour to sup or dine with most of the great People at Court,

Val. Why so hot, Sir?

Marq. And, Sir, my Person is not more known than my Valour ——— I have fought a Hundred Duels, and never fail'd to kill or wound, ——— without receiving the least Hurt myself.

Val. You had very good Luck, truly, Sir,——What does the Blockhead aim at? [*Aside.*

Marq. Sir, Fortune owes my Life Protection, for Sake of the noble Race from which I sprung———my Father's Grandfather's great Grandfather was Viceroy of *Naples.*

Val. Oh! One may see that in your Air, Sir.

Marq. Now, Sir, there is a certain Lady that has a Passion for my Person, not that I am in Love with her: Only Gratitude,———and I am inform'd by her Woman, that you make your Addresses there; now, Sir, I suffer no Man beneath my Quality, to mix his Pretensions with mine.

Val. The Lady's Name, Sir?

Marq. The Lady *Wealthy.*

Val.

Val. You are misinform'd upon my Word, Sir; that Lady is at your Service for me.

Marq. That Declaration comes not from your Heart ——your Encomiums on *Angelica* last Night, serv'd only to conceal your Love from me.

Val. So far from that, I did not know you till you had left the Room.

Marq. Sir, I say you must not pretend to vie with Quality.

Val. I know the Distance Fortune has put between us, Sir.

Marq. Then pray observe it, Sir;——don't think every Fellow we condescend to play with, fit Companions for us Men of Quality.

Val. [*Cocking his Hat.*] Fellow, Sir——

[*Laying his Hand on his Sword.*

Marq. Yes, Fellow, Sir.——He has a Heart, I find, I'll moderate my Passion. [*Aside.*

Val. You will have it then, I see. [*Draws.*

Marq. No, upon my Word, Sir, I was in Jest all the while.

Val. But I am in earnest, Sir,—and therefore draw ——What, does the Courage of your royal Ancestors, Vice-Roys of *Naples*, fail you?

Marq. Sir, I made a Vow never to kill another Man, ——and therefore pray put up, you have given me as much Satisfaction as I desired,——I thirst for no Revenge.

Val. Sir, I am not to be trifled with, the Wine is drawn, and you shall drink. [*Slaps him.*

Enter Hector.

Hect. Hey! what's the Matter?

[*Lays hold of the Marquis, who draws.*

Marq. Ha! Company! Nay, then—Sir, this is too much to bear.

Hect. Hold, hold, Sir, hold, what do you do?

Val. Ay, ay, pr'ythee let him go, he's not so dangerous as thou imagin'st, *Hector*,——Ha, ha, ha.

Hect. Why then let him go,——there, Sir, I have done.

Marq. I shall find a Time, Sir.

Val.

Val. To be kick'd——you have been used too civilly here.

Hect. A Time! For what, what the Devil do you come into our Nation, to crow over us—I believe we shall find a Time in this Campaign to teach you better Manners—your capering Country is fitter for Dancing-Masters than Soldiers——Ha, ha, ha.

Marq. It suits not with my Quality to answer the Impertinence of a Valet——Monsieur, adieu——*prenez garde une autre fois.* [*Exit.*

Val. Coxcomb below Resentment——[*Looking on his Watch.*] I have out-staid my Time.

Now Fortune be my Friend, I'll ask no more,
One lucky Hour may double all my Store.

Hect. *Or make you Bankrupt as you was before.* [Exit.

SCENE *Changes. A Table, with Pen, Ink and Paper on it.*

Enter Lady Wealthy, *sola.*

L. *Weal.* Which Way shall I contrive to disappoint my Sister's Wishes? Now would I give Half my Estate to feed my Vanity. Oh, that I could once bring *Valere* within my Power, I'd use him as his ill Breeding deserves; I'd teach him to be particular. He has promis'd *Angelica* to play no more: I fancy that proceeds from his Want of Money, rather than Inclination.—If I could be sure of that—I'll try however. If my Project takes, I shall again break their Union——and if I can't serve my Pride, I shall at least disturb their Peace; and either brings me Pleasure. [*Sits down and writes.*] Now how shall I convey this to his Hands——It is not proper to send any of my own Servants——Who's there?

Enter Mrs. Betty.

Betty. Did your Ladyship call, Madam?

L. *Weal.* Ay, get me a Porter.

Betty. A Porter! Madam: *Robin, John,* and *Nicholas* are all within.

L. *Weal.* And what then? Do as I bid you.

Betty. What can she want with a Porter!—I am resolv'd to watch. [*Exit.*

L. *Weal.*

L. *Weal.* 'Tis better being confin'd to a Desart, where one never sees the Face of Man——than not to be admir'd by all. [*Enter Porter.*] Here, carry this to Mr. *Valere:* Do you know him?

Port. Yes, an't please your Honour, very well.

L. *Weal.* Go, bring me an Answer then. [*Exit* Porter.

Enter Lovewell.

Ha! *Lovewell:* I must avoid his Presence, lest he discover this Intrigue———He'll be alarm'd at the Sight of a Porter in my Lodgings————Besides, my Soul resents the ill Treatment I have given him————He indeed merits better Usage———But I know not how, I cannot resolve on Matrimony. [*Exit.*

Love. Gone! Am I then shun'd like pestilential Air——yet doom'd to doat upon her cold Indifference————Oh! Give me Patience, or I burst with Rage——There must be more than her bare Temper in't—She loves——Ay, there's the Cause——Oh! the racking Thought: By all the Powers, it fires each vital Part and with a double Warmth strikes every active Sense.

Hear me, ye Pow'rs——And if you ne'er design
To make this dear, this scornful Beauty mine,
Grant in the Lieu—I may my Rival meet,
And throw him gasping at his Lady's Feet. [Exit.

Enter Angelica *and* Favourite, *with a Letter in her Hand.*

Ang. I shall not open it, indeed———If you venture to receive Letters again, without my Leave, I shall discharge you from your Attendance, Mrs. *Favourite.*

Fav. I do it for your Good, Madam.

Ang. For my Good! Impertinence—Am I to be govern'd by those I may command?

Fav. In spite of all that I can do, I shall lose my Salary: For when he finds the Cause go backwards, he'll fee no more. [*Aside.*

Enter Dorante.

Ang. So, he's here too, by your Appointment, I suppose.

Dor.

Dor. May I venture to approach the Rays of that Divinity, which dart into my Soul an impetuous Flame?

Ang. O dear Sir, there's a Fire in the next Room, whose Flames will warm you better than my Beauty, I believe.

Fav. Well, really, Madam, I think *Valere* could not have express'd himself finer.

Ang. Cease your odious Comparisons -- Mr. *Dorante* might I advise you, make your Addresses to my Woman —I'm sure you'll meet a kind Reception; ha, ha, ha.

Dor. Your Woman, Madam! I thought a Person of your Rank knew how to treat a Gentleman better.

Ang. And I thought a Person of your Years might have understood better, than to make Love to one of mine.

Dor. My Years, Madam! I'm not so old——Can I help my being in Love with you?

Ang. No more can *Favourite* being in Love with you.

Fav. You are always witty upon me, Madam—I'd have her to know I love a young Fellow as well as herself. [*Aside*.

Dor. 'Tis for my extravagant Nephew that I am despis'd; that complicated Piece of Vice, whose headstrong Courses, and luxurious Life, will ruin both your Peace and Fortune. I saw him a little while ago enter one of those Schools of Poverty, a Gaming-House in St. *Martin's Lane*.

Ang. 'Tis false,

Fav. Nay, Madam, I dare say 'tis true—Yonder goes his Man; I'll call him and convince you.

[*Exit, and Re-enters with* Hector.

Ang. He cannot be so ungrateful, after my last Favours.———*Hector*, where's your Master?

Hect. Where'er his Person is—his Heart is with your Ladyship, Madam; I dare answer for him.

Ang. That's foreign to my Question; where is he?

Dor. Yes, yes, he's a fit Person to enquire of, truly.

Hect. So I am, Sir: For nobody knows my Master's Out-goings and his In-comings better than myself.

Ang. Come, you shall tell me——*Dorante* says, he saw him go into a Gaming-House.

Hect. Discover'd—Nay then I must bring him off——Why, that is true, Madam.

Ang. Perfidious!

Hect. But, Madam, it is to take his Leave, upon my Word——He's gone to play, with a Design to play no more.

Fav. Now, Madam, who was in the right?

Ang. Is it possible a Man can be so base!

Dor. There are Men, Madam, that ne'er were guilty of such Crimes.

Hect. But, Madam, you won't hear me——my Master is making all the Speed he can to put himself in a Condition to keep his Word with you: He is shaking his Elbows, rattling the Box, and breaking his Knuckles for Haste——He has sent me Post for his last auxiliary Guineas, which, when he has thrown off, he'll lay himself at your Feet, with full Resolution never to touch Box or Dice more.

Ang. A likely Matter, truly.

Hect. So it is, Madam——For he'll put it out of his Power to offend again.

Dor. Till he has a new Recruit.

Hect. Madam, your Ladyship's most humble Servant, I must fly; for my Master will think every Hour Seven till I am there. [*Exit*.

Dor. Now, Madam, are you convinc'd——Will you yet accept a Heart devoted only to your Charms?

Ang. No more of your Fustian — 'tis unseasonable; don't provoke me to use you worse than good Manners will allow: I respect your Age, but hate your——

Dor. Well, scornful Maid, take up with your Gamester, do: You'll be the first that repents it. And so farewel. [*Exit*.

Ang. O, my too constant Heart! canst thou still hold the Image of this faithless Man——And yet methinks I'd fain reclaim him——I'll try the last Extremity.

For when from Ill a Proselyte we gain,
The goodness of the Act rewards the Pain:
But if my honest Arts successless prove,
To make the Vices of his Soul remove,
I'll die—or rid me from this Tyrant Love.

ACT IV.

Enter Valere *with a Box and Dice in his Hand, as from Play to a Porter*——Betty *listening.*

Betty. SO; thus far I have followed this Porter: Here I'll observe who he wants——I'm sure 'tis against the Interest of Mr. *Lovewell.*

Val. From a Lady, say'st thou? and must be deliver'd into my own Hand——

Betty. As I imagin'd.

Val. Pr'ythee, Fellow, dost know what 'tis to interrupt a Gamester, when his Fortune's at Stake——Seven or Eleven have more Charms now than the brightest Lady in the Kingdom—[*Opens the Letter.*] Reads——Humph—*Pursuant to what I told you before* Angelica, *that a Declaration of Love would not be disagreeable, I confirm my Words in a golden Shower*——*'Tis what I believe most acceptable to a Man of your Circumstances.* (Well guess'd, 'e Faith.) A Bill for One Hundred Pounds, payable at Sight—Monsieur le Porter, your very humble Servant——Tell the Lady, I am hers most obediently——It requires no other Answer, till I fly myself to return my Thanks.

Port. Yes, Sir. [*Exit* Porter.

Val. What must I do now? prove a Rogue, and betray my Friend *Lovewell*——If I accept this Present, I must make my Returns in Love; for when a Widow parts with Money, 'tis easy to read the valuable Consideration she expects:——But then *Angelica*, the dear, the faithful Maid——But then a Hundred Guineas, the dear tempting Sight! Ha, *Lovewell!* thou com'st in good Time; for my Virtue's staggering.

Enter Lovewell.

Lov. I have been seeking you all the Town over.

Val. And what News? Thou hast a very love-sick Countenance: The Widow has us'd thee scurvily, I know.

Lov. Beyond all bearing——*Valere*, thou ever wert

my

my Friend; pr'ythee instruct me——Help to find the cursed Rival out——'Tis not the Fool Marquis, I'm convinc'd; but some lurking Villain, some Wretch unworthy of her Charms——else her Vanity would ne'er conceal him.

Val. Hold, hold, Friend: you run on a little too fast——What would your Mightiness do now, supposing you discover'd this detested Rival?

Lov. I'd force him to renounce her; or lose my Life, and leave her free.

Val. Why then I have such a Respect for this Gentleman, that I must preserve him from your Lion-like Fury.

Lov. Ha! Do'st thou know him then—Oh! I charge thee by our past Years of Friendship, and by my Peace of Mind, which this cruel Woman takes eternally away, tell me but who he is, describe him to me: Is he a Gentleman?

Val. Yes, Faith.

Lov. And handsome?

Val. The Ladies think so.

Lov. Tell but his Name, that my Revenge may reach him. Hast thou a Friend more dear than I—No, no; thy Companions are no Friends; Gamesters and Profligates——whom in thy reflecting Hours I know thou hatest—She is not fit for one of these.

Val. The Spark is a little given to Gaming, I confess— yet holds his Nose as high as your Widow, I can tell you that.

Lov. Pr'ythee trifle no longer with me — nor do not jest with Pains like mine.

Val. Do you know her Hand?

Lov. Death! does she write to him?

Val. These Credentials will confirm she does.

[*Gives him her Letter with the Bill.*

Lov. Confusion to thee—And a Bill for Money——Away, it cannot be——By Hell, the Company thou keep'st has taught thee to be a Villain: Thou hast abus'd her Honour, which I will justify. Draw.

Val. Here's a Rogue now—When I have withstood a Temptation would have shook a Hermit—he'd cut my Throat for not taking his Mistress from him—Well,

 these

these romantic Lovers are whimſical Things——Harkye, *Charles*, I believe you know I am no Coward, and if your fighting Fit remains on you till To-morrow Morning—I'll meet you when and where you pleaſe; but I'm engag'd now—as you may ſee. Farewel——

[*Exit, ſhewing him the Box*, &c.

Lov. What Man but would forever ſcorn, deſpiſe this falſe Ingrate—But I'm a Slave to Love, and bound with ſuch a Chain, no Injuries can break—Something muſt be done; but what I know not. [*Exit.*

Mrs. Betty *comes forwards.*

Betty. So, my Lady has brought herſelf into a fine Præmunire. Well, I'm glad I heard this; and hope to make it turn to Mr. *Lovewell's* Advantage—who is a generous Man, and deſerves a Counteſs. [*Exit.*

SCENE *changes to Lady* Wealthy's *Lodgings.*

Lady Wealthy, *ſola.*

L. *Weal.* So, thus far I'm ſucceſsful: The Porter ſays he was tranſported with the Letter, and will inſtantly be here——Who's there? [*Enter Footman.*] Bid my Woman come hither.

Footm. She's not within, Madam.

L. *Weal.* How, not within!

Footm. Here ſhe comes.

Enter Betty.

L. *Weal.* Hey! where have you been to put yourſelf in this Heat?

Betty. Speaking to a Relation, Madam.

L. *Weal.* A Relation; ſure 'twas a warm Conference has left ſuch Signs on't in your Cheeks—Set my Toilet ——I'll throw theſe mournful Blacks away—adorn'd in chearful White, receive and charm my Hero.

Betty. Mr. *Lovewell*, Madam.

L. *Weal.* No, Fool; When did you ever ſee me dreſs at an old Lover? He's mine; ſecurely mine: But *Valere*, the Gay, the Rover, the unconquer'd Rambler; he, he alone deſerves my Care.

Betty. Madam, might I presume to speak——

L. *Weal*. Your Nonsense freely; I am in a good Humour, and can bear it all.

Betty. Then *Valere* is the most ungrateful—and Mr. *Lovewell* the most accomplish'd of any Man breathing.

L. *Weal*. Ha, ha, ha: And is this your Speech—— *Lovewell* is beholden to you truly; and Mr. *Valere* shall know his Friend.

Betty. I hate him, Madam: and you have Reason.

L. *Weal*. Peace. I find I gave you too much Liberty.

Enter a Footman.

Footm. Madam, a Letter for your Ladyship.

L. *Weal*. Humph! from *Lovewell*: I know the Hand; some Compliment, some dismal Madrigal, or tedious Ditty, in worse Prose, I am sure. [*Opens it.*] Ha, my own Bill! What means this—*Madam—You have bestow'd your Favours unworthily: Notwithstanding this Proof, I would have fought, defended you beyond Demonstration; but your new Choice declin'd the Sword————and that Love I so long languish'd for.*

Your neglected, injur'd, but still faithful
Lovewell.

Base Traytor! Is this a Man of Honour? this the Return to my Advances—It is impossible—He has way-laid the Porter, brib'd him, and deceiv'd me.

Betty. Indeed he has not, Madam.

L. *Weal*. Why, know you ought of this?

Betty. Yes, I can tell you all—if you will promise to interpret for the Good of him who loves you truly.

L. *Weal*. Come in, and let me hear the Story—If *Valere* has triumph'd o'er my Weakness, and expos'd my unrequested Bounty——

Such a Repulse may fix this wand'ring Heart:
And constant Love may meet its due Desert. [Going.

Enter the Marquis.

Marq. Turn back, bright Fair, and listen to an Action glorious as *Condé*, *Luxembourg*, or *Hess*, or any He that ever grac'd the Field.

L. *Weal.* More Plagues!——I begin to grow weary of this Train of Fools—Pray make your Story short, Sir.

Marq. I'll be as concise as the Heroic Deed—— *Veni, Vidi, Vici,* as *Cæsar* said.

L. *Weal.* Over whom was this Conquest? your Footman and your Taylor?

Marq. No, Madam, over my Rival, *Valere.*

L. *Weal.* Ha! where met you that Report?

Marq. Every where——The World says you are in Love with him—'Tis all the Discourse at the *Chocolate-House.*

L. *Weal.* Confusion! Am I become so wretched——I shall be sung in Ballads shortly.

Marq. Having a profound Respect for your Ladyship—away flew I to his Lodgings—where I had no sooner enter'd, but the Memory of your Wrongs——set the stormy Marks of Anger on my Brow——Sir, said I—Sir, said he, your most humble Servant—Sir, said I—here is a Rumour spread abroad, prejudicial to the Reputation of a Lady whom I have honour'd with my Esteem.

L. *Weal.* Honour'd! Oh, audacious!

Marq. And Report says you are the Author——Who I? said he, in the meekest, humblest Tone that ever Lover begg'd in—frightned out of his Wits———Her Name, I pray———which when I had told him, and bid him draw; he poorly disclaim'd his Passion, and said, I might take you with all his Heart, for he would not fight——— At which I stept up to him, saying, *Savez vous, Monsieur, du Lansquenet*———that is as much as to say, in *English,* a Flip of the Nose, Madam—at which the good Gentleman pull'd off his Hat, and made me the lowest Bow; and I, in Triumph, left——— Now, my Reward—my Reward, Madam.

L. *Weal.* Your Reward; never to see me more: For though I love Valour, I know this Story false—and you made up of Cowardice. Do'e hear—if ever my Doors are open [*Enter three Footmen*] to this bold Intruder more, I'll have your Liveries pull'd over your Ears. [*Exit.*

Marq. Gone! I durst have sworn she would have married me for the News———Now here's a good Invention

vention lost——Ah poor Monsieur *Markee*, thoul't never thrive with these Women of Quality——I must to some rich toothless City Dame—

On them my Courage and my Shame may pass:
These Court-end Wits discover me an' Ass. [Exit.

SCENE *the Street.*

Hector *solus.*

Hect. Well, I have not Patience any longer to see this Master of mine play——I find which Way he's going——Odso, here's his Father——How shall I send him away——For if he should see his Son come out of this Gaming-House, we shall be undone again—— [*Enter Sir* Thomas Valere.] Oh, Sir, I have been all over the Town to look you——

Sir *Tho.* For what, pray? Did my last Greeting please you so well, that you've a Mind to more on't—Where's the Rake your Master?

Hect. Oh, Sir, happy, happy beyond Expression——He's with *Angelica*, who has presented him with her Picture, set round with Gems of inestimable Value.

Sir *Tho.* Ha! Say'st thou so, Boy? And is he likely to carry *Angelica*?

Hect. Carry her, Sir; why the Business is done, and nothing wanting but your Presence, with a Lawyer, to fit 'em for the Priest—Good Sir, make haste——

Sir *Tho.* I'll be there in an Instant——And shall I be a Grandfather adad——I could find in my Heart to give thee Six-pence for thy News—And I will too——there *Hector*, drink your young Master's and Lady's Health, Sirrah——Ah my dear Boy *Jemmy*, I forgive thee all——I'm so transported, I think it an Age till I embrace thee. [*Exit.*

Hect. 'Fore *George* if this old Fellow finds me in a Lie, as he most certainly will; for if *Angelica* hears my Master is at play again, she'll never have him that's sure too——I must let him know what I have done, and get him in the Mind to go this Hour to *Angelica*——or *Hector*'s Bones will pay for't.

To serve my Master, I a Lie may tell,
But would not suffer, when I mean it well. [Exit.

SCENE *discovers a Gaming-Table, with* Valere, *Count* Cogdie, *and other Gentlemen at Hazard, with several Rakes and Sharpers, waiting round the Table; a Box-Keeper and Attendants.*

Cogd. Come ——— Seven ——— What do you set Gentlemen?

Box-K. Seven's the Main.

1st Gent. That.

2d Gent. Ten Pieces.

Val. The Devil's in the Dice—There, Sir, a Hundred Guineas. [*Angrily.*]

[Cogdie *rattling the Box, and considering where to throw.*

Box-K. Knock where you are, Sir.

Cogd. I am at the fairest only; [*Throws out the Dice.* Come, and that little Silver too.

Box-K. Four to Seven.

1st Rake. Mr. *Cogdie*, to three a Crown, shall I?

2d Rake. To three and eleven Guineas if you please.

1st Sharp. Here's three Crowns to eleven, and if I lose, by all that's good I know not where to eat.

Cogd. [*To 1st Rake.*] You go to three a Crown [*To 2d Rake.*] you to three, and eleven Guineas. [*To Sharper.* You shall go yours to eleven *Jack*.

Box-K. Pray, Sir, throw away, don't hold the Box all Night.

Cogd. There, [*Shakes the Box and throws three.*] you're in once, Gentlemen.

Both Rakes. We go again.

Cogd. With all my Heart. [*Shakes the Box again and throws four.*

Box-K. Four, Trey-Ace.

Cogd. There, Gentlemen, I have brought you off again. [*To the Rakes.*]

Val. You did not throw out your Dice fair, and I'll not yield it.

Cogd. Judgment, Gentlemen.

1st

1st Gent. I think 'twas fair enough.

2d. Gent. Ay, ay, a Man may throw his Dice how he pleases.

Val. Sir, I say this Hat's white. [*In a Passion.*]

Cogd. I say so too.

Val. 'Tis false, 'tis black.

Cogd. As you say, I think it is black.

Val. No, Sir, 'tis neither black nor white.

Cogd. Nay, very likely, Sir.——He hast lost his Money and now he grows mutinous.

Box-K. Come, pray Gentlemen don't quarrel, and I'll ask it round.

Cogd. Ask what, you Blockhead? whether his Hat's black or white? [*Tosses a Pair of Dice in his Face.*

Box-K. No, Master, whether you won the Money or not.

2d Gent. He won it fairly. Come *Valere*, I'll lend thee ten Pieces, set boldly, set boldly, I warrant thee Luck, Boy.

1st Gent. Ay, ay, come whose is the Box?

Cogd. 'Tis mine——

2d Gent. Throw a Main then.

Cogd. Five.

Box-K. Five's the Main.

Val. There——take all.

1st Gent. That——

2d Gent. That——

Cogd. Where I was last. Now little Dice.

Val. Shake your Dice.

Cogd. There, Sir, [*Shakes the Dice and throws Duce Ace.*] Oh, burn 'em.

Box-K. Duce Ace.

Val. Out——Give me the Box——Six.

Box-K. Six is the Main.

Cogd. There, Sir, if you dare throw at it.

1st Gent. That——

2d Gent. That——

Val. At you all—— [*Shakes the Box and throws Quatre Duce.*

Box-K. Six. Quatre Duce, you've won it, Sir.

Cogd. Um! [*Seems disorder'd.*]

Val. Come, Seven. [*Throws.*]

Box-K. Seven's the Main.

Cogd. A hundred Guineas.

Val. Now little Dice———

Cogd. Not another Nick ſure. [*Speaks as* Valere *is going to throw the Dice.*

Val. Nick by *Juno*———

Box-K. Cinque Duce.

Cogd. Oh! Blood! and Death and Fire! [*Riſes and walks about in a Paſſion.*

Val. Nine. [*Throws.*]

Box-K. Nine's the Main.

Cogd. There, Sir, I'll ſet you two hundred Guineas upon that Note.

Val. Note, Sir! Whoſe Note is it pray?

Cogd. Why 'tis very good, Sir, 'tis upon Sir *F—, Ch—d.*

Val. At it, Egad. [*Throws.*]

B. x-K. Nine, Cinque and Quatre, the Box is due.

Cogd Um! [*Throws away the Dice, Breaks the Box.*] Sir, I bar that Throw.

Val. Sir, I did not ſee you,—and I won it fairly.

Cogd. The Devil, I that underſtand Play ſo well, to be bubbled of my Money—Sir, I ſay this Hat's white —Who dare ſay the contrary?

Val. Not I, indeed, Sir.

Cogd. I ſay 'tis black.

Val. Why, as you ſay, I think 'tis black.

Cogd. I ſay, Sir, 'tis neither black nor white.

Val. Then it ſhall be green, blue red, or yellow, or what you pleaſe, Sir. I have more Manners than to quarrel now I'm on the winning Side, Ha, ha, ha,

1ſt Gent. Prithee don't quarrel with him, you'll get nothing by it. *Valere* will fight, you know.

Cogd. And ſo will I, Sir. You're all a Parcel of— If ever I play upon the Square again———I'll give 'em Leave to make Dice of my Bones.

Val. Ha, ha, ha, hold, let me pay my Debts. There Sir— [*to 2d Gent.*]

Box-K. You owe a Box, Sir, an't pleaſe you.

Val. There—[*Gives a Shilling.*]

Box-K. You owe me a Teaster for a back-hand Tip, a little while ago, Master.

Val. There you Dog. [*Gives him Six-pence.*]

Box-K. Thank you Master—I'll thank any Gentleman that will put that Shilling in the Box.

Enter Angelica *in Man's Cloaths.*

Ang. Ay, here he is.

Val. Come Seven.

Box-K. Seven's the Main.

1st Gent. That———

2d Gent. That———

Val. 'Tis mine.

Box-K. Eleven.

2d Gent. I never saw such Fortune.

1st Gent. Here's the last of a Hundred, if Luck turn not I'm broke.

Ang. Save you Gentlemen ——— may one fling off a Guinea or two with you? [*This while* Cogdie *sits disordered and plays by himself at another Table.*

Val. Ay, a hundred if you please, a pert young Bubble this, flung Six.

Box-K. Six is the Main.

Ang. Fifty Pieces, Sir.

Val. Well said Stripling—Down with 'em—Six or a Dozen Dice—Duce Ace—Ah split it———

[*Throws down the Box.*

Box-K. Duce Ace.

Ang. Out, Sir, give me Fifty Guineas, Sir.

Val. There 'tis, Sir.

[Cogdie *rises and comes to* Angelica.

Cogd. [*To* Angelica.] Sir, will you do me the Favour to let me go two Pieces with you; I am just stript.

Ang. With all my Heart, Sir. Come Gentlemen [*Throws.*] set boldly.

Box-K. Five's the Main.

Val. A hundred Guineas.

Ang. Along [*Throws.*] 'tis mine. [*Sweeps the Money.*]

Box-K. Five, Trey, Duce.

Ang. [*To* Cogdie.] There's your two Pieces, Sir.

Cogd. I go the four, Sir, if you please.

Ang. By and by, Sir, you shall.

1st Gent. I'm broke; but I'll be here again instantly. [*Exit.*

2d Gent. I'll throw off this Stake—If Luck turn not I must home for Recruits too.

Ang. Come on then, Sir, six. [*Throws.*

Box-K. Six is the Main.

Val. In my Conscience, I believe this young Dog will strip us all. There, Sir.

Ang. And there, Sir. [*Sweeps the Money.*

Box-K. A Dozen.

2d Gent. I hope you'll stay till my Return? [*Exit.*

Ang. If these Gentlemen can hold me play.

Box-K. I hope, Gentlemen, you won't stay late, for Fear of the Press-masters, here was two Gangs last Night before twelve o'Clock.

[*All the Sharpers sneak off, and leave* Angelica *and* Valere *together.*

Ang. Pshaw, hang the Press-masters, come, Sir, Five.

Box-K. Five's the Main.

Val. That upon Five.

Ang. Nick——

Box-K. Five, Quarter Ace, you owe me a Box, Sir.

Val. Confusion! Did ever Man see the like? That Watch at twenty Guineas. [*Sets a Gold Watch.*

Ang. Done, Sir, Nine. [*Throws.*

Box-K. Nine's the Main.

Ang. 'Tis mine. [*Throws.*

Box-K. Nine, Six, and Three, a Main above a Box.

Val. Furies and Hell—That Ring at ten Guineas.

Ang. Ha, ha, ha, with all my Heart, Sir, Six again. [*Throws.*

Box-K. Six is the Main.

Ang. Nick again, Ha, ha, ha.

Box-K. Six, Cinque Ace, two Mains above a Box.

Val. The Devil —— I'll set you a hundred Guineas upon Honour, Sir.

Ang. I beg your Pardon, Sir, I never play upon Honour with Strangers — If you have nothing else to set, your humble Servant.

Val. Death—shall he carry off my Money thus——

Hold,

Hold, Sir, Friends will be here presently, I'll borrow some of them.

Ang. That's baulking my Hand——I can't stay, Sir, have you nothing else?

Val. Yes, one Thing, but that is dearer to me than my Life. [*Takes out the Picture.*

Ang. What can that be pray?

Val. 'Tis a Picture, the Original of which is nearest to my Soul—— [*Kisses it.*

Ang. Pish—a Trifle——Oh my Heart——Yet you shan't say I'm ungenerous—whate'er you value it at, I'll answer it.

Val. Value it at—It is not to be valued.

Ang. Then you'll not set it; Sir, your Servant.

Val. Stay, Sir,—Luck may turn—I'll set the Diamonds at two hundred Guineas.

Ang. Oh Villain—Well, Sir, Seven——

Box-K. Seven's the Main.

[Angelica *throws at the Picture;*

Box-K. Four or Seven.

Val. I bar the first Throw.

Box-K. Bar.

[Angelica *throws two or three Times and then wins it.*

Ang 'Tis mine, Sir.

Box-K. Four, Trey, Ace; you owe me three Boxes, Sir.

Val. Eternal Furies——lost——He shall restore it, or I'll cut his Throat.——Well, Sir, take the Diamonds, but I must have the Picture.

Ang. The Picture, Sir.

Val. Ay, the Picture, Sir.

Ang. I won it, Sir, and I shan't restore it, I assure you.

Val. But you shall restore it, Sir, e'er you and I part.

Ang. If I should draw a Duel upon my Hands here ——I'm in a fine Condition—[*Aside.*] Nay, Sir, if you are angry, good by——

Val. Nay, nay, nay, [*Runs between her and the Door.*] you shan't carry off the Picture, by *Hercules*—Look'e Sir, either take my Bond, or fight me for't. [*Draws.*

Ang. Sir—[*Trembling.*] What shall I do? I must be oblig'd to discover myself—— [*Aside.*

Enter 1st and 2d Gentlemen.

1st Gent. Hold *Valere*.

2d Gent.

2d Gent. What's the Meaning of this?

[*Lays hold of* Valere.

Ang. Ha! A lucky Escape—— [*Runs off.*

Val. Away; stand off; or I shall make my Passage through you, Traytor, Dog—Oh I could tear my Flesh —Cut off these Hands that laid the Jewel down, and stab my Heart for having once consented——

[*Walks about raving.*

1st Gent. What can be the Cause of this Passion?

2d Gent. Ho, he has lost his Money—Pr'ythee don't let that trouble thee, I'll lend thee more—Come let's throw for the Box.

Val. Throw for the Devil—No, henceforth a Gamester is my Foe; nor should the *Indies* bribe me even to touch a Die; nor, after this Moment, will I e'er set Foot in such a House again.

1st Gent. The Man is mad.

2d Gent. Pr'ythee let's go seek out better Company.

[*Exeunt.*

Val. Now I behold what a Monster this darling Sin has made me, and loath myself for my long Race of Folly.

Now I repent, but oh it comes too late,
And 'tis but Justice now that she should hate:
He that flies Virtue still to follow Vice,
'Tis fit, like me he lose his Paradise.

The End of the FOURTH ACT.

ACT V.

SCENE Valere's *Lodgings.*

Valere *solus.*

Val. WHAT shall I do? There's no going near *Angelica.* The Action I have done carries such a Face that she can ne'er forgive me.

Enter

Enter Hector.

Hect. Another 'scape, Sir, another 'scape. Your Father was just at the Gaming-House Door upon the Hunt for you,—but Thanks to my Wit, I found a Way to send him packing. He's gone to *Angelica*'s with a Lawyer. Follow him, follow him, Sir,—If he gets there before you, the old Gentleman will believe me no more—for I told him you staid for him there ——— Ha; he minds me not. Sir, Sir; don't you hear me?

Val. No: I'll neither hear, nor see, nor eat, nor drink, nor ever rest again.

Hect. Ah, the Devil! I shall be as slender as a Hazel-Switch in a little Time then; for I suppose I must keep you Company in that thin Diet——Ah! what I dreaded is come to pass—What then is all the Money lost?

Val. Money! My Life, my Soul is lost.

Hect. Hey day! What's the Matter now?

Val. The Picture.

Hect. The Picture, Sir——— [*With a frightful Look.*] Mercy on us; shake your Pockets, shake your Pockets, Sir. [*Runs to* Valere *and shakes his Coat Pockets.*

Val. Hold off: I tell thee I've lost it at Play.

Hect. Why then you have play'd fair—Why what will you do now, Sir?

Val. Cut your Throat, Sirrah, and then my own. [*Clapping hold of* Hector.

Hect. 'Twas none of my Fault, Sir. [*Half weeping.*

Val. O no! it was my own: For had I taken thy Counsel, this Curse had been prevented.

Hect. Ay, Sir, but a Gamester's Life was the most genteel of any————their Fob was a Fund, and their Hands Philosophers Stones. Ay, Sir.

Val. No more—go fetch me a Book— [*Sits down.*

Hect. What Book, Sir?

Val. The first that comes to your Hand, no Matter which. [*Exit* Hector, *returns with a Book.*

Hect. Here's *Seneca*, Sir?

Val. Well, read—Was ever Man so unfortunate! [*Walking about in a thinking Posture.*

Hect. Who, I read *Seneca*, Sir?

Val. Why not?

Hect. I seldom read any Thing, Sir, but Almanacks.

Val. Oh read, read at a Venture ——— To lose upon Seven when the Chance was Four! Confusion! [*Stamps.*

Hect. [*Reads.*] — Be not taken with the glittering Dreams of Riches, their Possession brings Trouble: Tranquility is a certain Equality of Mind, which no Condition of Fortune can either exalt or depress. If his Fortune be good, he tempers it; if bad, he masters it.

Val. The Devil was in me, that I could not leave off when I was a Winner.

Hect. What is the End of Ambition and Avarice? We are but Stewards of what we falsely call our own. All those Things which we pursue with so much Hazard, for which we break Faith and Friendship, what are they but the mere Depositor of Fortune, and not ours, but already inclining towards a new Master.—Now will I be hang'd, if *Seneca* himself was not given to Gaming.—— Sir, don't you think this looks like a moral Reflection after a Loss.—In my Conscience, I'm half in the Mind that he play'd away a Mistress's Picture too——

Val. Ha! Name it not, for if thou dost, I'll shake thee into Atoms.— [*Shaking him.*

Hect. Ah, Sir, I've done, I've done,——— But, Sir, this *Seneca* was a wonderous Man —Was he ever in *London,* Sir?

Val. No, he lived at *Rome.*——— Not one in ten, Oh wretched Luck.

Hect. That's a long Way off—I thought indeed 'twas something made his Morals so little minded —— Come, Sir, Courage.

Val. Yes, I'll to the Camp, there, in the Service of my Country, expiate my Follies.

Hect. To the Camp, Sir, what do you mean? Odsbud, Sir, go to *Angelica,* this Minute, and marry her out of Hand, she does not know you have lost the Picture, and when once she's secure, if she asks for it, stop her Mouth with Kisses, Sir.

Val. Well, I will go, if but to take my Leave of her —For I much fear she'll read Guilt in my Face—

This I resolve, whatever Fate's in Store,
To touch the curst infectious Dice no more.

Hect.

Hect. Ay, stick you but there, and I warrant we prosper.

SCENE, *The Lady* Wealthy's *House.*

Enter Lady Wealthy, *Mrs.* Betty *to her.*

Betty. Madam, Mr. *Lovewell* to wait on your Ladyship.

L. *Weal.* How shall I see him! Shame and Confusion rises in my Face, yet it is not in my Temper to own myself in the wrong, if he upbraids me, this is his last Visit, bring him up———

Enter Mr. Lovewell.

I suppose you come triumphant, but know, I give Account of my Actions to no Man. Am free, and will so remain.

Love. 'Tis my hard Fortune still to be mistaken, my Love's too blind to think you do amiss —I have since been with *Valere,* sworn to him the Letter was a Plot of mine, the Hand and Bill all counterfeit, to satisfy my jealous Scruple, if there were Affairs between ye, he believed it, and your Honour's free from all ill Tongues—And the Wretch doom'd to be hated still,—Am come to take my everlasting Leave.

L. *Weal.* This Generosity shocks me—[*Aside.*] Farewel, you have clear'd me to your Rival, but to yourself can say she was ungrateful and despised me: Love without Esteem is a forc'd Plant and wants its Root, therefore my ill Conduct parts us, and thank your generous Carriage for this Confession,—Great Spirits hardly yield themselves to blame.

Lov. Nor are you; I have not watch'd so many Years your Temper, each Turn and Sally of your Mind, but I can judge it right, Honour is center'd in your Soul, nor would you wrong it in an essential Part. All your little Affectations are but the Effects your Glass produces, which tells ye, Beauty like yours, may take ten thousand Liberties.

L. *Weal.* You have chose a cunning Way to move my

Heart,

Heart, when I was arm'd with Accusations to extenuate my Faults. And if I could persuade myself to trust a Man, I think it would be you.

Lov. Oh cherish that kind Opinion, and if ever you do repent it, proclaim me to the World a Villain.

L. *Weal.* This I resolve in Favour of your noble Usage, to banish from my House that senseless Train of Fop Admirers, which I always laugh at, and only kept to feed my Vanity.

Lov. On my Knees I thank you: but do not, do not dash my Transports by Delay.——Your Year of Widowhood is just expir'd————reward my constant Love, and make me happy. A Husband will fright the Fool Pretenders from approaching, and these fond Arms secure you ever mine.

L. *Weal.* Bless me, is the Man mad? Here would be a strange Leap indeed, from Mortal Odds into Matrimony. No, no; a little longer Time must try you first.

Lov. If Time be now required, you may defer my Joys till Age has strew'd my Head with hoary Hairs; for from my very Infancy I have ador'd you—'Tis but a Month ago when my auspicious Stars inclin'd you to a Fit of Mercy.————I flew, got a Licence, came with eager Hopes, and you deny'd to see me. The same Authority will do now.————Nor will I leave you, till your Hand is mine.

Enter Betty.

L. *Weal. Betty,* come to my Aid; here's an audacious Man will marry me, in spite of my Teeth, this very Instant.

Betty. O Madam, the luckiest Moment in the World. I have been just looking on *Erra Pater*, and there's the happiest Conjunction————And the Chaplain sauntering about the Gardens ready for Employment.

Lov. Nay, look not back, your Eyes consent, and I'll have no Denial.

L. *Weal.* Well, this is the maddest Thing.

Lov. The happiest Thing————Thus————

The wand'ring Fair are by long Courtships kind,
And constant Love does luckiest Minutes find. [Exeunt.

Enter

Enter Angelica.

Ang. Lovewell and my Sister; happy Pair!—— I am only curst in a loose Reprobate, whom no Chance, no Obligations can fix. I must resolve to blot him from my Soul—but how hard 'tis to efface the first Impression— *Valere*, if I can part with thee, Mankind will be upon the Square. Thy Uncle may succeed; Old or Young: For I shall never look with loving Eyes again—Let me think—To lose my Picture—O unpardonable Fault.

Enter Dorante *and Mrs.* Favourite *at a Distance.*

Fav. Now, Sir, is your Time; she is horridly out of Humour. I know 'tis with *Valere*, for nothing else makes her so.

Dor. Madam, I hope you will pardon my Intrusion, when 'tis to warn you of approaching Danger. I can prove to you my Nephew has broke all his Oaths, and played with the veriest Rakes the Town affords, in a public Gaming-House.

Ang. Malice, Malice all

Dor. As this is true or false, may I your Love enjoy.

Ang. Suppose it true, am I confin'd to make my Choice in your Family—or indeed to choose at all——Perhaps I'll never marry.————

Dor. O say not so; let not so much Beauty lose the End of its Creation —You should bless the World with your Increase.

Ang. Methinks you are too much in the Wain to think of Increase— However, I am yet resolv'd on nothing —and desire to be freed from Importunity—'Tis well you

Enter Valere *and* Hector.

are come: Your Uncle has been using all his Rhetoric to supplant you.

Hect. The Day's our own: She's in a pure Humour, [*Aside.*

Val. No clandestine Dealings, Uncle, I beseech you: Give me fair Play and let the Lady choose————

Ang. With what Assurance he approaches. [*Aside.*

Dor. However her Choice may go, I know who de-

serves

serves her most —I'm no Gamester, Sir—Her peaceful Hours of Rest shall ne'er be broke by me.

Hect. That I dare swear. [*Aside*.

Val. No Reflections, Sir, on former Follies. You in your Youth doubtless had your Share—though now you are past 'em, and only rail at what you can't enjoy——But I in my full Strength and Vigour give 'em over, resolving never to indulge the tempting Vice again.

Dor. This you have often swore, and as often broke your Vows.

Val. I have; but 'tis not in the Power of Fate to make me do't again; and what's past this Lady has forgiven.

Ang. To end your Disputes, Mr. *Dorante*, I'll now own to you, that my Heart has been long since given to *Valere*———and this Morning I renew'd my Vows.

Val. O Transport! Now, Uncle, I hope you are satisfied.

Dor. No, Sir, I am not satisfied—nor can I believe what she says real, without condemning her Judgment.

Ang. A strange positive old Man this——*Valere*, pray clear his Understanding —Shew him the Present I made you to Day; then let him judge who I design my Heart for.

Val. Ha! What shall I say? [*Aside*.

Hect. O, I'm thunder-struck! [*Aside*.

Val. O spare his Age, Madam, I forgive him. He is my Uncle, and I would not triumph——'Twould make him mad, should I produce the Picture.

Ang. No, no, fear not; tis rather Charity: For since he refuses to believe my Words, 'tis but Reason he should have ocular Demonstration.

Val. He that doubts what's utter'd by that Tongue, is unworthy of your farther Care———Therefore pardon me, Madam; a Thing so sacred as your Image, never shall convince him.

Hect. Well hinted, I'faith. [*Aside*.

Ang. But when I desire it, methinks you should not refuse. Obedience becomes a Lover.

Hect. Lost again. [*Aside*.

Val. You ever shall command me———

[*Feeling first in one Pocket, then in t'other*.

Ha! Where did I put it?

Hect.

Hect. Humph. [*Lifting up his Eyes.*

Ang. I'm amaz'd at his Impudence. [*Aside.*

Val. Bleſs me! ſure I did not leave it in the Bed.—Which Way ſhall I come off?—[*Aside.*]—*Hector.*

Hect. Sir——— [*Looking very ſimply.*

Val. Did you not ſee a Picture any where to Day?

Hect. A Picture, Sir——— [*In a Kind of Fright.*

Val. Ay, a Picture. What makes you look ſo, Sirrah? Ha! I ſuſpect your Rogueſhip has done ſomething with it.

Hect. O dear Sir——— [*Trembling.*

Val. Where is it? Speak, Raſcal, or I'll cut your Ears off. [*Draws.*

Hect. O Sir, forgive me, and I'll tell you the whole Truth. [*Falls on his Knees.*

Ang. What means the Fellow? [*Aside.*

Val. What will you tell me, Sirrah?

Hect. Why, Sir, fearing that your Pocket might be pick'd, or your Lodgings robb'd, and you might loſe the Picture, and that I thought would break your Heart, knowing how much you did eſteem the Piece, I took it, Sir, to a famous Painter of my Acquaintance to have it copied, Sir, that's all.

Ang. A well invented Tale. [*Aside.*

Val. Fly, Sirrah, and fetch it. [*Slaps him on the Back.*

Hect. Yes, Sir. [*Going.*

Ang. Oh you may ſpare your Pains, Sir—the Picture is already here—[*Pulls it out.*] now, Sir, do you bluſh.

Val. I am amaz'd to think how ſhe came by it. [*Aside.*

Hect. Ruin'd paſt Redemption—Oh, oh, oh,—that ſuch a compleat Lye ſhould turn to no Account. [*Aside.*

Ang. Ungrateful Man.

Dor. How, how's this?

Ang. Is this the Price you ſet upon my Favours——the Sight of this would mind you of your Duty——if I remember, thoſe were your Words—But I preſume you meant it ſhould remind you of a laſt Stake—How have I been deceiv'd.————Is it poſſible thou couldſt be ſo baſe to expoſe my Picture at a common Board, amongſt a Crew of Revellers.

Val. Madam———

Ang. Be dumb, and make no impudent Excuſes.

Dor. Dol, dol, dery dol, dery dol. [*Sings.*

Val. No, Madam, I ſhall not ſtudy to excuſe myſelf, only this, I am not guilty of all your Charge, for there was none in Preſence when I loſt it, but the Youth that won it. Who had not liv'd to have brought it you, had not an unlucky Chance prevented me.

Ang. Then to conceal your Treachery, you would have committed Murder,—excellent Moraliſt ——But, Sir, the Privacy of the Act you boaſt of—Does not in the leaſt extenuate your Crime; I told you whilſt you kept that Picture, my Heart was yours, but you grew weary of the Trifle, and reſtor'd it back, and now I have Liberty to give it to whom I pleaſe.

Dor. I hope you are ſatisfied now, Nephew, ha, ha ha.

Val. I am with every Thing this Lady is pleaſed to inflict, I know ſhe can uſe me no worſe than I deſerve.— I own the Foulneſs of my Guilt, and will not hope for Pardon.

Enter Sir Thomas Valere, *with a Lawyer.*

Hect. Nay, then we are friendleſs, indeed,—Sir, Sir, ſhall I ſee what *Seneca* ſays upon this Head?

[*Aſide to* Valere.

Val. Away, and plague me not—Ha, my Father.—

Sir *Tho.* I'm bleſt, beyond Expreſſion bleſt.—Madam, I wiſh you Joy: My Son, I have brought Mr. *Demurr* the Lawyer,———I'll reſerve but Five Hundred a Year for myſelf———the Reſt is thine, Boy,———full Two Thouſand Pounds *per Annum.*

Ang. Sir *Thomas*, your Words carry a Meaning in 'em—which I am a Stranger to.

Sir *Tho.* Meaning, Madam,—I hope my Son and you underſtand one another's Meaning,———and I underſtand it too, Madam.——-Come, Mr. *Demurr*, where are the Writings of my Eſtate?——He ſhall make thee a ſwinging Jointure, my Girl.————

Ang. You muſt pardon me, Sir *Thomas*,—my Mind's alter'd.————

Sir *Tho.* How! Did you not promiſe?

Ang. Suppoſe I did. When a Man breaks all his Oaths to me, I know no Reaſon I ſhould keep my Word with him.

Hect,

Hect. Ah *Hector, Hector,* what will become of thee? [*Aside.*

Sir *Tho.* Why I underſtood theſe Quarrels were made up———and as a Token of your being reconcil'd, you made him a Preſent of your Picture.————

Ang. True,—And that's the Thing that parts us.

Sir *Tho.* What do you mean?

Dor. He gam'd it away, Brother; now do you underſtand her?

Sir *Tho.* Malice and Marriage, Brother, ill becomes your Years.—She does not mean it ſo.

Ang. Indeed but I do.—

Sir *Tho.* Say you ſo, Madam,—then I'll do you Juſtice immediately. [*Draws.*] Sirrah, I'll ſave the Hangman a Labour,—I will you Baſtard.

Val. Do, kill me, Sir; you ſhall find I will not vent one Groan,—for my Soul has ta'en its Flight already,—My baſe Ingratitude has deeper ſtabb'd my Heart, than now your Sword can do——

Sir *Tho.* Say you ſo, Sirrah,—then I hope you'll live to want Nothing, for I'll take Care you ſhall have Nothing to ſupport your Extravagance.— Mr. *Demurr,* I deſire you to make my Will this Minute,—and put the ungracious Rogue down a Shilling.—Sirrah, I charge you never to come in Sight of me or my Habitation more; nor, do you hear, dare to own me for your Father.—Go, Troop, Sirrah, I ſhall hear of your going up *Holbourn-Hill* in a little Time.—

Hect. So, there's all my Wages loſt.— [*Aſide.*

Ang. Ha! this Uſage ſhocks me. [*Aſide.*

Val. Sir, I promiſe you to obey you to a Tittle,——and this undutiful Child ſhall ne'er offend you with his Preſence more.—You but enjoin, but I before had choſe, for *England* now would be the worſt of Fates.

Ang. My Heart beats as if the Strings were breaking. [*Aſide.*

Val. Madam, there is but one Requeſt that I will make—then take my Leave for ever, and if you grant it not, I ſhall be ſo much more unhappy.——My being diſinherited weighs not a Hair, compar'd with what I've loſt in loſing you, whom my Soul prefers before all Wealth,

Wealth, Friends, or Family.——Then, where should I ask Pardon but where I most have injur'd?——Thus on my Knees, I beg you not to hate my Memory, nor suffer the Follies which I have now cashier'd for ever from my Breast;—(but oh too late) to drive my Name as distant as my Body from you, sometimes vouchsafe to think on lost *Valere*.

Ang. There is Nothing so indifferent but we think of it sometimes——

Sir *Tho.* Sirrah—begone I say. [*Pushes him.*

Val. I have done.—Now Madam, eternally adieu.

Ang. Shall I see him ruin'd—no—that would be barbarous beyond Example.——*Valere*, come back, should I forgive you all—Would my Generosity oblige you to a sober Life.—Can you upon Honour (for you shall swear no more) forsake that Vice that brought you to this low Ebb of Fortune?

Val. Ha! Oh let me fold thee in my repenting Arms—and whisper to thy Soul, that I am intirely chang'd—[*Embraces her.*] Yes, my Love, I swear the Course of Life that I've run hitherto—is grown more hateful to me than Toads or Adders; and I would as soon keep those Animals in my Bosom, whose Sting I know would kill me, as once indulge my former Follies.

Ang. Then I am happy.—Know I was the Youth that won the Picture, and you parted with it to myself.

Hect. I shall die with Joy, that's certain— [*Aside.*

Val. Then I did not break my Oath entirely, you were excepted, Madam.

Sir *Tho.* How lucky a Turn is this! Madam, your Example is too good not to be followed.—*Valere*, I forgive thee, and confirm my first Design:—Bless you both——Now Brother, I hope you'll believe you can't get my Boy's Mistress from him. Ha, ha, ha.

Dor. Nor he shan't get a Penny of my Estate, Brother, remember that.——

Sir *Tho.* He wants it not.——Ha! Who have we here——my Lady *Wealthy* and her old Lover.

Enter Lovewell *and Lady* Wealthy.

Love. Wish me Joy, Friends, wish me Joy.

Sir

Sir *Tho.* With all my Heart, for in my Conſcience thou deſerv'ſt her.———

Ang. I wiſh you Joy, Siſter; here let all Quarrels ceaſe. [*Salutes her.*

L. *Weal.* I over-heard your Reconciliation,——and I wiſh you the ſame.

Love. Oh my Friend! Sure never Man was bleſt like me. [*To* Valere.

Val. Yes, I can boaſt a Happineſs beyond thee,—I that merited her endleſs Scorn, am, by her ſweet forgiving Temper, rais'd to laſting Joy.———

Enter Marquis *of* Hazard.

Marq. I underſtand you are married, Madam; and come to wiſh you Joy.———I do it with a *bon cœur, le Diable m'en porte*———

L. *Weal.* O Monſieur *Marque*, I am infinitely oblig'd to you e'er ſince your Knight-Errantry with *Valere* in Defence of my Honour,

Marq. A Duce of that unlucky Story.——No Words on't now, Madam, I beſeech you.

Val. How's that?

Marq. By the Honour of *France* I ſhall be diſcover'd.

Enter Betty.

Betty. Madam, Mrs. *Security* has brought a Pair of very fine Diamond Ear-rings to ſhew you, they were loſt in Pawn, ſhe ſays,——and therefore ſhe can afford them an extraordinary good Pennyworth.

L. *Weal.* Bring her in.———

Enter Mrs. Security.

Well, Mrs. *Security*, are they very fine ones.

Mrs. *Sec.* As fine a Pair as ever your Ladyſhip ſaw in all your Life, Madam.———[*Gives her the Ear-rings.*] Bleſs me,—What do I ſee, my Couſin *Robin Skip*? I'm glad to ſee thee with all my Heart. [*To the* Marquis.

L. *Weal.* Do you know what you ſay, Mrs. *Security*? ——That is a *French* Nobleman.

Mrs. *Sec.* A Nobleman,———What do you think I don't know my Brother's Son?———

Marq. A Fox of ſuch Kindred—Now all will out—

Mrs. *Sec*. Why how long haſt thou been in *England*, *Robert*?——I heard thou wert Footman to the Prince of *Conti*.———Thy old Maſter, Sir *William*, aſks mightily how thou doſt.

Omnes. Ha, ha, ha,

Val. How's this, the Marquis of *Hazard* a Footman? Ha, ha, ha.

Hect. Brother, give me thy Hand———Hold, now I think on't keep your Diſtance, Friend,———for a *Valet de Chambre* is above a Footman.——— [*Struts*.

L. *Weal*. My Footman, Sir, will ſhew you into the Buttery; a Horn of ſmall Beer may quench your Thirſt of Honour. Ha, ha.

Val. This Morning he boaſted of his Royal Blood at my Lodgings,—but his Cowardiſe confirm'd me what he is.—

L. *Weal*. He told me he was at your Lodgings, and preſented you with a Tweague by the Noſe——

Val. How, Scoundrel, beneath my Sword, and therefore take this.——— [*Kicks him*.

Marq. Very fine, very fine Breeding, Gentlemen, truly.—Well this is my Maxim ſtill——

Who once by Policy a Title gains,
Merits above the Fool that's born to Means. [Exit.

Mrs. *Sec*. 'Tis dirtily done of you, Mr. *Valere*, ſo it is, to kick a Man for nothing;—His Father, though I ſay it, was as honeſt a Man as ever broke Bread, and I could find in my Heart to———

L. *Weal*. No more of your Noiſe, —— Wait without there.——— [*Exit Mrs*. Security.

Sir *Tho*. Come, come, enough of this Nonſenſe,—— Let's have a Dance.

A Country Dance.

Val. Now Virtue's pleaſing Proſpect's in my View,
With double Care I'll all her Paths purſue;
And proud to think I owe this Change to you. [*To* Ang.
Virtue that gives more ſolid Peace of Mind,
Than Men in all their vicious Pleaſures find;
Then each with me the Libertine reclaim,
And ſhun what ſinks his Fortune, and his Fame.

THE

THE PROLOGUE.

Written by N. ROWE, Esq;

Spoken by Mr. BETTERTON.

IF humble Wives that drag the Marriage Chain
With cursed dogged Husbands, may complain;
If turn'd at large to starve, as we by you,
They may, at least, for Alimony *sue.*
Know, we resolve to make the Case our own,
Between the Plaintiff-Stage, *and the* Defendant-Town.
When first you took us from our Father's *House,*
And lovingly our Interest did espouse;
You kept us fine, caress'd and lodg'd us here,
And Honey-Moon *held out above* Three Year;
At length, for Pleasures known do seldom last,
Frequent Enjoyments pall'd your sprightly Taste;
And though at first you did not quite neglect,
We found your Love was dwindled to Respect;
Sometimes, indeed, as in your Way it fell,
You stop'd, and call'd to see if we were well.
Now, quite estrang'd, this wretched Place you shun,
Like bad Wine, Business, Duels, or a Dun.
Have we for this increas'd Apollo's *Race?*
Been often pregnant with your Wit's Embrace?
And born you many chopping Babes of Grace?
Some ugly Toads we had, and that's the Curse,
They were so like you that they far'd the worse;
For this to-night we are not much in Pain,
Look on't, and if you like it, Entertain;
If all the Midwife says of it be true,
There are some Features too like some of you;
For us, if you think fitting to forsake it,
We *mean to* run away, *and let the* Parish take it.

EPILOGUE.

Spoken by Mrs. SANTLOW.

AS one condemn'd, and ready to become
For his Offences past, a Pendulum,
Does e'er he dies, bespeak the learned Throng.
Then, like the Swan, expires in a Song.
So I, though doubtful long which Knot to choose,
Whether the Hangman's, or the Marriage Noose)
Condemn'd good People, as you see, for Life,
To play that tedious, juggling Game, a Wife,
Have but one Word of good Advice to say,
Before the doleful Cart draws quite away.

You roaring Boys, who know the Midnight Cares
Of rattling Tatts, ye Sons of Hopes and Fears:
Who labour hard to bring your Ruin on,
And diligently toil to be undone;
Your'e Fortune's sporting Footballs at the best,
Few are his Joys, and small the Gamester's Rest:
Suppose then Fortune only rules the Dice,
And on the Square you play; yet, who that's wise,
Would to the Credit of a faithless Main,
Trust his good Dad's hard-gotten hoarded Gain?
But then such Vultures round a Table wait,
And hov'ring watch the Bubble's fickly State;
The young fond Gambler covetous of more,
Like Æsop's Dog, loses his certain Store.
Then the Spunge squeez'd by all, grows dry,—And now
Compleatly wretched turns a Sharper too;
These Fools, for Want of Bubbles too, play fair,
And lose to one another on the Square;
So Whores the Wealth from numerous Culls they glean,
Still spend on Bullies, and grew poor again.

This

EPILOGUE.

This Itch for Play has likewise fatal been,
And more than Cupid, *drawn the Ladies in,*
A Thousand Guineas for Basset *prevails,*
A Bait, when Cash runs low, that seldom fails;
And when the Fair One can't the Debt defray
In Sterling Coin does Sterling Beauty pay.

In vain we labour to divert your Care,
Nor Song, nor Dance can bribe your Presence here,
You fly this Place like an infectious Air.
To yonder happy Quarter of the Town,
You croud; and your own fav'rite Stage disown;
We're like old Mistresses, you love the Vice,
And hate us only 'cause we once did please.
Nor can we find how else 'tis we deserve,
Like Tantalus, *'midst Plenty thus to starve.*

THE

BASSET-TABLE.

A

COMEDY.

THE

PROLOGUE.

Spoken by Mr. PENKETHMAN.

IN all the Faces that to Plays resort,
Whether of Country, City, Mob, or Court,
I've always found, that none such Hopes inspire,
As you—dear Brethren of the Upper Tire.
Poets, in Prologues, may both preach and rail,
Yet all their Wisdom nothing will avail;
Who writes not up to you 'tis Ten to One will fail.
Your thundering Plaudit is that deals out Fame;
You make Plays run, tho' of themselves but Lame:
How often have we known your Noise commanding,
Impose on your inferior Masters Understanding;
Therefore, dear Brethren, (since I am one of you)
Whether adorn'd in Grey, Green, Brown, or Blue,
This Day stand all by me, as I will fall by you.
And now to let——
The poor Pit see how Pinky'*s Voice commands,*
Silence — Now rattle all your Sticks, and clap your grimy
Hands.
I greet your Love—and let the vainest Author shew,
Half this Command on cleaner Hands below,
Nay, more to prove your Interest, let this Play live by you.
So may you share good Claret with your Masters,
Still free in your Amours from their Disasters;
Free from poor House-keeping; where Peck is under Locks,
Free from cold Kitchens, and no Christmas-Box:
So may no long Debates i' th' House of Commons,
Make you in the Lobby starve, when Hunger summons;
But may your plenteous Vails come flowing in,
Give you a lucky Hit, and make you Gentlemen;
And thus preferr'd, ne'er fear the World's Reproaches,
But shake your Elbows with my Lord, and keep your Coaches.

THE

THE

EPILOGUE.

Spoken by Mr. Estcourt.

THIS goodly Fabrick, to a gazing Tar,
Seems Fore and Aft, a Three Deckt Man of War:
Abaft, the Hold's the Pit, from thence look up;
Aloft! that's Swabbers Nest, that's the Main-Top.
Side Boxes mann'd with Beau, and modish Rake,
Are like the Fore-Castle and Quarter-Deck.
Those dark-disguised, advent'rous black-nos'd few,
May pass for Gunners, or a Fire-Ship's Crew.
Some come like Privateers a Prize to seize,
And catch the French *within the Narrow Seas.*
The Orange Ladies, Virgins of Renown,
Are Powder-Monkies running up and down.
We've here our Calms, our Storms, and prosp'rous Gales,
And shift our Scenes as Seamen shift their Sails.
The Ship's well mann'd, and not ill woman'd neither,
So ballasted and stow'd, my Lads, she'll bear the Weather.
But greater Dangers vent'ring Players alarm;
This Night's Engagement's worse than any Storm.
The Poet's Captain, but half dead with Fright,
She leaves her Officers to maintain the Fight;
Yond middle Teer with Eighteen Pounders maul us,
That Upper-Deck with Great and Small Shot gaul us.
But from this Lower-Teer most Harm befals,
There's no opposing their prevailing Balls.
At either Foe or Friend their Chain-Shot flies,
We sink or swim, we conquer, fall or rise.
To fit and rig our Ships much Pains we take;
Grant we may now a Saving-Voyage make.
Here we're embark'd, and as you smile or frown,
You are our Stars, by you we live or drown.

Dramatis Personæ.

MEN.

Lord Worthy, *in Love with Lady* Reveller, *a Hater of Gaming,*	*Mr.* Mills.
Sir James Courtly, *an airy Gentleman, given to Gaming,*	*Mr.* Wilks.
Lovely, *an Ensign, in Love with* Valeria,	*Mr.* Bickerstaff.
Sir Richard Plainman, *formerly a Citizen, but now lives in* Covent-Garden, *a great Lover of a Soldier, and an inveterate Enemy to the* French,	*Mr.* Bullock.
Captain Hearty, *a Sea Officer, design'd by Sir* Richard, *to marry* Valeria,	*Mr.* Estcourt.
Sago, *a Drugster in the City, very fond of his Wife,*	*Mr.* Johnson.
Buckle, *footman to Lord* Worthy,	*Mr.* Penkethman.

WOMEN.

Lady Reveller, *a Coquetish Widow, that keeps a* Basset-Table,	*Mrs.* Oldfield.
Lady Lucy, *her Cousin, a religious sober Lady,*	*Mrs.* Rogers.
Valeria, *a philosophical Girl, Daughter to Sir* Richard, *in Love with* Lovely,	*Mrs.* Montford.
Mrs. Sago, *the Drugster's Wife, a gaming profuse Woman, great with my Lady* Reveller, *in Love with Sir* James,	*Mrs.* Cross.
Alpiew, *Woman to Lady* Reveller,	*Mrs.* Lucas.

Ladies, and Gentlemen, for the Basset-Table.

Chairmen, Footmen, &c.

SCENE, *Lady* Reveller's *Lodgings, in* Covent-Garden; *the Time, Four o'Clock in the Morning.*

THE

THE BASSET-TABLE.

ACT I.

SCENE, *A large Hall, a Porter with a Staff, ſeveral Chairs waiting, and Footmen aſleep, with Torches and Flambeaux ſtanding about the Room.*

Footman.

CERTAINLY they'll play all Night, this is a curſed Life.

Port. How long have you liv'd with your Lady?

Footm. A Month; too long by thirty Days, if this be her Way of Living, I ſhall be dead before the Year's out; ſhe games all Night, and ſleeps all Day.

Port. Then you ſleep too, what's the Matter?

Footm. I deny that; for while ſhe ſleeps I'm employ'd in Howd'ye's, from one End of the Town to the other.

Port. But you reſt while ſhe's gaming; What would you do if you led my Life? This is my Lady's conſtant Practice.

Footm. Your Lady keeps a *Baſſet-Table*, much good may do you with your Service——Hark, they are broke up. [*Within.*] Ha, hy, my Lady *Gamewell*'s Chair ready there—Mr. *Sonica*'s Servant. [*The Footmen wake in a Hurry.*

1ſt Footm. Where the Devil is my Flambeaux?

2d Footm. So-hey——*Robin*, get the Chair ready, my Lady's coming; ſtay, ſtay, let me light my Flambeaux.

3d Footm. [*Yawning*] Hey, hoa, what han't they done play yet?

Port. They are now coming down, but your Lady is gone half an Hour ago.

3d Footm. The Devil ſhe is! Why did not you call me?

Port. I did not ſee you.

3d Footm. Was you blind—She has loſt her Money, that's certain ——— She never flinches upon a winning Hand———Her Plate and Jewels walk To-morrow to repleniſh her Pocket—a Pox of Gaming, I ſay. [*Exit.*

[*Within.*] Mr. *Looſeall*'s Man——

4th Footm. Here—So-ho, who has ſtole my Flambeaux?

[*Within.*] My Lady *Umbray*'s Coach there—

5th Footm. Hey! *Will*, pull up there.

[*Exeunt omnes.*

Enter Lady Reveller *and* Alpiew, *her Woman.*

Lady. My Lady *Raffle* is horridly out of Humour at her ill Fortune, ſhe loſt 300 *l.*

Alp. She has generally ill Luck, yet her Inclination for Play is as ſtrong as ever.——Did your Ladyſhip win or loſe, Madam?

Lady. I won about 50 Pieces—Pr'ythee, what ſhall we do, *Alpiew?* 'Tis a fine Morning, 'tis pity to go to Bed.

Alp. What does your Ladyſhip think of a Walk in the Park?—The Park is pleaſant in a Morning, the Air is ſo very ſweet.

Lady. I don't think ſo; the Sweetneſs of the Park is at Eleven, when the Beau-Monde make their Tour there; 'tis an unpoliſh'd Curioſity to walk when only Birds can ſee one.

Alp. Bleſs me, Madam! Your Uncle—Now for a Sermon of two Hours.

Enter Sir Richard Plainman, *in a Night-Gown, as from Bed.*

Sir *Rich.* So, Niece! I find you're reſolv'd to keep on your Courſe of Life; I muſt be wak'd at four, with

Coach

Coach, Coach, Chair, Chair; give over, for Shame, and marry, marry, Niece.

Lady. Now would I forfeit the Heart of my next Admirer, to know the Cause of this Reproach. [*Aside*. Pray, Uncle, explain yourself; for I protest I can't guess what Crime I have unhappily committed to merit this Advice.

Sir *Rich*. How can you look me in the Face, and ask me that Question? Can you that keep a *Basset-Table*, a public Gaming-House, be insensible of the Shame on't? I have often told you how much the vast Concourse of People, which Day and Night make my House their Rendezvous, incommode my Health; your Apartment is a Parade for Men of all Ranks, from the Duke to the Fidler; and your Vanity thinks they all pay Devoir to your Beauty—but you mistake; every one has his several Ends in meeting here, from the Lord to the Sharper, and each their separate Interests to pursue—Some Fools there may be, for there's seldom a Crowd without.

Lady. Malice—some Fools? I can't bear it.

Alp. Nay, 'tis very affronting, truly, Madam.

Lady. Ay, is it not, *Alpiew*?—Yet, now I think on't, 'tis the Defect of Age to rail at the Pleasures of Youth, therefore I shall not disorder my Face with a Frown about it. Ha, ha, I hope, Uncle, you'll take peculiar Care of my Cousin *Valeria*, in disposing of her according to the Breeding you have given her.

Sir *Rich*. The Breeding I have given her! I would not have her have your Breeding, Mistress, for all the Wealth of *England*'s Bank; no, I bred my Girl in the Country, a Stranger to the Vices of this Town, and am resolv'd to marry her to a Man of Honour, Probity, and Courage.

Lady. What, the Sea Captain, Uncle? Faugh, I hate the Smell of Pitch and Tar; one that can entertain one with nothing but Fire and Smoke, Larboard and Starboard, and t'other Bowl of Punch; ha, ha, ha.

Alp. And for every Fault that she commits, he'll condemn her to the Bilboes; ha, ha.

Lady. I fancy my Cousin's Philosophy, and the Captain's courageous Bluster, will make Angelic Harmony.

Sir *Rich*. Yes, Madam; sweeter Harmony than your

Sept

Sept & Leva Fops, Rakes, and Gamesters; give me the Man that serves my Country, that preserves both my Estate and Life—Oh, the glorious Name of Soldier; if I were young, I'd go myself in Person, but as it is——

Alp. You'll send your Daughter——

Sir *Rich.* Yes, Minx, and a good Dowry with her, as a Reward for Virtue, like the Captain's.

Alp. But suppose, Sir, Mrs. *Valeria* should not like him?

Sir *Rich.* I'll suppose no such Thing, Mistress, she shall like him.

Lady. Why, there 'tis now; indeed, Uncle, you're too positive.

Sir *Rich.* And you too impertinent: Therefore I resolve you shall quit my House; you shan't keep your Revels under the Roof where I am.

Alp. I'd have you to know, Sir, my Lady keeps no Revels beneath her Quality.

Sir *Rich.* Hold your Tongue Mrs. *Pert*, or I shall display your Quality in its proper Colours.

Alp. I don't care, say your worst of me, and spare not; but for my Lady——my Lady's a Widow, and Widows are accountable to none for their Actions——Well, I shall have a Husband one of these Days, and be a Widow too, I hope.

Sir *Rich.* Not unlikely, for the Man will hang himself the next Day, I warrant him.

Alp. And if any Uncle pretends to controul my Actions——

Sir *Rich.* He'd lose his Labour, I'm certain——

Alp. I'd treat him——

Sir *Rich.* Don't provoke me, Hussy, don't.

Lady. Be gone, and wait in the next Room.

[*Exit* Alpiew.

Sir *Rich.* The Insolence of a Servant is a great Honour to the Lady, no doubt; but I shall find a Way to humble you both.

Lady. Lookye, Uncle, do what you can, I'm resolv'd to follow my own Inclinations.

Sir *Rich.* Which infallibly carry you to Noise, Nonsense, Foppery and Ruin; but no matter, you shall go out

out of my Doors, I'll promiſe you; my Houſe ſhall no longer bear the ſcandalous Name of a *Baſſet-Table*: Huſbands ſhall no more have Cauſe to date their Ruin from my Door, nor cry, There, there my Wife gam'd my Eſtate away—Nor Children curſe my Poſterity, for their Parents knowing my Houſe.

Lady. No more Threatning, good Uncle; act as you pleaſe, but don't ſcold, or I ſhall be oblig'd to call *Alpiew* again.

Sir *Rich*. Very well, very well, ſee what will come on't; the World will cenſure thoſe that game, and, in my Conſcience, I believe not without Cauſe.

For ſhe whoſe Shame no good Advice can wake,
When Money's wanting will her Virtue ſlake.

[Exit.

Lady. Advice! Ha, ha, ridiculous Advice.

Enter Lady Lucy.

No ſooner rid of one Miſchief but another follows— [*Aſide.*] I foreſee this to be a Day of Mortification, *Alpiew*.

Enter Alpiew.

Alp. Madam.

Lady My Uncle's gone, you may come in, ha, ha, ha.

L. *Lucy*. Fye, Couſin, does it become you to laugh at thoſe that give you Counſel for your Good?

Lady. For my Good! Oh, *mon cœur!* Now cannot I divine what 'tis that I do more than the reſt of the World to deſerve this Blame.

Alp. Nor I, for the Soul of me.

L. *Lucy*. Shou'd all the reſt of the World follow your Ladyſhip's Example, the Order of Nature would be inverted, and every Good deſign'd by Heaven, become a Curſe; Health and Plenty no longer would be known among us———You croſs the Purpoſe of the Day and Night; you wake when you ſhould ſleep, and make all who have any Dependance on you wake, while you repoſe.

Lady. Bleſs me! may not any Perſon ſleep when they pleaſe?

L.

L. *Lucy*. No; there are certain Hours that good Manners, Modesty, and Health, require your Care; for Example; disorderly Hours are neither heathful nor modest——And 'tis not civil to make Company wait Dinner for your Dressing.

Lady. Why does any Body dine before Four o'Clock in *London*? For my Part, I think it an ill-bred Custom to make my Appetite Pendulum to the Twelfth Hour.

Alp. Besides, 'tis out of Fashion to dine by Day-light; and so I told Sir *Richard* Yesterday, Madam.

L. *Lucy*. No doubt but you did, Mrs. *Alpiew*; and then you entertain such a Train of People, Cousin, that my Lady *Reveller* is as noted as a public Ordinary, where every Fool with Money finds a Welcome.

Lady. Would you have me shut my Doors against my Friends?—Now she is jealous of Sir *James Courtly* [*Aside*.] Besides, is it possible to pass the Evenings without Diversions?

Alp. No, certainly————

L. *Lucy*. I think the Playhouse the much more innocent and commendable Diversion.

Lady. To be seen there every Night, in my Opinion, is more destructive to the Reputation.

L. *Lucy*. Well; I had rather be noted every Night in the Front Box, than, by my Absence, once be suspected of Gaming; one ruins my Estate and Character, the other diverts my Temper, and improves my Mind. Then you have such a Number of Lovers.

Lady. Oh, *Cupid*! is it a Crime to have a Number of Lovers? If it be, 'tis the pleasantest Crime in the World. A Crime that falls not every Day to every Woman's Lot.

L. *Lucy*. I dare be positive every Woman does not wish it.

Lady. Because Wishes have no Effect, Cousin, ha, ha.

L. *Lucy*. Methinks my Lord *Worthy*'s Assiduity might have banish'd the admiring Crowd by this Time.

Lady. Banish'd 'em! Oh, *mon cœur*! what Pleasure is there in one Lover? 'tis like being seen always in one Suit of Cloaths; a Woman, with one Admirer, will ne'er be a reigning Toast.

L. *Lucy*. I am sure those that encourage more, will never have the Character of a reigning Virtue.

Lady.

Lady. I slight the malicious Censure of the Town, yet defy it to asperse my Virtue; Nature has given me a Face, a Shape, a Mein, an Air for Dress, and Wit and Humour to subdue: And shall I lose my Conquest for a Name?

Alp. Nay, and among the unfashionable Sort of People too, Madam; for Persons of Breeding and Quality will allow, that Gallantry and Virtue are not inseparable.

L. *Lucy.* But Coquetry and Reputation are; and there is no Difference in the Eye of the World, between having really committed the Fault, and lying under the Scandal; for my own Part, I would take as much Care to preserve my Fame, as you would your Virtue.

Lady. A little Pains will serve you for that, Cousin; for I never once heard you nam'd———A Mortification would break my Heart, ha, ha.

L. *Lucy.* 'Tis better never to be nam'd, than to be ill spoken of; but your Reflections shall not disorder my Temper. I could wish, indeed, to convince you of your Error, because you share my Blood; but since I see the Vanity of the Attempt, I shall desist.

Lady. I humbly thank your Ladyship.

Alp. Oh! Madam, here's my Lord *Worthy*, Sir *James Courtly*, and Ensign *Lovely* coming down; will your Ladyship see them?

Lady. Now have I a strong Inclination to engage Sir *James*, to discompose her Gravity; for if I have any Skill in Glances, she loves him. But then my Lord *Worthy* is so peevish since our late Quarrel, that I'm afraid to engage the Knight in a Duel; besides, my Absence, I know, will teize him more; therefore upon Consideration I'll retire. Cousin *Lucy*, good-Morrow. I'll leave you to better Company, there's a Person at hand may prevent your Six o'Clock Prayers. [*Exit.*

L. *Lucy.* Ha! Sir *James Courtly*—I must own I think him agreeable; but am sorry she believes I do. I'll not be seen, for if what I scarce know myself, be grown so visible to her, perhaps he too may discover it, and then I am lost.

While in the Breast our Secrets close remain,
'Tis out of Fortune's Power to give us Pain. [Exit.

Enter

Enter Lord Worthy, Sir *James, and Ensign* Lovely.

Sir *Jam.* Ha! was not that Lady *Lucy?*

Ensign. It was—Ah, Sir *James*, I find your Heart is out of Order about that Lady, and my Lord *Worthy* languishes for Lady *Reveller*.

Sir *Jam.* And thou art sick for *Valeria*, Sir *Richard*'s Daughter. A poor distressed Company of us.

Ensign. 'Tis true, that little She-Philosopher has made me do Penance more heartily than ever my Sins did; I deserve her by mere Dint of Patience. I have stood whole Hours to hear her assert, that Fire cannot burn, nor Water drown, nor Pain afflict, and Forty ridiculous Systems————

Sir *Jam.* And all her Experiments on Frogs, Fish, and Flies, ha, ha, without the least Contradiction.

Ensign. Contradiction, no, no, I allow'd all she said, with undoubtedly, Madam,———I am of your Mind, Madam, it must be so———natural Causes, *&c.*

Sir *Jam.* Ha, ha, ha, I think it is a supernatural Cause, which enables thee to go thro' this Fatigue; if it were not to raise thy Fortune, I should think thee mad to pursue her; but go on and prosper, nothing in my Power shall be wanting to assist you——My Lord *Worthy*, your Lordship is as melancholy as a losing Gamester.

Lord. Faith, Gentlemen, I'm out of Humour, but I don't know at what.

Sir *Jam.* Why then I can tell you; for the very same Reason that made your Lordship stay here to be Spectator of the very Diversion you hate, (Gaming) the same Cause makes you uneasy in all Company, my Lady *Reveller*.

Lord. Thou hast hit it, Sir *James*, I confess I love her Person, but hate her Humours, and her Way of Living; I have some Reasons to believe I'm not indifferent to her, yet I despair of fixing her, her Vanity has got so much the Mistress of her Resolution; and yet her Passion for Gain surmounts her Pride, and lays her Reputation open to the World. Every Fool that has ready Money shall dare to boast himself her very humble Servant; S'death, when I could cut the Rascal's Throat.

Sir *Jam.* Your Lordship is even with her one Way; for

for you are as testy as she's vain, and as fond of an Opportunity to quarrel with her, as she of a gaming Acquaintance; my Opinion is, my Lord, she'll ne'er be won your Way.

To gain all Women there's a certain Rule:
If Wit should fail to please, then act the Fool;
And where you find Simplicity not take,
Throw off Disguises, and profess the Rake;
Observe which Way their strongest Humours run,
They're by their own lov'd Cant the surest Way undone.

Lord. Thou'rt of a happy Temper, Sir *James*, I wish I could be so too; but since I can't add to your Diversion, I'll take my Leave; good Morrow, Gentlemen. [*Exit.*

Sir *Jam.* This it is to have more Love than Reason about one; you and I, *Lovely*, will go on with Discretion, and yet I fear it's in Lady *Lucy*'s Power to banish it.

Ensign. I find Mrs *Sago*, the Drugster's Wife's Interest, begins to shake, Sir *James*.

Sir *Jam.* And I fear her Love for Play begins to shake her Husband's Bags too. Faith, I am weary of that Intrigue, lest I should be suspected to have a Hand in his Ruin.

Ensign. She did not lose much to Night, I believe. Pr'ythee, Sir *James*, what kind of a temper'd Woman is she? Has she Wit?

Sir *Jam.* That she has—A large Portion, and as much Cunning, or she could never have manag'd the old Fellow so nicely; she has a vast Passion for my Lady *Reveller*, and endeavours to mimick her in every Thing. Not a Suit of Clothes, or a Top-knot, that is not exactly the same with her's. Then her Plots and Contrivances to supply these Expences, put her continually upon the Rack; yet to give her her Due, she has a fertile Brain that Way; but come, shall we go Home and sleep two or three Hours; at Dinner I'll introduce you to Captain *Hearty*, the Sea Officer, your Rival that is to be, he's just come to Town.

Ensign. A powerful Rival, I fear, for Sir *Richard* resolves to marry him to his Daughter; all my Hopes lie in in her Arguments, and you know Philosophers are very positive. And if this Captain does but happen to contradict one whimsical Notion, the Poles will as soon join, as they couple, and rather than yield, she would go to the *Indies* in search of *Dampier*'s Ants.

Sir *Jam.* Nay, she is no Woman if she obeys.

Women, like Tides, with Passions ebb and flow,
And like them too, their Source no Man can know.
To watch their Motions, is the safest Guide;
Who hits their Humour, sails with Wind and Tide. [Exit.

ACT II.

Enter Buckle, *meeting Mrs.* Alpiew.

Alp. GOOD-Morrow.

Buck. Good-Morrow.

Alp. Good-Morrow, good-Morrow, is that all your Business here? What means that affected Look, as if you long'd to be examin'd what's the Matter?

Buck. The Capricio's of Love, *Mademoiselle*; the Capricio's of Love.

Alp. Why! are you in Love?

Buck. I—in Love! No! the Devil take me, if ever I shall be infected with that Madness! 'tis enough for one in a Family to fall under the whimsical Circumstances of that Distemper. My Lord has a sufficient Portion for both; here—here—here's a Letter for your Lady; I believe the Contents are not so full of Stars, and Darts, and Flames, as they us'd to be.

Alp. My Lady will not concern herself with your Lord, nor his Letters neither, I can assure you that.

Buck. So much the better; I'll tell him what you say ———Have you no more?

Alp. Tell him it is not my Fault; I have done as much for his Service as lay in my Power, till I put her in so great a Passion, that 'tis impossible to appease her.

Buck. Very good—my Lord is upon the Square, I promise ye, as much inraged as her Ladyship to the full.

Well,

Well, Mrs. *Alpiew*, to the longest Day of his Life, he swears never to forget Yesterday's Adventure, that has given him perfect, perfect Liberty.

Alp. I believe so——What was it, pray?

Buck. I'll tell you; 'twas Matter of Consequence, I assure you, I've known Lovers part for a less Trifle by half.

Alp. No Digressions, but to the Point, what was it?

Buck. This——my Lord, was at the Fair with your Lady.

Alp. What of that?

Buck. In a Raffling-Shop she saw a young Gentleman, which she said was very handsome—At the same Time, my Lord praised a young Lady; she redoubles her Commendations of the Beau——He enlarges on the Beauty of the Belle; their Discourse grew warm on the Subject; they pause; she begins again with the Perfections of the Gentleman; he ends with the same of the Lady: Thus they pursued their Arguments, still finding such mighty Charms in their new Favourites, till they found one another so ugly—so ugly—that they parted with full Resolution never to meet again.

Alp. Ha, ha, ha, pleasant; well, if you have no more to tell me, adieu.

Buck. Stay a Moment, I see my Lord coming, I thought he'd follow me. Oh! Lovers Resolutions.

Enter Lord Worthy.

Lord. So, have you seen my Lady *Reveller*? [*To* Buck.

Alp. My Lord——

Lord. Ha! Mrs. *Alpiew*. [*Gives him his own Letter*.

Buck. Here's your Lordship's Letter.

Lord. An Answer! She has done me very much Honour.

Alp. My Lord, I am commanded——

Lord. Hold a little, dear Mrs. *Alpiew*. [*All this while he is opening the Letter, thinking it from the Lady*.]

Buck. My Lord, she would not——

Lord. Be quiet, I say——

Alp. I am very sorry——

Lord. But a Moment——Ha! Why this is my own Letter.

Buck.

Buck. Yes, my Lord.

Lord. Yes, my Lord—— What, ſhe'd not receive it then?

Buck. No, my Lord.

Lord. How durſt you ſtay ſo long.

Alp. I beg your Lordſhip not to harbour an ill Opinion of me; I oppoſed her Anger with my utmoſt Skill, prais'd all your Actions, all your Parts, but all in vain.

Lord. Enough, enough, Madam; ſhe has taken the beſt Method in the World—Well, then we are ne'er to meet again.

Alp. I know not that, my Lord———

Lord. I rejoice at it, by my Life I do; ſhe has only prevented me; I came on purpoſe to break with her——

Buck. [*Aſide*.] Yes, ſo 'twas a Sign, by the Pleaſure you diſcover'd in thinking ſhe had writ to you.

Lord. I ſuppoſe ſhe has entertain'd you with the Cauſe of this.

Alp. No, my Lord, never mention'd a Syllable, only ſaid, ſhe had forever done with you; and charg'd me, as I valu'd her Favour, to receive no Meſſage nor Letter from you.

Lord. May I become the very'ſt Wretch alive, and all the Ills imaginable fall upon my Head, if I ſpeak to her more; nay, ever think of her but with Scorn—Where is ſhe now? [*Walks about*.

Alp. In her Dreſſing-Room.

Lord. There let her be; I am weary of her fantaſtic Humours, affected Airs, and unaccountable Paſſions.

Buck. For half an Hour. [*Aſide*.

Lord. Do you know what ſhe's doing?

Alp. I believe, my Lord, trying on a Mantua; I left her with Mrs. *Pleatwell*, and that us'd to hold her a great while, for the Woman is ſaucily familiar with all the Quality, and tells her all the Scandal.

Lord. And conveys Letters upon Occaſion; 'tis tack'd to their Profeſſion—But, my Lady *Reveller* may do what ſhe pleaſes, I am no more her Slave, upon my Word; I have broke my Chain—She has not been out then ſince ſhe roſe.

Alp. No, my Lord.

Lord. Nay, if she has, or has not, 'tis the same Thing to me; she may go to the End of the World, if she will, I shan't take any Pains to follow her———Whose Footman was that I met?

Alp. I know not, my Lord, we have so many come with How-d'ye's, I ne'er mind them.

Lord. You are uneasy, Child; come, I'll not detain you, I have no Curiosity, I protest I'm satisfied if she's so; I assure ye, let her despise me, let her hate me, 'tis all one; adieu. [*Going.*

Alp. My Lord, your Servant.

Lord. Mrs. *Alpiew*, let me beg one Favour of you, [*turns back*] not to say I was here.

Alp. I'll do just as you please, my Lord.

Lord. Do that then, and you'll oblige me.

[*Is going, and comes back often.*

Alp. I will.

Lord. Don't forget.

Alp. Your Lordship may depend upon me.

Lord. Hold! now I think on't—Pray tell her you did see me, do you hear?

Alp. With all my Heart.

Lord. Tell her how indifferent she is to me in every respect.

Alp. I shan't fail.

Lord. Tell her every Thing just as I exprest it to you.

Alp. I will.

Lord. Adieu. [*Going.*

Alp. Your Servant.

Lord. Now I think on't, Mrs. *Alpiew*, I have a great Mind she should know my Sentiments from my own Mouth.

Alp. Nay, my Lord, I can't promise you that.

Lord. Why?

Alp. Because she has expresly forbid your Admittance.

Lord. I'd speak but one Word with her.

Alp. Impossible.

Lord. Pugh, pr'ythee let me see her. [*Intreating.*

Buck. So, now all this mighty Rage ends in a begging Submission.

Lord. Only tell her I'm here.

Alp.

Alp. Why ſhould you deſire me to meet her Anger, my Lord.

Lord. Come, you ſhall oblige me once.

[*Puts a Ring upon her Finger.*

Alp. O dear, my Lord, you have ſuch a Command over your Servant, I can refuſe nothing. [*Exit.*

Lord. Have you been at the Goldſmith's about the Bills, for I am fix'd on Travelling.

Buck. Your Lordſhip's ſo diſturb'd, you have forgot you countermanded me, and ſent me hither.

Lord. True.

Enter Mrs. Alpiew.

Alp. Juſt as I told your Lordſhip, ſhe fell in a moſt violent Paſſion at the bare mention of your Name: Tell him, ſaid ſhe, in an heroic Strain, I'll never ſee him more and commanded him to quit that Room, for I'm coming thither.

Lord. Tyrant, curſe on my Folly, ſhe knows her Power; well, I hope I may walk in the Gallery; I would ſpeak with her Uncle.

Alp. To be ſure, my Lord. [*Exit Lord* Worthy.

Buck. Learn, Miſtreſs, learn, you may come to make me mad in Time, ha, ha, ha.

Alp. Go, Fool, follow your Lord. [*Exit* Buck.

Enter Lady Reveller.

Lady. Well, I'll ſwear, *Alpiew,* you have given me the Vapours for all Day.

Alp. Ah! Madam, if you had ſeen him, you muſt have had Compaſſion; I would not have ſuch a Heart of Adamant for the World; poor Lord, ſure you have the ſtrangeſt Power over him.

Lady. Silly—one often fancies one has Power, when one has none at all; I'll tell thee, *Alpiew,* he vex'd me ſtrangely before this grand Quarrel; I was at *Piquet* with my Lady *Lovewit* four Nights ago, and bid him read me a new Copy of Verſes, becauſe, you know, he never plays, and I did not well know what to do with him; he had ſcarce begun, when I, being eager at a Pique, he roſe up and ſaid, he believ'd I lov'd the Muſic of my own

Voice,

Voice, (crying Nine and Twenty, Threeſcore) better than the ſweeteſt Poetry in the Univerſe, and abruptly left us.

Alp. A great Crime, indeed, not to read; when People are at a Game they are oblig'd to talk all the while.

Lady. Crime; yes, indeed was it, for my Lady loves Poetry better than Play, and perhaps before the Poem had been done, had loſt her Money to me. But I wonder, *Alpiew,* by what Art 'tis you engage me in this Diſcourſe, why ſhould I talk of a Man that's utterly my Averſion———Have you heard from Mrs. *Sago* this Morning?

Alp. Certainly, Madam, ſhe never fails; ſhe has ſent your Ladyſhip the fineſt Cargo, made up of Chocolate, Tea, *Montifiaſco* Wine, and fifty Rarities beſide, with ſomething to remember me, good Creature, that ſhe never forgets. Well, indeed, Madam, ſhe is the beſt-natur'd Woman in the World; it grieves me to think what Sums ſhe loſes at play.

Lady. Oh, fye, ſhe muſt; a Citizen's Wife is not to be endur'd amongſt Quality; had ſhe not Money, 'twere impoſſible to receive her———

Alp. Nay, indeed, I muſt ſay that of you Women of Quality, if there is but Money enough, you ſtand not upon Birth or Reputation, in either Sex; if you did, ſo many Sharpers of *Covent-Garden,* and Miſtreſſes of St. *James*'s, would not be daily admitted.

Lady. Peace, Impertinence, you take ſtrange Freedoms. [*Enter* Valeria *running.*

Why in ſuch Haſte, Couſin *Valeria?* [*Stopping her.*

Val. Oh! dear Couſin, don't ſtop me, I ſhall loſe the fineſt Inſect for Diſſection, a huge Fleſh Fly, which Mr. *Lovely* ſent me juſt now, and opening the Box to try the Experiment, away it flew.

Lady. I am glad the poor Fly eſcap'd; will you never be weary of theſe Whimſies?

Val. Whimſies! natural Philoſophy a Whimſy! Oh! the unlearned World.

Lady. Ridiculous Learning!

Alp. Ridiculous indeed, for Women; Philoſophy ſuits our Sex, as Jack-Boots would do.

Val. Cuſtom would bring them as much in Faſhion as

Furbeloes, and Practice would make us as valiant as e'er a Hero of them all; the Resolution is in the Mind —Nothing can enslave that.

Lady. My Stars! this Girl will be mad, that's certain.

Val. Mad! so *Nero* banish'd Philosophers from *Rome*, and the first Discoverer of the *Antipodes* was condemn'd for a Heretic.

Lady. In my Conscience, *Alpiew*, this pretty Creature's spoil'd. Well, Cousin, might I advise, you should bestow your Fortune in founding a College for the Study of Philosophy, where none but Women should be admitted; and to immortalize your Name, they should be called *Valerians*, ha, ha, ha.

Val. What you make a Jest of, I'd execute, were Fortune in my Power.

Alp. All Men would not be excluded; the handsome Ensign, Madam.

Lady. In Love! Nay, there's no Philosophy against Love; *Solon* for that.

Val. 'Pshaw, no more of this trifling Subject; Cousin, will you believe there's any Thing without Gall.

Lady. I am satisfy'd I have one, when I lose at play, or see a Lady address'd when I am by; and 'tis equal to me, whether the rest of the Creation have or not.

Val. Well, but I'll convince you then; I have dissected my Dove——and positively I think the vulgar Notion true, for I could find none,

Lady. Oh, barbarous! kill'd your pretty Dove. [*Starting.*

Val. Kill'd it! Why, what did you imagine I bred it up for? Can Animals, Insects, or Reptiles, be put to a nobler Use than to improve our Knowledge? Cousin, I'll give you this Jewel for your *Italian* Greyhound.

Lady. What to cut to Pieces? Oh, horrid! he had need be a Soldier that ventures on you; for my Part, I should dream of nothing but Incision, Dissection, and Amputation, and always fancy the Knife at my Throat.

Enter Servant.

Serv. Madam, here's Sir *Richard*, and a——

Val. A——What, is it an Accident, a Substance, a Material Being, or a Being of Reason?

Serv.

Serv. I don't know what you call a Material Being, it is a Man.

Val. 'Pſhaw, a Man, that's nothing.

Lady. She'll prove by and by, out of, *Deſcartes* that we are all Machines.

Enter Sir Richard, *and Capt.* Firebrand.

Alp. Oh, Madam, do you ſee who obſerves you? My Lord walking in the Gallery, and every Minute gives a Peep.

Lady. Does he ſo! I'll fit him for Eves-dropping—

Sir *Rich.* Sir, I like the Relation you have given me of your Naval Expedition; your Diſcourſe ſpeaks you a Man fit for the Sea

Capt. You had it without a Flouriſh, Sir *Richard*; my Word is this, I hate the *French*, love a handſome Woman, and a Bowl of Punch.

Val. Very blunt.

Sir *Rich.* This is my Daughter, Captain, a Girl of ſober Education; ſhe underſtands nothing of Gaming, Parks, or Plays.

Alp. But wanting theſe Diverſions, ſhe has ſupply'd the Vacancy with greater Follies. [*Aſide.*

Capt. A tight little Frigate [*Salutes her.*] 'Faith, I think ſhe looks like a freſh Man Sea-ſick——But here's a gallant Veſſel—with all her Streamers out, Top and Top-Gallant—with your Leave, Madam, [*Salutes her.*] Who is that Lady, Sir *Richard*?

Sir *Rich.* 'Tis a Niece of mine, Captain—tho' I am ſorry ſhe is ſo; ſhe values nothing that does not ſpend their Days at their Glaſs, and their Nights at *Baſſet*; ſuch who ne'er did good to their Prince, nor Country, except their Taylor, Peruke-maker, and Perfumer.

Lady. Fye, fye, Sir, believe him not, I have a Paſſion, an extreme Paſſion for a Hero—eſpecially if he belongs to the Sea; methinks he has an Air ſo fierce, ſo piercing, his very Looks commands Reſpect from his own Sex, and all the Hearts of ours.

Sir *Rich* The Devil——Now, rather than let another Female have a Man to herſelf, ſhe'll make the firſt Advances. [*Aſide.*

Capt. Ay, Madam, we are preferr'd by you fine Ladies, sometimes before the sprucer Sparks——there's a Conveniency in't; a fair Wind, and we hale out, and leave you Liberty and Money, two Things the most acceptable to a Wife in Nature.

Lady. Oh! ay, it's so pretty to have one's Husband gone Nine Months of the Twelve; and then to bring one home fine China, fine Lace, fine Muslin, and fine *Indian* Birds, and a thousand Curiosities.

Sir *Rich.* No, no; Nine is a little too long, Six would do better for one of your Constitution, Mistress.

Capt. Well, Madam, what think you of a cruising Voyage towards the Cape of Matrimony, your Father designs me for the Pilot; if you agree to it, we'll hoist Sail immediately.

Val. I agree to any Thing dictated by good Sense, and comprehended within the Borders of Elocution; the Converse I hold with your Sex, is only to improve and cultivate the Notions of my Mind.

Sir *Rich.* What the Devil is she going upon now? [*Aside.*

Val. I presume you are a Mariner, Sir——

Capt. I have the Honour to bear the Queen's Commission, Madam.

Val. Pray speak properly, positively, laconically, and naturally.

Lady. So; she has given him a Broadside already.

Capt. Laconically! Why, why, what is your Daughter, Sir *Richard*? ha.

Sir *Rich.* May I be reduc'd to wooden Shoes, if I can tell you, the Devil: had I liv'd near a College, the Haunts of some Pedant might have brought this Curse upon me; but to have got my Estate in the City, and to have a Daughter run mad after Philosophy, I'll ne'er suffer it in the Rage I am in; I'll throw all the Books and Mathematical Instruments out of the Window.

Lady. I dare say, Uncle, you have shook Hands with Philosophy——for I'm sure you have banish'd Patience, ha, ha, ha.

Sir *Rich.* And you Discretion—By all my Hatred for the *French*, they'll drive me mad: Captain, I'll expect you in the next Room; and you Mrs. *Laconick*, with your Philoſophy at your Tail. [*Exit.*

Lady. Shan't I come too, Uncle, ha, ha.

Capt. By *Neptune*, this is a kind of a whimſical Family. Well, Madam, what was you going to ſay ſo poſitively and properly, and ſo forth?

Val. I would have aſk'd you, Sir, if ever you had the Curioſity to inſpect a Mermaid———Or if you are convinc'd there is a World in every Star———We, by our Teleſcopes, find Seas, Groves and Plains, and all that; but what they are peopled with, there's the Quere.

Capt. Let your next Contrivance be how to get thither, and then you'll know a World in every Star—Ha, ha, ſhe's fitter for *Moorfields* than Matrimony; pray, Madam, are you always infected, Full and Change, with this Diſtemper?

Val. How has my Reaſon err'd, to hold Converſe with an irrational Being———Dear, dear Philoſophy, what immenſe Pleaſures dwell in thee!

Enter Servant.

Serv. Madam, *John* has got the Fiſh you ſent him in ſearch of.

Val. Is it alive?

Serv. Yes, Madam.

Val. Your Servant, your Servant, I wou'd not loſe the Experiment for any Thing, but the Tour of the new World. [*Exit.*

Capt. Ha, ha, ha, is your Ladyſhip troubled with theſe Vagaries too? Is the whole Houſe poſſeſt?

Lady. Not I, Captain, the ſpeculative Faculty is not my Talent; I am for the Practice, can liſten all Day to hear you talk of Fire, ſubſtantial Fire, Rear and Front, and Line of Battle—admire a Sea-man, hate the *French*—love a Bowl of Punch: Oh! nothing ſo agreeable as your Converſation, nothing ſo jaunty as a Sea Captain.

Alp. So; this engages him to play,—if he has either Manners or Money. [*Aſide.*

Capt. Ay; give me the Woman that can hold me tack in my own Dialect—She's mad too, I ſuppoſe, but I'll humour her a little. [*Aſide.*] Oh, Madam, not a fair Wind, nor a rich Prize, nor Conqueſt o'er my Enemies, can pleaſe like you; accept my Heart without Capitulation——'Tis yours, a Priſoner at Diſcretion. [*Kiſſes her Hand.*

Enter Lord Worthy.

Lord. Hold, Sir, you muſt there contend with me; the Victory is not ſo eaſy as you imagine.

Lady. Oh, fye, my Lord, you won't fight for one you hate and deſpiſe? I may truſt you with the Captain; ha, ha, ha. [*Exit.*

Capt. This muſt be her Lover——and he is mad another Way: This is the moſt unaccountable Family I ever met with. [*Aſide.*] Look ye, Sir, what you mean by contending, I know not; but I muſt tell you, I don't think any Woman I have ſeen ſince I came aſhore, worth fighting for. The philoſophical Gimcrack I don't value of a Cockle-Shell. And am too well acquainted with the Danger of Rocks and Quick-ſands, to ſteer into t'other's Harbour.

Lord. He has diſcover'd her already; I, only I am blind. [*Aſide.*

Capt. But, Sir, if you have a mind to a Breathing, here, tread upon my Toe, or ſpeak but one Word in favour of the *French*, or againſt the Courage of our Fleet, and my Sword will ſtart of itſelf, to do its Maſter and my Country Juſtice.

Lord. How ridiculous do I make myſelf———Pardon me, Sir, you are in the right. I confeſs I ſcarce knew what I did.

Capt. I thought ſo, poor Gentleman, I pity him: this is the Effect of Love on Shore--When do we hear of a Tar in theſe Fits, longer than the firſt freſh Gale--Well, I'll into Sir *Richard*, eat with him, drink with him; but to match into his Generation, I'd as ſoon marry one of his Daughter's Mermaids. [*Exit.*

Lord. Was ever Man ſo ſtupid as myſelf? But I will rouſe from this lethargic Dream, and ſeek elſewhere what is deny'd at home; Abſence may reſtore my Liberty.

Enter

Enter Mr. Sago.

Sago. Pray, my Lord, did you ſee my *Keecky?*

Lord. *Keecky*, what's that?

Sago. My Wife, you muſt know, I call her *Keecky*, ha, ha.

Lord. Not I, indeed——

Sago. Nay, pray my Lord ben't angry, I only want to tell her what a Preſent of fine Wine is ſent her juſt now; and ha, ha, ha, ha what makes me laugh—is, that no Soul can tell from whence it comes.

Lord. Your Wife knows, no doubt.

Sago. No more than myſelf, my Lord—We have often Wine and Sweatmeats; nay, whole Pieces of Silk, and the Duce take me if ſhe could deviſe from whence; nay, ſometimes ſhe has been for ſending them back again, but I cry'd, whoſe a Fool then.

Lord. I'm ſure thou art one in Perfection, and to me inſupportable. [*Going.*

Sago. My Lord, I know your Lordſhip has the Privilege of this Houſe, pray do me the Kindneſs, if you find my Wife, to ſend her out to me. [*Exit.* Lord.] I ne'er ſaw ſo much of this Lord's Humour before; he is very ſurly, methinks——Adod, there are ſome Lords of my Wife's Acquaintance, as civil and familiar with me, as I am with my Journeyman—Oh! here ſhe comes.

Enter Mrs. Sago, *and* Alpiew.

Mrs. *Sago.* Oh, Puddy, ſee what my Lady *Reveller* has preſented me withal.

Sago. Hey, Keecky, why ſure you riſe—as the Saying is, for at Home there's four Hampers of Wine ſent ye.

Mrs. *Sago.* from whence, dear Puddy?

Sago. Nay, there's the Jeſt, neither you nor I know. I offer'd the Rogue that brought it a Guinea to tell from whence it came, and he ſwore he durſt not.

Mrs. *Sago.* No, if he had, I'd never have employ'd him again. [*Aſide.*

Sago. So I gave him half a Crown, and let him go.

Mrs. *Sago.* It comes very opportunely; pray, Puddy, ſend a Couple of the Hampers to my Lady *Reveller*'s, as a ſmall Acknowledgment for the rich Preſent ſhe has made me.

Sago. With all my Heart, my Jewel, my Precious.

Mrs. *Sago*. Puddy I am ſtrangely oblig'd to Mrs. *Alpiew*; do, Puddy, do, dear Puddy.

Sago. What?

Mrs. *Sago*. Will ye, then? Do, dear Puddy, do, lend me a Guinea to give her, do.

[*Hanging upon him in a wheedling Tone.*

Sago. 'Pſhaw, you are always wanting Guineas; I'll ſend her half a Pound of Tea, Keecky.

Mrs. *Sago*. Tea—ſha—ſhe drinks Ladies Tea; do, dear Puddy do; can you deny, Keecky, now?

Sago. Well, well, there. [*Gives it her.*

Mrs. *Sago*. Mrs. *Alpiew*, will you pleaſe to lay the Silk by for me, till I ſend for it, and accept of that?

Alp. Your Servant, Madam, I'll be careful of it.

Mrs. *Sago*. Thank ye, borrow as much as you can on't, dear *Alpiew*. [*Aſide to her.*

Alp. I warrant you, Madam. [*Exit.*

Mrs. *Sago*. I muſt raiſe a Sum for *Baſſet* againſt Night.

Sago Pr'ythee, *Keecky*, what kind of humour'd Man is Lord *Worthy*? I did but aſk him if he ſaw thee, and I thought he wou'd have ſnapp'd my Noſe off.

Mrs. *Sago*. Oh, a mere Woman, full of Spleen and Vapours, he and I never agree.

Sago. Adod, I thought ſo—I gueſs'd he was none of thy Admirers—ha, ha, ha; why there's my Lord *Courttall*, and my Lord *Horncit*, bow down to the Ground to me where ever they meet me.

Enter Alpiew.

Alp. Madam, Madam, the Goldſmith has ſent in the Plate.

Mrs. *Sago*. Very well, take it along with the Silk.

[*Aſide to her.*

Alp. Here's the Jeweller, Madam, with the Diamond Ring, but he don't ſeem willing to leave it without Money. [*Exit* Alpiew.

Mrs. *Sago*. Humph! I have a ſudden Thought; bid him ſtay, and bring me the Ring———Now for the Art of Wheedling———

Sago.

Sago. What are you whiſpering about? Ha! Precious———

Mrs. *Sago.* Mrs. *Alpiew* ſays, a Friend of her's has a Diamond Ring to ſell, a great Pennyworth, and I know you love a Bargain, Puddy.

Enter Alpiew, *gives her the Ring.*

Sago. 'Pſhaw, I don't care for Rings; it may be a Bargain, and it may not; and I can't ſpare Money; I have paid for a Lot this Morning; conſider Trade muſt go forward, Lambkin.

Alp. See how it ſparkles.

Mrs. *Sago.* Nay, Puddy, if it be not worth your Money, I don't deſire you to buy it; but don't it become my Finger, Puddy? See now———

Sago. Ah! that Hand, that Hand it was which firſt got hold of my Heart; well, what's the Price of it? Ha, I am raviſh'd to ſee it upon *Keecky*'s Finger———

Mrs. *Sago.* What did he ſay the Price of it was? [*To* Alpiew.

Alp. Two hundred Guineas, Madam. [*Aſide to Mrs.* Sago.

Mrs. *Sago.* Threeſcore Pounds, dear Pudd:—The Devil's in't if he won't give that. [*Aſide.*

Sago. Threeſcore Pounds! Why 'tis worth a Hundred, Child, richly—'tis ſtole—'tis ſtole———

Alp. Stole! I'd have you to know, the Owner is my Relation, and has been as great a Merchant as any in *London*, but has had the Misfortune to have his Ships fall into the Hands of the *French*, or he'd not have parted with it at ſuch a Rate; it coſt him two hundred Guineas.

Mrs. *Sago.* I believe as much; indeed it is very fine.

Sago. So it is, *Keecky*, and that dear little Finger ſhall have it too; let me bite it a little tiny Bit— [*Bites her Finger.*

Mrs. *Sago.* Oh! dear Pudd, you hurt me.

Sago. Here—I han't ſo much Money about me, but there's a Bill, Lambkin——there now, you'll buſs poor Puddy now, won't you?

Mrs. *Sago.* Buſs him—yes, that I will, agen and agen, and agen, dear Pudd. [*Flies about his Neck.*

Sago. You'll go home with Puddy now to Dinner, won't you?

Mrs. *Sago.* Yes—a—dear Puddy, if you desire it—— I will—but—a—

Sago. But what?

Mrs. *Sago.* But I promis'd my Lady *Reveller* to dine with her, Deary—Do, let me, Pud—I'll dine with you To-morrow-day.

Alp. Nay, I'm sure my Lady won't eat a Bit, if she don't stay.

Sago. Well, they are all so fond of my Wife; my *Keecky*, shew me thy little Finger agen——O dear little Finger, my *Keecky!* [*Exit.*

Mrs. *Sago.* My nown Pudd—— Here *Alpiew*, give him his Ring agen, I have my End; tell him 'tis too dear. [*Aside.*

Alp. But what will you say when Mr. *Sago* misses it?

Mrs. *Sago.* I'll say—that it was too big for my Finger, and I lost it; 'tis but a Crying-bout, and the good Man melts into Pity.

I'th' married State, this only Bliss we find,
An easy Husband to our Wishes kind.
I've gain'd my Point, replenish'd Purse once more,
Oh! cast me, Fortune, on the winning Shore:
Now let me gain what I have lost before. [Exit.

ACT III.

The SCENE *draws, and discovers* Valeria *with Books upon a Table, a Microscope, putting a Fish upon it, several Animals lying by.*

Val. 'PSHAW! Thou fluttering Thing — So, now I've fix'd it.

Enter Alpiew.

Alp. Madam, here's Mr. *Lovely*; I have introduced him

him as one of my Lady's Visitors, and brought him down the Back-Stairs.

Val. I'm oblig'd to you, he comes opportunely.

Enter Lovely.

O Mr. *Lovely!* come, come here, look through this Glass, and see how the Blood circulates in the Tail of this Fish.

Lov. Wonderful! but it circulates prettier in this fair Neck.

Val. 'Pshaw—be quiet—I'll shew you a Curiosity, the greatest that ever Nature made.— [*Opens a Box.*] In opening a Dog the other Day, I found this Worm.

Lov. Prodigious! 'Tis the Joint-Worm, which the Learned talk of so much.

Val. Ay; the *Lumbricus*, *Lætus*, or *Fæscia*, as *Hippocrates* calls it, or vulgarly in English, the Tape-Worm—*Thudæus* tells us of one of these Worms found in a Human Body, two hundred Feet long, without Head or Tail.

Lov. I wish they be not got into thy Brain. [*Aside.* Oh, you charm me with these Discoveries.

Val. Here's another Sort of Worm call'd *Lumbricus teres Intestinalis.*

Lov. I think the first you shew'd me the greatest Curiosity.

Val. 'Tis very odd, really, that there should be every Inch a Joint, and every Joint a Mouth——Oh, the profound Secrets of Nature!

Lov. 'Tis strangely surprizing——But now let me be heard, for mine's the Voice of Nature too; methinks you neglect yourself, the most perfect Piece of all her Works.

Val. Why, what Fault do you find in me?

Lov. You have not Love enough; that Fire would consume and banish all Studies but its own; your Eyes would sparkle, and spread I know not what, of Lively and Touching, o'er the whole Face; this Hand when press'd by him you Love, would tremble to your Heart.

Val. Why so it does——Have I not told you twenty Times I love you?——for I hate Disguise; your Temper being adapted to mine, gave my Soul the first Impreſſion;——You know my Father's poſitive,——but do not believe he ſhall force me to any Thing that does not love Philoſophy.

Lov. But that Sea Captain, *Valeria.*

Val. If he was a Whale, he might give you Pain, for I ſhould long to diſſect him; but as he is a Man, you have no Reaſon to fear him.

Lov. Conſent then to fly with me.

Val. What, and leave my Microſcope, and all my Things for my Father to break in Pieces?

Sir *Rich.* *Valeria, Valeria.* [*Within.*

Val. O Heavens! he is coming up the Back-Stairs. What ſhall we do?

Lov. Humph; ha, can't you put me in that Cloſet there?

Val. Oh, no, I han't the Key.

Lov. I'll run down the great Stairs, let who will ſee me. [*Going.*

Val. Oh no, no, no, no, not for your Life;—here, here, get under this Tub.

[*Throws out ſome Fiſh in haſte and turns the Tub over him.*

Sir, I'm here.

Enter Sir Richard.

Sir *Rich.* What, at your Whims—and Whirligigs, ye Baggage! I'll out at Window with them.

[*Throwing away the Things.*

Val. Oh! dear Father, ſave my *Lumbricus Lætus.*

Sir *Rich.* I'll Lamprey and Latum you; what's that I wonder? Ha! Where the Devil got you Names that your Father don't underſtand? Ha? [*Treads upon them.*

Val. Oh, my poor Worm! Now you have deſtroy'd a Thing, that, for ought I know, *England* can't produce again.

Sir *Rich.* What is it good for? Anſwer me that. What's this Tub here for? Ha? [*Kicks it.*

Val. What ſhall I do now?——it is a—'tis a——Oh dear Sir! don't touch the Tub——for there's a Bear's young Cub that I have bought for Diſſection,——but I dare not touch it till the Keeper comes.

Sir *Rich.* I'll Cub you, and Keeper you, with a Vengeance

geance to you; is my Money laid out in Bears Cubs? — I'll drive out your Cub—[*Opens the Door, stands at a Distance off, and with his Cane lifts up the Tub*, Lovely *rises*.

Lov. Oh the Devil! discover'd; your Servant, Sir. [*Exit*.

Sir *Rich*. Oh! your Servant, Sir—What is this your Bear's Cub? Ha, Mistress! His Taylor has lick'd him into Shape, I find——What did this Man do here? Ha, Hussy?—I doubt you have been studying Natural Philosophy, with a Vengeance.

Val. Indeed, Sir, he only brought me a strange Fish, and hearing your Voice, I was afraid you would be angry, and so that made me hide him.

Sir *Rich*. A Fish! 'tis the Flesh I fear; I'll have you married To-night —— I believe this Fellow was the beggarly Ensign, who never march'd farther than from *Whitehall* to the *Tower*, who wants your Portion to make him a Brigadier, without ever seeing a Battle — Hussy, ha—tho' your philosophical Cant, with a Murrain to you—has put the Captain out of Conceit, I have a Husband still for you; come along, come along, I'll send the Servants to clear this Room of your Baubles. [*Pulls her off*.] I will so.

Val. But the Servants won't, old Gentleman, that's my Comfort still. [*Exit*.

Re-enter Lovely.

Lov. I'm glad they are gone, for the Duce take me if I could hit the Way out.

Enter Sir James.

Sir *Jam*. Ha—Ensign! luckily met; I have been labouring for you, and I hope done you a Piece of Service. Why, you look surpriz'd.

Lov. Surpriz'd! so wou'd you, Sir *James*, if you had been whelm'd under a Tub, without Room to breathe.

Sir *Jam*. Under a Tub! ha, ha, ha.

Lov. 'Twas the only Place of Shelter.

Sir *Jam*. Come, come, I have a better Prospect; the Captain is a very honest Fellow, and thinks if you can bear with the Girl, you deserve her Fortune; here's your

your Part, [*Gives a Paper.*] he'll give you your Cue; he ſtays at his Lodgings for you.

Lov. What's the Deſign?

Sir *Jam.* That will tell you; quick Diſpatch.

Lov. Well, Sir *James*, I know you have a prolific Brain, and will rely on your Contrivances, and if it ſucceeds, the Captain ſhall have a Bowl of Punch large enough to ſet his Ship afloat. [*Exit.*

Enter Lady Reveller, *Lady* Lucy, *and Mrs.* Sago.

Sir *Jam.* The Tea-Table broke up already! I fear there has been but ſmall Recruits of Scandal To-day.

Mrs. *Sago.* Well, I'll ſwear I think the Captain's a pleaſant Fellow.

Sir *Jam.* That's becauſe he made his Court to her. [*Aſide.*

L. *Revel.* Oh—I nauſeate thoſe amphibious Creatures.

Sir *Jam.* Umph, ſhe was not addreſs'd to.

L. *Lucy.* He ſeems neither to want Senſe, Honour, nor true Courage; and methinks there is a Beauty in his plain Delivery.

Sir *Jam.* There ſpoke Sincerity without Affectation.

L. *Revel.* How ſhall we paſs the Afternoon?

Sir *Jam.* Ay, Ladies, how ſhall we?

L. *Revel.* You here! I thought you had liſted yourſelf Volunteer under the Captain, to board ſome Prize, you whiſper'd ſo often, and ſneak'd out one after another.

Sir *Jam.* Who would give one ſelf the Pains to cruiſe Abroad, when all one values is at Home?

L. *Revel.* To whom is this directed? Or will you monopolize and ingroſs us all?

Sir *Jam.* No,—tho' you would wake Deſire in every Beholder, I reſign you to my worthy Friend.

L. *Lucy.* And the reſt of the Company have no Pretence to you.

Mrs. *Sago.* That's more than ſhe knows. [*Aſide.*

Sir *Jam.* Beauty, like yours, would give all Mankind Pretence.

Mrs *Sago.* So, not a Word to me; are theſe his Vows? [*In an uneaſy Air.*

L. *Lucy.* There's one upon the Teize already. [*Aſide.*

L. *Revel.* Why, you are in Diſorder, my Dear; you look

look as if you had loſt a *Trant Leva:* What have you ſaid to her, Sir *James?*

Sir *Jam.* I ſaid, Madam! I hope I never ſay any Thing to offend the Ladies. The Devil's in theſe married Women, they can't conceal their own Intrigues, though they ſwear us to Secrecy. [*Aſide.*

L. *Lucy.* You miſtake, Couſin; 'tis his ſaying nothing to her has put her upon the Fret.

L. *Revel.* Ah! your Obſervations are always malicious.

Mrs. *Sago.* I deſpiſe them dear Lady *Reveller*, let's in to Picquet; I ſuppoſe Lady *Lucy* would be pleas'd with Sir *James* alone to finiſh her Remarks.

L. *Lucy.* Nay, if you remove the Cauſe, the Diſcourſe ceaſes.

Sir *Jam.* [*Going up to her.*] This you draw upon your ſelf; you will diſcover it. [*To her.*

Mrs. *Sago.* Yes your Falſhood.

L. *Revel.* Come, my dear Sir *James*, will you make one at a Pool?

Sir *Jam.* Pardon me, Madam, I'm to be at *White*'s in half an Hour, anon at the *Baſſet-Table*. I'm yours.

Mrs. *Sago.* No, no, he can't leave her.

[*Going, ſtill looking back.*

L. *Lucy.* They play Gold, Sir *James.*

Sir *Jam.* [*Going up to Lady* Lucy.] Madam, were your Heart the Stake, I'd renounce all Engagements to win that, or retrieve my own.

L. *Lucy.* I muſt like the Counter-ſtake very well, e'er I play ſo high.

Mrs. *Sago.* Sir *James*, harkye, one Word with you.

[*Breaking from Lady* Reveller'*s Hand, pulling Sir* James *by the Sleeve.*

L. *Lucy.* Ha, ha, I knew ſhe could not ſtir; I'll remove your Conſtraint, but with my wonted Freedom, will tell you plainly—your Huſband's Shop would better become you than Gaming and Gallants. Oh Shame to Virtue, that Women ſhould copy Men in their moſt reigning Vices!

Of Virtue's wholſome Rules unjuſtly we complain,
When Search of Pleaſures give us greater Pain.
How ſlightly we our Reputation guard,
Which loſt but once can never be repair'd.

Lady

L. *Revel.* Farewel Sentences.

Enter Alpiew.

Alp. Madam——— [*Whispers her Lady.*

Mrs. *Sago.* So then, you perſuade me 'twas the Care of my Fame.

Sir *Jam.* Nothing elſe I proteſt, my dear little Rogue; I have as much Love as you, but I have more Conduct.

Mrs. *Sago.* Well, you know how ſoon I forgive you your Faults.

Sir *Jam.* Now to what Purpoſe have I lyed myſelf into her good Graces, when I would be glad to be rid of her? [*Aſide.*

L. *Revel.* Booted and ſpurr'd ſay you! Pray ſend him up, Sir *James*; I ſuppoſe truſty *Buckle* is come with ſome diverting Embaſſy from your Friend.

Enter Buckle *in a Riding-Dreſs.*

Mr. *Buckle,* Why in this Equipage?

Buck. Ah! Madam————

L. *Revel.* Out with it.

Buck. Farewel, Friends, Parents, and my Country; thou, dear Play-Houſe, and ſweet Park, Farewel.

L. *Revel.* Farewel, why, whither are you going?

Buck. My Lord and I am going where they never knew Deceit.

Sir *Jam.* That Land is inviſible, *Buckle.*

L. *Revel.* Ha, ha, ha.

Sir *Jam.* Were my Lord of my Mind, your Ladyſhip ſhould not have had ſo large a Theme for your Mirth. Your Servant Ladies. [*Exit.*

L. *Revel.* Well, but what's your Buſineſs?

Buck. My Lord charg'd me in his Name to take his everlaſting Leave of your Ladyſhip.

L. *Revel.* Why, where is he going pray?

Buck. In Search of a Country where there is no Women.

Mrs. *Sago.* Oh dear! Why what have the Women done to him, pray?

Buck. Done to him, Madam! He ſays they are all proud, perfidious, vain, inconſtant Coquets in *England.*

Mrs.

Mrs. *Sago*. Oh! he'll find they are every where the ſame.

L. *Revel*. And this is the Cauſe of his whimſical Pilgrimage? Ha, ha.

Buck. And this proceeds from your ill Uſage, Madam; when he left your Houſe—he flung himſelf into his Coach with ſuch a Force, that he broke all the Windows—as they ſay—for my Part I was not there—When he came home, he beat all his Servants round to be reveng'd.

Alp. Was you there, *Buckle?*

Buck. No, I thank my Stars, when I arriv'd, the Expedition was over—in haſte he mounted his Chamber—flung himſelf upon his Bed—burſt out into a violent Paſſion—Oh that ever I ſhould ſuffer myſelf to be impos'd upon, ſaid he, by this coquettiſh Beauty!

L. *Revel*. Meaning me, *Buckle*, Ha, ha.

Buck. Stay till I have finiſhed the Piece, Madam, and your Ladyſhip ſhall judge——ſhe's as fickle as ſhe's fair—ſhe does not uſe more Art to gain a Lover, ſaid he, than to deceive him when he is fix'd——Humph.

[*Leering at her.*

L. *Revel*. Pleaſant——and does he call this taking Leave?

Mrs. *Sago*. A comical Adieu.

Buck. Oh! Madam, I'm not come to the tragical Part of it yet; ſtarting from his Bed—

L. *Revel*. I thought it had been all Farce—if there be any Thing Heroic in't, I'll ſet my Face and look grave.

Buck. My Relation will require it, Madam, for I am ready to weep at the Repetition: Had you but ſeen how often he travers'd the Room, [*Acting it.*] heard how often he ſtamp'd, what diſtorted Faces he made, caſting up his Eyes thus, biting his Thumbs thus.

L. *Revel*. Ha, ha, ha, you'll make an admirable Actor—ſhall I ſpeak to the Patentees for you?

Mrs. *Sago*. But pray how did this end?

Buck. At laſt, Madam, quite ſpent with Rage, he ſunk down upon his Elbow, and his Head fell upon his Arm.

L. *Revel*. What, did he faint away?

Buck. Oh, no.

Mrs. *Sago.* He did not die?

Buck. No, but he fell asleep.

L. *Revel.* Oh brave Prince *Prettiman!*

Omnes. Ha, ha, ha.

Buck. After three Hours Nap, he wak'd—and calling hastily—my dear *Buckle*, said he, let's to the End of the World; and try to find a Place where the Sun shines not here and there at one Time———for 'tis not fit that it should at once look upon two Persons whose Sentiments are so different— She no longer regards my Pain, ungrateful, false, inhuman, barbarous Woman.

L. *Revel.* Foolish, fond, believing, easy Man; there's my Answer—Come, shall we to *Picquet*, my Dear?

Buck. Hold, hold, Madam, I han't half done——

Mrs. *Sago.* Oh! Pray my Lady *Reveller*, let's have it out, 'tis very diverting.——

Buck. He call'd me in a feeble Voice; *Buckle*, said he, bring me my little Scrutore—for I will write to Lady *Reveller* before I part from this Place, never to behold her more—What, don't you cry, Madam?

L. *Revel.* Cry—No, no; go on, go on.

Buck. 'Tis done, Madam—and there's the Letter. [*Gives her a Letter.*

L. *Revel.* So, this compleats the Narration. [*Reads.*

Madam, *Since I cannot live in a Place where there is a Possibility of seeing you without admiring, I resolve to fly; I am going to* Flanders: *Since you are false I have no Business here—I need not describe the Pain I feel, you are but too well acquainted with that—therefore I'll chuse Death rather than return*—Adieu.

Buck. Can any Man in the World write more tenderly, Madam? Does he not say 'tis impossible to love you, and go for *Flanders?* and that he would rather hear of your Death than return———

L. *Revel.* Excellent, Ha, ha.

Buck. What, do you laugh?

Mrs. *Sago.* Who can forbear?

Buck. I think you ought to die with Grief; I warrant Heaven will punish you all. [*Going.*

Alp. But harkye, *Buckle*, where are you going now?

Buck.

Buck. To tell my Lord in what Manner your Lady receiv'd his Letter; Farewel—now for *Flanders*—

Alp. A fair Wind and a good Voyage to you.

[*As he goes out enter Lord* Worthy.

Buck. My Lord here! So, now may I have my Head broke for my long Harangue, if it comes out.

L. *Revel.* Oh miraculous—my Lord! you have not finish'd your Campaign already, have you? Ha, ha, ha; or has the *French* made Peace at hearing of your Lordship's intended Bravery, and left you no Enemies to combat?

Lord. My worst of Foes are here—here, within my Breast; your Image, Madam.

L. *Revel.* O dear, my Lord, no more of that Theme, for *Buckle* has given us a Surfeit on't already——even from your breaking the Glasses of your Coach—to your falling fast asleep, Ha, ha, ha.

Lord. The Glasses of my Coach! What do you mean, Madam—Oh Hell! [*Biting his Thumbs.*

Buck. Ruin'd quite——Madam, for Heaven's Sake, what does your Ladyship mean? I ly'd in every Syllable I told you, Madam.

L. *Revel.* Nay, if your Lordship has a Mind to act it over again, we will oblige you for once—*Alpiew*, set Chairs——Come, dear *Sago*, sit down—and let the Play begin—*Buckle* knows his Part, and upon Necessity could act yours too, my Lord.

Lord. What has this Dog been doing? When he was only to deliver my Letter, to give her new Subject for Mirth—Death, methinks I hate her—Oh that I could hold that Mind——What makes you in this Equipage? Ha, Sirrah? [*Aside.*

Buck. My Lord, I, I, I, I,

Lord. Peace, Villain———— [*Strikes him.*

Lady. Hey—This is changing the Scene.

Buck. Who the Devil would rack his Brains for these People of Quality, who like no Body's Wit but their own?———— [*Aside.*

Mrs. *Sago.* If the Beating were Invention before, thou hast it now in reality; if Wars begin, I'll retire. They may agree better alone perhaps. [*Exit.*

Lady. Where did you learn this Rudeneſs, my Lord, to ſtrike your Servant before me?

Lord. When you have depriv'd a Man of his Reaſon, how can you blame his Conduct?

Buckle. Reaſon—Egad—there's not three Drams of Reaſon between you both—as my Cheek can teſtify. [*Aſide*.

Lady. The Affront was meant to me—nor will I endure theſe Paſſions—I thought I had forbid your Viſits.

Lord. I thought I had reſolv'd againſt them too.

Alpiew. But Reſolutions are of ſmall Force of either Side. [*Aſide*.

Lord. Grant me but this one Requeſt, and I'll remove this hated Object.

Lady. Upon Condition 'tis the laſt.

Lord. It ſhall—I think it ſhall at leaſt—Is there a Happy Man for whom I am deſpiſed?

Lady. I thought 'twas ſome ſuch ridiculous Queſtion; I'm of the Low-Church, my Lord, conſequently hate Confeſſors! ha, ha, ha.

Buckle. And Penance too I dare ſwear. [*Aſide*.

Lord. And every Thing but Play.

Lady. Dare you, the Subject of my Power—you, that petition Love, arraign my Pleaſures? Now I'm fixt—and will never ſee you more.

Buckle. Now wou'd any Body ſwear ſhe's in earneſt.

Lord. I cannot bear that Curſe—ſee me at your Feet again. [*Kneels*.] Oh! you have tortur'd me enough, take Pity now dear Tyrant, and let my Sufferings end.

Lady. I muſt not be Friends with him, for then I ſhall have him at my Elbow all Night, and ſpoil my Luck at the *Baſſet-Table*. [*Aſide*.] Either Cringing or Correcting, always in Extreams—I am weary of this Fatigue.

He that would gain my Heart, muſt learn the Way
Not to controul, but readily obey;
For he that once pretends my Faults to ſee,
That Moment makes himſelf all Faults to me. [Exit.

Buckle. There's the Inſide of a Woman. [*Aſide*.

Lord. Gone—now Curſes on me for a Fool—the worſt of Fools—a Woman's Fool—

Whoſe

Whose only Pleasure is to feed her Pride,
Fond of her Self, she cares for none beside:
So true Coquets their numerous Charms display,
And strive to conquer, purpose to betray.

ACT IV.

Enter Lord Worthy *and Sir* James.

Sir *James.* WELL, my Lord, I have left my Cards in the Hand of a Friend to hear what you have to say to me. Love I'm sure is the Text, therefore divide and subdivide as quick as you can.

Lord. Coud'st thou infuse into me thy Temper, Sir *James*, I should have thy Reason too; but I am born to love this Fickle, Faithless Fair—What have I not essay'd to raze her from my Breast; but all in vain! I must have her, or I must not live.

Sir *James.* Nay, if you are so far gone, my Lord, your Distemper requires an able Physician—What think you of *Lovely*'s bringing a File of Musketteers and carry her away, *Vi & Armis?*

Lord. That Way might give her Person to my Arms, but where's the Heart?

Sir *James.* A Trifle in Competition with her Body.

Lord. The Heart's the Gem that I prefer.

Sir *James.* Say you so my Lord? I'll engage three Parts of *Europe* will make that Exchange with you; Ha, ha, ha.

Lord. That Maxim wou'd hold with me perhaps in all but her; there I must have both or none; therefore instruct me, Friend, thou who negligent in Love, keeps always on the Level with the Fair—What Method shall I take to sound her Soul's Design? For tho' her Carriage puts me on the Rack when I behold that Train of Fools about her, yet my Heart will plead in her Excuse, and calm my Anger spite of all Efforts.

Sir *James.* Humph? I have a Plot, my Lord, if you will comply with it.

Lord. Nothing of Force.

Sir *James.* What e'er it be you shall be Witness of it, 'twill

'twill either quench your Flame, or kindle hers. I only will appear the Guilty; but here's Company, I'll tell you all within.

Enter Captain and Lovely, *dress'd like a Tar.*

L. *Wor.* I'll expect you. [*Exit.*

Sir *James.* Ha, Captain, how sits the Wind between you and your Mistress? Ha?

Capt. North and by South, Faith; but here's one sails full East, and without some unexpected Tornado, from the old Man's Coast—he makes his Port I warrant ye.

Lovely. I wish I were at Anchor once.

Sir *James.* Why, thou art as errant a Tar, as if thou had'st made an *East-India* Voyage, ha, ha.

Lovely. Ay, am I not, Sir *James?* But Egad I hope the old Fellow understands nothing of Navigation; If he does, I shall be at a Loss for the Terms.

Sir *James.* Oh! no Matter for Terms—look big, and bluster for your Country—describe the *Vigo* Business—publick News will furnish you with that, and I'll engage the Success.

Capt. Ay, ay, let me alone, I'll bear up with Sir *Richard,* and thou shalt board his Pinnace with Consent, ne'er fear—ho, here he comes full Sail.

Enter Sir Richard.

Sir *Richard,* I'm glad to see you; this is my Kinsman which I told you of; as soon as he landed I brought him to kiss your Hands.

Sir *Rich.* I honour you, you are welcome.

Lovely. I thank you, Sir—I'm not for Compliments; 'tis a Land Language, I understand it not; Courage, Honesty, and Plain-dealing Truth, is the Learning of our Element; if you like that I am for ye.

Sir *James.* The Rogue does it to a Miracle, [*Aside to the Captain.*

Capt. He's an improving Spark, I find, ha, ha.

Sir *Rich.* Like it, Sir? why 'tis the only Thing I do like, hang Compliments and Court breeding, it serves only to make Men a Prey to one another, to encourage Cowardice and ruin Trade—No, Sir, give me the Man that

that dares meet Death and Dinner with the ſame Appetite — one who rather than let in Popery, would let out his Blood; to maintain ſuch Men I'd pay double Cuſtom; nay, all my Gain ſhou'd go for their Support.

Sir *James*. The beſt Well-wiſher to his Country of an *Engliſhman* I ever heard.

Lovely. Oh! Sir *Richard*, I wiſh the Nation were all of your Mind, 'twou'd give the Soldiers and the Sailors Life. Captain launch off a round Lye or two.

Capt. And make us fight with Heart and Hand; my Kinſman, I'll aſſure, fits your Principle to a Hair; he hates the *French* ſo much, he ne'er fails to give them a Broadſide where'er he meets them; and has brought in more Privateers this War than half the Captains in the Navy; he was the firſt Man that boarded the *French* Fleet at *Vigo*—and in *Gibraltar* Buſineſs—the *Gazetteer* will inform you of the Name of Captain *Match*.

Sir *James*. Is this that Captain *Match*?

Lovely. For want of a better, Sir.

Sir *James*. Sir, I ſhall be proud of being known to you.

Sir *Rich*. And I of being related to you, Sir—I have a Daughter young and handſome, and I'll give her a Portion ſhall make thee an Admiral, Boy; for a Soul like thine is only fit to command a Navy—what ſay'ſt thou? art thou for a Wife?

Sir *James*. So, 'tis done, ha, ha, ha. [*Aſide*.

Capt. A proſperous Gale I' faith

Lovely. I don't know, Sir *Richard*, mehap a Woman may not like me; I am rough and Storm-like in my Temper, unacquainted with the Effeminacy of Courts; I was born upon the Sea, and ſince I can remember, never liv'd two Months on Shore; if I marry, my Wife muſt go Aboard, I promiſe you that.

Sir *Rich*. Aboard Man? Why ſhe ſhall go to the *Indies* with thee—Oh! ſuch a Son-in-Law—how ſhall I be bleſs'd in my Poſterity? now do I foreſee the Greatneſs of my Grand-Children; the Sons of this Man ſhall, in the Ages to come, make *France* a Tributary Nation.

Lovely. Once in an Engagement, Sir, as I was giving Orders to my Men, comes a Ball and took off a Fellow's Head, and ſtruck it full in my Teeth; I whipp'd it up, clap'd it into a Gun, and ſhot it at the Enemy again.

Sir

Sir *Rich*. Without the leaſt Concern!

Lovely. Concern, Sir—ha, ha, ha, if it had been my own Head I would have done the like.

Sir *Rich*. Prodigious Effect of Courage!—Captain I'll fetch my Girl, and be here again in an Inſtant—What an Honour will it be to have ſuch a Son. [*Exit*.

Capt. Ha, ha, ha, ha, you outdo your Maſter.

Sir *James*. Ha, ha, ha, ha, the old Knight's tranſported.

Lovely. I wiſh it was over, I'm all in a Sweat; here he comes again.

Enter Sir Richard *and* Valeria.

Sir *Rich*. I'll hear none of your Excuſes — Captain your Hand—there take her, and theſe Gentlemen ſhall be Witneſſes, if they pleaſe, to this Paper, wherein I give her my whole Eſtate when I die, and twenty thouſand Pounds down upon the Nail; I care not whether my Boy be worth a Groat — get me but Grandſons and I'm rich enough.

Capt. Generouſly ſaid, I'faith — much Good may do him with her.

Lovely. I'll do my Endeavour, Father, I promiſe you.

Sir *James*. I wiſh you Joy, Captain, and you, Madam.

Val. That's impoſſible; can I have Joy in a Species ſo very different from my own? Oh my dear *Lovely!*—We were only form'd for one another; — thy dear Enquiring Soul is more to me—than all theſe uſeleſs Lumps of animated Clay: Duty compels my Hand—but my Heart is ſubject only to my Mind,—the Strength of that they cannot conquer; — no, with the Reſolution of the Great Unparallel'd *Epictetus*, — I here proteſt my Will ſhall ne'er aſſent to any but my *Lovely*.

Sir *Rich*. Ay, you and your Will may philoſophize as long as you pleaſe,—Miſtreſs,—but your Body ſhall be taught another Doctrine, — it ſhall ſo, —— Your Mind and your Soul quotha! Why, what a Pox has my Eſtate to do with them? Ha? 'Tis the Fleſh Houſewife, that muſt raiſe Heirs, — and Supporters of my Name; —— and ſince I knew the getting of the Eſtate, 'tis fit I ſhould diſpoſe of it, ——and therefore no more Excuſes,

this

this is your Husband, do you, see, ——take my Word for it.

Val. *The outward empty Form of Marriage take,*
But all beyond I keep for Lovely'*s Sake.*
Thus on the Ground for ever fix my Eyes;
All Sights but Lovely *shall their Balls despise.*

Sir *Rich.* Come, Captain,—my Chaplain is within, he shall do the Business this Minute: If I don't use the Authority of a Father, this Baggage will make me lose such a Son-in-Law, that the City's Wealth can't purchase me his Fellow. [*Aside.*

Lov. *Thanks dear Invention for this timely Aid:*
The Bait's gone down, he's by himself betray'd.
Thus still where Arts both true and honest fail,
Deceitful Wit and Policy prevail.

Val. To Death, or any Thing,—'tis all alike to me. [*Exit cum* Valeria.

Sir *Rich.* Get you in I say,———Hussey, get you in. In my Conscience my Niece has spoil'd her already; but I'll have her married this Moment: Captain, you have bound me ever to you by this Match; command me and my House for ever; — But shall I not have your Company, Gentlemen, to be Witnesses of this Knot, this joyful Knot?

Capt. Yes, Faith, Sir *Richard*, I have too much Respect for my Kinsman to leave him,—till I see him safe in Harbour; I'll wait on you presently.

Sir *James.* I am engag'd in the next Room at Play, I beg your Pardon, Sir *Richard*, for an Hour; I'll bring the whole Company to congratulate the Bride and Bridegroom.

Sir *Rich.* Bride and Bridegroom! Congratulate me, Man! Methinks I already see my Race recorded amongst the foremost Heroes of my Nation; — Boys, all Boys,— and all Sailors.

They shall the Pride of France *and* Spain *pull down,*
And add their Indies *to our* English *Crown.* [Exit.

Sir *James.* Ha, ha, ha, never was Man so bigotted before;

ſore;——how will this end when he diſcovers the Cheat? Ha, ha, won't you make one with the Ladies, Captain?

Capt. I don't Care if I do venture a Piece or two; I'll but diſpatch a little Buſineſs, and meet you at the Table, Sir *James*.

Enter-Lady *Lucy*.

Sir *James*. Ha, Lady *Lucy!* is your Ladyſhip reconcil'd to *Baſſet* yet? Will you give me Leave to loſe this Purſe to you, Madam?

L. *Lucy*. I thank Fortune, I neither wiſh, nor need it, Sir *James*; I preſume the next Room is furniſh'd with Avarice enough to ſerve you in that Affair, if it is a Burthen to you; or Mrs. *Sago*'s ill Luck may give you an Opportunity of returning ſome of the Obligations you lie under.

Sir *James*. Your Sex, Madam, extorts a Duty from ours, and a well bred Man can no more refuſe his Money to a Lady, than a Sword to his Friend.

L. *Lucy*. That Superfluity of good Manners, Sir *James*, would do better converted into Charity; this Town abounds with Objects,——wou'd it not leave a more glorious Fame behind you to be the Founder of ſome pious Work, when all the Poor, at mention of your Name, ſhall bleſs your Memory, than that Poſterity ſhou'd ſay you waſted your Eſtate on Cards and Women.

Sir *James*. Humph, 'tis pity ſhe were not a Man, ſhe preaches ſo emphatically. [*Aſide.*] Faith, Madam, you have a very good Notion, but ſomething too early;—— when I am old, I may put your Principles in Practice, but Youth for Pleaſure was deſign'd.—

L. *Lucy*. The trueſt Pleaſure muſt conſiſt in doing good, which cannot be in Gaming.

Sir *James*. Every Thing is good in its Kind, Madam; Cards are harmleſs Bits of Paper, Dice inſipid Bones— and Women made for Men.

L. *Lucy*. Right, Sir *James*,—but all theſe Things may be perverted.——Cards are harmleſs Bits of Paper in themſelves, yet through them, what Miſchiefs have been done? What Orphans wrong'd? What Tradeſmen ruin'd? What Coaches and Equipage diſmiſs'd for them?

Sir

Sir *Jam*. But then, how many fine Coaches and Equipages have they ſet up, Madam?

L. *Lucy*. Is it the more honourable for that? How many Miſſes keep Coaches too? Which Arrogance in my Opinion only makes them more eminently ſcandalous———

Sir *Jam*. Oh! thoſe are ſuch as have a Mind to be damn'd in this State, Madam;—but I hope your Ladyſhip don't rank them amongſt us Gameſters.

L. *Lucy*. They are inſeparable, Sir *James*; Madam's Grandeur muſt be upheld — tho' the Baker and Butcher ſhut up Shop.

Sir *Jam*. Oh! Your Ladyſhip wrongs us middling Gentlemen there; to ruin Tradeſmen is the Quality's Prerogative only; and none beneath a Lord can pretend to do't with an honourable Air, ha, ha.

L. *Lucy*. Their Example ſways the meaner Sort; I grieve to think that Fortune ſhou'd exalt ſuch vain, ſuch vicious Souls,———whilſt Virtue's cloath'd in Rags.

Sir *Jam*. Ah! Faith, ſhe'd make but a ſcurvy Figure at Court, Madam; the Stateſmen and Politicians wou'd ſuppreſs her quickly;——but whilſt ſhe remains in your Breaſt ſhe's ſafe,———and makes us all in love with that fair Covering,

L. *Lucy*. Oh! Fie, fie, Sir *James*, you could not love one that hates your chief Diverſion.

Sir *Jam*. I ſhou'd hate it too, Madam, on ſome Terms that I cou'd name.

L. *Lucy*. What wou'd make that Converſion, pray?

Sir *Jam*. Your Heart.

L. *Lucy*. I cou'd pay that Price—but dare not venture upon one ſo wild.—[*Aſide*.] Firſt let me ſee the Fruit, e'er I take a Leaſe of the Garden, Sir *James*.

Sir *Jam*. Oh! Madam, the beſt Way is to ſecure the Ground, and then you may manure and cultivate it as you pleaſe.

L. *Lucy*. That's a certain Trouble, and uncertain Profit, and in this Affair, I prefer the Theory before the Practice: But I detain you from the Table, Sir *James*. —you are wanted to Tally——your Servant.— [*Exit*.

Sir *Jam*. Nay, if you leave me, Madam, the Devil

will tempt me,———She's gone, and now can't I ſhake off the Thought of ſeven Wins, eight Loſes——for the Blood of me,———and all this grave Advice of her's is loſt,———Faith,—tho' I do love her above the reſt of her Sex;——ſhe's an exact Model of what all Women ought to be,—and yet your merry little coquettiſh Tits are very diverting;—well, now for *Baſſet*; let me ſee what Money have I about me.—Humph! about a hundred Guineas,——half of which will ſet the Ladies to cheating—falſe Parolies in abundance.

Each Trifling Toy wou'd tempt in Times of Old,
Now nothing melts a Woman's Heart like Gold.
Some Bargains drive, others more nice than they,
Who'd have you think they ſcorn to kiſs for Pay;
To purchuſe them you muſt loſe deep at Play.
With ſeveral Women, ſeveral Ways prevail;
But Gold's a certain Way that cannot fail. [Exit.

The SCENE *draws, and diſcovers Lady* Reveller, *Mrs.* Sago, *and ſeveral Gentlemen and Ladies round a Table at* Baſſet.

Enter Sir James.

L. *Revel.* Oh! Sir *James*, are you come? We want you to tally for us.

Sir *Jam.* What Luck, Ladies?

L. *Revel.* I have only won a *Sept & leva.*

Mrs. *Sago.* And I have loſt a *Trante & leva,*——my ill Fortune has not forſook me yet I ſee.

Sir *Jam.* I go a Guinea upon that Card.

L. *Revel.* You loſe that Card.

Mrs. *Sago.* I maſe Sir *James*'s Card double.

Banker. Seven wins, and five loſes; you have loſt it, Madam.

Mrs. *Sago.* Again?——ſure never was Woman ſo unlucky———

Banker. Knave wins, and ten loſes; you have won, Sir *James.*

L. *Revel.* Clean Cards here.

Mrs.

Mrs. *Sago*. Burn this Book, 't has an unlucky Air, [*Tears them*.] Bring some more Books.

Enter Captain.

L. *Revel*. Oh! Captain,——here set a Chair; come. Captain, you shall sit by me—now if we can but strip this Tarr. [*Aside*.

Capt. With all my Heart, Madam;——come, what do you play Gold?—that's something high tho';—well, a Guinea upon this honest Knave of Clubs.

L. *Revel*. You lose it for a Guinea more.

Capt. Done. Madam.

Banker. The Five wins, and the Knave loses.

L. *Revel*. You have lost it, Captain.

Sir *Jam*. The Knave wins for two Guineas more, Madam.

L. *Revel*. Done, Sir *James*.

Banker. Six wins,—Knave loses.

Sir *Jam*. Oh! the Devil, I fac'd, I had rather have lost all.

Banker. Nine wins, Queen loses,—you have won.

Mrs. *Sago*. I'll make a Paroli,—I mase as much more; your Card loses, Sir *James*, for two Guineas, yours, Captain, loses for a Guinea more.

Banker. Four wins, Nine loses; —— you have lost, Madam.

Mrs. *Sago*. Oh! I could tear my Flesh—as I tear these Cards;—Confusion!—I can never win above a wretched Paroli; for if I push to *Sept & Leva*, 'tis gone. [*Walks about disorderly*.

Banker. Ace wins, Knave loses.

Capt. Sink the Knave, I'll set no more on't.

L. *Revel*. Fac't again;—what's the Meaning of this ill Luck to Night; Bring me a Book of Hearts, I'll try if they are more successful, that on the Queen; yours and your Card loses.

Mrs. *Sago*. Bring me a fresh Book; bring me another Book; bring me all Diamonds.

[*Looks upon them One by One, then throws them over her Shoulders*.

L. *Revel*. That can never be lucky; the Name of Jewels don't become a Citizen's Wife. [*Aside*.

Banker. King wins, the Tray loses.

Sir *Jam.* You have great Luck to Night, Mr. *Sharper.*

Sharper. So I have, Sir *James,*—I have won *Soneca* every Time.

L. *Revel.* But if he has got the knack of winning thus, he shall sharp no more here, I promise him. [*Aside.*

Mrs. *Sago.* I mase that.

L. *Revel.* Sir *James,* pray will you Tally.

Sir *Jam.* With all my Heart, Madam.

[*Takes the Cards and shuffles them.*

Mrs. *Sago.* Pray give me the Cards, Sir.

[*Takes 'em and shuffles 'em, and gives 'em to him again.*

Capt. I set that.

L. *Revel.* I set Five Guineas upon this Card, Sir *James.*

Sir *Jam.* Done Madam,——Five wins,—Six loses.

Mrs. *Sago.* I set that.

Sir *Jam.* Five don't go, and Seven loses.

Capt. I mase double.

L. *Revel.* I mase that.

Sir *Jam.* Three wins, Six loses.

Mrs. *Sago.* I mase, I mase double, and that—Oh ye malicious Stars!—— again.

Sir *Jam.* Eight wins, Seven loses.

Capt. So, this *Frante & leva* makes some amends;—Adsbud, I hate cheating—What's that false Cock made for now? Ha, Madam?

L. *Revel.* Nay, Mrs. *Sago,* if you begin to play foul.

Mrs. *Sago.* Rude Brute, to take Notice of the Slight of Hand in our Sex;—I protest he wrongs me, Madam, —there's the *Dernier* Stake, and I'll set it all,——now Fortune favour me, or this Moment is my last.

L. *Revel.* There's the last of fifty Pounds,—what's the meaning of this?

Sir *Jam.* Now for my Plot; her Stock is low I perceive. [*Slips a Purse of Gold into the Furbelows of Lady* Reveller's *Apron.*

L. *Revel.* I never had such ill Luck,——I must fetch more Money: Ha, from whence came this? This is the genteelest Piece of Gallantry; the Action is Sir *Harry*'s, I see by his Eyes.

[*Discovers a Purse in the Furbelows of her Apron.*

Sir

Sir *Jam.* Nine wins, Six loſes.

Mrs. *Sago.* I am ruin'd and undone for ever; Oh, oh, oh, to loſe every Card, Oh, oh, oh. [*Burſts out a crying.*

Capt. So, there's one Veſſel ſprung a-Leak, and I am almoſt aſhore;——if I go on at this Rate, I ſhall make but a lame Voyage on't I doubt.

Sir *Jam.* Duce wins, King loſes.

Capt. I maſe again,—I maſe double, I maſe again;—now the Devil blow my Head off if ever I ſaw Cards run ſo; damn 'em. [*Tears the Cards, and ſtamps on 'em.*

Sir *Jam.* Fie, Captain, this Concern among the Ladies is indecent.

Capt. Damn the Ladies,—mayn't I ſwear,——or tear my Cards, if I pleaſe; I'm ſure I have paid for them: Pray count the Cards, I believe there's a falſe Tally.

Sir *Jam.* No, they are right, Sir. [*Sir* James *counts 'em.*

Mrs. *Sago.* Not to turn one Card! Oh, oh, oh.

[*Stamps up and down.*

L. *Revel.* Madam, if you play no longer, pray don't diſturb thoſe that do.—Come, Courage, Captain, Sir *James*'s Gold was very lucky.—Who cou'd endure theſe Men, did they not loſe their Money? [*Aſide.*

Capt. Bring another Book here;—that upon Ten,—and I maſe that.— [*Puts down a Card, and turns another.*

Sir *Jam.* King fac't, Eight wins, Ten loſes.

Capt. Fire and Gunpowder. [*Exit.*

L. *Revel.* Ha, ha, ha, what is the Captain vaniſh'd in his own Smoke?—Come, I bett it with you, Mr. *Sharper*; your Card loſes.

Re-enter Captain, pulling in a Stranger, which he had fetch'd out of the Street.

Capt. Sir, do you think it poſſible to loſe a *Trante & leva*, a *Quinze-leva*,—and a *Sept leva*,—and never turn once.

Stranger. No ſure, 'tis impoſſible.

Capt. Ounds you lye, I did Sir.

[*Laying his Hand on his Sword.*

All the Women. Ah, ha, ah, ha. [*Shriek and run off.*

Capt. What the Devil had I to do among theſe Land-Rats?—Zounds, to loſe forty Pounds for nothing, not ſo much as a Wench for it; Ladies, quotha,—a Man had as good be acquainted with Pick-pockets. [*Exit.*

Sir *Jam.* Ha, ha, ha, the Captain has frightened the Women out of their Wits,——now to keep my Promise with my Lord, tho' the Thing has but an ill Face, no Matter.

They join together to enslave us Men,
And why not we to conquer them again.

ACT V.

Enter Sir James *on one Side, and Lady* Reveller *on the other.*

L. *Revel.* SIR *James*, what have you done with the rude Porpoise?

Sir *Jam.* He is gone to your Uncle's Apartment, Madam, I suppose.———I was in Pain till I knew how your Ladyship did after your Fright.

L. *Revel.* Really, Sir *James*, the Fellow has put me into the Spleen by his ill Manners. Oh, my Stars! that there should be such an unpolish'd Piece of Humanity, to be in that Disorder for losing his Money to us Women—I was apprehensive he would have beat me, ha, ha.

Sir *Jam.* Ha, ha, your Ladyship must impute his ill Breeding to the Want of Conversation with your Sex; but he is a Man of Honour with his own, I assure you.

L. *Revel.* I hate out of fashion'd Honour.———But where's the Company, Sir *James*? Shan't we play again?

Sir *Jam.* All dispers'd, Madam.

L. *Revel.* Come, you and I will go to Picquet then.

Sir *Jam.* Oh, I'm tir'd with Cards, Madam, can't you think of some other Diversion to pass a chearful Hour?—I cou'd tell you one, if you'd give me leave.

L. *Revel.* Of your own Invention? Then it must be a pleasant One.

Sir *Jam.* Oh, the pleasantest one in the World.

L. *Revel.* What is it, I pray?

Sir *Jam.* Love, Love, my dear Charmer. [*Approaches her.*

L.

L. *Revel.* Oh, *Cupid!* How came that in your Head?

Sir *Jam.* Nay, 'tis in my Heart, and except you pity me, the Wound is mortal.

L. *Revel.* Ha, ha, ha, is Sir *James* got into Lord *Worthy*'s Clafs?——You that could tell me I fhould not have fo large a Theme for my Diverfion, were you in his Place, ha, ha, ha: What, and is the gay, the airy, the witty, inconftant Sir *James* overtaken? ha, ha.

Sir *Jam.* Very true, Madam,——you fee there is no jefting with Fire.——Will you be kind?

[*Gets between her and the Door.*

L. *Revel.* Kind? What a difmal Sound was there?—I'm afraid your Fever's high, Sir *James*, ha, ha.

Sir *Jam.* If you think fo, Madam, 'tis time to apply cooling Medicines. [*Locks the Door.*

L. *Revel.* Ha, what Infolence is this? The Door lock'd! What do you mean, Sir *James?*

Sir *Jam.* Oh, 'tis fomething indecent to name it, Madam, but I intend to fhew you. [*Lays hold on her.*

L. *Revel.* Unhand me, Villain, or I'll cry out——

Sir *Jam.* Do, and make yourfelf the Jeft of Servants, expofe your Reputation to their vile Tongues,—which, if you pleafe, fhall remain fafe within my Breaft; but if with your own Noife you blaft it, here I bid Defiance to all Honour and Secrefy,—and the firft Man that enters, dies. [*Struggles with her.*

L. *Revel.* What fhall I do? Inftruct me Heaven.—Monfter! is this your Friendfhip to my Lord? And can you wrong the Woman he adores?

Sir *Jam.* Ay, but the Woman does not care a Soufe for him; and therefore he has no Right above me; I love you as much, and will poffefs.

L. *Revel.* Oh! Hold,——Kill me rather than deftroy my Honour;—what Devil has debauch'd your Temper? Or, how has my Carriage drawn this Curfe upon me? What have I done to give you Caufe to think you ever fhould fucceed this hated Way? [*Weeps.*

Sir *Jam.* Why this Queftion, Madam? Can a Lady that loves Play fo paffionately as you do,—that takes as much Pains to draw Men in to lofe their Money, as a Town Mifs to their Deftruction,——that careffes all

Sorts of People for your Intereſt, that divides your Time between your Toilet and *Baſſet-Table*; can you, I ſay, boaſt of innate Virtue?—Fye, fye, I am ſure you muſt have gueſs'd for what I play'd ſo deep;———we never part with our Money without Deſign,—or writing Fool upon our Foreheads;——therefore no more of this Reſiſtance, except you would have more Money.

L. *Revel.* Oh! horrid.

Sir *Jam.* There was fifty Guineas in that Purſe, Madam,——here's fifty more; Money ſhall be no Diſpute. [*Offers her Money.*

L. *Revel.* [*Strikes it down.*] Periſh your Money with yourſelf———you Villain——there, there; take your boaſted Favours, which I reſolv'd before to have paid in *Specie*; baſeſt of Men, I'll have your Life for this Affront———what ho, within there.

Sir *Jam.* Huſh!——'Faith, you'll raiſe the Houſe. [*Lays hold on her.*] And 'tis in vain—you're mine; nor will I quit this Room 'till I'm poſſeſs'd. [*Struggles.*

L. *Revel.* Raiſe the Houſe! I'll raiſe the World in my Defence; help, Murther! Murther———a Rape, a Rape———

Enter Lord Worthy *from another Room with his Sword drawn.*

Lord. Ha! Villain, unhand the Lady——or this Moment is thy laſt.

Sir *Jam.* Villain, back my Lord———follow me. [*Exit.*

L. *Revel.* By the bright Sun that ſhines, you ſhall not go—-no, you've ſav'd my Virtue, and I will preſerve your Life—let the vile Wretch be puniſh'd by viler Hands—yours ſhall not be prophan'd with Blood ſo baſe, if I have any Power———

Lord. Shall the Traytor live?—Tho' your barbarous Uſage does not merit this from me, yet in Conſideration that I lov'd you once—I will chaſtiſe his Inſolence.

L. *Revel.* Once——Oh! ſay not once; do you not love me ſtill? Oh! how pure your Soul appears to me above that deteſted Wretch. [*Weeps.*

Sir *Jam.* [*Peeping.*] It takes as I cou'd wiſh—

Lord.

Lord. Yet how have I been ſlighted; every Fop preferr'd to me—Now you diſcover what Inconveniency your Gaming has brought you into———this from me would have been unpardonable Advice—now you have prov'd it at your own Expence.

L. *Revel.* I have, and hate myſelf for all my Folly—Oh! forgive me—and if ſtill you think me worthy of your Heart——I here return you mine———and will this Hour ſign it with my Hand.

Sir *Jam.* How I applaud myſelf for this Contrivance.

Lord. Oh the tranſporting Joy, it is the only Happineſs I covet here.

Haſte then my Charmer, haſte the long'd-for Bliſs,
The happieſt Minute of my Life is this. [Exit.

Sir *Jam.* Ha, ha, ha, ha; how am I cenſur'd now for doing this Lady a Piece of Service, in forcing that upon her, which only her Vanity and Pride reſtrain'd.

So bluſhing Maids refuſe the courted Joy,
Tho' wiſhing Eyes, and preſſing Hands comply;
Till by ſome Stratagem the Lover gains,
What ſhe deny'd to all his amorous Pains.

As Sir James *is going off, enter Lady* Lucy *meeting him.*

Sir *Jam.* Ha, Lady *Lucy!*——Having ſucceeded for my Friend, who knows but this may be my lucky Minute too?———Madam, you come opportunely to hear. [*Takes her by the Hand.*

L. *Lucy.* Stand off, baſeſt of Men, I have heard too much; coud'ſt thou chuſe no Houſe but this, to act thy Villanies in? And coud'ſt thou offer Vows to me, when thy Heart, poiſon'd with vicious Thoughts, harbour'd this Deſign againſt my Family?

Sir *Jam.* Very fine, 'Faith, this is like to be my lucky Minute with a Witneſs; but Madam—

L. *Lucy.* Offer no Excuſe, 'tis height of Impudence to look me in the Face.

Sir *Jam* 'Egad ſhe loves me——Oh! happy Rogue——this Concern can proceed from nothing elſe. [*Aſide.*

L. *Lucy.* My Heart till now unus'd to Paſſion ſwells with this Affront; wou'd reproach thee————wou'd reproach myſelf, for having harbour'd one favourable Thought of thee.

Sir *Jam.* Why did you, Madam?—'Egad I owe more to her Anger than ever I did to her Morals.

L. *Lucy.* Ha! What have I ſaid?

Sir *Jam.* The only kind Word you ever utter'd.

L. *Lucy.* Yes, Impoſtor; know to thy Confuſion, that I did love thee, and fancy'd I diſcover'd ſome Seeds of Virtue amongſt that Heap of Wickedneſs; but this laſt Action has betray'd the fond Miſtake, and ſhew'd thou art all o'er Fiend.

Sir *Jam.* Give me leave, Madam———

L. *Lucy.* Think not this Confeſſion meant to advance thy impious Love, but hear my final Reſolution.

Sir *Jam.* 'Egad I muſt hear it——I find; for there's no ſtopping her.

L. *Lucy.* From this Moment I'll never———

Sir *Jam.* [*Clapping his Hand before her Mouth.*] Nay, nay, nay, after Sentence no Criminal is allow'd to Plead; therefore I will be heard—not Guilty, not Guilty, Madam, by—if I don't prove that this is all a Stratagem, contriv'd, ſtudy'd, deſign'd, proſecuted, and put in Execution, to reclaim your Couſin, and give my Lord Poſſeſſion—may you finiſh your Curſe, and I be doom'd to everlaſting Abſence—'Egad I'm out of Breath——

L. *Lucy.* Oh! Coud'ſt thou prove this?

Sir *Jam.* I can, if by the Proof you'll make me happy; my Lord ſhall convince you.

L. *Lucy.* To him I will refer it, on this Truth your Hopes depend.

In vain we ſtrive our Paſſions to conceal,
Our very Paſſions do our Loves reveal;
When once the Heart yields to the Tyrant's Sway,
The Eyes our Tongue will ſoon the Flame betray. [Exit.

Sir *Jam.* I was never out at a critical Minute in my Life.

Enter Mr. Sago *and two Bailiffs meeting* Alpiew.

Sago. Hark ye, Miſtreſs, is my Wife here?

Alp. Truly, I ſhan't give myſelf the Trouble of ſeeking her for him, now ſhe has loſt all her Money—your Wife is a very indiſcreet Perſon, Sir.

Sago. I'm afraid I ſhall find it ſo to my Coſt.

Bailiffs

Bailiffs. Come, come, Sir, we can't wait all Day—the Actions are a thousand Pounds——You shall have Time to send for Bail, and what Friends you please.

Sago. A thousand Pounds! [*Enter Mrs.* Sago.] Oh Lambkin! have you spent me a thousand Pounds?

Mrs. *Sago.* Who, I Pudd? Oh! undone for ever——

Sago. Pudd me no Pudd—Do you owe Mr. *Taby* the Mercer two hundred Pounds, ha?

Mrs. *Sago.* I, I, I don't know the Sum, dear Pudd—but, but, but, I do owe him something; but I believe he made me pay too dear.

Sago. Oh! thou Wolfkin instead of Lambkin——for thou hast devour'd my Substance; and do'st thou owe Mr. *Dollar* the Goldsmith, three hundred Pounds? Do'st thou? Ha, speak Tygress.

Mrs. *Sago.* Sure it can't be quite three hundred Pounds. [*Sobbing.*

Sago. Thou Island Crocodile thou——and do'st thou owe *Ratsbane* the Vintner an hundred Pounds? And were those Hampers of Wine which I receiv'd so joyfully, sent by thyself to thyself, ha?

Mrs. *Sago.* Yes, indeed, Puddy——I, I, I beg your Pardon. [*Sobbing.*

Sago. And why did'st not thou tell me of them, thou Rattle-Snake?——for they say they have sent a hundred Times for their Money—else I had not been arrested in my Shop.

Mrs. *Sago.* Be, be, be because I, I, I was afraid, dear Puddy. [*Crying.*

Sago. But wer't thou not afraid to ruin me tho', dear Pudd? Ah! I need ask thee no more Questions, thou Serpent in Petticoats; did I doat upon thee for this? Here's a Bill from *Callico* the Linen-Draper; another from *Setwell* the Jeweller——from *Coupler* a Mantua-maker, and *Pimpwell* the Milliner; a Tribe of Locusts enough to undo a Lord-Mayor.

Mrs. *Sago.* I hope not, truly, Dear, Deary I'm sure that's all.

Sago. All, with a Pox——no Mrs. *Jezebel*, that's not all; there's two hundred Pounds due to myself for Tea, Coffee, and Chocolate, which my Journeyman has confess'd, confess'd, since your Roguery came out—that you have embezzled, Hussy, you have; so, this comes of your keeping Quality Company——e'en let them keep you now, for I have done with you, you shall come no more within my Doors, I promise you.

Mrs. *Sago*. Oh! Kill me rather; I never did it with Design to part with you, indeed, Puddy. [*Sobbing*.

Sago. No, no, I believe not, whilst I was worth a Groat. Oh!

Enter Sir James.

Sir *Jam*. How! Mrs. *Sago* in Tears, and my honest Friend in Ruffians Hands; the Meaning of this?

Sago. Oh! Sir *James* —— my hypocritical Wife is as much a Wife as any Wife in the City —— I'm arrested here in an Action of a thousand Pounds, that she has taken up Goods for, and gam'd away; get out of my Sight, get out of my Sight, I say.

Mrs. *Sago*. Indeed, and indeed, [*Sobbing*.] dear Puddy, but I cannot—no, here I will hang for ever on this Neck. [*Flies about his Neck*.

Sago. Help, Murder, Murder; why, why, what will you collar me?

Sir *Jam*. Right, Woman; I must try to make up this Breach——Oh! Mr. *Sago*, you are unkind——'tis pure Love that thus transports your Wife, and not such base Designs as you complain of.

Sago. Yes, yes; and she run me in Debt out of pure Love too, no doubt.

Mrs. *Sago*. So, it was, Pudd.

Sago. What was it, ha, Mistress, out of Love to me that you have undone me? Thou, thou, thou, I don't know what to call thee bad enough.

Mrs. *Sago*. You won't hear your Keecky out, dear Pudd; it was not out of Love for Play——but for Lo, Lo, Love to you, dear Pudd; if you'll forgive me, I'll ne'er play again. [*Crying and Sobbing all the while*.

Sir *Jam*. Nay, now, Sir, you must forgive her.

Sago. What! Forgive her that would send me to Jail?

Sir *Jam*. No, no, there's no Danger of that, I'll bail you, Mr. *Sago*, and try to compound those Debts—— You know me, Officers.

Officers.

Officers. Very well, Sir *James*, your Worſhip's Word is ſufficient.

Sir *Jam.* There's your Fees then, leave here your Priſoner, I'll ſee him forth-coming.

Officers. With all our Hearts; your Servant, Sir. [*Exit.*

Sago. Ah thou wicked Woman, how have I doated on thoſe Eyes! How often have I kneel'd to kiſs that Hand! Ha, is not this true, Keecky?

Mrs. *Sago.* Yes, Deary, I, I, I, I do confeſs it.

Sago. Did ever I refuſe to grant whatever thou aſk'd me?

Mrs. *Sago.* No, never Pudd— [*Weeps ſtill.*

Sago. Might'ſt not thou have eaten Gold, as the Saying is, ha?—Oh Keecky, Keecky! [*Ready to weep.*

Sir *Jam.* Leave crying, and wheedle him, Madam, wheedle him.

Mrs. *Sago.* I do confeſs it; and can't you forgive your Keecky then, that you have been ſo tender of, that you ſo often confeſt your Heart has jump'd up to your Mouth when you have heard my Beauty prais'd.

Sago. So it has I profeſs, Sir *James*,—I begin to melt ——I do; I am a good-natur'd Fool, that's the Truth on't: But if I ſhould forgive you, what would you do to make me amends? For that fair Face, if I turn you out of Doors, will quickly be a cheaper Drug than any in my Shop.

Sir *Jam.* And not maintain her half ſo well—promiſe largely, Madam. [*To Mrs.* Sago.

Mrs. *Sago.* I'll love you for ever, Deary.

Sago. But you'll jig to *Covent-Garden* again.

Mrs. *Sago.* No, indeed, I won't come within the Air on't, but take up with City Acquaintance, rail at the Court, and go twice a Week with Mrs. *Outſide* to *Pin-makers-hall.*

Sago. That would rejoice my Heart. [*Ready to weep.*

Sir *Jam.* See, if the good Man is not ready to weep; your laſt Promiſe has conquer'd—Come, come, buſs and be Friends, and end the Matter—I'm glad the Quarrel is made up, or I had had her upon my Hands. [*Aſide.*

Mrs. *Sago.* Pudd, don't you hear Sir *James*, Pudd?

Sago. I can hold no longer.———Yes, I do hear him, ———come then to the Arms of thy nown Pudd.

[*Run into one another's Arms.*

Sir

Sir *Jam*. Now all's well; and for your Comfort, Lady *Reveller* is by this Time married to my Lord *Worthy*, and there will be no more Gaming, I assure you, in that House.

Sago. Joys upon Joys. Now if these Debts were but accommodated, I should be happier than ever; I should indeed, *Keecky*.

Sir *Jam*. Leave that to me, Mr. *Sago*, I have won Part of your Wife's Money; and will that Way restore it you.

Sago. I thank you, good Sir *James*, I believe you are the first Gamester that ever refunded.

Mrs. *Sago*. Generously done,——Fortune has brought me off this Time, and I'll never trust her more.

Sir *Jam*. But see the Bride and Bridegroom.

Enter Lord Worthy *and Lady* Reveller, *Lady* Lucy, Buckle *and* Alpiew.

L. *Lucy*. This Match which I have now been Witness to, is what I long have wish'd; your Course of Life must of Necessity be chang'd.

L. *Revel*. Ha, Sir *James* here!—Oh if you love me, my Lord, let us avoid that Brute; you must not meet him.

Sir *Jam*. Oh, there's no Danger, Madam———My Lord, I wish you Joy with all my Heart; we only quarrel'd to make you Friends, Madam, ha, ha, ha.

L. *Revel*. What, am I trick'd into a Marriage then?

Lord. Not against your Will, I hope.

L. *Revel*. No, I forgive you; tho' had I been aware of it, it should have cost you a little more Pains.

Lord. I wish I could return thy Plot, and make this Lady thine, Sir *James*.

Sir *Jam*. Then I should be paid with Interest, my Lord.

L. *Lucy*. My Fault is Consideration you know, I must think a little longer on't.

Sir *Jam*. And my whole Study shall be to improve those Thoughts to my own Advantage.

Sago. I wish your Ladyship Joy, and hope I shall keep my Keecky to myself now.

Lady.

Lady. With all my Heart, Mr. *Sago,* ſhe has had ill Luck of late, which I am ſorry for.

Mrs *Sago.* My Lord *Worthy* will confine your Ladyſhip from Play as well as I, and my Injunction will be more eaſy when I have your Example.

Buck. Nay, 'tis Time to throw up the Cards when the Game's out.

Enter Sir Richard, *Captain* Hearty, Lovely, *and* Valeria.

Capt. Well, Sir *James,* the Danger's over; we have doubled the Cape, and my Kinſman is ſailing directly to the Port.

Sir *Jam.* A boon Voyage.

Sir *Rich.* 'Tis done, and my Heart is at Eaſe.—Did you ever ſee ſuch a perverſe Baggage? Look in his Face, I ſay, and thank your Stars; for their beſt Influences gave you this Huſband.

Lov. Will not *Valeria* look upon me? She us'd to be more kind when we have fiſh'd for Eels in Vinegar.

Val. My *Lovely,* is it thee! And has natural Sympathy forborn to inform my Senſe thus long? [*Flies to him.*

Sir *Rich.* How! how! This *Lovely?* What, does it prove the Enſign I have ſo carefully avoided?

Lov. Yes, Sir, the ſame; I hope you may be brought to like a Land-Soldier, as well as a Seaman.

Sir *Rich.* And, Captain, have you done this?

Capt. Yes, 'Faith, ſhe was too whimſical for our Element; her hard Words might have conjur'd up a Storm for ought I know,———ſo I have ſet her aſhore.

L. *Revel.* What, my Uncle deceiv'd with his Stock of Wiſdom? ha, ha, ha.

Buck Here's ſuch a Coupling, Mrs. *Alpiew,* han't you a Month's Mind?

Alp. Not to you, I aſſure you.

Buck. I was but in Jeſt, Child; ſay nay, when you're aſk'd.

Sir *Jam.* The principal Part of this Plot was mine, Sir *Richard.*

Sir *Rich.* Wou'd 'twas in my Power to hang you for't. [*Aſide.*

Sir

Sir *Jam.* And I have no Reaſon to doubt you ſhould repent it; he is a Gentleman, tho' a younger Brother; he loves your Daughter, and ſhe him, which has the beſt Face of Happineſs in a marry'd State; you like a Man of Honour, and he has as much as any one, that I aſſure you, Sir *Richard.*

Sir *Rich.* Well, ſince what's paſt is paſt Recal, I had as good be ſatisfied as not; therefore take her, and bleſs ye together.

Lord. So now each Man's Wiſh is crown'd, but mine with double Joy.

Capt. Well ſaid, Sir *Richard*, let's have a Bowl of Punch, and drink to the Bridegroom's good Voyage to-Night——ſteady, ſteady, ha, ha.

Sago. I'll take a Glaſs with you, Captain,——I reckon myſelf a Bridegroom too.

Buck. I doubt *Keecky* won't find him ſuch. [*Aſide.*

Mrs. *Sago.* Well,—poor *Keecky*'s bound to good Be-(haviour,
Or ſhe had quite loſt her Puddy's Favour.

Shall I for this repine at Fortune?——No,
I'm glad at Heart that I'm forgiven ſo.
Some Neighbours Wives have but too lately ſhewn,
When Spouſe had left 'em, all their Friends were flown.
Then all you Wives that wou'd avoid my Fate,
Remain contented with your preſent State.

Love

Love at a Venture.

A

C O M E D Y.

THE

PROLOGUE.

LEST any here shou'd blame our Author's Toil,
For strolling with her Brat a Hundred Mile.
By me to such, She does this Reason give,
Seeing how many Men by Ventures live.
She straight embark'd, and hoisted Sail to try,
What pure good Nature in these Bottoms lye.
Beside, she hop'd, she might divert you too,
By adding to your Pleasures something new.
The Virtue of these Baths had ne're been known,
If or'e these Hills, no Man had ventur'd down.
Here Doctors Venturing, come in Hopes of Fees,
And Patients Venture, on their Skill for Ease,
For Wealth, the Merchant Ventures on the Seas.
The Lawyer Ventures upon any Cause,
And Venturing Client's beggar'd by the Laws.
The Lover Ventures, to Address the Fair,
With broken Speeches, and dejected Air,
She runs a Venture, who relieves his Care.
The Gamester Ventures, to improve his Store,
And having lost, he Ventures on for more.
The London *Punk, in Garret shut all Day,*
At Night, with last Half-crown she Ventures to the Play.
The Amorous Cully meeting with the Miss,
Ventures at Water-Gruel for a Kiss.
Since every Man, Adventures in his Way,
Hither our Author Ventur'd with her Play.
And hopes her Profits will her Charge defray,
If that bright Circle Ventures to adorn her Day.

THE

THE

EPILOGUE.

Spoken by Miſs JACOBELLA POWER.

IN Spight of dull inſipid Rules, I'm come,
To learn what Fate attends my Virgin Bloom.
Strange Things I've heard this Night, that makes me fear,
Leaſt I ſhou'd find ſuch Entertainment here.
You Men are grown ſo witty in Deceit,
That We, poor Girls, are often ruin'd by't.
'Tis Pity——but I hope to croſs this Play,
And be reveng'd on you ſome other Way.
Well———but conſider, We are tender Things,
That Innocence, and ſprightly Beauty brings.
Soft Accents, broken Words, and yielding Air,
Are all the Weapons, that attend the Fair.
And can you long reſiſt, the ſweet Temptation,
Give us at leaſt a Bill of Reformation.
That the ſucceeding Age may ſay of you,
You dare be Civil, tho' you can't be true.
But if at laſt no Charms have Power to win ye,
You're paſt Repentance——or the Devil's in ye.

[Runs off.

Drama-

Dramatis Personæ.

MEN.

Belair, *a Gentleman just come from Travel, an Airy Spark.*

Sir William Freelove, *Friend to* Belair, *in Love with* Beliza.

Sir Thomas Belair, *Father to* Belair.

Sir Paul Cautious, *a Whimsical, Desponding, Old Fellow.*

Ned Freelove, *younger Brother to Sir* William.

Wou'dbe, *a Silly, Projecting Coxcomb.*

Positive, *Father to* Camilla.

Robin, *Servant to* Belair.

WOMEN.

Lady Cautious, *Wife to Sir* Paul, *and Sister to Sir* William.

Beliza.

Camilla, *Cousin to* Beliza, *a great Fortune.*

Patch, *Maid to* Beliza.

Flora, *Maid to Camilla.*

LOVE AT A VENTURE.

ACT I.

SCENE *Sir* Paul Cautious's *House.* *Sir* William Freelove's *Apartment.*

Enter Belair *and* Robin, *meeting Sir* William.

Belair.

OH Sir *William*, I am ſo tranſported, I cannot ſpeak in the common Strain of Mankind.

Sir *Will.* And pry'thee, *Belair*, What occaſions this Tranſport?

Bel. Had'ſt thou been my profeſt Enemy all thy Life, and done me as much Miſchief as the *Turk* in *Hungary*, or the *French* in *Flanders*; if thou'lt but help me now, thou woud'ſt make Amends for all—ſuch a Creature! ſuch an Angel!

Sir *Will.* What Viſions! Apparitions?

Bel. Cou'd I but hope to ſee her once more, I'd change the happieſt half of my Life for that one Moment.

Sir *Will.* If you pleaſe to deſcend from your high-flown Raptures, and walk Hand in Hand with my Underſtanding.

Bel. You'l lead me to her. [*Haſtily.*

Sir *Will.* Ha, ha, ha, what, before I know where ſhe

is

is——you wou'd be landed at your Port before you have taken Shipping, or told the Place you design for.

Bel. Pho; you know all my Designs.

Robin. When a Woman's concern'd. [*Aside.*

Sir *Will.* Are extravagant——you have more Intrigues upon your Hands, than a handsome young Poet on the Success of his first Play——like a Dog in a Herd, you run at all, and catch none, because you run with such ungovern'd Heat, you spring the Quarry before you can draw your Net.

Bel. But if I miss Sitting, I commonly hit 'em Flying—but this is nothing to the Purpose; the Lady, Man, the Lady———

Sir *Wil.* Ay, the Lady; what of her?

Bel. Which I saw last Night——Oh, such a Creature!

Sir *Will.* At what Window?

Bel. Such a charming Air.———

Sir *Wil.* What House was it at?

Bel. As much Youth as wou'd serve to recover half the decay'd Faces in the Town.

Sir *Will.* What Street?

Bel. Wanton as a Nun, yet look'd demure as a Quaker———

Sir *Will.* Z'death, where, where, is this rare Creature to be seen?

Bell. Then her Features, Sir *Willam!* Oh, such Features; she is the most perfect Piece in the World——her Shape clean and easy——a profuse Quantity of dark brown Hair—and such a Complexion, as the Gods form when they design a Miracle of Beauty.

Sir *Will.* Nay, since you will have your own Way, I'll strike in with you———a charming high Forehead.

Bel. Ay, and such a Mouth———

Sir *Will.* Sparkling black Eyes———

Bel. And such a Cast———

Sir *Will.* Such Dimples in her Cheeks———

Bel. Ay, ay, Rapture, Rapture.

Sir *Will.* Ah, he's got above the Clouds already—when you have recover'd your Senses, *Belair*, you may be fit for Conversation; I have a little Business to dispatch———and must beg your Pardon———

Bel. Thou wilt not leave me.

Sir

Sir *Will.* Why, what Service can I do you?

Bel. You must assist me in the Management of this Affair.

Sir *Will.* What Affair? Who is she? Where did you see her?

Bel. Why, when I left you last Night, I took a Boat resolving to go up the River for a little Air, when the luckiest Occasion presented to make me the happiest Man living.

Rob. I have known a hundred of these lucky Occasions; in a Month's Time the most unlucky Occasions, that ever Man had. [*Aside.*

Sir *Will.* What was it?

Bel. A Lady designing to land at *Whitehall* Stairs, stepping short from the Boat, fell into the Water, I jumpt in after her, caught her in my Arms, and brought her safe ashore.

Rob. Who cou'd have believ'd he shou'd be burnt in the Middle of the *Thames* now.

Sir *Will.* What's her Name?

Bel. I know not, she enquir'd mine, and where I liv'd; gave me a thousand Thanks, and promis'd I shou'd hear from her.

Sir *Will.* Well, and what can I do for you?

Bel. I'll tell you, I must have Lodgings in this House, for here I directed her; told her my Name was *Constant*, tho', Faith, *Bellair* was at my Tongue's End; but you know my Reasons for concealing my Name, least my Father hear I'm in *England*, before I'd have him, and force me to marry the Woman he commanded me Home for, which, for ought I know, may be ugly, old, ill-natur'd, foolish, conceited, vain, and so forth—at least, I shall think her such, because of his chusing—I like no Caterer in Love's Market—

Sir *Will.* You shall have these Lodgings to oblige you, good Mr. *Constant*—but what have you done with the other Lady you told me of Yesterday; you was then dying for her?

Bel. Faith, I like her still——but t'other, t'other, is a perfect Venus——

Rob. Pray, Sir, what is your Name to her? I shall certainly forget all these Names.

Bel. Colonel *Revel*, you Sot.

Rob. Just come from where, Sir?

Bel. From *Portugal*, Blockhead.

Rob. And —— are you an —— Officer too in t'other Place with your new Amour; Co, co, co, con, pray, Sir, do me the Favour to tell me your Name to this Incognita once more?

Bel. *Constant*, Coxcomb.

Rob. And what are you, Sir, pray, what are you?

Bell. An *Oxfordshire* Gentleman; remember that, Sirrah, come up to Town about a Law-Suit.

Rob. Yes, Sir— Colonel *Revel* just come from *Portugal*, — Mr. *Constant*, an *Oxfordshire* Gentleman, come-up to Town about a Law-Suit.——Very well, I have it now, Sir, I warrant you.

Sir *Will.* Well but do you think to manage both these Intrigues with Secresy.

Bel. I do; and in order to't, I'll keep my own Lodgings, that are known to the other, and these for my Incognita, and I'll engage to play my Part with both.

Sir *Will.* To what Purpose?

Bel. Why, since my old Dad will have me marry, I would willingly chuse for my self; now, you must know, I design to take my swing of Love and Liberty——if, in the Chase, I chance to meet one that can fix me, her I'll marry; till when I'll, like the Bee, kiss every Plant, and gather Sweetness from every Flower——Youth is the Harvest of our Lives, Sir *William.*

Sir *Will.* Well, in my Conscience, Travel has given thee a large Assurance.

Enter a Servant.

Serv. Here is Mr. *Wou'dbe* to wait on you.

Bel. Who's he?

Sir *Will.* The projecting Coxcomb, I told you of Yesterday.

Bel. What, he that mimicks thee in his Cloaths?

Sir *Will.* The same —— now, for hard Words, and soft Sense; bring him up. [*Exit Servant.*

Bel. I'll not stay——I expect a Message from my t'other Mistress at my Lodgings; I'll send a Night-Gown, and

and a Suit of Cloaths hither; and *Robin* ſhall wait to call me, if my Fair unknown ſends——Oh the Pleaſure of Intrigue; it finds Employment for every Senſe, ſharpens the Wit, and gives a Life to all our Faculties.

When pall'd with one, another ſtill ſupplies,
Thus different Women give us different Joys.
Beauty in one; in t'other Wit we find;
In this a Shape, in that a ſpacious Mind;
But Change, dear Change, thou Life of human Kind.
[Exit.

Enter Wou'dbe.

Wou'd. Dear, Sir *William*, my Stars are ſuperabundantly propitious, in adminiſtring the ſeraphick Felicity of finding you alone.

Sir *Will.* Oh, Mr. *Wou'dbe*——ſpare me, I beſeech you——

Wou'd. My Soul's inhabited; or, rather canoniz'd, with an Alacrity to ſee you.

Sir *Will.* I know not how his Soul's inhabited; but his Head might paſs for a Colony, in *Greenland*, it is ſo thinly Peopled. [*Aſide.*

Enter Ned Free Love.

Ned. Brother, good Morrow; Mr. *Wou'dbe*, yours.

Wou'd. Sir, I am moſt obſequiouſly your Servant.

Ned. What Gentleman was that I ſaw go out juſt now?

Sir *Wil.* A Friend of mine, who, for ſome Reaſons, I have promis'd this Apartment to; I hope Sir *Paul* won't be alarm'd; I think 'tis beſt not to let him know it, if he does not find it out.

Ned. Much the beſt, for he'll aſk ſo many impertinent Queſtions about him, and be in ſuch a Fright, he'll call in half the Pariſh to watch with him——Who is the Gentleman?

Sir *Will.* If you remember, I told you, when I was in *Spain*, a Gentleman reſcu'd me from the Hands of Ruffians, when I was ſet upon in the Night; this is he, and ever ſince we have held a ſtrict Friendſhip —— Perhaps he may have kill'd his Man, I know not; he deſires Privacy——and I am bonud, in Honour, to give it.

Ned. Doubtless———What's his Name?

Sir *Will.* *Constant.*

Enter Servant.

Serv. Sir, the Taylor has brought home your Cloaths.

Sir *Will.* Bring him in.

Wou'd. But, Sir *William*, pray, how do you like my Way of greeting——I never want Words, you see——I hate those dull Rogues, that have no better Expressions at meeting their Friends than, dear *Jack*, how is't?

Enter Taylor, and Sir William *dresses.*

Meer Fustian,———ha! What do I see? Another Suit——and, upon my Veracity, a charming one——I must put down the Trimming exactly, I shall obliterate half else. [*Takes out a Book and writes.*

Ned. Our *English* Tongue is much oblig'd to you, Mr. *Wou'dbe.*

Sir *Will.* Is it not too short Mr. *Measure*? [*To the Taylor.*

Tayl Not at all, Sir.

Wou'd. The Suit my Taylor is making, is the very same Colour; I'll send, and have it trimm'd exactly like that. [*Aside.*

Sir *Will.* How do you like my Fancy in this Suit, Mr. *Wou'dbe?*

Wou'd. Sir *William*, I reverence the Sublimity of your Fancy——If mine be not done by Play-time, I'll break my Taylor's Head, and never pay the Bill. [*Aside.*

Ned. But what new Discoveries have you made lately, Mr. *Wou'dbe*; Never a Project, ha!

Wou'd. Yes, Sir, I am going to erect an Office for Poetry.

Ned. How! An Office for Poetry?

Wou'd. Ay, Sir, where all Poets may have free Access, paying such a Moiety of their Profits, and be furnish'd with all Sorts of refin'd Words adapted to their several Characters.

Sir *Will.* The Poets will be very much oblig'd to you truly, Sir.

Wou'd. I think so———hark ye, I'm upon another Project, which you'll not guess for a Wager?

Sir

Sir *Will.* No, really, Mr. *Wou'dbe*; 'tis not in my ſhallow Capacity, to fathom the Profundity of your Wit.

Wou'd. Oh, Sir *William*, ſuch accumulated Kindneſs will bankrupt my poor Acknowledgements —— Profundity of your Wit——ſpoke like a Gentleman, and a Scholar —— thou art expenſively obliging, therefore I will communicate——tho' it is not grown to a full Maturity, yet——'tis this——for the Good of the Public, I am contriving how to ſave the Charges of Hackney-Coaches; the Raſcals are ſo ſaucy, eſpecially to Ladies, there's no enduring them; I reſolve to deſtroy their Conſtitution.

Ned. As how, pry'thee?

Sir *Will.* They are the moſt neceſſary Things in the World; a Hackney-Coach carries us from one End of the Town to the other in a Trice.

Wou'd. Ay, Sir *William* ——— but my Project carries 'em quicker——and without going out of their Houſes.

Ned. That's a Stratagem, indeed, beyond my Comprehenſion.

Sir *Will.* If you can do that, Mr. *Wou'dbe*, you need not fear a Patent; the Ladies will be all of your Side.

Wou'dbe. They will have Reaſon, Sir, for they may dreſs, patch, paint, drink Tea, or play at Piquet, all the while they are going to the Play-houſe —— Is not this an excellent Project?

Sir *Will.* Excellent, indeed; but, pry'thee, how is it?

Ned. Ay, ay, how is it, you muſt deal with the Devil certainly.

Wou'd. No, without his Help, I aſſure you, 'tis all my own———this individual Brain contriv'd it ——— were I known at Court, I ſhou'd be a great Man———a moſt magnificent Man.

Sir *Will.* Oh, this Project, Sir, will do your Buſineſs.

Wou'd. I know you are impatient for the Secret; you are my Friends, or I'd not impart a Matter of this Conſequence.

Sir *Will.* I hope you don't doubt our Secreſy?

Wou'd. Not in the leaſt——to convince you, 'tis this, I'll make the Streets to move.

Ned. Ha, ha, the Streets move! Pry'thee, how wilt thou do that?

Wou'd. Oh, by Clock-work, Sir.

Sir *Will.* By Clock-work? What make the solid Earth move by Clock-work?

Wou'd. Ay, Sir——I affirm that's possible——You mistake, the Earth is not solid; read but *Baker*'s Chronicle, and you'll find a whole Field walk'd ten Mile in Queen *Bess*'s Days.

Ned. But not by Clock-work, Mr. *Wou'dbe.*

Wou'd. Humph——ha——I can't be positive in that, but——if it can walk at all——why can't it be made walk by Clock-work——but in a Month's Time I shall be able to answer that, and all other Objections——For, you must know, Yesterday I began my Study, in order to search out the Curiosity of every Country, Language, Art and Science——you shall hear how I have canton'd out the Day——I rise about five, my first Hour is laid out upon Law——'tis fit a Gentleman shou'd understand the Laws of his Country, tho' I hate the confounded Study, 'tis so crabbed——At Six, I read a Lesson of Greek——at Seven, one of Hebrew——Eight, is for Italian——Nine, for Spanish——Ten, for French——Eleven, Astronomy——Twelve, is proper for Geometry, then the Sun Beams are perpendicular——

Ned Excellent, ha, ha, ha.

Wou'd. At One, I dine——then repose an Hour for Digestion——at Three, I study Physic——, that, if I'm poison'd by the Vintners, I may not be kill'd by the Doctors——at Four, Logic——at Five, Philosophy——at Six, Husbandry——that when my Father dies, my Steward and Tenants mayn't cheat me.

Sir *Will.* A politic Thought——

Wou'd. Hawking, hunting, fishing, fowling, at Seven——Architecture, at Eight——for to understand the Art of Building, is of mighty Consequence towards raising a Man's Fortune, you know,——Nine, for Poetry, in Honour of the Nine Muses——because I love the Ladies Company towards Bed-time——Thus, in a Month, I hope to become Master of all these Things; how like you my Rules, Gentlemen, ha?

Ned. Oh, wonderfully, ha, ha.

Wou'd.

Wou'd. Well, Poetry is one of the noblest Parts of the Mathematics — but we have such Factions now on Foot, that Music has put Poetry quite out of Tune—but that Suit—I must to my Taylor immediately. [*Aside.*

Ned. But, Mr. *Wou'dbe*, the Town say you are much in *Beliza*'s Favour———you won't rival my Brother, will you?

Wou'd. Not I, upon my Soul —— but does the Town really say so?

Ned. Why shou'd I tell you so else?

Wou'd. Nay, the Elegance of my Fabric, has titulated the Imagination of many a fine Lady, I assure you.

Sir *Will.* Ha, ha, ha, the Fool believes you.

Wou'd. Where do you dine, Sir *William*?

Sir *Will.* With my Sister *Cautious*.

Wou'd. If *Beliza* likes me ——I'm a happy Mortal; I'll make some Advance, and give her to understand I'm not inexorable. [*Aside.* I'll rendezvous you at the Portal of her Apartment after Dinner; your most obsequious— [*Exit.*

Ned. He took particular Notice of your Cloths, Brother; I'll venture a Guinea, the next Time he appears, he's equipt to a Hair, if either Money or Credit be in his Power; ha, ha, ha.

Sir *Will.* I believe that, but I'll give him enough on't if he is—'tis the most whimsical Coxcomb I ever saw.—

Ned. Well, but how goes it between you and *Beliza*, Brother?

Sir *Will.* I begin to doubt a Rival there, but who, I can't find out——She is grown indifferent of late, often abroad, and seldom in Humour, when at Home; if there be a Favourite in reserve, let her take Care to conceal him, for Faith, I have suck'd in the *Spaniard*'s Jealousy with their Air, and shou'd breath a Vein without Scruple————

Ned. Well, if ever I be in Love———of all Passions which agitate the Mind of Man———grant I may never be infected with Jealousy.

Sir *Will.* Thou prayest against the only Thing that gives Love a Relish.

Love like to luscious Meat, will Surfeits breed,
And hurt the Stomach which they're sent to feed.
Without a Grain of Jealousy apply'd,
Your Appetite, your Health, and Life's destroy'd. [Exit.

The SCENE *changes to* Belair's *Lodgings.*

Enter Belair *meeting Mrs.* Patch.

Bel. I foresee this Day, Mrs. *Patch*, will be a lucky Day——the Sight of thee——

Patch. Will not please you, I dare be positive, my Lady can't see you to Day. being oblig'd to go abroad.

Bel. Oh, propitious Disengagement—— Now, if my Incognita does but send— [*Aside.*] I'll wait for her return, let it be never so late——

Patch. Not to Day, sweet Sir —— your Love runs on Wheels——Pray, more softly, Sir.

Bel. This Girl's very pretty, I never minded her so much before —— Harkye, Child, I will come, if I miss thy Lady, thou shalt keep me Company.

Patch. You are merry, Sir.

Bel. I must be so, when I am near any Thing—— belonging to *Beliza* —— Methinks I entertain her whilst thou art near me.

Patch. I can't tell how you mean it, Sir——but I assure you, as fine Gentlemen as yourself, have paid their Devotions to me, before now——

Bel. Why not? he must be insensible, that so much Beauty cannot warm. [*Kisses her.*

Enter Robin.

Rob. Why, the Devil's in my Master——egad, I shall starve with him in Love's Kitchen, for he engrosses all Sorts of Flesh, I find, [*Aside.*

Patch. Not so close, I beseech you, Sir. [*Pushing him away.*

Bel. I protest my Heart feels a thousand Emotions for thee——

Patch. Pray stop your Emotions, Sir——and don't load me with your Heart for I have so many already I don't don't know where to put 'em, without choaking one another.

Rob. She need never fear that, he'll not stay so long.—

Bel. I protest it is a Pleasure to look on thee——

Rob. He does not love to be idle, I'll say that for him; but I bring him Employment and must disturb him—Sir.

Patch. I am not surpriz'd at that—for I take Pleasure to look on my self, and generally do it a thousand Times a Day.

Rob. Sir,—Sir,—Sir.

Bel. Ha! has she sent? [*Aside to* Robin.

Rob. The Maid stays for you, Sir.

Bel. Oh! Transport—run—fly, let every Thing be ready for my Change of Dress, I'll be there in an Instant—I wish this Girl were gone.

Rob. So, the Tide's turn'd already—Why, what a hurrying Life's this I lead. [*Exit.*

Patch. Well, what more fine Things, Sir.

Bel. Nay, I see you don't believe what I have said already—and an, an——pish pox——how shall I get rid of her————

Patch. You are out of Humour, Sir, I hope, I——

Bel. No, no, no, no, Child, I, I, I,—what the Devil shall I say—this is the most unlucky Accident.

Patch. What is, Sir?

Bel. A good Hint—why, my Man tells me there is a Friend of mine wounded in a Duel, and desires me to bring a Surgeon immediately—so dear little Rogue, excuse me, this Kiss to thy Lady, and tell her *Revel* lives not in her Absence—if this don't do't, I shall go distracted, that's certain——— [*Aside.*

Patch. Nay, I have done my Message, so your Servant. [*Exit.*

Bel. So, now for my dear unknown———Let me see, what am I?—ho, a Country Gentleman—I must restrain my Humour—a little Gravity will be necessary to adorn that Character—besides, the Invention's new, and gives the Intrigue the greater Gusto—

To gain my Point, I'll every Art improve,
All Policy's allow'd in War and Love. [Exit.

ACT II.

Beliza's Lodgings.

Beliza *and* Camilla.

Beliz. AND you are really in Love with this Stranger, Cousin?

Cam. I fear so, *Beliza.*

Beliz. To what Purpose?

Cam. To no Purpose at all, without thy Help.

Beliz. You are assur'd of me— but pr'ythee, in what can I help thee? You neither know who he is, nor what he is——he may, for ought you know, be a Wretch unworthy of your Esteem.

Cam. Impossible——I tell thee he's a Country Gentleman, which the Term brought up to Town on Business.

Beliz. Then how are you sure he is not married in the Country?

Cam. Start no Objections, I beseech you—I am sure he is not married——he did not look as if he was.

Beliz. Well, suppose he is what you'd have him be, you know your Father has dispos'd of you, and I'm afraid won't be prevail'd upon to alter his Mind.

Cam. Ay, there's the only Bar to all my Wishes; why shou'd our Parents impose upon our Inclinations, in that one Choice which makes us ever happy, or ever miserable?

Beliz. 'Tis an unjust Prerogative Parents have got, from whence I see no Deliverance without an Act of Parliament.

Cam. If thou art my Friend, *Beliza*, I may chance to cross my Father's Design, without the Help of the Senate.

Beliz. I confess I am a Well-wisher to Disobedience in Love Affairs——there's my Hand, instruct me how I may be serviceable.

Cam. Thus: I have sent *Flora* to give him an Invitation hither.———

Beliz. Hither!——to my Lodgings; 'tis well I sent Colonel *Revel* Word I shou'd not be at Home. [*Aside.*

Cam.

Cam. Yes, I hope you'll forgive the Liberty I have taken, I was not willing he ſhou'd know mine, till I had your Approbation of him.

Beliz. But how if my Lover, Sir *William*, ſhou'd happen to come, who is grown a perfect *Spaniard* ſince his Travels, and has of late been apprehenſive of a Rival, tho' from what Cauſe I know not ——— the Country Gentleman wou'd be in Danger, I aſſure you.

Cam. To prevent his being ſeen, I have order'd him to be brought in the Back-way——he is yet a Stranger to every Thing that concerns me —— he neither knows my Name nor Family——nor ſhall he, if you approve him not; therefore, after I have thank'd him for the Service he did me, I'll give him to underſtand I have a a Relation whoſe Judgment I rely on——and from her Mouth he muſt receive his Hopes, then I'll call you in and retire.

Beliz. You have a very good Opinion of me, Couſin.

Cam. I have ſo.

Enter Flora.

Flo. He waits your Pleaſure, Madam.

Cam. Bring him in———Couſin, you'll be at Hand.

Beliz. In the next Room. [*Exit* Beliza.

Enter Bellair, *gravely dreſt*.

Bel. This is an Honour ſo much above my Merit, Madam———that I receive it with Confuſion, and ſhall be uneaſy till you inform me how I may return this wonderous Favour———I am caught by *Venus*: What Eyes are there.

Cam. Rather inſtruct me, Sir, how I may return the Obligations I have to you; they are no common Ones—you purchas'd my Life at the Hazard of your own, and it ſhall be the Buſineſs of that Life you ſav'd (if ever ought falls within my Power) to ſerve you.——Oh, my Heart. [*Aſide*.

Bel. On that kind Promiſe will I build my Hopes; nay, I will rely upon it ——and now, Madam, I muſt declare that it is in your Power to over-pay the Hazard you have mention'd; the only Woman I could be content to take, for Better for Worſe, I ever ſaw; egad, I'm upon the very Precipice of Matrimony, if ſhe conſents. [*Aſide*.

Cam. Gratitude obliges generous Souls———then be aſſur'd, and aſk——pray Heaven his Deſigns be honourable——that he aſks the Right. [*Aſide.*

Bel. 'Tis done, faith, [*Aſide*] your Heart—I fear you'll think I am too bold in my Deſires———but you commanded me to ſpeak———and I durſt not tell you a Lye—yourſelf wou'd have diſcover'd it, for your beauteous Image is drawn ſo lively in my Breaſt, that you are Miſtreſs of every Thought, and every Wiſh about it.

Cam. My Soul tells him, thro' my Eyes, (I fear) that his Requeſt is granted, [*Aſide.*] I confeſs you have ſurpriz'd me, Sir, and I know not well what to anſwer you; only this———were I free to diſpoſe of my Perſon, with my Heart, your Services ſhou'd not go unrewarded.

Bel. Ha! what ſay you, Madam! your Words ſhake me like an Ague Fit—you are not—(forbid it Heaven) married?

Cam. Not married.

Bel. Nor vow'd againſt it?

Cam. Neither—but I've a Father to whom my Duty muſt ſubmit, without his Leave I meaſure not a Foot of his Eſtate, tho' I'm his only Child.

Bel. Let him keep it then,—if Love had any Power o'er your Soul——or had I Charms to wound like you, this wou'd be no Obſtacle.

Cam. You have too many, and I find my Heart but too inclining—were it poſſible, but my Duty————

Bel. Oh, Extaſy! I ſhan't contain myſelf [*Aſide.*] it is, it ſhall be poſſible——give me to underſtand your Father, Madam, that I may apply myſelf to him; if Avarice affects him, and Wealth be his only Aim, I am Heir to an Eſtate, perhaps, as large as he can wiſh.

Cam. But how are you ſure your Father will conſent; and why wou'd you hazard his Diſpleaſure for a Stranger, Sir?

Bel. The Eſtate's intail'd, he cannot hurt me there, and here I muſt be happy, or not at all——may I not know your Family?

Cam. Yet you muſt not.

Bel. Why ſhou'd you deny me——Is it not in my Power to know———Can I not enquire when I go out, whoſe Houſe this is?

Cam.

Cam. Without any Benefit by it——for these are a Friend's Lodgings, whose Judgment I esteem, you shall consult her; if she approves it, perhaps, you may know mine before Night—Who's there?

Enter Flora.

Desire *Beliza* to walk in————

Bel. Ha! Did she not name *Beliza?* I hope it is not that *Beliza* I know——if it shou'd, I'm in a fine Condition———— [*Enter* Beliza *and* Patch.] by ill Luck—the very She—what the Devil shall I do? [*Aside.*

Cam. Cousin, this is the Gentleman I'm so much oblig'd to——Mr. *Constant*, this is a Relation of mine.

Beliz. What do I see? Colonel *Revel* here————

Pat. Ay, tis even he.

Bel. There is no Excuse to be made now—thou never failing Power of Impudence assist me. [*Aside.*] I must honour every Thing that's related to you, Madam. [*Salutes her.*

Beliz. How grave he is in this Disguise—picques me, methinks, tho' I had no Design upon him.

Pat. How sober he looks————

Cam. This is the Friend I refer you to, Mr. *Constant.*

Pat. *Constant!*—Yes, he is constant with a Witness.

Cam. What she promises, I'll confirm. [*Exit.*

Bel. I'm in a hopeful Way, faith————Egad I'm so confounded, I know not how to look—but I'm resolv'd to carry it off, and persuade her I'm not the Man. [*Aside.* Madam, I'm oblig'd to my Stars, however, tho' they conceal the Family, and Name of her I adore, they give me an Opportunity of knowing her second Self, you being made so by the strictest Bonds of Friendship——This is the hardest Task I ever went thro', by *Jupiter.* [*Aside.*

Beliz. I don't wonder that you know me——but I am surpriz'd at your Impudence.

Bel. This is the first Time I was ever accus'd of that by a fair Lady: Wherein have I incurr'd your Displeasure?

Beliz. Pray, Sir, do you act this Part upon a Wager, or do you think I have lost my Senses—very pretty, truly—

Bel. A Wager.—Part—and Senses——What do you mean, Madam?—Oh, mischievous Encounter. [*Aside.*

Beliz. Colonel *Revel* can inform Mr. *Constant* of my Meaning.

Bel. Colonel *Revel!* Who's he?——A Pox of the Name. [*Aside.*

Pat. So, he don't know himſelf——

Beliz. You don't know ſuch a Man as Colonel *Revel?*

Bel Not I, upon my Word, Madam——

Beliz. Well, ſuch an Aſſurance I never ſaw, and do you think this will paſs upon me?

Bel. I hope ſo, [*Aside.*] I proteſt, Madam, I can't gueſs what you aim at——

Pat. Were I in your Place, Madam, I'd have him toſt in a Blanket.

Bel. Well ſaid, Mrs. *Patch:* Egad, wou'd I were well out of their Hands. [*Aside.*

Beliz. Lookye, Sir, your Declaration for my Couſin concerns me not; for from the Firſt, to me you appear'd as indifferent as now——But if you think to impoſe upon my Underſtanding, you'll draw my utmoſt Malice on your Head;

Bel. And I need no more——for the Malice of a Woman exceeds the Devil's. [*Aside.*] Your Rallery is very pleaſant, Madam, but very different from what I expected—for I confeſs, I am a Stranger to your Meaning.

Beliz. Oh, you ſhift your Shape ſo often, you may eaſily forget—an excellent Contrivance, to take as many Names as you make Miſtreſſes.

Pat. Conſult your Pocket-Book, Sir; and you'll find your Name was *Revel* two Hours ago——

Bel. This is a new Way of treating Strangers, Madam; Do you call this telling me the Secrets of the unknown Fair? This will make the pretrieſt Novel in the World—— [*Aside.*

Beliz. The Secrets of the unknown Fair; yes, ſhe ſhall know your Secrets, I promiſe you, and who you are——believe me, your Affairs are done with her; you ſhall neither know her Name, nor Quality.

Bel. Recal that Sentence, Madam; or, let me fall a Sacrifice, to your ſuppoſed Reſentments——never to know my lovely, dear Incognita is Death, with all the additional Racks *Barbarians* e'er invented, to ſeparate

Soul

Soul and Body. I begin to grow perfect in my double Art, I find. [*Aside.*

Beliz. This is the most bare-fac'd Impostor I ever saw. [*Aside.*] Really, now in my Opinion, Colonel, you act the same Person too long—Come, come, pull off the Mask, and I'll forgive you, ha, ha.

Bel. That Wheedle shan't take, I'm in, and must go thro' it. [*Aside.*] Mask, Madam! by all the Pangs of Love I feel for your beauteous Friend, I wou'd wear no Disguise to any Thing that belongs to her——

Pat. Well, was I my Lady, I'd have that Tongue pull'd out of your Head.

Bel. Pray, Madam, who is that pretty Enemy? is she Friend, or some Relation?

Pat. Do, do, seem ignorant, poor Devil—you don't know me; not long since, you knew me for this Lady's Maid, and lik'd me well enough, to think me worth a Compliment.

Beliz. Make Love to my Woman! Pray, Sir, what Name wou'd you have taken to her, ha, ha.

Bel. You are in a pleasant Humour, Ladies, I hope I shall find the Benefit of it; to my Knowledge, I never saw any of you till this Hour——This is a Master-piece of Art, to face down two Women at once. [*Aside.*]

Pat. Nay, if I had believ'd all he said to me, I shou'd have registered him amongst my Lovers. That is not true neither.

Bel. As the rest—Poor Gentlewoman, I pity thee; pr'ythee, get Advice, before thy Frenzy increase too much.

Beliz. So, you'll persuade us we are mad by and by—and you don't bear a Colonel's Commission, and have not been in *Portugal* with *Charles* the Third?

Bel. No, upon my Honour, Madam—My Name is *Constant*, born in *Oxfordshire*, and come up about a Suit in *Chancery*; and know this Colonel no more than you know me; if you please, I'll give you my Oath on't——which I can do without Perjury, that's my Comfort. [*Aside.*

Beliz. A pleasant Quibble, ha, ha.

Pat. This Story has cost you some Pains————

Bel. I wish I cou'd see this Gentleman which you take me for: Can you believe I cou'd be so base to make Love to another, if once I had presum'd to mention it to you—your Charms are full Security against such Proceedings; I am concern'd, that Nature has made any Resemblance between us: I shall hate myself for being like him.

Beliz. Well, whether you will, or you will not be him, it is the same Thing——provided you'll tell him, that I suffer'd his Addresses only for my Diversion, and that I never had any Passion for him, but loath, detest, and hate him.

Bel. Tell him———where shall I find him?

Beliz. I have done, and desire you'd know your Way out.

Bel. I wou'd not willingly disobey a Lady; but here, Madam, you must pardon me, since my future good or ill depends on you; I cannot stir from hence, till I obtain your Promise to assist my Suit, and give me hopes that I, at last may know my beauteous Fair.

Beliz. Ha, ha, ha, all that I can say, Colonel, is, that you are very unlucky in this Affair, not but you counterfeit to a Miracle; but the Mischief is, that I have all my Senses, can see Colonel *Revel*, hear Colonel *Revel*, and understand Colonel *Revel* too well to solicit his Cause, I assure you.

Pat. There's your Answer, Sir,——and if you please to follow me, I'll shew you a Way out better known to you than that you came in by.

Bel. Pray, good Mrs. *Civility*, be not so hasty—give me leave, at least, to see your Cousin before I go, Madam.

Beliz. To what End, pray?

Bel. To convince you of your Error.

Beliz. That's the hardest Task that you ever undertook, Colonel, and not to be effected; therefore, once more I tell you, you have seen your last of her, and your Absence wou'd oblige me.

Bel. 'Tis very hard, Madam, that because Nature has made me resemble another Person, who may, for ought I know, be a Man of Honour too, tho' unhappily under your Displeasure, I shou'd have the ill Fortune to suffer for Nature's Fault.

Beliz. That wou'd, indeed, be unjust——but I shall not be prevail'd upon to believe Nature in the Fault here; therefore pray retire, the Scene is long enough, 'tis time to change it; good Colonel don't oblige one to treat you below your Title.

Pat. Don't you understand my Lady, Sir?

Bel. Yes, yes, Madam, but too well; and if I must go without the Satisfaction I expected, let me implore this Favour; tell her, I die hers. [*Exit.*

Pat. And every Body's, I dare swear, in his turn.

Beliz. This Man is the very Epitome of his Sex; the compleatest Juggler I ever saw: I protest his Assurance has put me quite out of Countenance,

Re-enter Camilla.

Cam. Well, how do you like him, Cousin: Is he not a charming Fellow?

Beliz. I think not.

Cam. Pish! I know you do.

Bel. Indeed I don't; and if you knew as much as I, you wou'd think him as ugly as I do.

Cam. Ugly! Can any Mortal think that Man ugly? But pr'ythee, what have you discover'd—— won't you tell me?

Beliz. Yes, if you promise to make right use on't.

Cam. What do you mean?

Beliz. That your pretended Lover is a Villain.

Cam. How! Pray, Cousin, explain yourself within the Rules of good Manners.

Beliz. He deserves it not.

Cam. I don't understand you——and the Introduction grows tedious—of what do you accuse Mr. *Constant*?

Bel. In the first Place, his Name is not *Constant*, but *Revel.*

Cam. How know you that?

Beliz. From his own Mouth.

Cam. When?

Beliz. A Week ago.

Cam. Where?

Beliz.

Beliz. Here in this House.

Cam. In this House, how came he hither?

Beliz. Upon his Legs, I think.

Cam. On what Business, pray?

Beliz. Much upon the same Errand—Love.

Cam. Love! to whom?

Beliz. To your Friend and Servant.

Cam. Ha, ha, ha, now I find your Drift——you like him yourself, and this is an Artifice to blast my good Opinion—'tis poorly done, *Beliza.*

Beliz. No, my Constitution is not so warm as yours—remember you took Fire in the middle of Water; I despise him.

Cam. We never despise indifferent Things——I little expected this from a Friend.

Beliz. If you'd have the Friend continu'd, don't provoke me to return Suspicions, Cousin.

Cam. Don't you provoke me, by traducing of the Man I love—he has not been in Town two Days, and you'd persuade me he has made Overtures of Love to you a Week ago.

Beliz. If I don't prove this is Colonel *Revel*, lately come from *Portugal*, and been in Town this Fortnight, and made me several Visits under Pretence of Courtship *A-la mode*, I'm content to forfeit both Friendship and Estate.

Cam. How shall it be prov'd? 'Tis sure impossible.

Beliz. Write to him, and tell him what I have confirm'd; desire him to come hither to justify himself, if he expects any farther Favours from you—at the same Time I'll send for him by the Name of *Revel*, and appoint him here also, if there appear two Men exactly the same, (as I am sure they are) then I'll own myself in the Wrong, and ask your Pardon; if not, you shall mine.

Cam Agreed, I'll in, and write to him this Moment; pray Heaven there be two Socia's. [*Exit.*

Enter Sir William.

Sir *Will.* I am pleas'd.

Beliz. That's more than I am, I assure you, Sir *William.*

Sir *Will.* To find you alone, I meant, Madam; I am not

not ſurpriz'd at your being out of Humour, for I have ſeldom found you in it of late, the Reaſon of which I'm yet to learn, not being conſcious of having given you any Cauſe, except the trueſt Paſſion that e'er poſſeſs'd the Heart of Man be one.

Beliz. Sometimes, and in ſome Perſons it is ſo; but from whence you derive your Suſpicions, I can't imagine.

Sir *Will.* From your exceſſive Coldneſ ——for ſome Days paſt, I have beheld ſuch a Reſerve in all your Carriage to me, very different from what it us'd to be, and I begun to fear your Heart had entertain'd ſome new Amour.

Bel. I hope he has not diſcover'd this Impoſtor, he could not meet him, ſure. [*Aſide.*] You have no Reaſon to doubt my Sincerity, Sir *William*; I am not ſubject to fall in Love, I may venture to ſay, you hold the greateſt Share in my Heart.

Sir *Will.* That's kind—but this thin airy Diet of Hope and Expectation, *Beliza,* ſtarve thoſe which feed on't—will you not admit me to the Banquet of Poſſeſſion——when ſhall I receive from this Hand the Confirmation of thoſe Lips. [*Kiſſes her Hand.*

Beliz. When I can bring my Heart to a Reſolution, Sir *William*, of quitting all theſe little innocent Pleaſures a ſingle Life permits, you ſhall have timely Notice for a Licenſe.

Enter Patch.

Pat. Madam, your Couſin *Camilla* deſires one Word with you.

Beliz. Pardon my leaving you in my own Lodgings, Sir *William*, ſome Affairs of my Couſins, who is lately come to Town, preſs me at preſent; I ſhall come to Cards at Lady *Cautious*'s in the Evening. [*Exit.*

Sir *Will.* I'll not fail being at home——there's ſomething more in this than I can fathom; I reſolve to watch her narrowly, if I have a Rival, and 'ſcapes me, I forgive him. [*Exit.*

ACT

ACT III.

Sir William's *Lodgings.*

Sir William *meeting Lady* Cautious.

Sir *Will.* IN Tears, Sister, what's the Matter?

Lady. What shou'd be the Matter, but my Husband? that doating, old, disponding Wretch, whose Fears, Mistrusts and Jealousies, is enough to distract any Body, still doubting Providence, and fearing every Wind ——yet you are so far from pitying my Condition, you add to my Misfortunes, by making my Confinement stricter, under Pretence of the Honour of our Family—I hope I'm of Age to know how far that concerns me.

Sir *Will.* Ay, Sister, but the Wife that is displeas'd with the Husband–and the Husband that does not please the Wife, are always in Danger——she of liking some Body else—and he of being a Cuckold——now, while there is such a Probability, the Honour of our Family requires a Guard.

Lady. Why was I marry'd then to that I cannot love?

Sir *Will.* My Father knew his Reasons, doubtless, Sister.

Lady. Yes, and I know 'em too——Sir *Paul* took me without a Fortune, by which yours is the greater, yet the Consideration has no Weight with you; it pleases you to see your Sister condemn'd to the idle Fancies, and whimsical Mistrusts of this impertinent Dotard; he is so apprehensive of Death, that he allows a Surgeon a Hundred a Year perpetually to attend him, and wou'd not set a Step without him for a Thousand—nay, he lays in the same Chamber———just now he fancied himself call'd three Times, which he takes for an Omen of his Death, pray Heaven it prove so—and has sent for twenty People to watch by him.

Sir *Will.* Ridiculous Folly—but you must bear with it, Sister; he is old———

Lady. That's the worst Argument under the Sun, for a young Woman to bear with. [*Aside.*] Pray, Brother, what Gentleman is that which you have oblig'd with these Lodgings?

Sir

Sir *Will.* Ha! has ſhe ſeen him—Why do you aſk?

Lady. Is it a Crime to aſk who is in my own Houſe?

Sir *Will.* Yes, if they are not in your own Apartment—'tis not Modeſty in your Sex to inquire after ours—now I foreſee my Error too late, in letting him have theſe Lodgings—How came you to know there was a Man here?

Lady. I muſt not ſay, I have ſeen him— [*Aſide.*] my Woman brought me Word, there was a Stranger dreſſing himſelf, when I ſent her this Morning, to aſk if you wou'd not drink ſome Chocolate with me.

Sir *Will.* Then you did not ſee him yourſelf?

Lady. No.

Sir *Will.* I'm glad to hear that, for he is Libertine enough to engage her.

Lady. But ſuppoſe I had, where had been the Crime?

Sir *Will.* Nay, no Crime, Siſter———only I wou'd not have you affronted; therefore, pray take care not to come near this Apartment, for he hates the Sight of Women.

Lady. That's falſe, to my Knowledge—for he ſaid the ſofteſt Things to me that Love cou'd form; [*Aſide.*] ſay you ſo, Brother? an unpoliſhed Brute, I hope he is not to continue long here?

Sir *Will.* Only, for two or three Days.——

Lady. Oh, my Heart—ſo ſhort a Stay. [*Aſide.*

Sir *Will.* Ho, here he comes, retire Siſter.

Lady. I muſt ſee him again——tho' you prevent me now; if I don't break through this Conſtraint, ſay, Woman wants Contrivance. [*Exit.*

Enter Belair *and* Robin.

Rob. Why then, this prov'd a confounded Miſtake, Sir, but were it poſſible you cou'd not know the Houſe again?

Bel. How cou'd I, when I was convey'd the back Way into an Apartment, where I never was before; the cunningeſt Man alive, might have been deceived, as well as I——but the Gift of Impudence is a wonderful Gift; ha! Sir *William*, I did not ſee thee.

Sir *Will.* I believe not, Love and Variety clouds thy Sight, but what is the Diſappointment you ſpeak of?

Bel.

Bel. I am an unlucky Dog, that's all———I fell into the Company of both my Mistresses, at once.

Sir *Will.* This 'tis to have more Intrigues than one can manage, ha, ha, ha,; and how did you behave yourself?

Bel. Faith en'cavalierement — I stuck close to the Name of *Constant*, and my Incognita—for I like her best.

Rob. Till he sees somebody he likes better. [*Aside.*

Bel. And swore I never saw t'other, in my Life, nor never heard of the Name of *Revel*—but was as downright a Country Gentleman, and made Love as gravely, as ever a Squire of 'em all.

Sir *Will.* And did the Imposition pass?

Bel. Not without Scruple——but I'll undertake to make myself two distinct Persons, as clear as the Sun at Noon-day, if thou'lt assist me.

Sir *Will.* How? for the Frolick's sake, I care not if I do———

Bel. Then, as I have Occasion, you shall receive Instructions, I want a Messenger in my Interest.

Sir *Will.* That I can procure you—but to what Purpose.

Bel. You shall know in Time—I shall want thy personal Appearance too.

Sir *Will.* You shall want nothing, in my Power—but pr'ythee do you like either of 'em well enough to marry?

Bel. In my Conscience I think I cou'd be content with the Noose, if my Incognita's Family be answerable to her Beauty———

Rob. Nay, if he grows honourably in Love, I may hope for some Rest at last. [*Aside.*

Sir *Will.* Why will ye not quit the other then?

Bel. T'other is related, and a Friend—if I deceive her not, she'll maliciously spoil my Intrigue; besides, 'tis a pretty Amusement, and the Design so Novel, that I must pursue it for the Pleasure of Invention, and I think it possible to perform; we have seen two People so very like, that when absent they cou'd not be distinguish'd from one another.

Sir *Will.* But if the Faces wore Resemblance, the Voice or Shape discover'd it.

Bel.

Bel. But a good Aſſurance ſolves all that.

Rob. Why, Sir, if the worſt come to the worſt—that they will both have you—why e'en marry them both, keep one for yourſelf, and t'other to entertain your Friends—or, if you pleaſe, Sir,—to do you a Service, I don't care if I take one of 'em off your Hands.

Sir *Will.* Then you'l venture to rely upon your Maſter's Choice, ha, ha, ha.

Rob. Ay, Sir, ſooner than ere a Man in *England*; my Maſter has taſted ſo many of thoſe Diſhes — that I dare truſt to his Palate.

Bel. You are witty, Raſcal, ha! Who have we here, thy Mimick.

Enter Wou'dbe, *dreſt like Sir* William, *and* Ned. Freelove.

Wou'd. Well, I have ſurprized ſome Ladies, ſtrangely, that ſtop'd their Coach, and call'd out Sir *William*, Sir *William*; and when I turn'd back, and they diſcover'd their Miſtake, they bluſh'd intolerably, ha, ha, ha. [*Aſide to* Ned.

Ned. Nay, your Dreſs is exactly the ſame with his; the Miſtake was very eaſy.

Sir *Will.* Mr. *Wou'dbe*, your Servant.

Wou'd. Surprizing! another Suit!

Bel. Ha, ha, ha, what a Conſternation you have put him in?

Ned. What's the Matter with you, Sir? This Minute you look'd as gay, and pleaſant as the Month of *June*, and now it is *December* at leaſt — he has diſcover'd you, Brother.

Wou'd. Moſt beatifically expreſt, and worthy of Quotation. [*Takes out a Pocket-book and writes.*

Bell. I preſume, Sir, you are examining, what Aſſignations fall out this Hour, that you may not diſappoint the Ladies.

Wou'd. No, Sir, I am taking Cognizance of the Gentleman's Wit.

Bel. I hope you are not one of thoſe Spungy-brain'd Poets, that ſuck ſomething from all Companies to ſqueeze into a Comedy, at acting of which, the Pit and Boxes may laugh at their own Jeſts.

Ned.

Ned. Where each may claim his Share of Wit.

Bel. And by my Consent, shou'd claim a Share of the Profits too, ha, ha.

Wou'd. This is a Gentleman of an intellectual Sublimity—— No, Sir, I contemn the terrene Extraction of those poor Animals, whose barren Intellects thrusts such spurious Brats abroad; when I write, it shall be all my own I assure you.

Sir *Will.* Oh, Mr. *Wou'dbe* can never want Assistance of that kind.

Wou'd. What shall I do with these Cloths! I wou'd not give a Farthing for 'em, now he has left 'em off—and that's ten Times the prettier Suit in my Opinion—Well, he is the most genteel Fellow in *Europe*.

Enter Robin.

Rob. Sir, Sir, the Incognita's Maid, Sir, has brought you this Letter, and stays for an Answer.

[*Gives him a Letter.*

Bel. Ha! Reads — *My Cousin has a strange Opinion of you, and nothing but your Personal Appearance immediately can prevent my giving Credit to her Story; make Haste, if you expect any farther Favours from your Incognita* —— any farther Favours! Yes, I do expect farther Favours, or I'd never take half this Pains—Let me see [*Pauses.*

Wou'd. I wish'd I cou'd sell this Coat——I shall never indure the Sight of it, that's certain. [*Aside.*

Bel. Hark ye, Sirrah, do you tell the Maid, I'll not fail the Summons——and do you hear, follow her at a Distance, till you see her Hous'd; if she goes to *Beliza*'s, do you ask to speak with *Beliza*'s Cousin, and tell her you left me in the Street talking to somebody, but that she might not think me long, I sent you before; besure you make no Blunders, Sirrah.

Rob. I warrant you, Sir, Lying is become my Vocation; but, Sir, what Name, Sir?

Bel *Constant*, you forgetful Blockhead.

Rob. Ha, I have it, the Country Gentleman, Sir——

Bel. Ay, ay, away. [*Aside to* Robin.] [*Exit.* Robin.

Sir *Will.* What, another Billet-doux?

Bel. 'Tis from my unknown — now for thy Assistance.

Wou'd.

Wou'd. What Contrivance ſhall I have for ſuch a Dreſs—my Rogue of a Taylor will not truſt, that's certain. Let me think——that won't do—nor that——ho, I have it————

[*Takes out his Book and writes,*

Bel. This Meſſenger muſt be had immediately, Sir *William.*

Sir *Will.* I'll procure you one inſtantly.

Bel. Then I'm Maſter of my Art.

Wou'd. Sir *William,* I recommend that to your Peruſal [*Gives him the Tablets.*] If this Project takes not, I'm undone———— [*Aſide.*

Sir *Will.* What's this [*Reads.*] *We whoſe Names are here ſubſcrib'd, do promiſe to make our Perſonal Appearance in the Side-Box, the third Day of a new Play, either Tragedy, Comedy, Farce, or Opera, that ſhall be written by* Timothy Wou'dbe, *Eſq; and play'd at one of the Houſes or both, as the Players can agree about that, on Forfeit of a Guinea, which we have depoſited in the Hands of the Author.*

Ned. Ha, ha, ha, a pretty Contrivance for another Suit.

Bel. This is new, indeed, ha, ha, ha.

Sir *Will.* I love to encourage Ingenuity, he has flung away many a Guinea after me, now I'll give him one —pray enter me down Mr. *Wou'dbe.*

Wou'd. Let me intreat your own Hand, for the Incouragement of others. [*Sir* William *writes.*

Bel. I'll not be out at a Frolic, there's mine, Sir.

Sir *Will.* There, Brother, enter your Name too————

[*Gives* Ned *a Guinea.*

Ned. Ha, ha, with all my Heart there is *Belvil, Loveil,* and *Freewit*—you may depend on Mr. *Wou'dbe.*

Wou'd. I'll wait on 'em incontinently.

Bel. But, when is this Play to be writ, Sir?

Wou'd. That I muſt conſider on, Sir; too many Things at once deſtroy the Thought, and dull the Fancy.

Ned. But ſuppoſe it ſhou'd not live till the third Day, the Town is very capricious.

Wou'd. I know it, Sir, for that Reaſon I took this Method; when their Gold is at Stake, they'll bring in their Bodies, to ſave their Bail —— egad, I ſhan't have

Money enough—Let me ſee——I'll ſell theſe Clothes, to make it up——Gentlemen, I'm your moſt oblig'd——
[*Exit.*

Ned. Ha, ha, ha, he is upon the Wing, with his Subſcription, I'll follow, and ſee if he goes to their Lodgings.
[*Exit.*

Sir *Will.* Now, for thy Buſineſs, *Belair*, where ſhall I find you half an Hour hence?

Bel. Here, for I muſt now dreſs me.

Sir *Will.* Very well. [*Exit.*

Bel. So, thus far I'm right——now for half an Hours Reſpite from the Fatigue of Buſineſs——egad, I wiſh the pretty Creature, I ſaw in the Morning, wou'd fall in my Way—who the duce is ſhe, I wonder—no Matter who, ſhe's handſome—and that's Knowledge enough, to recommend her———Ha! here ſhe comes by *Jove.*

Enter Lady Cautious.

Lady. Here he is! a charming handſome Fellow—what Excuſe ſhall I make?—ha—I thought Sir *William* had been here—Sir, I beg your Pardon———

Bel. He's juſt gone out, Madam, he's a happy Man, to have ſo much Beauty in Queſt of him.

Lady. Beauty's an Epithet your Sex never fail to make Uſe of to raiſe our Vanity, when preſent, but the Object once remov'd, you ſoon recall your Praiſes.

Bel. Sometimes, Madam, good Manners produce Adulation; but here Flattery dares not ſhow her Face, your Charms are ſo conſpicuous, they need no Art to inform your Knowledge, nor I no Cunning to inſlave myſelf; I am chain'd already, your Eyes at firſt Sight reduc'd me, and the ſhort Moments which we paſs'd this Day together, made ſuch an Impreſſion on my Heart, that I have thought of nothing ſince but how to ſee you again.

Lady. Oh! how his Words run thro' my Soul——alas, Sir, to what Purpoſe ſhou'd you ſee me, I am married.

Bel. Good———

Lady. Wretchedly married.

Bel. Better and-better—wretchedly married, ſay you?

Lady.

Lady. Wretchedly—— to an old peevish desponding Wretch.

Bel. As I cou'd wish—her Dislike of her Husband is my first Step to Possession——— [*Aside.*

Lady. Forc'd by my Friends to wed him, by which all my Happiness in this World is lost.

Bel. Banish that Thought my charming Creature—— 'tis a false one; there are Joys, inestimable Joys in Store, give me but Leave, and I'll inform you where they may be reap'd. [*Taking her Hand.*

Lady. Not by me without a Crime.

Bel. The Crime be on their Heads that forc'd your Marriage, Nature ne'er design'd these Charms shou'd wither in the Arms of Age, and destin'd only to a Clod ——besides your not consenting to the Match makes it invalid, and of no Force to hold you—take Pity, then, both of yourself and me, I languish, sigh, despair—nay, e'en die for you.

Lady. Help me, Heaven, I have no Power to speak—

Bel. Oh! do not struggle so, nor dash my rising Hopes, leave me not, except you wish my Death, which I resolve the Moment you depart———

Lady. Forbid that Thought, I cannot see you die—yet must not yield; let me go for Virtue's sake———

Bel. Love forbids it—Oh! I shall faint with Extacy of Pleasure—no Jessamin nor Rose has half the Sweets that dwell upon these Lips, 'tis Essence from the Throne of *Jove*—this Neck, this Breast—Oh! every Part about thee is Celestial, Loadstone like, thy Breath attracts and draws my Lips to thine. [*Kissing her.*

Lady. Oh! the Difference between his Kisses, and my Husbands, what shall I do———

Bel. Do! Consent to bless the Man that loves you.

Lady. But how long will he do so?

Bel. That's ever the Womens Question—ask not that; can I prove false to so much Beauty, oh, no, faithful as the Needle to its Pole, or Turtle to his Mate, secret as a Priest——and loving as the Vine——give me Possession once, and bind the truest of his Sex for ever. [*Pulling her.*

Sir Paul *within.*

Sir *Paul*. *Basilicon*———

Lady. Ah, [*Shrieks.*] my Husband's Voice.

Sir *Paul*. [*Within.*] Ah, Thieves, Thieves.

Bel. A Curse of all ill Luck —Just in the critical Minute when she was yielding——— 'Death, what shall I do, Madam, can, can, can, can, you put me no where?

Lady. Impossible, he'll search all the House—now the Duce take me for shrieking——— [*Aside.*

Bel. Then there's no way—but to cut his Throat.

Lady. Now help me, dear, dear Invention [*Pauses.*

Sir *Paul*. *Basilicon*, why where's my Surgeon there—I shall be murder'd here's Thieves got into my House.

Lady. A lucky Hint, improve it.

Bel. Improve what?

Enter Sir Paul, *and Servants.*

Sir *Paul*. What's here, a Man, a Thief, a Thief, fall on, fall on.

Bel. I shall be apprehended for a Rogue, here—make your Mermidons be civil, Sir, or I shall whip you thro' the Guts, by *Hercules*. [*Lays his Hand on his Sword.*

Sir *Paul*. *Basilicon*, keep near me *Basilicon*———

Lady. Oh! Hold, hold, Sir *Paul*, What do you do! Abuse a Gentleman that came to save your Life.

Bel. What the Devil does she mean now—some Turn to bring me off, if I can but hit her right.

Lady. Tell him you saw the House beset with Rogues, tell him, tell him, any Thing. [*Aside to* Bel.

Bel. Humph, ha, Oh, witty Rogue———

Sir *Paul*. Ha, how's that?

Bel. Yes, Sir, I came to do you Service.

Sir *Paul*. As how, pray, sweet, Sir? To lye with my Wife, ha!

Bel. No, Sir, coming by your House I saw four Men, and heard 'em say, that's the Door, dog him to some convenient Place, and then secure him.

Sir *Paul*. Secure me, for what, Sir? I owe no-body nothing, I have no Employment in the State, Sir.

Bel. Your Riches is much talk'd on, Sir, and People imagine

imagine you have got that which we call the Philosopher's Stone; I believe they design to rob and murder you, I heard 'em mutter something of ripping you up, and Diffecting you.

Sir *Paul.* Oh! Bloody Villains.

Lady. Excellent Fellow——. [*Aside.*

Bel. They talk'd as if you swallow'd the Stone every Morning, and kept it in your Body for greater Security all Day.

Sir *Paul.* Monstrous!

Bel. I find their Design is to search for that Stone, which, if they get it, will make them as rich as Aldermen ever after.

Sir *Paul.* Barbarous— Sir, if you'l believe me, I don't know what they mean by the Philosopher's Stone, as I hope for long Life——I have no Stone worth a Groat, except the Stone of this Ring.

Bel. Nay, I know nothing of that, Sir, I thought myself bound in Honour, tho' unknown to you, to give you Notice of your Danger.

Sir *Paul.* Sir, I heartily thank you—My Coachman, indeed, told me there was four Men behind my Coach last Night, which made me not go abroad to Day; these must be the Rogues.

Lady. It passes as I would have it——but I wish he had been at the Bottom of the Sea, when he interrupted us, for that charming Fellow has got my Heart, I find that. [*Aside.*

Bel. Pox take him for his unseasonable Intrusion. [*Aside.*

Sir *Paul.* I thought I heard you shriek out, Wife.

Lady. I wish I had been dumb when I did—yes, my Dear, with design to raise the House, to pursue, and take the Rogues, this Gentleman told me of, at least disperse 'em, that my Love might be in no Danger.

Sir *Paul.* Oh, was it that, very well—come, you and I will retire to my Closet, and return Thanks for this Deliverance, *Basilicon*; come you along with us, Sir, I thank you. [*Exit.*

Lady. I never had less Religion about me in my Life. *Exit.*

Bel. If thou had'st stay'd but one Quarter of an Hour longer, Old Noll, thou shou'dst have had something to have thank'd me for.

Enter a Servant.

Serv. Sir *William* sends to tell you, that he, and the Gentleman you want, stays for you at the Coffee-house, Sir.

Bel. I come— [*Exit Servant.*] was there ever such a promising Project crost; I must have her—and I find she must have me too———

What various Hazards do we Rovers run,
To purchase what we slight as soon as won;
And Women know it too, yet long to be undone.

The End of the THIRD ACT.

ACT IV.

Robin, *solus.*

Rob. HERE she went in!—let me see—I am to say—what am I to say?—pox on't, my Master gives me so many different Lessons, one knocks t'other out of my Head—he is doing—doing, no, no, he did not bid me say he was doing—he was stopt in the Street—ay, ay, that's right, and his Name——ads bud, I have forgot his Name now——but here's the Maid, and so 'tis no Matter.

Enter Flora.

Flor. Ha! *Robin!* is your Master come?

Rob. He's coming, Child—a Lawyer, I believe, for he had a swinging Stroke with his Tongue, stopt him in the Street, about his Law-Suit, I suppose, so he sent me Express, fraught with his eager Wishes, to beg thy Lady's Patience for two Minutes only, and then he'll throw him-

self

ſelf at her Feet———egad, I think I have made as noble a Speech as ever a Courtier of 'em all. [*Aſide.*

Flora. Why don't you come in, and deliver your Meſſage, then?

Rob. Now I have ſeen thee I dare not.

Flor. Why, what do you fear?

Rob. Thoſe pinking Ogles of thine—But now I think on't, if my Maſter and your Lady Couple, thou'lt fall to me of Courſe.

Flor. To you——I believe not, Sir.

Rob. But I believe yes — are not we Perquiſites made for one another?——our Station's the ſame—our Employment alike——you dreſs your Lady—— ſo do I my Maſter—you receive and deliver Meſſages, ſo do I—and lying is the common Vocation of us both.

Flor. You are very familiar in your Courtſhip.

Rob. 'Tis my Way—but I know Truth is an out-of-faſhion'd Courtſhip, which your Sex is not us'd too. Ha! my Maſter. [*Enter* Belair *dreſt for* Revel.] Sir, I did your Meſſage.

Bel. My Meſſage, Fellow, what Meſſage? This Dog will ſpoil all by his Blunders; he does not ſee that I'm *Revel* now; [*Aſide.*] do you know who you ſpeak too?

Rob. By my Troth, I don't know—and yet methinks I ſhou'd know too.

Flor. 'Tis very ſtrange if he ſhou'd not know his Maſter.

Rob. Why, Sir, pray are not you my Maſter, co, co, co.

Bel. I'll tell you, Raſcal. [*Strikes him a Box on the Ear.*

Rob. Egad, I'm in the wrong, but where I can't tell—his Fingers are grown plaguy flippant of late.

Bel. Is *Beliza* within, my Dear, doſt know?

Flor. I believe ſhe is, Sir — I'll let her know you'd ſpeak with her, if you'll pleaſe to ſignify what Name you'll wear at preſent———

Bel. Name! Why, my own Name, Child, *Revel*; what Name ſhou'd I wear? Thou art pleaſant, ha, ha, ha.

Rob. There was my Miſtake, now. [*Aſide.*

Flor. Here ſhe comes, Sir.

Enter Beliza.

Bel. So darts the Sun thro' all the thick wrought Clouds, to chear the labouring Swain. [*Catching her in his Arms.*

Beliza. Hold, Sir! Who are you pray? The Colonel, or the Country Gentleman —— the grave, serious, formal Lover, or the gay rakish Soldier? — let me know, I beseech you, that I may square my Conversation to yours.

Bel. Ha, ha, ha, Why these Interrogatories? Madam, do you walk in your Sleep? — now I fancy you are in a Dream; ay, it is so, faith ——— and I cannot resist the Opportunity for Gloves. [*Kisses her.*

Beliza. Away, thou exquisite Dissembler——— How can you look me in the Face?

Bel. Because I don't know a Face in *Europe* that pleases me half so well——but pr'ythee, why this Air of Indifference, or rather, Resentment? Look ye, Madam, if you affect this Quarrel by the Way of poignant Sauce—— you have no Need of those little Recourses of your Sex ——*Revel* loves as much as ever, and dare promise——

Beliza. More than you perform.———

Bel. Accuse me not before you try me—but why these cross Purposes—ha, my Incognita! now *Belair*, play thy Part. [*Aside.*

Beliza. Here's one will inform you.———

Enter Camila.

Cam. Oh, Mr. *Constant*, are you come?

Bel. *Constant!* Yes, Faith, Madam, I'm as constant as any Man——— this Lady can witness for me.

Beliza. Not in the Court of Conscience, Sir.

Bel. Then you have no Conscience at all.

Rob. If my Master took up Lying by the Week, what a confounded Interest 'twou'd come to in a Year. [*Aside.*

Cam. Do you know why I sent for you so soon, Mr. *Constant?*

Bel. No, Madam—nor that you sent for me at all.

Beliz. You mistake, Cousin, this is Colonel *Revel*, ha, ha.

Cam. Colonel fiddle, is it not?--sure I know Mr. *Constant.*

Bel. *Constant!* Who is he, Madam?

Cam. Who's he? Why, are not you he?

Bel. Not that I know of.

Beliza. Ha, ha, ha, you shall be *Revel*, Sir, till *Constant* comes, if my Cousin will give you Leave———

Cam.

Cam. I'm supriz'd at his Impudence—pray, were not you here two Hours ago, Sir?

Bel. Not that I remember—

Cam. Impossible—did not you save me from drowning, yesterday.

Bel. 'Twas in my Sleep, then—for waking I'm sure I did not.

Cam. Distraction—Nor is not your Name *Constant*? And *Oxfordshire*.

Bel. Quite wrong——this is a pretty *Christmas* Game Lady——but, pray let me have some Commands, as well as all Questions.

Cam. Nor don't you know this Footman?

Bel. Again—No, Madam, never saw him in my Life.

Rob. Oh Lord, Oh Lord, who am I now——for he has renounc'd me heartily. [*Aside.*

Beliza. What say you Friend, don't you know this Gentleman neither?

Rob. No more than I do the great *Mogul*, Madam.

Cam. Who do you belong to——

Rob. Belong to, Madam! why, why, why, a Pox of his 'tother Name, now I can't think on't, if I were to be hang'd. [*Aside.*

Cam. Ay, who do you belong to, I say, again?

Rob. Why, I belong to my Master, Madam.

Beliza. And what is that Master's Name, pray?

Rob. Name, Madam—his Name is—ad, now I think on't, I won't tell his Name——why, sure I'm too big to be catechis'd.

Bel. This Dog will betray me. [*Aside.*

Flor. You challeng'd this for your Master, just now.

Rob. What if I did, Mistress, what then? He is not, it seems, without his being double, as you pretend—the Devil shou'd have doubled me too.

Cam. What Business have you here?

Rob. Business! why I brought a Message from my Master to one of you——and so good by——

Cam. Hold, stay, Sir—pray, what was that Message?

Rob. Why, that my Master wou'd be here, presently—

Bel. Oh, I suppose, this is Mr. *Constant*'s Man, that you mistake me for—ah, Pox of his Memory. [*Aside.*

Rob. You have hit it, Sir—Mr. *Constant* is my Master. now his Name's out———

Cam. I'm astonish'd! Cousin, did you ever hear the like?

Beliza. Yes, the very same——— but I traduc'd Mr. *Constant* then, you know———What say you, *Revel*, did I?

Bel. Hey, Ladies! do you design to bait me, if so, give me fair Play, at least———hark ye, draw off your Cousin, and confess your Plot———or egad I'll humour her Frenzy, take the Name of *Constant*, and make Love to her before your Face.

Beliza. With all my Heart, 'tis not the first Time——— and I have no further Services for you, ha, ha, ha.

Rob. So, he's in a fair Way to lose 'em both. [*Aside.*

Enter Messenger and Attendant.

Mess. I arrest you, Sir, in an Action of High Treason.

Bel. Treason, Sir! Sure you mistake the Man.

Beliza. Ha! how's this?

Mess. Your Name's *Revel*, Sir.

Bel. My Name is *Revel*, Sir, but guilty of no such Crime.

Rob. Here's a Turn now—I must second him. [*Aside.*

Mess. That must be prov'd, 'tis no Business of mine, I am only to execute my Orders.

Cam. I am concern'd for him methinks——— won't you take Bail, Sir?

Mess. In these Cases no Bail is admitted, Madam.

Beliza. My Mind misgives me this is a Trick.

Mess. Come, Sir, I can't stay———

Rob. Hold, hold, Sir, pray enter my Action too, for a Box of the Ear he gave me just now———this is some Comfort, however, I shall see him hang'd.

Bel. Come, Gentlemen, I can easily prove my Innocence—if I stand fair in this Lady's Opinion, I cannot fear the World. [*To* Beliza.] [*Exit with Messengers.*

Beliza. I wish you a good Deliverance, Colonel ——I know not what to think.

Rob. I'll see him lodg'd, I'm resolv'd [*Exit.*

Cam. Nor I ——to what End can a Man affect these Disguises?

Beliza. Out of Gallantry, Cousin—I shall hardly be con-

convinc'd without I ſaw them both together———I pity the Colonel's unhappy Diſgrace; but, believe me, now he is arreſted, *Conſtant* is no more, his Man following him plainly ſhew'd the Cheat.

Cam. Nay, I confeſs, they are extremely alike, but obſerving very narrowly, I think their Features are not exactly the ſame.

Flor. You are of my Mind, Madam—for methinks, he is half an Inch taller than Mr. *Conſtant.*

Cam. And ſomething about his Face, I don't know what—

Flor. I fancy his Noſe is ſomething longer.

Cam. Thou haſt hit it; it is his Noſe, I'm ſure.

Enter Belair *for* Conſtant.

Beliza. You are both mad, I'm ſure——ha, ha, ha,——bleſs me! Pray Heaven it ben't the Devil that thus deludes us.

Bel. I am come, Madam, according to your Commands——but if my Reception prove like the laſt, the Pleaſure of ſeeing you will very much abate—I am firſt at the Rendezvous, I perceive.

Cam. Now, Couſin, you are convinc'd, I hope.

Beliza. You are, I ſee.

Flor. Now, Madam, I can tell you the very Difference, his Eyes are a little-little larger.

Cam. Nay, I think they are a great deal larger.

Bel. Why do you ſurvey me ſo Madam? is it poſſible that you can be deceiv'd too—Where is this Colonel to be found? Will he not come?

Cam. He is juſt gone.

Beliza. He has diſengag'd himſelf, Sir, to leave you Room to act your Part.

Bel. Why did you not keep him, I ſent my Man before me to let you know, I would inſtantly be here.

Beliza. How could we when the Queen's Authority favour'd his Retreat.

Bel. How ſay you, Madam? has the Queen ſent for him.

Beliza. How cunningly you diſſemble—but that's not new, Diſſimulation ſeems your natural Gift.

Bel. Still these Reproaches, will nothing that I say convince you?——Why did you consent to let him go?

Cam. Why, do you really think this is still the same? [*To* Beliza.

Beliza. I do really——the Trap was laid with too much Policy to be prevented, knowing the Messenger I never suspected the Truth of the Action—but I may change to counter-plot you yet. [*Exit.*

Bel. So, she is gone to the Prison——but she'll return as unsatisfied as she went. [*Aside.*] Why do you take Pleasure to insult the Man, your Beauty has inslav'd? If my Visits be offensive—tho' I die without you——I prefer your Peace so much above my own, I'll never disturb you with my Presence more.

Cam. He looks, methinks, with such an honest Face, it can be only *Constant*; [*Aside.*] you must own, I have Reason to suspect you—but you have a powerful Advocate within, which pleads in your Excuse, and fain wou'd justify you.

Enter Robin.

Rob. At last, I am satisfied—the Spark is Cag'd.

Flo. Did you follow him?

Rob. Do you doubt it;

Bel. Whom, speak?

Rob. Oh, Sir, are you there?——you'll be hang'd in Effigy To-morrow———

Bel. How, Sauce-box!

Rob. Ay, Sir, he did box me, but I shall have a swinging Revenge.

Bel. Revenge, for what?

Rob. Why, Sir, your Likeness—that here has been such a Sputter about—is taken up for Treason, Murder, Robbery, and the Devil and all———

Bel. Oh, Misfortune! to be like such a Rascal.

Rob. Ay, so it is indeed, Sir—I thought he wou'd have been pull'd to-pieces in the Street—there were Girls of Fourteen, and Women of Fourscore, with Actions of Ravishment against him——and Tavern, and Eating-house Bills in abundance.

Bel. The Rogue has improv'd the Hint admirably [*Aside.*

Rob. (Tis an ill-bred Scoundrel, he is very like you, Sir, that's the Truth on't) he gave me the damndest Box on the Ear, only because I mistook him for you——he has a swinging Fist, Sir, that was all the Distinction I cou'd make between you—— but I shall see him truss'd up for it, that's my Comfort.

Cam. I am extremely pleas'd to find they are two different Persons.

Enter Sir William.

Sir *Will.* *Constant!* I can't believe my Eyes.

Bel. Why, what surprizes thee?

Sir *Will.* I met thy very Likeness in Custody of a Messenger, and stop'd 'em to examine the Reason—— the Spark snapp'd me up short, and told me 'twas none of my Business, bad 'em pass on——I admir'd at the Meaning, for I cou'd have sworn it had been the—ha! that is *Beliza*'s Lodgings, certainly. [*Aside.*

Bel. Was he drest like me too?

Sir *Will.* No, that was the only Distinction I found about him——I wish *Beliza* ben't the other Woman——

Bel. Now, Madam——are you still in Suspence?

Cam. I'm convinc'd, and over-joy'd, to find you what I wish you.

Sir *Will.* If my Suspicions be true, I have a pretty Kind of an Employment here——serving my Rival against myself. [*Aside.*

Enter a Servant.

Serv. Madam, your Father wants you——he talks of having you married to Night——

Rob. How's that, egad, my Master will be fobb'd at last, I fear. [*Aside.*

Cam. Oh, Unfortunate——

Sir *Will.* If it be so, 'tis some Pleasure at least to know the Man, [*Aside.*

Bel. What do I hear? Oh, Madam, if ever Pity touch'd your Soul, exert it now—think where you are going, think too, who you leave—give me some Assurance

ance to support my Hope, that you will disobey your Father—or I am miserable.

Cam. Believe me, my Surpize is as great as yours, I promise to use my utmost Arguments against it; if I fail, you shall then know my Father, and use your own Discretion. [*Exit with* Flora.

Bel. That's all I ask—unexpected Turn of ill Fortune; this News has chang'd the very Countenance.

Sir *Will.* Why, one wou'd swear thou wer't really in Love.

Bel. And not be forsworn, Sir *William*; for, faith, I do love her heartily, and am ready to capitulate for better for worse, as soon as she pleases.

Sir *Will.* I'm glad to hear that—one Thing, pray, tell me, without Reserve———

Bel. Most willingly———

Sir *Will.* What Design have you upon the other? for you can't marry 'em both?

Bel. Humph—faith, no Design at all, if I cou'd come off handsomely; tho' she's very pretty, but too well acquainted with my Incognita, to have any Intrigue with.

Sir *Will.* Does she love you *Belair*?

Bel. Not that ever I cou'd discover, to say the Truth.

Sir *Will.* One Thing more———is not her Name *Beliza*?

Bel. Ha! does he know her——I'm afraid my Plot's spoil'd again. [*Aside.*] Nay, Sir *William*, don't force me to tell Names, especially after the Stratagem I have made Use of.

Sir *Will.* Nay, nay, I am conviuc'd 'tis the same; had I apprehended it sooner, Friend, you had not carried your Design thus far.

Bel. So, I have made my Rival my Confident; I find I am a lucky Fellow, now, may he, out of pure Revenge discover me. [*Aside.*] If I have committed any Fault, Sir *William*, 'twas a Fault of Ignorance; could I divine the Lady was your Acquaintance — so that I am assur'd your Friendship must forgive me.

Sir *Will.* What Friendship must forgive, Love denies —as I imagin'd, here she comes.

Bel. Well, Sir *William*, whatever Satisfaction you demand

mand I'm ready to return——this Favour let me obtain, as you are a Gentleman betray me not, to my fair Unknown—this 'tis the most unfortunate Thing. [*Exit.*

Rob. Quite undone again. [*Exit.*

Enter Beliza.

Beliza. I am confounded! I know not whether there be two or not—— the Messenger affirms that *Revel* is in his Custody, but his Orders run so strict, that none must be admitted to see him———ha, Sir *William.*

Sir *Will.* Pray, what was the Subject of your Ladyship's Contemplation———Colonel *Revel.*

Beliza. He has found it then at last———why, do you know Colonel *Revel*, Sir *William?*

Sir *Will.* You do, I find —— perfidious Woman—— have I discovered thy Falshood—all thy Turnings and Windings of Indifference, had their Source from hence.

Beliza. The readiest Way to stop his Tongue is to let loose mine. [*Aside.*] Do, do, exalt your Voice, and raise your Passion higher—but know! your jealous Rage shall extort no Submission from me, tho' I cou'd clear my Innocence with Ease—but the Man that dares suspect my Conduct —— and start a Quarrel Husband-like, e'er I have confirmed his Title, I scorn to disabuse——so leave him to what Method he thinks best. [*Exit.*

Sir *Will.* Oh, Guilt! What an Assurance dost thou give, Oh, Hell, Hell.

What Fate than this cou'd more injurious prove,
Deceiv'd by Friendship, and destroy'd by Love. [Exit.

SCENE *changes to Sir* William's *Lodgings.*

Enter Bellair *and* Robin.

Rob. You act your Part very well, Sir, but there was one Thing superfluous in that of *Revel.*

Bel. What was that, pr'ythee?

Rob. The Box o'th' Ear, Sir; 'twas very uncomfortable.

Bel. Oh, there's a Cordial for thee. [*Gives him Money.* 'twas only to teach you a good Decorum.

Rob.

Rob. Oh, Sir, your humble Servant, I am ready to be taught, Sir, when ever you pleafe.

Bel. But how are you fure my Father knows I am in Town.

Rob. Sure on't, Sir! why I faw him, and told him you came but two Hours ago — and that, you'd wait upon him as foon as you had refrefh'd yourfelf with clean Linen———

Bel. Z'death, and why did you fo, Sirrah?

Rob. Becaufe, Sir, that was the firft Excufe that came at my Tongue's End—and you know there is no humming and hawing with my old Mafter, Sir.

Bel. I am in a bleffed Condition, — in Love, with I know not who, to be found I know not where——undoubtedly out of Favour with my Father, if I refufe his Choice, as I moft certainly fhall———

Rob. Nay, good, Sir, be'nt over certain———may be fhe's as handfome as t'other — and you may like her as well.

Bel. And, in all Probability, in Danger of a Duel with my Friend——to rectify all thefe Matters, require a Machivilian Brain—go you wait at t'other Lodgings.

Rob. Yes, Sir. ——— Now has he fo many Women upon his Hands, he knows not what to do with 'em—— the firft Time I ever faw him puzzled in thefe Matters—

[*Exit.*

Lady Cautious *paffing over the Stage.*

Bel. My Charmer! the Sight of thee difpels my Melancholly, and revives the Joy within my Breaft, which firft thofe Eyes infpired———

Lady. Why, were you melancholly, Sir? impoffible.

Bel. How fhou'd I be otherwife in the Abfence of my Love.

Lady. Abundance of Love, but not a Grain of Conftancy I fear.

Bel. As conftant as the Sun my Faireft———

Lady. What, like him, court all you meet, and quit as foon as tafted——Nature never defign'd my Sex to feed your Luxury—but for Health, Content and Neceffaries.

Bel. Right, why then can you deny the Man that endeavours to engrofs thofe Neceffaries you fpeak of.

Lady.

Lady. Where they are lawful —— but upon second Thoughts, I find I have Scruples.——

Bel. Vapour, Vapours, all——lawful! Why the mechanical Notion I have of the World, is a rich Banquet, set off with all the choicest Things of the Creation—— where Man's the Guest—and would it not be the Height of ill Manners to snatch a Dish, and run away with it, when, perhaps, twenty more had a Mind to the same Meat.

Lady. And wou'd it not be the Extremity of Folly to taste of every Dish—when your Curiosity may bring a Surfeit——

Bel. Then there's Physicians enough in Town to cure me—

Lady. Or kill you.

Bel. With all my Heart —— because a House may fall on my Head——must I therefore lie in the Field— but what have we to do with Philosophy?

For softer Pleasures was your Sex design'd,
Heaven form'd, and sent 'em to delight Mankind.
No Rule or Custom, did we first obey,
But freely lov'd where Nature led the Way.

[Embracing her.

Lady. Bless me! you'l smother me———

Bel. Let us not in cold disputing waste the Time, least Fortune, angry at our dull Delay, send another Interruption———

Lady. Well, you was born to ruin me——but do not, pray, do not—use your Force—for well I find my Weakness——— [*In a yielding Tone.*

Bel. A good Hint — sure Fortune will not jilt me again—but hold, I'll secure the Door— [*Shuts the Door.* now shew me a Man possest of half an Hour's Happiness above me. [*Takes Hold of her.*] [*Knocking without.*

Lady. Undone for ever—— there's some body at the Door, if I'm discover'd——Ruin attends me.

Bel. Another malicious Devil has crost me again—— why, why, why—which Way shall I get out? Is there no back Stairs, nor Trap-Door—I, I, I, I'll jump out of the Window.

Lady. By no Means—— what will come of me——— here, here, get into that Closet. [*Knocks again.*

Bell.

Bel. Ay, ay, any where — oh, Succeſs, Succeſs, thou haſt forſaken me. [*Exit.*

[*She ſhuts the Door, then opens 'tother.*

Lady. Who knocks with that Authority? Brother, is it you! what ſhall I ſay? [*Aſide.*

Sir *Will.* What Buſineſs have you here——Confuſion, how ſhall I contain myſelf? [*Aſide.*

Lady. If he has diſcover'd me, I'm a dead Woman. [*Aſide.*] Why do you look ſo angry, Brother—— Is it a Crime to be in your Lodgings?

Sir *Will.* Yes, I forbad you——and what was the Door ſhut for, ha?

Lady. I ſhall be found out, there's no avoiding it—— becauſe I was afraid the Stranger which you ſay hates Women ſhou'd ſurpriſe me—I came hither to be private, and to avoid the Impertinency of Sir *Paul* — I tremble every Joint. [*Aſide.*

Sir *Will.* Ay, ſhe did come to avoid Sir *Paul*, that's plain enough——Oh Natute, Nature, why did'ſt thou make a Woman——I'm ſure I heard his Voice— far off he cannot be — that Cloſet muſt conceal him— I'm glad to find you was ſo circumſpect, Siſter——I am out of Humour——you'll forgive me——how ſhall I get rid of her [*Aſide.*

Lady. Better than I expected—— [*Aſide.*

Sir *Will.* Pray, oblige me with Pen, Ink, and Paper, I have loſt the Key of my Scrutore, and can't come at mine——

Lady. With all my Heart, Brother —— a fortunate Eſcape. [*Exit.*

Sir *Will.* Let me conſider ſhall I ſacrifice his Blood to my injur'd Honour—no, I owe this Life to him which now I bear— and a ſolemn League of Friendſhip join'd our Souls — I lodg'd him here — and ſhall I break the Laws of Hoſpitality? — no—firſt, let me know how far my Honour is concern'd—if my Siſter has betray'd her Virtue—and I prove it— my juſt Reſentment then ſhall fall on both—'tis reſolv'd—— [*Puts out the Candle, goes to the Cloſet and knocks.*] Sir, Sir— [Belair *opens the Door, and comes out.*

Bel. Are they gone, my Life, my Love——

Sir

Sir *Will.* My, Life, my Love! Damnation [*Aside.* they are gone, hush, make no Noise for your Life, I expect my Husband every Minute, therefore if you love me retire instantly—

Bel. Love thee; do I live? But, oh, I fear these curst malicious Planets ne'er will crown my Wishes. [*Exit.*

Sir *Will.* By that I find he has not enjoy'd her—now know how far she's inclin'd.———

[*Goes into the Closet, and shuts the Door after him.*

Enter Lady Cautious *with Pen, Ink, and Paper,*

Lady. Here's Pen and Ink, Brother—— ha, in the dark, Brother — Brother — ha! gone — lucky Opportunity—let me 'scape now, and I'll never run the Danger more—— [*Goes to the Closet.*] you may come out, the Coast is clear.

Enter Sir William.

Sir *Will.* Then I'm happy—now let's lose no Time—but improve the precious Moments—— conduct me to some more private Place, there let me breathe my Soul into your Bosom, and pay the Hazards which we have both run———

Lady. This is no Time except you wish my Ruin—— my Brother is alarm'd and may return this Minute, and sacrifice me to his jealous Fears——— have you no Regard for my Safety——yet will you loiter to undo me.

Sir *Will.* Destruction seize thee. [*Aside.*] I will go, but first tell me when, and where I shall be blest again.

Lady. Press me not to further Folly—I own the tender Sentiments of my Heart——and I fear I love you——

Sir *Will.* Excellent Confession——— [*Aside.*

Lady. But my Fears grow strong, and represent Vice in hideous Forms—— twice this Day Surprize preserv'd my Virtue.

Sir *Will.* Twice! Oh, Traiteress. [*Aside.*

Lady. And now by all the Virtuous Stars, I'll never see you more. [*Flings from him.*] [*Exit.*

Sir *Will.* I'm glad to hear that—— but did not she know me, so took her Opportunity to start from my Vengeance? It may be so, and this be all a Lye—— it

must

must be so —— and now I cou'd rip that Bosom where her Heart, her hot lustful Heart resides —— yes, if thou be'st guilty — these Hands shall strait let out thy tainted Blood, to wash the Stains thou hast thrown upon our Family.

Enter Sir Paul *with a Candle.*

Sir *Paul.* Mercy on me, what a Noise is here in this House—Adsbud, it were a Blessing to be deaf—what did I say—Heaven forgive me—if I shou'd be struck deaf now, what a lamentable Thing 'twou'd be——humph—ha— in my Conscience, my Ears sing, I have a strange Humming in my Head — pray, Heaven, I grow not deaf in earnest—Well, my Wife has so many Relations—that lodge here, and visit her together— I shall certainly be undone—it costs me, at least, five Pounds a Week in Coffee—Tea— Chocolate— and Ratafee — Mercy upon me— if I shou'd come to want now in my old Age —— I may thank Marriage for it — if I shou'd come to be maintain'd by the Parish now — Oh, sad — Oh, sad — or shou'd live to be blind——and led with a Dog and a Bell—what shall I do, if I come to that, and who knows but I may—Let me see, let me see, I'll try how I can walk in the Dark. [*Puts out the Candle.*

Enter Belair.

Bel. The Devil take these Disappointments, I say—— I have peep'd into every Room I cou'd find open, but no Sight of her——well, if my Incognita——falls to my Lot at last, 'twill be some Amends——

Sir *Paul.* What a wretched Condition is it to be depriv'd of Sight——the very Apprehension puts me in a Sweat all over—ah, ah, within there, Lights, Lights.

Bel. I can't imagine into what Part of the House I'm got. [*Runs against Sir* Paul.

Sir *Paul.* What's that? Thieves, Thieves.

Bel. Pox take this old Cuff, how came I to stumble on him.

Sir *Paul.* *Basilicon*, why *Basilicon*, I say, Murder, Murder.

Enter

Enter Servants, with Lights, and Basilicon.

Bel. Sir, I'm glad to see you with all my Heart——

Sir *Paul.* That's a Lye, I believe——but what's your Business here now, Sir? Answer me that— do you come to bring me another Information of Rogues, ha! I know you again——either you come, Sirrah, to make me a Cuckold—or to rob my House——but I'll have you laid by the Heels——I will so——

Bel. Very fine, Faith — my next Step will be to *Tyburn.*

Sir *Paul.* Bind his Hands, there——

Bel. Keep off Scoundrels — without you'l have your Guts full of Oylet-holes.

Sir *Paul.* Oh, *Basilicon,* see, see, am I not wounded? Keep close to me.

Enter Sir William.

Bas. Not in the least, Sir.

Sir *Will.* How now, what's the Matter here—

Bel. Oh, Sir *William,* you come opportunely, to save me from these Rascals.

Sir *Will.* Sir *Paul,* why these Disorders? Of what are you Apprehensive —— this Gentleman is a Friend of mine.

Sir *Paul.* But how came he here, Sir, in the Dark——

Bel. I mistook this for Sir *William*'s Apartment——

Sir *Will.* Oh, Hippocrisy——but e'er you and I have done, you'll own t'was upon another Score, [*Aside.*] it must be so, Sir *Paul,* I lent my Lodgings to the Gentleman for two or three Days — curse of my shallow Reason—I did not tell you of it, Sir, not thinking it material enough to trouble you about.

Sir *Paul.* Say you so, Sir—— then Cuckoldom is nothing material, you shall all out of my House—— you shall so, every Mother's Child of you——

Sir *Will.* What you please, Sir *Paul*—— hark ye, *Belair,* there's something to adjust between you and I, which require more Privacy—follow me. *Exit.*

Bel. So my Affair goes swimmingly. [*Exit.*

Bel.

Sir *Paul.* What the Devil had I to do with a young Wife?

They who in Age will drag the Marriage Chain,
Like me they'll find the Hopes of Comfort vain;
But if Relations usher in the Wife,
There needs no greater Curse to Human Life. [Exit.

The End of the FOURTH ACT.

ACT V.

SCENE *Sir* William's *Lodgings.*

Enter Sir William *and Belair.*

Sir *Will.* THUS far, Sir, I have had a strict Regard to the League we made in *Spain* — serv'd you in the minutest, as well as greatest Things, even beyond the Character of a Gentleman, in helping you to impose upon a Lady, making good Manners subservient to my Friendship.

Bel. Pr'ythee, Sir *William*, let me know the Sum at once, without this regular Account.

Sir *Will.* 'Twill be cast up immediately—at your Request, resign'd my own Lodgings, to oblige you, kept your Secret, even to the Woman I lov'd—tho' you abus'd her—

Bel. Nay, there's a false Tally, Sir *William*——I never abus'd a Lady in my Life——

Sir *Will.* Have you not abus'd *Beliza?*

Bel. Which Way? I never ask'd a Favour that cou'd put her to the Blush—or promis'd Marriage, and declin'd my Word.

Sir *Will.* Have you not pass'd by a wrong Name to her.

Bel. But the Person is the same, when once a Woman likes the Man—she seldom finds Fault with the Name.

Sir

Sir *Will.* Look'e, *Belair*, you may affect what Air you please—but supplanting my Love, and dishonouring my Family, are Things not to be repair'd with a Smile——

Bel. The dishonouring of your Family! What mean you, Sir? Such Accusations are not like a Friend.

Sir *Will.* Nor such Actions, therefore draw—[*Draws.*

Bel. I'll never draw my Sword—till I know the Cause you allege; I endeavour'd to supplant you: I deny it.—I wou'd not supplant my Friend, tho' I dy'd for the Woman—but this was only Gallantry—and I ignorant of your Pretences; and before I knew you lov'd *Beliza*, I had fix'd upon her Friend—that Point is clear'd with any reasonable Man—but the other Article it is that stings me——How have I dishonour'd your Family?—— for there my Honour, Faith and Friendship are concern'd——

Sir *Will.* Are they gone, my Life——my Love——

Bel. Ha! my own Words!

Sir *Will.* And spoke to my Sister, Sir——

Bel. The Devil they were.

Sir *Will.* What! are you astonish'd, Sir? Draw instantly——or by the base Affront you offer'd me——

Bel. Nay, nay, hold, hold, Sir *William*, for Faith I will not fight thee——one Word—— were it possible that I cou'd know thy Sister by instinct? Or, deny a fair Lady in Distress.

Sir *Will.* Trifle no longer with my just Resentment—

Bel. Hear me out, and if I plead not within the Rules of Reason, Justice, and Probability, pass Sentence on me freely——she's young and handsome — her Husband old and impotent——he full of Whimsies, she full of Love; he wrinkled and decay'd—— she warm and wishing; I young and vigorous——she married against her Will—— I not married at all—— we met by Accident——she lamented her Misfortune——I pitty'd her —— and what Return she might have made——no Man—— not yourself, cou'd have refus'd, had the Case been yours——Oh, but then she proves the Sister of my Friend—— but my Friend never told me that ——- consequently he is the Aggressor—— Now, Sir *William*, will you put yourself upon your Guard, or put up your Sword, ha, ha, ha.

Sir

Sir *Will.* My Friend, again —— I confess thy Arguments are unanswerable —— those we do not trust, can ne'er betray us.

Enter Robin *hastily.*

Rob. Oh, Sir, your Father, Sir *Thomas*, has found your Lodgings, and hears you have been in Town this Fortnight—— and swears if I don't find you out immediately, he'll slice me into Hash-meat; he says, he shall forfeit a Thousand Pounds if you come not presently——

Bel. What shall I conclude on—— is he at my Lodgings?

Rob. No, Sir, he's upon the Hunt like any Bloodhound; I run down twenty Bye-ways, least he shou'd dog me —— for you know, Sir, I am your most careful Servant.

Sir *Will.* That thou art indeed —— you must resolve to see him.

Bel. And if I see him, there will be no avoiding this hated Match——

Rob. Without, Sir, you shou'd take another Name, and persuade him you are not his Son —— I have the same honest, lying Face, Sir, still, I'll swear you are none of my Master. [*Knocks without.*

Bel. No, Sirrah, that won't do with him —— ha, see who knocks.

Rob. If it be my old Master—what shall I say, Sir, must I lye, or speak Truth.

Bel. Which you will, the Condition's desperate.

Re-enter Robin *with a Letter.*

Rob. Safe, Sir, safe, a Letter from your Incognita, Sir. [*Gives him the Letter.*

Bel. Thou dear Cordial to my love-sick Mind [*Kisses it.* [*Reads.*] *I have us'd all my Rhetoric without Effect; my Father resolves this Night to give me to thy Rival — therefore if thou hast any Stratagem to relieve me, be quick in the Execution—— We are now coming to Sir* Paul Cautious's, *who, it seems, is an old Friend of my Father's, you being in the same House, renders you capable of seeing — your Incognita* —now, Sir *William*, I'll throw off Disguise, confess who

I

I am, and ask her of her Father —— if he refuse, my Rival must measure Blades with me; you'll be my Second, if it come to a Push, Sir *William*.

Sir *Will*. My Sword is still at my Friend's Service.

Bel. Have at him, then——I'll to my Lodgings, Dress, and return in an Instant—— Now all ye Stars, that favour faithful Lovers, prevent my meeting with my Father. [*Exit*.

Rob. And his Cane meeting my Shoulders. [*Exit*.

Enter Sir Paul, *pulling in Lady* Cautious.

Sir *Pal*. You, troop, troop —— there, Sir, take your Sister, and get out of my House—do so—you shan't bring Gallants under my Nose, and lend your Lodgings to Rascals that wou'd cut my Throat —— Mercy upon me, 'tis a Miracle the House don't tumble on our Heads—— I admire I'm alive———

Lady. Thou art alive, indeed, and that's all———

Sir *Paul*. All, Housewife, why, why, why, you han't poison'd me, or wounded me, have you?

[*Looking and feeling about him*.

Enter Basilicon.

Why, where are you, Rascal? Look, am I hurt — do I Bleed any where?

Basil. Not a Drop, Sir.

Sir *Paul*. Can you know by my Eyes or Hands, or any Thing, if all be right within me?

Basil. Very easily, Sir—you are in perfect Health—

Sir *Paul*. You are sure on't?

Basil. I am sure on't, Sir!

Sir *Paul*. Why then, Mistress, what do you Mean, ha!

Lady. That thou art an old doating,—despicable Wretch.

Sir *Will*. Hold, Sister — better Language to your Husband wou'd become you—and for you, Sir, since your ill Manners proceeds from groundless Jealousies, taxing a Gentleman with Crimes of which I know him innocent—making that a Pretence to traduce the Virtue of your Wife—I advise you to recall your Temper, and use her like my Sister——or I shall use you like my Enemy.

Sir *Paul*. And run me thro' the Guts, I suppose—was ever Man thus plagu'd before!

Lady. [*Weeping*.] This is the Life I lead—my Virtue still suspected—my Innocence accus'd, and the Quiet of my Life destroy'd —— Did I truly merit his Abuses— Patience and Submission wou'd become me—but I defy, even the Tongue of Malice, to asperse my Fame or Conduct — and do you think, Brother, I'll endure this —— tamely to submit and cringe to what I hate.

Sir *Will.* One Word, Madam— [*Pulls her aside.*] Boast not of your Conduct, nor your Virtue — vile audacious Woman— the Closet, Mistress, think on the Closet.——

Lady. Does he know that? now, I'm lost for ever.——

Sir *Will.* Now, vent your clamorous Virtue —— while those in whose Hands you lodge it, Echo back, you have none.

Lady. What sure Disgrace attends unlawful Love; had I really fall'n, I now shou'd die with shame.

Sir *Paul.* What are they whispering about, Now— contriving to make me away, ten to one, *Basilicon.*

Bas Oh, Sir, I defy 'em to do that whilst I am near you.

Lady. Oh, Brother, forgive me; 'twas the only Slip I ever made—— methinks I hate myself, for having, but in Wish, consented, and grow in Love with Virtue.—— Since I have not stain'd my Family—— the most was Thought, for some good Angel still did interpose to prop my nodding Virtue.

Sir *Will.* Take heed it nods no more.

Lady. I will, for now the Shame and Ruin that must have attended me, are so conspicuous to my Sight, that I will shun even the Resemblance of a Crime like this; if you'll but pardon me, I'll vow never to fall again from Duty.

Sir *Will.* On that Condition I do—and, now, Sister, since your Marriage-Knot can never be dissolv'd, till Nature slips it— shew yourself the Pattern of a virtuous Wife, indulge his Age——and that Way preserve your Ease, and by your Meekness and Humility, fix your Reputation.

Lady. I readily obey—Sir *Paul*, my Youth has hitherto engaged me in a foolish Passion, contradictory to your Will, but my Brother's Instructions has so far inform'd me of my Duty, that my Behaviour, for the future, shall give you no Cause for Complaint.

Sir *Will.* I'll engage my Honour for the Performance of her Promise.

Sir

Sir *Paul.* Here's a Turn; who can find what Plot is going forward——Are you both in Earnest now, or not?

Sir *Will.* Pray, be less suspicious, and more a Man—the less you suspect, the more you are secur'd, Sir *Paul.*

Lady. A generous Confidence, will always oblige your Wife.

Sir *Paul.* Well, for once I will trust thee——come to my Arms then——hold, hold, let me see——you have no Penknife nor Pistol about you, have you?

Lady. To what Purpose, my Dear——Nay, did you not say, you'd trust me——

Sir *Paul.* Well, so I will then. [*Embrace.*

Enter a Servant.

Serv. Sir, here's a Gentleman, calls himself *Positive*, to wait on you, Mrs. *Beliza*, and another young Lady, with him.

Sir *Paul.* Bring them in immediately, I have not seen him this many a Year——and your Mistress too *Will*, we'll have a Match before you part, a Faith we will, my old Friend——

Enter Mr. Positive, Beliza, Camilla, Patch, *and* Flora.

Welcome, I'm glad to see thee with all my Heart, Ladies, you are welcome—

Pos. Sir *Paul*, your Hand——I cou'd not come to Town without seeing you, Faith——this is your Lady, I suppose; by your Leave, Madam. [*Salutes her.*] This is my Daughter, Sir *Paul*, I am come up to marry her.

Sir *Paul.* Why then, I wish her much Joy.

Lady. I shou'd be proud of being better known to you.

Cam. And I of your Acquaintance.

Lady. Dear *Beliza*, how do you expect I shou'd forgive your long Absence? Not see me in two Days.

Beliz. I confess my Fault.

Sir *Will.* The readiest Way to be pardon'd, is not to persist in the Wrong, indeed, Madam.

Beliz. But who shall judge between Right and Wrong?

Sir *Will.* Our Reason, Madam.

Beliz. That very often deceives us, especially if we put too much Trust in the Person.

Sir *Will.* It requires Judgment therefore, to make a proper Choice, for every Accident depends on that; but why this Indifference, Madam?

Beliz. Why, that Question?

Sir *Will.* Because Love requires more Freedom.

Beliz. But Jealousy forbid it, Sir *William.*

Sir *Will.* Only the Effect of too much Love; I ask your Pardon for all past Offences.

Beliz. Rather of too much Folly.

Enter Belair.

Ha, *Revel,* at Liberty again——and here, what can this mean?

Bel. Ladies and Gentlemen, your Servant—

[*Sir* William *takes him aside.*

Lady. Ha! the handsome Stranger—lie still my Heart, and think not of him. [*Aside.*

Cam. Now am I distracted, to know whether this be her Lover, or mine. [*Aside.*

Sir *Will.* Sir, here's a Gentleman begs Leave to unfold a Secret to you—— [*To Mr.* Positive.

Pos. To me——out with it then.

Sir *Paul.* Has he a Secret for him too.——This Spark is full of Secrets. [*Aside.*

Bel. Sir, I presume you are the Father of this Lady.

Cam. This is *Constant*, that's certain. [*Aside.*

Beliza. So, now the Game's up —— as I suspected, all one Man. [*Aside.*

Pos. And, what then, Sir?

Bel. Then, my Request is, to be admitted for your Son-in-Law.

Pos. For my Son-in-Law——

Bel. Yes, Sir, provided I make it appear my Fortune and Family are equal to yours——

Pos. Sir, in one Word — if you cou'd prove your Descent from the Blood-royal, and as many Acres of Land as the *Po* has engross'd, 'twou'd not avail you that, do you see [*Snaps his Fingers.*] my Word's my Word, she's dispos'd of already, and so give yourself no farther Trouble.

Cam. Heart-breaking Sentence. [*Aside.*

Bel. Is this your final Resolution, Sir?

Pos. Why, Sir, what Reason have you to believe, I shou'd alter it?

Bel. Because, Sir, I have some Reasons to believe, your Daughter loves me — and I hope you'll not force her Inclinations——

Pos.

Pos. You have some Reasons to believe she loves you— what Reasons, Sir, what Reasons? You have not lain with her, have you? for that's the surest Reason a Man can build upon.

Bel. You surprise me, with your Question, Sir,—and make me blush, to hear you give Utterance to a Thought like that ——— Your Daughter's Virtue needs no Guard against such foul Advances.

Pos. I hope not———

Cam. I ne'er shall give you Cause, to doubt my Virtue, Sir, and 'tis unkindly urg'd——I own, I love this Gentleman.

Pos. What, this is he, that you have pick'd up since you came to Town, is it?

Cam. This is he, that sav'd my Life, Sir——and if I have him not, I ne'er can love another; yet your Commands shall fix me as you please.

Sir *Paul.* Well said.

Pos. As to your Love, and Liking, that's out of my Power, but your Portion and Person are not——so whether you consent or not, 'tis the same Thing——look ye, my Word's my Word, so never trouble yourself about that.

Bel. Is it so, I'll not leave the Sight of her—till I see my Rival——and then the best Arm carry her.

Beliza. And, this is your worthy Friend, you have so often mention'd, Sir *William*?

Sir *Will.* The same, another Time I'll inform you of every Thing, and hope to obtain your Pardon for him.

Beliza. Nay, I'm inclining to be good-natur'd; I like his Humour mightily———

Cam. But, Sir, have you no Regard to the Hazards which he run to save my Life; had not his generous Care preserv'd me, you had now been Childless in your Age.

Pos. Humph! Why, to say Truth, I wou'd be grateful, but I want the Means—he says, his Estate is large, so that he's above a Present—and I know not what to offer him——Sir, I thank you for the Service which you did my Daughter, and had I not given my Word, I might have chose you, as soon as another, but now there's no Help for't—if you'll be one of her Bride-men, you shall have a Favour to keep for her Sake.

Sir *Paul*. That's something.

Lady. Rude unpolished Monster. [*Aside*.

Bel. Insult me not, Sir, ——— the Favour I wou'd wear you have refus'd.

Enter Robin.

Rob. Sir, here's your Father will come in, in Spite of my Teeth——or he swears he'll have a File of Musquetteers, and blow the House up. [*Aside to* Bel.

Sir *Will*. What News brings *Robin*?

Bel. That my Father is at the Door, I must go and try to appease him.

[*Goes towards the Door, and meets Sir* Thomas.

Sir *Tho*. Give me Entrance, or, I'll knock you down, you Dogs———

Enter Sir Thomas.

Where is this graceless Rogue.

Bel. [*Kneeling*.] Your Blessing, Sir, and with it your Pardon, for having thus long conceal'd myself, but when you shall know my Reasons———

Sir *Tho*. Reasons, Sirrah, what Reasons have you to shun your Father —— and a handsome Woman; come along, come along, [*Pulling him*] the Parson and the Bride, has waited this two Hours, while I have been hunting you all over the Town, Sirrah.

Bel. And now you have found me, Sir, I cannot comply with what you propose.

Sir *Tho*. How, how's this?

Bel. There stands the Lady that destroys my Duty—

Sir *Tho*. Ha! What do I see?

Bel. Now, Sir, shew a true Paternal Love, and force me not to wed against my Will; for tho' the Lady you have chose, shou'd have all the Charms that bounteous Nature gave the whole Sex—there I am fix'd—and must, and will, refuse her.

Pos. Ha! Is not that Sir *Thomas Belair*?

Sir *Tho*. Sayst thou so—why, then, take her, my Boy; [*Throws him into* Camilla's *Arms*.] for this is she, thy Father did design for thee.

Bel. Oh, Transport, oh, unexpected Happiness!

Cam. Oh, Excess of Pleasure! [*They embrace*.

Sir

Sir *Tho.* Mr. *Positive*, your Servant; there's my Son.

Pos. So I see, Sir, and am glad of it with all my Heart.

Bel. Now, Sir, your Consent I hope is free.

Sir *Paul.* Why, this is the prettiest Turn I ever saw.

Rob. I, I, I, am so overjoy'd, I shall jump out of my Skin———

Pos. Camil.—there take him.

[*Calls her to him, and throws her to* Belair.

Bel. My Love, my Life——— my Soul's best Comfort———

Beliza. I am pleas'd to see the Event so lucky.

Sir *Will.* So am I, Love is the strongest Guard to restrain Liberty.

Cam. Look up my *Constant*, and bless our friendly Stars that thus have turn'd our Disobedience into Duty.

Bel. Oh, I was lost in Rapture, the powerful Torrent rowl'd too fast, and sinks me down with Pleasure; now no more that Name, but know thy Husband wears that of *Belair*———and now, Madam, I must ask your Pardon too—and you my Friend, I give you a thousand Thanks, and wish you as happy in *Beliza*'s Love———

Beliz. I'm glad to see you out of Prison, Sir; but how?

Bel. Those Stratagems are vanish'd now, and I rely on your good Nature to forgive me.

Sir *Paul.* Nay, Niece; I seldom ask Favours, therefore must not be deny'd; you, and my Wife's Brother, must make the second Couple.

Lady. I must second Sir *Paul*, in that Request.

Cam. Compleat my Happiness, and bear me Company.

Bel. Augment my Joys, by crowning of my Friends.

Sir *Will.* Let not all intreat in vain, Madam.

Beliz. Well, Sir *William*, I'll run the dangerous Venture of a Jealous Husband, for once; but let me caution you, aforehand———the more you suspect my Conduct, the less I shall consult your Humour? the more you watch me, the more I shall study to deceive you——— Leave then, your Spanish Airs——— and put the true English Husband on, that is the only Way to have a virtuous Wife.

Sir *Will.* Your Advice is so reasonable, that you shall be Mistress both of yourself, and me.

Sir *Paul.* Well said, Brother, thy Example shall be my Guide, for the future; come, we'll be merry, I'm resolv'd; who is within there?

Enter Servant.

Go to the Play-House, and desire some of the Singers and Dancers to come hither; I am not often in this Humour, but will be merry while it lasts.

Sir *Will.* Go in my Name——they'll not refuse me.

Bel. No, thou art a good Benefactor to 'em.

Enter Ned.

Ned. Ladies and Gentlemen, I wish you Joy, I overheard the Conclusion of your Happiness——and to crown your Mirth, here's a comical Figure upon Enterance.

Enter Wou'dbe, *in his Waistcoat.*

Sir *Will.* Ha, ha, ha, Mr. *Wou'dbe*, without his Clothes — what dost thou design this for a Masquerade, at my Wedding.

Wou'd. Married, and to *Beliza*, then the good Opinion *Ned* said she had of me, is come to nothing, I find [*Aside.* Oh, Sir *William*, I am undone for ever, robb'd of my new Coat, that I but just put upon my Back, by the most whimsical Stratagem you ever hear'd.

Beliza. Ha, ha, ha, Mr. *Wou'dbe* out-plotted.

Sir *Will.* How was it, pr'ythee?

Wou'd. Why, Sir, you must know I had just made up such a Suit of Cloaths as that you have on—— and was coming hither, but meeting your Brother *Ned*, he wou'd needs press me to the Tavern, to give him Beveridge, so in we went, the Fellow that waited on us, told me I had a Cut cross the Shoulder of my new Coat; I look'd, and found I had—— he said there liv'd a Fine-drawer at the next Door——he wou'd draw it up in a Minute; Wherefore I gave it him, but my Eyes ne'er encounter'd him since.

Omnes. Ha, ha, ha, ha, ha.

Bel. Is your Subscription come to this, ha, ha, ha; why did not you examine the House.

Wou'd. I did, and they say he came in with me, and told them he was my Servant.

Ned.

Ned. And that he never suffer'd a Drawer to wait on him, and therefore borrow'd an Apron of them to attend us.

Wou'd. To cheat me of my Coat——nothing vexes me so much, as that I have not been seen in it, had I but made the Tour of St. *James*'s, and both Play-houses, my Passion for it would have ebb'd to an Indifference—and then——

Beliza. That was an unparallel'd Grievance, indeed.

Bel. Mr. *Wou'dbe*, might I advise you as a Friend, leave off this foolish Whim of Mimicking; Sir *William* he's a Gentleman of a plentiful Fortune, and can afford Change of Cloaths for every Day; but you, whose slender Allowance from a Father's Hand, admits of no Profuseness——to imitate him is Madness.

Rob. What a grave Piece of Advice is there——well, Marriage has chang'd my Master already, I find.

Beliza. I heard you was about writing a Play, Mr. *Wou'dbe*, I'd advise you to make your top Character a Sharper——you see they can't out-wit a Gentleman; he has shew'd you Plot for Plot.

Wou'd. With what Courage can I proceed with the Play, when this Rascal is run away with the Subscription—Well, I'll into the Country, and never see this damn'd Town again. [*Exit.*

Enter Servant.

Omnes. Ha, ha, ha, ha.

Serv. The Singers and Dancers are come, Sir.

[*Here is Songs and Dances.*

Sir *Will.* Bring 'em in, come, Gentlemen, take your Seats, but you forget *Belair*—*Robin* is unrewarded yet.

Bel. Why, he shall chuse between the two Maids.

Rob. Ah, *Patch!*

Patch. Me do you chuse?

Rob. Thou tempts me, and if I shou'd look any longer, perhaps the Devil might be more cunning than I.

Patch. You don't like me then?

Rob. Look ye, Marriage is a lasting Thing——if it were for six Months only, I might venture upon thee——but for all the Days of my Life——Mercy upon me——thy Features are too high

Priz'd

Priz'd Fu-niture for House keeping, especially where they must let Lodgings —— therefore, *Flora*, have at thee————

Flora. Why will you quit her for me?

Rob. To shew the Extremity of my Love, I will.

Patch. Fool, didst thou think I wou'd have had thee? Dost thou know that I have had my Nativity cast, and am told that I shall marry a Knight, at least, if not a Lord.

Rob. Oh, good Night to your Ladyship, then.

Ned. Well, *Patch*, stay till my Brother dies, and I'll marry thee, to make good thy Calculation, ha, ha.

Patch. Though you shou'd make me a Lady, you'd not better my Fortune much by being your Wife, our Humours wou'd quickly consume our Estate; —— I love fine Cloaths, ——— fine Coach, ——— fine Equipage, and fine House; ——— Your Drinking, Wenching, Gaming, and, so forth———that when I wanted a New Suit, in the Morning, you have flung off your Money over Night.————

Sir *Will.* She has hit you home, Brother, for your jesting.

Ned. Well, since we know one another's Infirmities so well, we'll keep as we are————

Bell. Now, my fair *Camilla*, I am happy —— these Arms shall fix my rambling Heart.

Ungovern'd Youth, of Taste not over-nice,
Roves thro' the various Fields of Pois'nous Vice.
Cheated with Health, they ride thro' Pleasure Post,
To purchase Liberty, what e'er it cost.
True English like, that Idol they adore,
And fear the Marriage Knot, as much as Gallick *Power.*
But if once Reason checks the looser Reins,
And bring sound Judgment into Play again,
Then all must own————
The truest Joy that waits on human Life,
Is a constant Temper——and a virtuous Wife.

THE

THE

EPILOGUE.

Spoken by Mr. PENKETHMAN.

THE Plodding Tribe are so resolv'd of late,
To model and refine our little State.
I fear to Great *Ones we have this relation,*
They'll ruin us at last by Reformation!
What heavy Race so far without the City,
Cou'd think of plaguing us for being Witty?
But were we broke (disbanded I wou'd speak,
For nothing but a Shopkeeper shou'd break!)
Men of our Quality's wou'd rise by falling,
And grow more eminent in any Calling.
Our various Virtues wou'd fit all Conditions;
They that want Piety might turn Physicians.
A Door-keeper whose Cheats we can't prevent,
Wou'd surely thrive in any State-Employment.
He that his Hopes from Impudence does draw,
Might turn his happy Genius to the Law.
The Under Fry a little Thing will serve,
For by the Laws of England, *younger Brothers starve.*
No Change of Government the Women drop, [Putting on a Mask.
For—Eighteen Pence in Velvet sets them up.
As for my self; may Marriage be my Fate,
Chain'd to a Cross, I may repent, tho' late;
Grow fit to turn Informer to the Town,
And thrive by the same Means I was undone.

THE

STOLEN HEIRESS:

OR THE

Salamanca Doctor Outplotted.

A

COMEDY.

PROLOGUE.

Spoke by Mrs. PRINCE.

OUR Author fearing his Success to Day,
Sends me to bribe your Spleen against his Play,
And if a Ghost in Nelly's *Time cou'd sooth ye,*
He hopes in these that Flesh and Blood may move ye,
Nay, what is more, to win your Hearts, a Maid!
If ever such a Thing the Play house had.
For Cold and Shade the waxen Blossom's born,
Not to endure the Regions of the Sun,
Let every Beau then his Applause begin,
And think the Rarity was born for him:
Your true-bred Knights for fancy'd Dames advance,
And think it Gallantry to break a Launce,
And shall a real Damsel e'er be found
To plead her Cause in vain on English *Ground,*
Unless that dreadful Prophecy's begun,
In which Seven Women are to share——one Man!
But thanks my Stars that Danger I disown,
For in the Pit, I see 'tis—one—to one.
And while the Fair can all their Rights enjoy,
We'll keep our Title up to being Coy,
So let your Praise be noisy as your Wine,
And grant your Favours, if you'd purchase mine.

A SONG design'd to be sung by Mr. DOGGET.

THE Man you Ladies ought to fear,
Behold and see his Picture here.
With Arms a-cross, and down-cast Eyes
Thus languishes, and thus he dies,
Then gives his Hat a careless Pull,
Thus he sighs, and thus looks dull,
Thus he ogles, thus he sneers,
Thus he winks, and thus he leers.
This, this is he alone can move,
And this the Man the Ladies love.

EPI-

THE

EPILOGUE.

Spoke by Mr. DOGGET,

YOU have seen what Scholar is in Cap and Gown,
Before his Breeding's polish'd by this Town:
'Tis not enough, that he can Hebrew speak,
Greek, Latin, Chaldeac, and Arabick;
He may perform his Task in Church and School,
Ne'er drop a Word, that is not Grammar-Rule.
Run through the Arts; can each Degree commence,
Yet be a Freshman still, to Men of Sense.
Tho' the learn'd Youth, can all the Sages quote,
Has Homer, Hesiod, and the rest by Wrote;
Yet what's all this to Picquet, Dress or Play?
Or to the Circle, on a Visiting-Day?
A finish'd Beau; for such fine things I have seen,
That heretofore, has of some College been:
But that Despising, nothing now retains,
For Learning is a Thing requires Brains;
And that's a Perquisite the Gentleman disdains.
The Great Dull Ass, from breaking Head of Priscian;
Hither he comes, and writes approv'd Physician.
The Noise of Chariot brings the Patients in;
Grant them Patience, that Physick for their Sin.
Well then——
Since Learning's useless, I'll the Task defy;
Practice to Ogle, Flatter, Swear and Lye;
For that's the Way the Ladies Hearts to gain,
Burn all my Books; my Studies are but vain:
To gain their Looks, each Shape and Dress I'll try;
Smile when they Smile; and when they Frown, I Die.

Dramatis Personæ.

MEN.

Governor of Palermo,	*Mr.* Bowman.
Count Pirro, *Nephew to the Governor,*	*Mr.* Griffith.
Gravello, *a* Sicilian *Lord, Father to* Lucasia,	*Mr.* Freeman.
Larich, *his Brother,*	*Mr.* Fieldhouse.
Lord Euphenes, *an old* Sicilian *General,*	*Mr.* Arnold.
Palante, *Son to* Euphenes *but unknown in Love with* Lucasia,	*Mr.* Powel.
Clerimont, *his Friend,*	*Mr.* Baile.
Eugenio, *Son to* Gravello *in Disguise under the Name of* Irus	*Mr.* Booth.
Alphonso, *formerly an Officer under* Euphenes,	*Mr.* Knap.
Francisco, *in Love with* Lavinia,	*Mr.* Pack.
Sancho, *a Pedant, bred at* Salamanca, *design'd by* Larich, *a Husband for* Lavinia,	*Mr.* Dogget.
Tristram, *his Man,*	*Mr.* Lee.
Rosco, *Servant to Count* Gravello,	*Mr.* Bright.

WOMEN.

Lucasia, *Daughter to* Gravello, *in Love with* Palante,	*Mrs.* Barry.
Lavinia, *Daughter to* Larich, *in Love with* Francisco,	*Mrs.* Prince.
Laura, *Woman to* Lucasia,	*Mrs.* Lawson.

The SCENE *in* PALERMO.

The STOLEN HEIRESS:
OR, THE
SALAMANCA DOCTOR Out-plotted.

ACT I. SCENE I.

Enter Count Gravello *and* Rosco.

Gravello.

ROSCO!

Rosco. My Lord.

Grav. Hast thou divulg'd the News that my Son died at *Rome?*

Rosco. Yes, my Lord, with every Circumstance, the Time, the Place, and Manner of his Death; that 'tis believed, and told for Truth with as much Confidence, as if they had been Spectators of his End.

Grav. That's well, that's very well, now *Rosco* follows my Part, I must express a most unusual Grief, not like a well-left Heir for his dead Father, or a lusty Widow for an old decrepit Husband; no, I must conterfeit in a far deeper Strain; weep like a Parent for an only Son: Is not this a hard Task? Ha, *Rosco?*

Rosco. Ah, no, my Lord, not for your Skill; in your Youth your Lordship saw Plays, convers'd with Players, knew the fam'd *Alberto*.

Grav. 'Tis true, by Heav'n, I have seen that Knave paint Grief in such a lively Colour, that for false and acted Passion he has drawn true Tears, the Ladies kept Time with his Sighs, and wept to his sad Accents as if he had truly been the Man he seem'd, then I'll try my Part, thou hast still been privy to my Bosom Secrets; know'st Wealth and Ambition are the Darlings of my Soul; nor will I leave a Stratagem unessay'd to raise my Family.

My

My Son is well and ſafe, but by Command from me he returns not this three Months. My Daughter, my *Lucaſia*, is my only Care, and to advance her Fortune have I fram'd this Project; how doſt like it *Roſco*, ha!.

Roſco. Rarely, my Lord, my Lady will be now ſuppos'd the Heir to all your vaſt Revenues, and peſter'd with more Suitors than the *Grecian* Queen, in the long Abſence of her Lord. You'll have the Dons, Lords and Dukes ſwarm about your Houſe like Bees.

Grav. My Aim is fix'd at the Rich and Great, he that has Wealth enough, yet longs for more, Count *Pirro*, the Governor's Heir and Nephew, that rich Lord that knows no End of his large Fortunes, yet ſtill gapes on, for Gold is a ſure Bait to gain him, no other Loadſtone can attract his Iron Heart, 'tis Proof againſt the Force of Beauty, elſe I ſhould not need this Stratagem, for Nature has not prov'd a Niggard to my Daughter.

Roſco. To him, I'm ſure, ſhe's play'd the Step-Dame, I much fear *Lucaſia* will not reliſh ſuch a Match.

Grav. Ha! not reliſh it! has ſhe any other Taſte but mine, or ſhall ſhe dare to wiſh ought that may contradict my Purpoſe—But hold, perhaps you know how ſhe's inclin'd, you may be confederate with her, and manage her Intrigues with that Beggar *Palante*, who is only by Lord *Euphene*'s Bounty, my mortal Enemies, kept from ſtarving.

Roſco. Who I, my good Lord? Heav'n knows, I have learnt by your Lordſhip's Example, always to hate the Poor, and like the Courtier, never to do ought without a Bribe.

Enter a Servant.

Serv. My Lord, Count *Pirro*, to wait upon your Lordſhip.

Grav. Conduct him in. [*Exit. Serv.*] Now *Roſco*, to my Couch; if my Plot takes, I'm a happy Man.

Enter Count Pirro.

Pirro. Is your Lord aſleep?

Roſ. I think not, my Lord, but thus he lies, Heav'n knows when this Grief will end — My Lord, my Lord, the Count of *Pirro*.

Grav. I pray your Lordſhip pardon me, at this Time I'm not fit to entertain Perſons of your Worth.

Pir.

Pir. Alas! my Lord, I know your Grief.

Rof. Ay, 'twas that brought his good Lordſhip hither.

Pir. You have loſt a worthy, and a hopeful Son, but Heav'n that always gives, will ſometimes take, and there's no Balſam left to cure theſe Wounds but Patience; there's no diſputing with it, yet if there were, in what could you accuſe thoſe Pow'rs, that elſe have been ſo liberal to you, and left you to bleſs your Age a beauteous Daughter.

Rof. Now it begins to work. [*Aſide*.

Pirro. Your Blood is not extinct, nor are you Childleſs, Sir, from that fair Branch may come much Fruit to glad Poſterity; think on this, my Lord.

Grav. I know I ſhould not repine, my Lord, but Nature will prevail, I cannot help reflecting on my Loſs; alas, my Lord, you know not what it is to loſe a Son; 'tis true, I have ſtill a Child, Heav'n has now confin'd my Care to one, to ſee her well beſtow'd ſhall be the Buſineſs of my Life — Oh! my *Eugenio*.

Rof. Egad, he does it rarely. [*Aſide*.

Pirr. How ſhall I manage, that he may not ſuſpect my Love to his Daughter proceeds from his Son's Death, [*Aſide*.] I was juſt coming to make a Propoſal to your Lordſhip as the News reach'd my Ear, I much fear the Time's improper now to talk of Buſineſs.

Grav. Pray Heav'n it be the Buſineſs I wiſh; were my Grief more great, if poſſible, yet would I ſuſpend it to hear my Lord of *Pirro*.

Rof. Cunningly inſinuated. [*Aſide*.

Pirro. Your Lordſhip is too obliging.

Grav. Not at all, pray proceed, my Lord.

Pirro. It was, my Lord, to have aſk'd the fair *Lucaſia* for my Wife.

Rof. So he has ſwallow'd the Bait. [*Aſide*.

Grav. As I could wiſh. [*Aſide*.

Pirro. 'Twas not out of any Conſideration of her preſent Fortune, my Lord, I hope you'll not believe, ſince I deſigned it e'er I knew *Eugenio* dead. I wiſh he may believe me. [*Aſide*.

Grav. If 'twas, my Lord of *Pirro* does deſerve it all, nor would I wiſh my Child a better Match. But 'tis too ſoon to treat of Marriage after ſuch a Loſs.

Roſca.

Rosco. Dear Sir, consent to this good Lord, so will your Care be over, and hopeful Grandsons make up poor *Eugenio*'s Loss.

Grav. What would you have me think of Joy and Death at once, and mingle the Grave and Marriages together.

Pirro. If you'll consent, my Lord, a private Marriage may be had, and so dispense with the usual Solemnities of Joy. If you refuse me, I shall think you slight my Claim.

Grav. That Argument alone prevails: No, I will never give the Count of *Pirro* Cause to doubt of my Esteem.

Rosco. Consider, my Lord, she's an Heiress, that may set bold desperate Youths on rash Attempts; and tho' they know *Sicilian* Laws gives Death to him that steals an Heiress, yet I'll not warrant her Safety till to-morrow Night.

Pirro. He's in the right, my Lord.

Grav. Away, and call her, tho' she's disorder'd with her Griefs. Now thou hast rais'd another Fear, and my poor Heart trembles for *Lucasia*, as it for *Eugenio* bleeds.

[*Ex*. Rosco.

Pirro. Within my Arms she shall be safe and happy, the Governor, my noble Uncle, and my Friend, her great Protector.

Enter Rosco *with* Lucasia.

Grav. Come near *Lucasia*, like the Ambassadors from this World's great Rulers, I bring thee Grief and Joy, pause not upon a Brother's Loss, tho' 'twas a dear one; but fix thy Thoughts here, upon this Lord; thus I bequeath thee to the illustrious Count of *Pirro*.

Pirro. Thus I with Extasy receive her.

[*Kneels and kisses her Hand*.

Luc. You'll give me Leave, my Lord, to wake from this Confusion:
Is't possible! do I behold my Father?
Can he resolve, at once, to part with both
His Children, my Brother, the best of Men,
No more will bless his Roof, no more will grace
This Palace with his Presence——
Must I be cast out too, far more unblest
Than he who's lodg'd within the peaceful Grave.
Oh, send me to him, e'er you condemn me

To

To perpetual Bondage, to a Life of Woe;
To a Marriage unthought of, unforeseen.

Pirro. Madam——

Grav. Mind her not, my Lord, 'tis Grief, 'tis mere Distraction, she shan't dispute my Will. Please to walk in, my Lord, we'll peruse the Writings of your Estate, and hear what Settlement you'll make her, and to-morrow the Priest shall join you, to alleviate her Griefs, and Mine.

Pirro. But to see her weep thus, damps all my rising Joy.

Grav. They are but Virgin Tears, pray come with me, Daughter, you know my Will, I expect you be obedient; you know 'tis your Duty.

Luc. I know 'tis Sir.——
But you, I hope, will give my tortur'd Heart
Your Leave to break, and that may shew my Duty.

Pirro. Fair *Lucasia.*

Luc. Oh, Distraction! [*Flings from him.*

Grav. Pray come, my Lord, let her have her Way, the Fits of Women's Grief last not long, at least when I command she shall obey. [*Exeunt, all but* Lucasia.

Luc. A dismal Sentence, it strikes me upon my Soul,
And raises Terrors far more grim than Death;
Forgive me, Brother, if t' thy Memory
I pay not one Tear more, all now are due
To Love, and my *Palante.*

Enter Laura.

Lau. You name the Man that waits by me conceal'd,
For one blest Minute to comfort his *Lucasia.*

Luc. All Minutes now are curs'd, no chearful day,
Will ever bring the lost *Lucasia* Peace.

Lau. Come forth, Sir, I believe you'll prove the best Physician.

Enter Palante.

Luc. Oh *Palante,* art thou come prepar'd to weep,
Else, for me, thou art no fit Companion,
For I have News will rack thy very Soul.

Pal. Yes, I have heard of brave *Eugenio*'s Death;
He was thy Brother, and my early Friend:
Thus doubly ty'd, thou need'st not doubt I mourn
Him truly——

Luc. Oh poor *Palante!*
So wretched *Alcione* did at Distance grieve,
when she beheld the floating Corps,
Ard knew not 'twas her Husband.

Pal. What means my Love?

Luc. Dost thou not love me, my *Palante?*

Pal. Oh! after so many Years of faithful Service,
Why am I ask'd that Question?

Luc. It were better that thou didst not, for when
Thou hear'st the Story 'twill turn thee into Marble;
'Twill shock thy manly Heart, and make each Nerve
Lose its accustomed Faculty, chill all
Thy Blood, and make thine Eyes run o'er like mine,
For we must part for ever.

Pal. Can that Voice pronounce a Sound so dreadful?
Art thou then alter'd with thy Fortune? Must
I lose thee?

Luc. O thou unkind one to suspect my Love,
My promis'd Faith, or think me in the least
Consenting to my rigid Father's Will,
Who, but now has given me to the Count of *Pirro*.

Pal. Ha! to the Count of *Pirro*, that Lump of Deformity:
My Sword has been my Fortune hitherto,
And ne'er was wont to fail its Master, and
Whilst this Arm can hold it, I'll maintain my Right.

Luc. Which Way rash Man, is he not surrounded
By numerous Friends, and waiting Slaves?
Does not inevitable Death attend
Thy desperate Purpose?

Pal. Then let that same Sword, the old Acquaintance
Of my Arm, pierce its lost Master's Breast, and
End my Sorrows.

Luc. Forbid it Heaven, is there no other Way?

Pal. But one, and that I dare not name.

Luc, Oh! how has thy *Lucasia*, since first our
Mutual Vows were plighted, given Cause for Doubt.
Why dost thou fear to ask, since all is thine, within
The Bounds of Honour.

Pal. When I attempt ought against *Lucasia*,
Contrary to the nicest Rules of Virtue,
May Heaven, and she, forsake me.

Luc. Oh, I know it, and when I refuse what
May advance our Loves, may I be curst
With that hated Count of *Pirro*. Speak, my *Palante*,

Pal. Can I—Ye all-seeing Powers, move so bold a Suit,
Oh! let me humbly ask it on my Knees,
To quit her cruel Father's House,
And all the Grandeur of a pompous Court.
To bear a Part in my hard Fortunes;
Oh! 'tis too much to think, to wish, to hope.

Luc. Yes, dear *Palante*, more than this I'd do for thee.
What's Pomp and Greatness when compared with Love?
Oh! that thou wert some humble Shepherd on
Our *Sicilian* Plain, I thy chearful Mate,
Wou'd watch with Pleasure till the Ev'ning Tide,
And wait thy blest Return, with as much Joy
As Queens expect victorious Monarchs, and
Think myself more blest than they. But, oh *Palante*!
Thou know'st our Country's Laws gives Death without
Reprieve to him that weds an Heiress against her Parents
Tho' with her own Consent. Will,

Pal. Who would not die to purchase thee? For I
Must die without thee.

Luc. No, live *Palante*, we'll together tread
The Maze of Life, and stand the Shock of Fate.
The Power's Decree, or both our Happiness,
Or both our Miseries, where shall we meet?
For I will leave this loathsome House, before their
Watch grows stricter.

Pal. Will thou then forsake the World for thy *Palante*?
Everlasting Blessings fall around thee,
And crown thy Days and Nights with Peace and Joy.
Oh! my fond Heart, I cannot half express
The Raptures thou hast rais'd, thou Treasure of
My Soul, let me embrace thee, and while thus
I hold thee in my Arms, I'm richer than
The *Eastern* Monarch, nor wou'd I quit thee
To be as great as he——
Oh! let but what my Arms infolds be mine;
Take all the rest the World contains, my Life.

Luc. My *Palante*——

Pal. I have an only Friend, faithful and just
As Men of old before Deceit became

A Trade, he ſhall aſſiſt us in our Flight;
He ſhall prepare a Prieſt, if thou wilt meet
Me in the *Eaſtern* Grove; when we are wed
We'll fly to *Spain*, till Time and Friends procure
My Pardon.

Luc. In ſome Diſguiſe I'll meet thee there,
Juſt at the Hour of Noon,
For then my Father ſleeps, and I will take
The Opportunity——
And, oh! I fear no Danger but for thee.

Pal. For me there's none, whilſt thou'rt ſafe, and with
Me thy Loſs alone can make *Palante* die.

Enter Laura.

Laura. Madam, your Father——

Luc. Away *Palante*, may all the Pow'rs preſerve thee.

Pal. And thou the beſt of Woman-kind.

[*Exeunt ſeverally.*

Luc. *O Love, thou that haſt join'd a faithful Pair,*
Guard my Palante, *make him all thy Care.*
Fate's utmoſt Rigor we reſolve to try,
Live both together, or together die.

Enter Count Gravello, Larich *and* Lavinia.

Grav. Brother, you are welcome to the Houſe of Sorrow; but I have learnt ſo much Philoſophy, to ceaſe to mourn when the Cauſe is paſt Redreſs. Once more, forgetting Grief, you are welcome, you, and my fair Niece.

Lar. Thank you Brother— the Girl's a fooliſh Girl — Marriageable, but fooliſh—You underſtand me.

Lavin. I thank you, Sir.

Larich. Why, are you not a Fool, Huſſy—look'e Brother, I have provided the Mynx a rich Huſband, a Scholar too, Body of me bred all his Youth at *Salamanca*, learn'd enough to commence Doctor—I love a learned Man, eſpecially when Riches too concur; he's the Son and Heir of my old Friend *Don Sancho*, of *Syracuſe* — and the Baggage cries *I hate him*, and yet has never ſeen him; but ſhe is in Love, forſooth, with a young beggarly Dog, not worth a Groat; but I'll prevent her, I'll warrant her.

Grav. Juſt, juſt my Caſe, we are Brothers in every Thing, my Daughter too thinks her Judgment wiſeſt, and flies a Fortune for a Princeſs, but her Reign's at an End, to-morrow I'm rid of her; I warrant you, Brother, we'll hamper the young Sluts.

Lavin. You may be both miſtaken, old Gentlemen, if my Couſin is of my Mind.

Larich. What's that you mutter, Mrs. *Littlewit*.

Lavin. I ſay, I long to ſee my Couſin *Lucaſia*, Sir, I hope that's no Crime.

Grav. No, no, *Roſco*, wait of her in to my Daughter, and doſt hear *Lavinia?* Pr'ythee let Obedience be thy Study, and teach it her.

Lavin. I'll warrant you, Sir, I'll teach her to be Obedient, if ſhe'll but follow my Advice, [*Aſide*] but 'tis ſomething hard, though Uncle, to marry a Man at firſt Sight one's heard but an indifferent Character of.

Larich. How, Huſſy, are you a Judge of Characters? Is he not a Scholar? Anſwer me that.

Lavin. A meer Scholar is a meer——You know the old Proverb, Father.

Larich. Do you hear the perverſe Baggage; get you out of my Sight, Huſſy.

Lavin. I am obedient, Sir,—I dare ſwear I ſhall find better Company, than two old arbitrary Dons.

[*Exit with* Roſco.

Larich. Did you ever ſee ſuch a Slut? body o'me theſe wild Wenches are enough to make old Men mad.

Grav. My Daughter is of another Strain, ſolid as Man, but obſtinate as Woman; but no Matter, when ſhe is married my Care is over, let Count *Pirro* look to't.

Larich, Count *Pirro!* body o'me a mighty Fortune for my Couſin; why, he's rich enough to buy a Principality; my Son's rich too, and a great Scholar, which I admire above all Things.

Enter Roſco.

Roſco. Oh! Sir, ſuch News, ſuch a Sight, Sir!

Larich. What's the Matter?

Roſco. Don *Sancho* come to Town in his *Salamanca* Habit, his Dreſs, and grave Phiz has alarm'd the Mob, that there's ſuch a crowd about the Inn Door, I'll maintain't his Landlord gives him free Quarter for a Twelve-month, if he'll let him expoſe him to Advantage, ha, ha, ha, he makes as odd a Figure, Sir, as the famous *Don Quixot*, when he went in Search of his *Dulcinea*.

Larich. Brother, pray correct your Servant, I like not his ridiculous Jests upon the Habit of the Learned, my Son-in-Law that is to be, minds nothing but his Books.

Rosco. Sir, I ask your Pardon, my niggard Stars have not allow'd Line enough to my Judgment, to fathom the Profundity of your Son's Shallow Capacity— [*Bowing comically.*

Grav. Peace, Sirrah—Come, Brother, now your Son's arriv'd, I hope we shall have a double Match to-morrow—— We'll not consult the Women, but force them to their Happiness.

Experienc'd Age knows what for Youth is fit;
With wise Men, Wealth out-weighs both Parts and Wit.

[Exeunt.

ACT II. SCENE I. Lucasia's *Chamber.*

Enter Lucasia *and* Lavinia.

Lavin. UPON my Life, Cousin, I think my Condition worse than yours, and yet you see I am not so much dejected.

Luc. Oh! What Condition is't can equal mine?
Much less exceed it; to be oblig'd to
Break my Vow, to part from my *Palante*;
Forc'd to the Arms of a mishapen Monster,
Whom Nature made to vex the whole Creation.
Nor is his crooked Body more deform'd
Than is his Soul, Ambition is his God;
He seeks no Heav'n but Interest; nor knows he
How to value ought but Gold.
Oh! my dearest Brother, had'st thou but liv'd
I had been truly happy, but now am
Doubly miserable, in losing thee and my *Palante.*

Lavin. For Heaven's Sake don't afflict yourself at this Rate, but study rather to avoid the Ill, if you would counterplot my Uncle; dry up your Eyes, and let the Woman work, I warrant you may contrive some Way to get rid of this Lump of Worms-meat; I don't fear giving my Father the drop, for all his Care, yet tho' he made me ride post to Town, to meet the Fool he has pick'd out for me; it shall cost me a Fall, if I don't marry the Man I have a Mind to; I shall see who's the best Politician, my Dad, or I.

Luc. Thy Courage gives fresh Life and Liberty,
To poor *Lucasia*'s tired restless Soul,
Such Pow'r have chearful Friends t'ease our Sorrows.

Oh! my *Lavinia*, may thy Counsel prove
Prophetic, I'm going now, in this Disguise, to meet my
Dear *Palante*; may no malignant Star
Interpose to cross our mutual Wishes.
May thy Designs successful prove,
To fix thee ever in *Francisco*'s Arms.

Lavin. And make *Palante* yours.

SCENE *the Street*.

Sancho *and* Francisco *meeting*.

Fran. Don *Sancho* your Servant; who thought of seeing you at *Palermo*, I thought you had been at the University of *Salamanca*?

Sancho. I came lately from thence.

Fran. Pr'ythee, what brought you hither?

Sanc. Why, that that brings some Men to the Gallows, a Wench.

Fran. What, I warrant, you have got your Bed-maker with Child, and so are expell'd the College.

Sancho. That's a Mistake.

Fran. What, thou art not come hither to take Physic, ha!

Sancho. No, not the Physic you mean; but am going to enter into a Course, that is, the Course of Matrimony.

Fran. Matrimony, with who, pr'ythee?

Sanc. Why, with Don *Larich*'s Daughter: Do you know her?

Fran. Ha! Is this my Rival? This was a lucky Discovery, [*Aside*] know her; ay, very well, Sir. I can assure you she's very handsome, and as witty as she's fair: Thou wont visit her in that Dress, sure?

Sancho. To chuse, Sir, 'tis an Emblem of Learning; nay, I design my Man shall carry a Load of Books along with me too, that she may see what he is Master of, that is to be Master of her.

Fran. Indeed, my Friend, you'll never succeed upon those Terms.

Tristr. Sir, my Master has such an Itch to this foolish Learning, that he bestows more Money yearly upon Books, than would build an Hospital for all the Courtesans in *Italy*.

Sancho. No more, or you'll displease me, *Tristram*.

Tristr. I can't help that, Sir,---Sir, will you believe me, I have spent two Days in sorting Poets from Historians, and as many Nights in placing the Divines on their own Chairs, I mean their Shelves; then separating Philosophers, from those People that kill with a License, cost me a whole Day's Labour; and tho' my Master says Learning is immortal, I find the Sheets it is contain'd in savours much of Mortality.

Sancho. I hope my Books are in good Case, *Tristram*?

Tristr. Yes, yes, Sir, in as good Case as the Moths-have left 'em.

Sancho. Od'so, I had forgot, to get me *Suarez Metaphysicks*, *Tolet de Anima*, and *Granados Commentaries*, on *Primum Secundæ Thomæ Aquinatis*.

Tristr. How the Devil does he do to remember all these Author's hard Names, I dare swear he understands not a Syllable of their Writings——Sir, would not the famous History of *Amidis de Gaul* do as well.

Fran. Ay, better, better far, Man, hark'ee *Sancho*, you are not at *Salamanca* now, amongst your square Caps, but in *Palermo*, come up to see your Mistress the fair *Lavinia*, the Glory of the City; go and court her like a Gentleman, without your Tropes and Figures, or all the Physics, Metaphysics, and Metaphors, will streight be made pitiful Martyrs.

Sancho. Martyrs, Sir, why, I thought—

Fran. Thyself an errant Idiot, thy Brain's more dull than a *Dutch* Burghers. Is this a Dress fit for a Gentleman to court his Mistress in? Away, away, the Lady you speak of, I can assure you is too much a Gallant to be taken with a Band and a square Cap—If you would succeed, you must throw off that Pedant, and assume the Gentleman, learn the Toss of the Head, and know the Principles of each Man by the Cock of his Hat.

Sancho. How's that, pray?

Fran. Oh! I'll teach you: If you be but willing to improve, I'll warrant you carry the Lady.

Sanch. But I am to be married to her as soon as I see her, so my Father told me, and that her Father admired a Scholar above all Things.

Fran. I'll improve that Hint—Ay, as I told you, a Scholar that is read in Men, not in Books.

Sancho. In Men, what's that? in Men! *Tristram*, what does he mean? what Man is to be read? In Men! I don't understand you; but you'll teach me, you say.

Fran. Ay, ay, I'll give you a Lesson upon that Subject.

Sancho. Very well; but what shall I do for Cloaths to dress like a Gentleman?

Fran. If you please to step into my Lodgings here, I'll equip

equip you with a Suit of mine till you can have one made, and there I'll teach you a little of the Town breeding, and I warrant you you'll succeed.

Sancho. Come on; faith I long to become thy Scholar.

Fran. And I to make you an Ass. [*Exit*.

Enter Eugenio *and his Man*.

Eug. What can this mean; where e'er I come the News is current of my Death, yet not two Days since, I wrote and received Letters from my Father, and here the Rumour goes, I have been dead this fortnight! I am resolv'd to know the Grounds, if possible. *Pedro*, go get me some Disguise, and for your Life discover not who I am, I'll stay here at this Inn 'till you return, and in the mean Time think what Method to pursue my Project in. [*Exit*.

SCENE *changes to the Grove*. Lucasia *sola*.

Lucasia. Methinks this silent solitary Grove
Should strike a Terror to such Hearts as mine;
But Love has made me bold, the Time has been,
In such a Place as this, I should have fear'd
Each shaking Bough, and started at the Wind,
And trembled at the Rushing of the Leaves;
My Fancy would have fram'd a thousand Shapes;
But now it seems a Palace,
Delightful as the Poets feign
The *Elizian* Fields; Here do I expect
To meet my Love, my faithful, dear *Palante*.
Why does he stay thus long? when last we
Parted, each Hour he said wou'd seem a Year,
Till we were met again, and yet I'm here
Before him; I'll rest a while, for come I
Know he will. [*Goes and sits down*.

Enter Palante *and* Clerimont.

Pal. This, *Clerimont*, this is the happy Place,
Where I shall meet the Sum of all my Joys,
And be possest of such a vast Treasure
As wou'd enrich a Monarch to receive;
And thou, my Friend, must give her to my Arms.

Luc. 'Tis my *Palante*'s Voice. [*Comes forward*.

Pal. My Life, my Soul, what here before me? still
Thou prevent'st me in the Race of Love, and
Makest all my Endeavours poor in Competition
With thy large Favours———
But I forget, Dearest; bid my Friend here welcome,

This is he whom I dare trust, next my own
Heart, with Secrets.

Luc. I must admire him that loves *Palante*;
Friendship's a noble Name, 'tis Love refin'd;
'Tis something more than Love, 'tis what I wou'd
Shew to my *Palante.*

Cler. It is indeed a Beauty of the Mind, a Sacred Name,
In which so brightly shines that Heavenly Love,
That makes th' immortal Beings taste each others Joy;
'Tis the very Cement of Souls. Friendship's
A Sacred Name, and he who truly knows
The Meaning of the Word, is worthy of Estimation.
No Pains he'll spare, no Difficulties start,
But hazard all for th' Int'rest of his Friend.

Pal. Ay! Now methinks I'm Emperor of the World,
With my inestimable Wealth about me:
To such a Mistress, such a Friend, what can be
Added more to make me happy?——
Oh! thou darksome Grove, that wont to be call'd
The Seat of Melancholy, and Shelter
For the discontented Souls! sure thou'rt wrong'd!
Thou seem'st to me a Place of Solace and Content!
A Paradise! that gives me more than Courts
Cou'd ever do: Blest be then thy fair Shades,
Let Birds of Musick always chant it here;
No croaking Raven, or ill-boding Owl,
Make here their baleful Habitation:
But may'st thou be a Grove for Loves fair Queen
To sport in, for under thy blest Shade two faithful
Lovers meet——Why is my *Lucasia* sad?

Luc. I know not, but I long to quit this Place,
My Thoughts seem to divine of Treachery,
But whence I know not; no Creature's conscious
To our meeting here but *Laura*; I have always
Found her honest, and yet I would she did not know it.

Pal. 'Tis only Fear assaults thy tender Mind;
But come, my Friend, let's to the Cell adjoining
To this Grove, and there the Priest
Shall make us one for ever. *Exeunt.*

Enter Larich *and* Lavinia.

Lar. Come, set your Face in order, for I expect young *Sancho* here immediately, he arriv'd in Town last Night, and sent me Word but now, he'd be here in an instant.

Lav.

Lav. But, Sir.

Lar. Sir me no Sirs, for I'm reſolv'd you ſhall be married to Night.

Enter a Servant.

Serv. Sir, here's a Gentleman to wait on you calls himſelf Don *Sancho*.

Lar. Odſo, ſhew him up; now, you Baggage, you ſhall ſee the Pink of Learning, one that can travel thro' the whole World in an Afternoon, and ſup in *Palermo* at Night, ha! you ſhall; you'll be as wiſe as the *Sibyls* in a Month's Time, with ſuch a Huſband, and will bring forth a Race of Politicians that ſhall ſet the World together by the Ears, then patch it up again in the ſupping of a poach'd Egg.

Enter Sancho *and* Triſtram.

Lar. Save you, Sir.

Sanc You don't think me damn'd, Sir, that you beſtow that Salutation upon me?

Lar. By no Means, Sir, 'tis only my Way of expreſſing a hearty Welcome.

Sanc. Sir, your humble Servant: Is this your fair Daughter, Sir?

Lar. Yes, Sir.

Sanc. She's very handſome, Faith.

Lar. She's as Heaven made her.

Sanc. Then ſhe ſhou'd be naked; the Taylor ſhou'd have no Hand in her — I ſuppoſe you know my Buſineſs, ſhall we be married inſtantly?

Lar. Won't to-morrow ſerve, Sir? I wou'd firſt hear a little of your Proceedings in the Univerſity; came you from *Salamanca* now, Sir?

Sanc. From *Salamanca!* What do you ſee in my Face, that ſhou'd make you judge me ſuch a Coxcomb?

Lar. Your Father writ me word, that his Son that was to marry my Daughter, was a Scholar, wholly given up to Books.

Sanc. My Father was an errant Aſs for his Pains, I ne'er read a Book in my Life but what I was beat to, and thoſe I forgot as ſoon as I left School: A Scholar! he lies in his Throat that told you ſo.

Lav. In my Conſcience, Sir, you may believe him; I dare ſwear he never ſaw a Book except the Chronicle chain'd in his Father's Hall.

Lar. Hold your Tongue, Huſſy; how now?

Sanc. Sir, I underſtand a Horſe, a Hawk, or Hound, as well as any Man living; nay, I underſtand Men too; I know now that you are an old covetous Hunks, by the ſett of your Hat now; but no Matter for that, your Daughter is the better Fortune.

Lav. The Fool has hit right upon my Father, we ſhall have rare Sport preſently.

Sanc. I have ſtudied Men, Sir—— I know each Man's inward Principle by his out-ſide Habit.

Lav. Does your profound Knowledge reach to Women too, Sir?

Lar. You will be prating——

Sanc. Look you, Sir, obſerve the Management of my Hat now——This is your bullying Gameſter.

[*Three Corners ſhort Pinch.*

Lar. What the Devil have we here! z'death this can never be Don *Sancho*'s Son?

Lav. This is indeed the Pink of Learning, Sir—I ſhall be as wiſe as the *Sybils* with ſuch a Huſband; ha, ha, ha.

Sanc. Your Beaus wear their Hats [*Offering to put it on.*] no, hold, thus, Sir; [*Clapping it under his Arm.*] your conceited Wit, thus, [*Putting it on over the left Eye*] and your travell'd Wit thus [*Over the right Eye without a Pinch.*] your Country 'Squire, thus, [*Putting it behind his Wig.*]

Lar. I wonder how an Aſs wears it, I'm ſure thou art one; I am amaz'd! this muſt be ſome Trick certainly. [*Aſide.*

Lav. What think you now, Sir, ſhall we get a Race of Politicians? In my Conſcience this falls out as well as I could wiſh. Oh that I could but once ſee *Franciſco.* [*Aſide.*

Lar. Huzzy, hold your Tongue, or——or——

[*Holds up his Cane.*

This may be ſome of your Contrivance, for ought I know. This is a very great Blockhead; Ounds, I— I— I— have a good Mind to add one Faſhion more to your Hat, and knock it down to your Crown.

Sanc. Evermore, Sir, when you ſee a Man wear his Hat thus, [*Pulling it down on both Sides.*] he's a Projector, a Projector, Sir, or a Member of the Society of the Reformation of Manners, [*In another Tone.*] What think you of this, old Gentleman? ha! is not this a greater Knowledge than ever Man attain'd to by Books? ha!

Lar. I admire that my old Friend, knowing my Averſion for theſe fooliſh Fopperies, ſhou'd breed up his Son to 'em,

then

then write me Word he had made him a Scholar, purposely because I was a Lover of Learning; pray, Sir, was you ever in *Palermo* before?

Sanc. No, Sir; but I like it very well now I am in't.

Lar. I must be satisfied that you are Seignor *Sancho*'s Son, e'er I shall like you for mine. [*Aside.*

Sanc. What think you of a Glass of Champaign, Sir? If you'll go to the Tavern, I'll give you a Bottle of the best the House affords; what say you, old Dad? ha! and there we will consult about our Marriage.

Lar. If you'll go to the Tavern that joins to the Piazza, I'll wait on you in a quarter of an Hour.

Sanc. Sir, I shall wait your Pleasure.

Lar. I took the Hint, to get rid of him, what shall I do to find the Truth of this? [*Exeunt.*

Enter a Servant.

Serv. Sir, a Scholar enquires for you.

Lar. A Scholar! admit him immediately.

Enter Francisco *in* Sancho'*s Habit.*

Fran. So, I watch'd *Sancho* out, now for my Cue. [*Aside.* If you be the venerable Man to whom this goodly Mansion is impropriated; I come to negociate about authentic Business.

Lav. This rather shou'd be Don *Sancho*'s Son —— his Words and Habit speak him most learned —— I am the Person, pray let me be bold to crave your Name.

Fran. My Appellation, or *pro Nomen*, as the Latins term it, is call'd *Jeremie*; but my *Cognomen*, in our Mother Tongue, is call'd *Sancho*.

Lav. Ha! upon my Life 'tis *Francisco*; oh, for an Opportunity to speak to him: I hope to Heaven, my Father won't find out the Cheat. [*Aside.*

Lar. Ay, this is he, this is he; what Don *Sancho*'s Son?

Fran. The *Nominals*, the *Thomists*, and all the Sects of old and modern School-men, do oblige me to pay to that Gentleman filial Duty.

Lar. I am glad to hear it with all my Herrt, I know the other must be an Impostor, but I'm resolv'd to apprehend and punish him: Sir, you are welcome; I guess your Business, my Daughter is yours.

Fran. My Business is about Propagation, as the civil Lawyers do learnedly paraphrase, is of Concomitance, or Cohabitation, or what you please to term it.

Lar. How am I bleſt that this wonderful Scholar ſhall be match'd into my Family—— Daughter, what ſay you now, here's a Huſband for you now, here's a Huſband for you.

Lav. Pray Heaven you hold but in the Mind 'till you have made him ſuch. [*Aſide*.

Lar. Does he not ſpeak like an Oracle? 'egad I'll maintain't, he ſhall put down ten Univerſities and Inns of Court in twenty Syllables —— Pray, Sir, ſpeak learnedly to my Girl, for, tho' I ſay it, ſhe has a good Capacity.

Fran. Moſt rubicund, ſtilliferous, ſplendant Lady, the occular Faculties by which the Beams of Love are darted into every Soul, or human Eſſence, have convey'd into my Breaſt the Luſtre of your Beauty; and I can admire no other Object; therefore pardon me, Sir, if I only expreſs myſelf in Terms Scholaſtic, and in Metaphors, my Phraſe to her.

[*Turning to* Larich.

Lar. Learned, learned, young Man, how happy am I in thee?

Lav. Now do I long to ſee my Father's Back turn'd, that he might change his learned non-ſenſe, and talk more modern, to talk more wiſe; you may ſpare your Rhetoric, Sir, unleſs you come down to my Underſtanding; but I know juſt enough of your Meaning, to tell you it does not ſuit with my Inclination.

Lar. What don't ſuit with your Inclination, ha, forſooth?

Lav. Marriage, Sir.

Lar. 'Tis falſe, huſſy, you have an Inclination, and you ſhall have an Inclination; not an Inclination, quoth the Baggage: Sir, I ſay ſhe's yours, come into the next Room, and I'll have the Settlement drawn immediately, and you ſhall be married to Night. Not an Inclination! [*Exit*.

ACT III. SCENE *the Street*.

Enter Eugenio.

Eug. THUS in Diſguiſe I ſhall diſcover all,
And find the Cauſe of my reported Death,
Which does ſo much amaze me.
A Month ago my Father ſent me Word, that I ſhou'd haſten my Journey to *Palermo*; and I met the Poſt upon the Road, that gave me a Letter, wherein he ſtrictly charges me not to come this three Months: No ſooner had I enter'd the Town, but

but I met the Rumour of my Death, which still surpris'd me more; but this Letter shall help me to the Knowledge of the Truth. [*Shews a Letter, goes to the Door and knocks.*

Enter Rosco.

Ros. Who'd you speak with, Friend?

Eug. With the Lord *Gravello*, if you please, Sir.

Ros. Marry gap, and can't I serve your Turn? Nothing but my Lord, good lack! I guess he knows you not; pray what's your Business? What's your Name? From whence come you? What do ye want? I believe you are of no such Extraction, that you shou'd be introduc'd to my Lord; let me be judge, whether your Affair require his Lordship's Ear, else, Friend, I shall bring you but a scurvy Answer; either he's busy, or a-sleep, or gone abroad, any of these are sufficient for your Quality, I suppose.

Eug Thus great Men always are abus'd, because there's no Access, but through such Knaves as thee? then I'll return my Message back unto his Son, and bid him employ a finer Fellow, if he expects that he should see his Father. [*Going.*

Ros. Ha! his Son! stay, Sir, and forgive me; here comes my Lord.

Enter Count Gravello, Rosco *goes and whispers him.*

Grav. Wou'd you ought with me, Friend?

Eug. If you be the Lord *Gravello.*

Grav. The same.

Eug. I came from *Rome*, my Lord; laden, I hope, with happy Tidings, and after the sad Report I have met with, I dare say, welcome; your Son *Eugenio* lives, and with his Duty, recommends this Letter to your Lordship's Perusal.

Grav. How! does my Boy live? Oh! I'm overjoy'd, for I thought him dead. *Rosco*, reward him for his Tidings, reward him largely, *Rosco.*

Ros. There's a Pistole for you, eat like an Emperor, d'ye hear, till that be out.

Grav. He writes me Word that you are a Gentleman fallen to Decay, and begs that I would take you into my Service: I have no Place vacant at present, but the first that falls worth your Acceptance, shall be yours; in the mean Time command my House, [*I must not let him suspect I knew* Eugenio *was alive*] the happy News that thou hast brought me, has rais'd me from the Vale of Death; but tell me, Friend, hast thou reveal'd this to any in *Palermo*, but myself?

Eug. To none. For tho' I met the tragic Story in every Street through which I pass'd, still I conceal'd the Truth, intending your Lordship's Ear should first receive it.

Grav. Thou hast done exceeding well; *Rosco*, give him a double Reward, a double Welcome; I have some private Reasons to myself, that it should still be kept a Secret, which if thou'rt faithful, thou in Time shalt know.

Eug. Fear not, my Lord, I am no Blab; I ever thought a slippery Tongue Mankind's Shame. What can this mean? [*Aside.*

Ros. This is a notable Fellow.

Grav. *Rosco*, bid him welcome; tell him my House is his, bid him be free.

Ros. As long as you have Occasion for him——Sir, I am your most obedient, most devoted, and thrice humble Serviteur; command the Pantry, Cellar, Maids, Chambers——for in these I rule, and these are at your Service, Sir. [*Bowing low.*

Eug. I thank you my quondam Friend; but a quiet Residence in my Lord's House, the Time I stay, satisfies my Desires.

Ros. A worthy Man, upon my Faith. Oh! my Lord, here comes the Bridegroom, I know by this Fellow's being out of Breath.

Enter a Servant.

Serv. My Lord Count *Pirro* so fine, so brisk, so ugly.

Grav. How, how, Sirrah, ugly?

Serv. So handsome, I mean, Sir; Pox on't, how came my Head to run so of Ugliness?

Ros. Seeing the Count, I warrant thee *Jack*.

Grav. Be gone, Varlet, and attend his coming. [*Exeunt.*

Eug. Ha! Count *Pirro*, the Bridegroom — and, my Life a Secret; I begin to find the Cause. [*Aside.*

Enter Count Pirro.

Pir. I came, my Lord, to claim your Promise, and receive into my Arms the beautiful *Lucasia*.

Grav. And I'll acquit myself instantly. Within there—call *Lucasia*.

Enter Laura.

Laura. My Lord.

Grav. My —— call your Lady; what does your Flurtship do here? I want your Mistress —— why don't the Wench stir?

Laura.

Laura. My Lord, I don't know.——

Grav. What don't you know? nay, no grinding between your Teeth, ſpeak out.

Laura. Why then, my Lord, I don't know where ſhe is.

Grav. 'Tis falſe, 'tis impoſſible; when went ſhe out? and whither? Speak ye confederate Miſchief; how long ago, I ſay? Confeſs, or I'll have ye rack'd.

Laura. She would not take me with her to prevent Suſpicion; and now all muſt out, for my Limbs will never bear ſtretching, that's certain. [*Aſide.*

Grav. What are you inventing a Lye? —— don't ſtand muttering your Devil's Pater-noſter there, but ſpeak quickly—or— [*Draws his Sword.*

Laura. Oh hold, it was, my Lord, my Lord, a, a, a——

Grav. What was it? ſpeak.

Laura. It was a great while ago, my Lord.

Grav. Ha, ſpeak to the Purpoſe, or thou dy'ſt.

Laura. No, no, no, my Lord, it was——it was juſt now; what ſhall I ſay to ſave my unhappy Miſtreſs? [*Aſide.*

Pirro. You terrify the Creature ſo, that we ſhall never learn the Truth, my Lord; don't tremble ſo, Sweetheart, but tell when went your Lady out, and whither?

Grav. Away, my Lord, my Sword ſhall fetch the Secret forth; Huzzy, ſpeak, or by this Hand, this Minute is thy laſt. [*Holds his Sword to her Breaſt.*

Laura. Oh, hold Sir, and I will tell you all; I do confeſs.

Grav. What?

Laura. It muſt out; that my Lady's fled to meet *Palante* in the Eaſtern Grove, and I believe, by this, they are married.

Grav. Fly, and eſcape my Fury, thou more than Devil. [*Straps her with his Sword, ſhe ſhrieks and runs off.*

Now, my Lord of *Pirro*, you that ſo kindly came this Day to comfort me, how ſhall I look you in the Face? or what Reparation can I make you, if my Daughter's loſt? Within there! raiſe the Houſe, take Officers immediately, I charge you; fly to the Eaſtern Grove, and ſeize my Daughter and all that you find with her: We'll have Revenge, my Lord, at leaſt.

Pirro. There's yet a Pleaſure left in that, and I'm reſolv'd my Arm ſhall give him Death; let's to the Grove, my Lord.

Roſco. Do you conſider, my Lord, the Danger of your raſh Attempt, the Law will do you right; 'tis preſent Death

in

in *Sicily*, to ſteal an Heireſs without her Friends conſent; firſt ſecure him, and his Life's yours.

Eug. 'Tis as I ſuppoſe; oh Treachery! [*Aſide.*

Grav *Roſco*, thou art an Oracle, that Way the Revenge is more ſecure and certain. I'll after 'em, and ſee the Traitor brought to condign Puniſhment. [*Exit with* Roſco.

Pirro. I'll to the Governor, and prepare him for the Judgment, my Intereſt there will ſurely ſign his Death. [*Going.*

Eug. Am I alive? do I breathe? can I have a human Soul, and ſuffer this Injuſtice to proceed? Poor *Palante*, muſt thou die, becauſe Fortune has not bleſt thee with her Favours; No, ſomething I will do to ſave thee; and yet, if poſſible not diſcover who I am. My Lord——

[*Pulls Count* Pirro *by the Sleeve as he goes out.*

Pirro. What art thou?

Eug A poor Poet, my Lord, little beholden to Fortune.

Pirro. None of thy Profeſſion are, take up ſome more thriving Occupation; turn Pimp, Sollicitor, Gameſter, any Thing will do better than Rhiming; there's ſomething for thee, I'm in Haſte now.

Eug. My Lord, I thank you for your Charity, and your good Advice; but I have ſome for you too.

Pirro. For me! what is't?

Eug. I underſtand, my Lord, that you are to marry my Lord *Gravello*'s Daughter.

Pirro. Yes, an Heireſs——

Eug. No Heireſs, my Lord, her Brother is alive.

Pirro. The Fellow's mad.

Eug. What I ſay is certain Truth; and to my Knowledge, his Father gives out the Report of his Death only as a Bait for you.

Pirro. Ha! where is he?

Eug. In this Town conceal'd till your Marriage be over; know I hate this Family, and that makes me diſcover it.

Pirro. Does he hate the Family? then perhaps he has only forg'd this Lye to hinder *Lucaſia* from marrying into mine; I'll try him farther. [*Aſide.*
Art thou ſure he is alive?

Eug. As ſure as that I live myſelf; my Lord, I ſaw him not two Hours ago; I wiſh he was not, for your Lordſhip's ſake: I am his Domeſtic, and come now to learn Intelligence;

gence; I loath my Servitude, deteſt the proud Family, and ſhou'd rejoice to ſee 'em ruin'd.

Pirro. From whence proceeds thy Hate? the World reports *Eugenio* a Man of Honour, Honeſty and Courage.

Eug. That Part of the World that thinks him ſuch, ſees thro' the wrong End of the Proſpective; his Honour's but Pretence, his Honeſty Hypocriſy, and his Courage Lewdneſs; he raviſht a Siſter of mine at *Rome*, for which I never can forgive him.

Pirro. This Fellow, I find is ripe for Miſchief; and if I durſt truſt him, wou'd, for a large Reward, remove *Eugenio*, and make *Lucaſia* indeed an Heireſs; and 'twere but juſt, ſince Count *Gravello* did deſign to wrong me of his Eſtate, why ſhou'd not I rob him of his Son? where could be the Danger of this Act? I can't fore-ſee any, for he has already given it out he's dead, and therefore dares not ſearch into the Matter; but is it ſafe to truſt this Stranger, he may betray my Purpoſe, or not do it; yet 'tis reaſonable to think the contrary, for he hates him for his Siſter's Rape, and therefore would be glad to meet Occaſion to revenge it, eſpecially when uſher'd in by a great Sum: I'm reſolv'd to break it to him. [*Aſide*.] What is your Name, Friend?

Eug. *Irus*, my Lord.

Pirro. Your Name as well as Habit ſpeak you poor.

Eug. I'm poor enough, my Lord.

Pirro. Very poor?

Eug. Very poor, my Lord.

Pirro. Would you not gladly mend your Fortunes.

Eug. I wiſh your Lordſhip wou'd ſhew me the Way.

Pirro. What think you now of taking Revenge for your Siſter's Rape, ha?

Eug. Alas! my Lord, that I wou'd have done long ago, but Want prevented my Eſcape.

Pirro. Say'ſt thou ſo? my Friend: well, poiſon this *Eugenio*, and thou ſhalt not want; for thy Reward, a thouſand Crowns are thine.

Eug. Think it done, my Lord, nor will I receive my Hire till I have brought you a certain Proof *Eugenio* is no more; all I aſk is but your Hand to the Agreement, my Lord, that I may be ſure of my Reward.

Pirro. I'll give it thee——We muſt be ſafe, for his Father will be aſham'd to proſecute, after his reported Death. I muſt confeſs I lov'd *Lucaſia* as an Heireſs, but was ſhe ten

time-

times as fair, I would not marry her without the Dowry, therefore make sure my Fortune by thy Master's Death.

Eug. He dies this Night.

SCENE *changes to the Grove.*

Enter Palante, Lucasia, *and* Clerimont.

Pal. 'Tis done, 'tis done, the sacred Knot is ty'd,
And bright *Lucasia* is for ever mine.
I ne'er 'till now did taste the Sweets of Life;
Or the transporting Extasy of Joy.
Burst not ye feeble Ministers of Nature,
With the vast Excess of swelling Pleasure.
Oh! my Friend, what shall I say to thee?

Cler. This is no Time for Talk, or Transports,
Make Use of my Fortune, and fly till the Pursuit is over.

Pal. Oh! *Clerimont*, I'm bankrupt every Way,
Both to thee, and to my fair *Lucasia*.
Still thou art sad, my Love.

Luc. My Sadness does proceed from Fear for thee,
Take your Friend's Counsel, let us fly this Place.
Hark! What Noise is that? ah me, we're lost.

Enter Gravello, Eugenio, Rosco, *and Officers.*

Grav. Fall on Officers, there they are.

Cler. Thieves.

Pal. Villains!

Grav. Thou art thyself the Thief and Villain too;
Give me my Daughter, thou Ranter.

Pal. First take my Life.

Grav. Fall on, I say; down with 'em if they resist,

Luc. Oh! we are undone, wicked, wicked *Laura.*

Pal. Come on, Slaves. [*They fight, but are disarm'd by*

Cler. We shall not surrender tamely. [*the Multitude.*

Grav. So, keep 'em fast, we'll have 'em faster shortly.
For you, Minion, I shall secure you from a second 'Scape.

Luc. Yet do but hear me, Father.

Grav. Call me not Father, thou disobedient Wretch,
Thou Vagabond, thou art no Child of mine;
My Daughter was bred up to Virtue:

Luc. For you my Mother wou'd have done as much:
If Need had so required;
Think not that my Mind e'er stray'd from Virtue;
Oh! listen to the Voice of my Prayer, and Crown
It with rich Mercy.

Grav.

Grav. Off, Strumpet, Officers away with the Criminals,
They both shall die.

Pal. Now I must speak, oh spare my Friend, for he
Is innocent.

Cler. If thou must die, *Palante*, I have no
Other Wish, but to suffer with thee.

Grav. That Wish assure thyself thou shalt obtain.

Luc. Oh stay blood-thirsty Men, stay and hear me
But a Word, and that shall be my final Resolution.
If thou, my cruel Father wilt not hear,
But dost proceed to spill the Blood of him
In whom my Life subsists, remember, Sir,
I am your Daughter, once you did love me;
Oh! tell me then, what Fault can be so great
To make a Father Murderer of his Child?
For so you are in taking his dear Life;
Do not think that I will stay behind him.
No, whilst there's Asps, and Knives, and burning Coals;
No *Roman* Dame's Example shall outgo
My Love.

Pal. Oh! my *Lucasia*, thou hast touch'd my Soul!
Barely but to imagine thou must die,
Will make me restless in my silent Grave.
Is not my Death sufficient, barbarous Man?
But must *Lucasia*'s Woe be added too?
Dry up those Tears my Wife, my lovely Bride,
Or thou wilt make me truly miserable,
Preserve thy Life, that I may after Death,
In thee my better Part survive.
For thee and for my Friend my only Prayers shall be,
If you both live, *Palante* dies with Pleasure.

Grav. Away with 'em, and let the Law decide it.

Luc. I too alike am guilty;
Oh let me share the Punishment with them,
Thou shalt not go alone, take me with thee;
Here are my willing Hands, quick bind 'em fast, [*Runs and*
Else here I'll hold 'till my last Breath expires. [*clasps* Palante.

Grav. Ungracious Viper, let go the Traitor.

Luc. What to die? Oh, never!

Pal. Had I a hundred Lives, the Venture had
Been small for such a Prize.
A Face not half so fair as thine has arm'd
Whole Nations in the Field for Battle ripe:

And

And brought a thousand Sail to *Tenedos*,
To sack lamented *Troy*, and shou'd I fear
To hazard one poor Life for thee, my Fair?
A Life that had been lost without thy Love,
For thou'rt both Life and Soul to thy *Palante*.

Luc. I'll clasp him like the last Remains of Life, [*Holds him*.
And struggle still with never dying Love.

Grav. Then thus I dash thee from him, thou Stranger [*Pushes her, and falls down*.
To my Blood, there lie and grovel on the Earth, and thank the Powers I do not kill thee; away to Justice with the Traitors.

Pal. If there be a Torment beyond this Sight,
Then lead me to it, that I may taste all
The Variety of Misery, and
Grow compleatly wretched.
Oh, inhuman Cruelty!
Slaves give me Way, that swift as Lightning,
I may dash him dead that wrong'd *Lucasia*.
You spiteful Powers show'r all your Curses down,
Augment the Weight, and sink me all at once.

Grav. Away with the Traitor.

Pal. Oh! Let me first embrace my Love, my Wife.

Grav. By Hell, he shall not.

Pal. *So when a Ship by adverse Winds is tost,*
And all the Hopes to gain the Port is lost,
The trembling Mariners to Heaven cry,
And all in vain, for no Relief is nigh.
Around fierce Terrors strike their aking Sight;
So I when shut from that all-charming Light,
Like them must plunge in everlasting Night.
[Exit. forc'd off.

Grav. I'll to the Governor, and urge my injur'd Suit. *Rosco* and *Irus*, guard that wretched Woman; take Care that she neither sends nor receives a Message. [*Exit*.

Rosco. Yes, my Lord.

Eug. My very Heart bleeds to see two such faithful Lovers parted; methinks my Lord's too cruel in this Action.

Ros. Ay, ay, Friend; but we are to obey, not to dispute his Will.

Eug. I can scarce forbear revealing myself, but I will reserve it for a fitter Hour; her Griefs so great, I fear it has deprived her of her Senses; look up, Madam.

Luc. Where's my *Palante*, gone to death? Oh Heav'n!

Then

Then shall I be mad indeed? what are you,
Officers of Justice? I'm ready, Sir.

Eug. No, Madam, I am one my Lord your Father left to attend you.

Luc. Attend me! alas, I need no Attendance.

Eug. Do not reject my Service.

Luc. All Service comes too late to miserable me;
My Fortune's desperate grown.

Eug. Believe me, Madam, I have a feeling Woe;
A greater your own Brother could not have:
Think not I'm suborn'd to do you wrong,
By all the Powers I'm your trusty Friend,
Command me any Thing, and try my Faith.

Ros. This is a rare spoken Fellow; I can't put in a Word.

Luc. Oh! 'tis most prodigious;
Cou'd I lose Pity in a Father's Breast,
And find it in a Stranger's? I shall not
Live to thank you, Sir, but my best Prayers go
With you.

Eug. 'Tis not for Thanks, nor for Reward I look,
But the sacred Love I bear to Virtue,
Makes me offer this.

Luc. Surely this poor Man is nobly bred, howe'er
His Habit speaks him. [*Aside*.
All Physic comes too late to my sick Mind,
Since there's no Hopes of my *Palante*'s Life.

Eug. Unless the Governor will please to pardon him, 'twas good that he were mov'd.

Ros. Be not so forward, Friend, I say; in my Conscience this Fellow will betray *Eugenio* lives.

Eug. Peace, Fool.

Ros. You are something free, methinks.

Luc. Who shall dare to make that Supplication?
My Father and the Count of *Pirro* rules;
Yet I wou'd venture, if I knew which Way.

Eug. So meritorious is the Act, that I wou'd stand the Test in giving you the Liberty to sue.

Ros. How, Sir?

Eug. Peace, Muckworm, or my Sword shall stop thy Breath for ever.

Ros. A desperate Fellow this, I dare not contradict him.

Luc.

Luc. A thousand Blessings on you for your Care,
Yes, I will go, grant it ye Powers above;
If you had e'er Regard to injur'd Love:
Teach me such Words as may his Pity move;
Let it pierce deep into his stony Heart,
In all my Sufferings make him feel a Part.
Oh make him feel the Pangs of sharp Despair,
That he may know what wretched Lovers bear:
My Sighs and Tears shall with Intreaties join,
That he would save Palante's *Life, or sentence mine:*
But if relentless to my Prayers he be,
And he must fall, then welcome Destiny.
Fate does our Lives so close together twine,
Who cuts the Thread of his unravels mine. [Exeunt.

SCENE *the Governor's House*.

Enter the Governor and Count Pirro.

Gov. Welcome, my dearest Nephew, you are grown a Stranger to the Court of late, tho' you know my aged Sight receives no Joy without you; but I can forgive you since Love is the Cause: I hear you have the Lord *Gravello*'s Consent to marry the fair *Lucasia*.

Pirro. I had, my Lord, but am unjustly robb'd of that fair Prize you mention; my promis'd Bride is stolen by *Palante*, Lord *Euphenes*'s Foster-Son, a Man far unworthy of *Lucasia*'s Love; her Father with Officers are gone to apprehend 'em——and bring 'em here before you to receive their Doom: Oh, Uncle, if ever you had a Kindness for me; if the being ally'd to you by Blood, or aught I have done, or can hereafter do, let me intreat you to give the Law its utmost Course: Young *Clerimont* too assisted in the Rape.

Gov. Fear not, Nephew, the Law shall have its Course, and they shall surely die.

Enter Euphenes *and Count* Gravello *at several Doors*.

Euph. My Lord, the Governor, I am come begging to you, for *Palante* my Foster-Son, whom, Childless, I adopted for my own; for him I plead.

Gov. What is his Offence?

Euph. No heinous Crime, my Lord, no treasonable Plot against your Person or the State, for then these aged Cheeks wou'd blush to ask Pardon. No crying Murder stains his Hands, his Fault is only Love: Unfortunately he has married the Daughter and Heiress to that proud Lord that follows, and seeks the last Extremity.

Grav.

Grav. I seek no more than what the Law will give; I am abus'd, my Lord, my Daughter is stoll'n, the only Comfort of my Age: Justice, my Lord, 'tis Justice that I ask.

Pirro. To his just Suit I bend my Knees—be not biass'd by aught but Justice.

Euph. Thou speakest like an Enemy, call it Revenge—— not Justice——My Lord.——

Gov. I'll hear no more, be silent; if the Law will save him, he shall live, if not, he dies; yes, my Lord, you shall have Justice —— [*Exeunt*.

SCENE *changes to* Gravello's *House*.

Enter Larich, Francisco, *and* Lavinia.

Lar. Body o'me! here's mad Work abroad, my Niece is stolen: I'm resolv'd to make sure of you; the Priest shall join you instantly.

Fran. Haste, Sir, to consummate our Joy:
I'll call the Muses from their sacred Hill,
To emulate your Daughter's Beauty;
And I'll, myself, in lofty Numbers sing my own
Epithalamium.

Lar. First, I'll punish that Impostor —— Here, bring in the Prisoner.

Lav. Oh! I fear we are undone, *Francisco*,

Fran. Pray, Father, delay not my exorbitant Desires.

Lar. But for a Moment, learn'd Son,
And thy exorbitant Desires shall be satisfied.

Enter Sancho *and* Tristram, *forc'd in by Servants*.

San. Hey day! What's the Matter now: Is the old Gentleman grown generous? Must we take a Bottle in his own House, ha?

Lar. Sirrah, you are a very impudent Impostor.

San. Hey, what's here, Frank in my Cloaths? what is there a Play to be acted? ha? what Part must I play? I have acted a Part at the College e'er now, Pox on't, that College will run in my Head, pr'ythee what am I to play, *Francisco*.

Fran. The Fool, Sir.

San. That's something blunt tho' *Frank*.

Lar. Ha! what do I hear? *Francisco*? sure that's the Fellow my Daughter is in Love with, I must enquire into this.

Fran. My Reverend Patree, I hope you'll not credit this illiterate Idiot, you knew me by my Scholastic Breeding.

San. Why what does he mean now? Breeding! why, why,

why, why, you wer'nt half ſo long at *Salamanca* as I, *Frank,* if you go to that *Triſtram,* where are my Books, *Triſtram?* we'll ſoon ſee who's moſt learn'd.

Γέρων πίθηκος ὐχ ἁλίσκεται πάγις.

You muſt not think to catch old birds with Chaff.

Δὶς διὰ πασῶν ἐςι παρὰ ἄλληλα.

He knows not a Hawk from a Handſaw.

Fran. The Man's diſtracted, Sir, away with him to Priſon.

San. To Priſon! nay, then the Truth ſhall out, that Habit's mine, and theſe Cloaths are his, he told me that this Lady wou'd hate a Scholar, and taught me how to act the Bully, fackins he did now, aſk *Triſtram* elſe.

Lar. Here's ſtrange juggling, I believe neither of you is Seignior *Sancho*'s Son.

Triſt. Bleſs me, Sir, do you doubt my Maſter? why he's as like my old Maſter as if he was ſpit out of his Mouth.

Lav. Methinks now by the Deſcription, Father, this Scholar muſt needs be Don *Sancho,* and this aukward Beau but a Pretender.

Lar. Peace, I'll have none of your Judgment.

San. A Pretender, odſbud, I find ſhe is in Love with a Schol[illegible], [illegible]t a Sot was I to be perſuaded to change my Hab[illegible] [illegible]hall be fobb'd of my Miſtreſs, by and by, why F[illegible] G[illegible]y thou wilt not fob me wilt thou.

Lar. Right, that Project will take, —— come who produces me a Letter from my Friend, I know the Hand, and that ſhall decide the Buſineſs.

Triſt. Here, here, Sir, here's Letters. [*Pulls out a Leather Pouch with Letters, and gives it to* Larich.

San. That's my Father's Hand, I can aſſure you, Sir, but the Stile is *Solomon*'s, they are freight with Wiſdom, but my Father pays the Poſtage.

Lav. Now we're undone, we are certainly betray'd.

Fran. Have Courage, I will ſtill be near thee, and prevent this Marriage or loſe my Life.

Lav. My Woman ſhall give you Notice of their Proceedings.

Lar. I am convinc'd, and worthy Sir, I aſk your Pardon, what an Eſcape have I had.

San. Pr'ythee *Frank* don't frown ſo, faith I forgive thee with all my Heart.

Fran. Away you Dolt——

San.

San. Fackings *Tristram,* he's woundy out of Humour, I have fob'd him now Faith, he, he, he.

Lar. Sir, I desire your scholastic Breeding wou'd quit my temporal Habitation to *Francisco,* least I commit you to a closer Place, and thank this Gentleman for your Liberty, 'tis because he has some small Acquaintance with you, that I don't proceed in a rougher Manner.

Fran. I am defenceless now, but I shall find a Time. [*Exit.*

Lar. To be hang'd I hope, come Mrs. I suppose you had a Hand in this wise Plot, I'll prevent your Stratagems, I'll noose and fetter you in the Chains of Wedlock, then if you plot, let *Sancho* look to't.

For when they are wed the Father's Care is done,

Trist. *And the poor doting Husband's just begun.*

ACT IV. SCENE *the Governor's House. The Governor in a Chair reading.*

Gov. I Have been searching over all our *Sicilian* Laws, and know they cannot find one Clause to save *Palante.*

Enter a Servant.

Serv. A Lady without, my Lord will not be deni[ed] Presence.

Gov. Admit her.

Enter Lucasia.

Luc. Pardon me, Sir, for pressing thus rudely
On your Privacy, I know 'tis boldness.
But I hope the Hour's propitious to me,
Finding you alone, and free from Business,
I promise myself I shall be heard with Patience.

Gov. Were the Business of the World at stake, such
Beauty would claim a Hearing, speak Madam.

Luc. Thus low I beg for poor *Palante*'s Life.

Gov. Ha!

Luc. Oh, Sir.
If ever Pity touch'd your gen'rous Breast,
If ever Virgin's Tears had Power to move,
Or if you ever lov'd and felt the Pangs
That other Lovers do, pity, great Sir,
Pity and pardon two unhappy Lovers.

Gov. Your Life is not in Question, Madam,

Luc,

Luc. If *Palante* dies, I cannot live, for we
Have but one Heart, and can have but one Fate.

Gov. What I can do, I will to ſave him, but Law muſt have its Courſe, riſe Madam.

Luc. Never till———
The gracious Word of Pardon raiſes me,
There's Pity in your Eye, oh! ſhew it, Sir!
And ſay that he ſhall live, 'tis but a Word,
But oh, as welcome as the Breath of Life,
Why will you part two Hearts that Heav'n has join'd?
He is my Huſband, Sir, and I his wedded Wife.

Gov. That can plead no Excuſe, for 'tis your Crime, but if I ſhou'd incline to pity you, what wou'd you return? what wou'd you do to purchaſe the Life of him you hold ſo dear?

Luc. You cannot think the Thing I would not do.
Speak, Sir, and lay it but in my Power,
And even beyond my Power I will attempt.

Gov. You wou'd be thankful then ſhou'd I pardon him?

Luc. If I were ever thankful unto Heav'n
For all that I call mine, my Health and Being.
Cou'd I then be unthankful unto you,
For a Gift I value more than thoſe?
Without which all other Bleſſings will be taſteleſs.

Gov. Thoſe that are thankful ſtudy to requite, wou'd you do ſo?

Luc. As far as I am capable I will,
Tho' I can ne'er make ample Satisfaction,
All my Services to you are Duty,
But to thoſe Pow'rs above that can requite
That from their waſteleſs Treaſure daily heap
Rewards more out of Grace than Merit on
Us Mortals;
To thoſe I'll pray that they wou'd give you, Sir,
More Bleſſings, than I have Skill to aſk.

Gov. There riſes one Way and but one to ſave him.

Luc. Oh! name it, Sir, that———
Swift as the Arrow from the Archer's Hand
My trembling Feet may fly to ſave him,
Oh! you have rais'd me from the Gulph of Grief
To that bleſt comfortable Region, Hope,
My Senſes all dance in the Cirque of Joy.
My raviſh'd Heart leaps up to hear your Words,
And ſeems as 'twou'd come forth to thank you.

Say,

Say, how, how shall I save him?

Gov. Marry my Nephew *Pirro* and *Palante* lives.

Luc. Oh! unexpected Turn of rigid Fate,
Cruel, Sir, far more cruel than my Father.
Why did you raise me to a Height of Joy?
To sink me in a Moment down again,
In what a sad Dilemma stands my Choice,
Either to wed the Man my Soul most loaths,
Or see him die for whom alone I live.
To break my sacred Vows to Heav'n and him,
To save a Life which he would scorn to take
On Terms like those, name any Thing but that,
You are more just than to enforce my Will,
Why should I marry one I cannot love,
And sure I am I cannot love Count *Pirro*,
Love him! no, I shou'd detest and loath him,
The Cause that made him mine, wou'd hourly add
Fresh Matter for my Hate.

Gov. You have your Choice, I swear by Heaven never to pardon him, but upon these Conditions.

Luc. Oh! I am miserable.

Gov. 'Tis your own Fault, come consider Madam, *Palante* will thank you for his Life, and if you let him die, you are the Tyrant.

Luc. I shou'd be such if I shou'd save him thus.
Since you have swore not to save him upon
Other Terms, I'll shew a duteous Cruelty
And rather follow him in Death than so,
To buy his Life, no, I despise the Price.
Why do I breathe my Woes, or beg for Mercy here;
Or hope to find plain Honesty in Courts?
No, their Ears are always stopp'd against Justice,
Avarice and Pride supplies the Place of Pity.
So may just Heav'n when you for Mercy sue,
As you have pitied me so pardon you. [Exeunt severally.

SCENE *Count* Gravello's *House*.

Enter Larich, Lavinia, Sancho *and* Tristram.

San. Is the Priest ready *Tristram?*

Trist. Yes, yes, Sir, a Priest and a Lawyer are always in Readiness, their Tongues are the chief Instrument belonging to their Trade, with which they commonly do more Mischief than all the Surgeons in the Kingdom can heal, he waits in the next Room, Sir, if you can get the Lady in the Mind.

Lar. You are witty Sirrah, but no more of your Jests, do ye hear, least I make you experience, there's something else can do Mischief besides their Tongues, come Mistress what you are in the Dumps now, are you? dry up your Eyes and go about it chearfully, or I'll turn you out of Doors, I assure you.

Lav. Good, Sir, consider.

Lar. Consider! no I won't consider, nor shall you consider upon ought but what I'd have you.

Lav. Sir, do you persuade him [*To* Sanch.] think how unhappy I shall make you.

San. Make me happy first, and then I'll do any Thing you'd have me.

Trist. The wisest Bargain I ever heard my Master make.

Lav. What wou'd you do, Sir, with me that cannot love you? Alas I was engaged long before I saw you, you may be happier far elsewhere, go court some Nymph whose Heart's intirely free, such only can be worthy of your Love.

San. For my Part I don't know what to say.

Lar. 'Zdeath she'll persuade him by and by to quit his Pretences to her,——come, come, come Mistress no more of your Cant. [*Pulls her by the Arm*.] It shall avail you nothing I'll promise you.

Lav. Good, Sir, hold a little, Don *Sancho* seems disposed to hear Reason.

San. Why ay truly, for my Part methinks 'tis a Pity to vex the Lady so.

Lav. Besides, Sir, 'tis for his sake I do it, to make him easy, and to prevent his eternal Shame and Torture.

San. Poor Fool, how hard it is, ay, ay, I know 'tis for my Sake, pray, Sir, hear her—pray do for my Sake as she says.

Lar. Pooh Fool.

San. Shall she say more for my Sake, than you'll hear Father that is to be.

Lar. Well Huzzy, consider what you say, for if it be'nt to the Purpose, as I'm sure it won't———look to't?

Lav. Before your hasty Rashness betrays me to eternal Woe, revoke your harsh Commands.

Lar. Ay, I knew that would follow, and this is all you have to say, Mistress, ha? come, come Woe, I'll woe you.

Lav. Something I have to speak, but know not in what Words to dress my Thoughts fit for me to speak, or you to

hear,

hear, oh ſpare the poor Remains of my already too much violated Modeſty, -- Heav'n can I do this, but there is no other Way. [*Aſide*.

Lar. How? how? how's that? Modeſty! why what a Duce is the Matter with your Modeſty, ha?

Lav. Oh! Sir, force me not to wrong a Man whoſe Father I have ſo often heard you ſay, you lov'd, think what ſure Diſgrace will follow, how will it reflect upon your Name and Family, when I ſhall be found no Virgin.

Lar. Ha! no Virgin? take Heed Minion that you ſtain not the Honour of my Houſe, for if you do, I ſwear by the beſt Blood in *Sicily*, my Sword ſhall do me Juſtice.

Lav. Now help me Courage, and forgive me Heaven my Reſolutions, Death or my *Franciſco*. [*Aſide*.
I throw myſelf beneath your Feet, thus proſtrate beg for Mercy, that I have deſerved Death my guilty Bluſhes own, the mighty Secret hangs upon my Tongue, but Shame refuſes Utterance to my Words.

Lar. I'm all of a cold Sweat, Heav'ns! how I dread the End of her Diſcourſe.

San. Pray Father let her riſe, or I ſhall weep too.

Triſt. Nay, I'll ſay that for my Maſter, he's as tractable as a Monkey, and generally does what he ſees other People do. [*Aſide*.

Lav. Oh! let it ſtill remain unknown, and rather baniſh me, confine me to ſome horrid Deſart, there to live on Roots and withered Graſs, and with the falling Dew, ſtill quench my Thirſt, and laſtly to ſome ſavage Monſter be a Prey, e'er I divulge my Shame.

San. I can hold no longer. [*Cries aloud*.

Lar. On, for I'll hear it all, tho' thou ſhalt live no longer than thou haſt told thy Tale.

Lav. Sure ne'er before was Maid thus wretched, Oh *Franciſco*! I give thee here the greateſt Proof of Love that ever Woman gave—— if it muſt out, then with it take my Life, but Oh! ſpare the innocent Babe.

Lar. Ha! the Babe?

Lav. Oh! I am with Child.

Lar. Then die both, and both be damn'd. [*Offers to ſtab her, but is prevented by* Sancho *and* Triſtram.

Sanc. Oh, Lord, Sir, for Heavens Sake, Sir, are you mad, help *Triſtram*.

Lar. 'Zdeath a Whore! Oh thou Scandal of my Blood.

San. Egad I'm resolv'd to own the Child, and bully this old Fellow a little now —— a Whore, Sir! who dares call my Wife a Whore? the Child is mine, Sir, let me see who has any Thing to say to't.

Lar. Away, don't trifle with me, I shall not give you Credit.

San. What care I whether you do or no, I say again the Child is mine, Madam, dry your Eyes, I like you ne'er the worse, and the World will like me the better for't, it will bring me into Reputation.

Lav. Oh Heavens! what will come on me now, Oh! fly me, Sir, as you wou'd shun Contagion, cou'd you receive into your Arms a Wretch polluted by another.

San. Pish, shaw, pish, shaw, 'tis the least Thing in a thousand, thou said thou didst it for my Sake just now, and sure I shou'd return the Kindness, Ingratitude is worse than the Sin of Witchcraft.

Lar. Oh! the audacious Strumpet, give me Way, that I may punish the Offence as it deserves. [Francisco *within*.

Fran. Slaves give me Way, he dies that barrs my Entrance.

Lav. Ha! 'tis my *Francisco*'s Voice—Oh! blest Minute.

Lar. Ha! what Noise is that? [*Help, Murder cry'd within*.

San. How Murder within and Murder without too, this is a barbarous House, I wish I was safe out on't. *Tristram* stand by thy Master.

Tristr. Oh, Sir, I had rather run with you, for I hate Murder in cool Blood.

Enter Francisco *with his Sword drawn*.

Lar. Help within there, murder, you won't murder me Sirrah, ha? [*Enter three or four Servants*.] run for the Corregidore, I shall be murder'd in my own House.

Fran. No, Sir, this Sword can never hurt the Father of *Lavinia*, nor will my Arm guide it to any Act unjust, nor is it drawn for aught but to defend my Wife.

Lar. Impudent Rascal, can'st thou look me in the Face, and know how thou hast injur'd me, thou hast dishonour'd my Daughter.

San. Sir, I say no Man has dishonour'd her but myself, and I wonder you shou'd tax this honest Gentleman with it.

Fran. Ha, Villain! re-call what you have said, or by Heaven 'tis thy last, 'tis safer playing with a Lion, than with *Lavinia*'s Fame. [*Holding his Sword at his Teeth*.

San. *Lavinia*'s Fame, what Fame, what makes you so choc eric, I thought I shou'd do the Lady a s in it.

Trist. Many a Man wou'd have been glad to have got rid of it so.

Lav. Humour my Father in what he says, for 'twas my last Stratagem to defer my Marriage. [*Aside to* Francisco.

Lar. *Lavinia*'s Fame! No Monster, thou hast robb'd, robb'd her of her Fame.

Fran. The Wrong my Love has done your fair Daughter, 'tis now to late too wish undone again, but if you please it may be clos'd up yet without Dishonour, I will marry her.

Lar. Marry her! she'll have a mighty Bargain of that, marry a Beggar, what Jointure canst thou make her?

Fran. I am poor, I must confess in regard of your large Wealth, but I swear by all Things that can bind, 'twas not your Wealth was the Foundation of true-built Love, it was her single uncompounded self, her self without Addition that I lov'd, which shall ever in my Heart out-weigh all other Womens Fortunes with themselves, and were I great, great as I cou'd wish myself for her Advancement, no such Bar as Fortune's Inequality shou'd stand betwixt our Loves.

Lar. Say you so, Sir, why then take her —— there hang, drown'd or starve together, I care not which, but never come within my Doors more. [*Throws her to him. Exit.* Larich.

San. Hey day, what have I lost my Mistress then, why what must I say to my Father, *Tristram*, who'll run stark mad without Hopes of a Grandson.

Tristr. Oh, Sir, if this Gentleman had not put in his Claim, here had been one ready to his Hands.

San. Ah Pox on't, 'tis damn'd unlucky, but come let's to the Tavern and drink away Sorrow. [*Exeunt.*

Fran. Come my fair *Lavinia,* and find a Father in thy Husband's Arms, oh thou charming Excellence, thou something better sure than ever Woman was, the matchless Proof that thou hast given of thy Love shall be recorded to Posterity——

Lav. It is a matchless one indeed, and I struggled long e'er I cou'd bring myself to own a Deed so distant from my Heart, but it has serv'd my Purpose, and I glory in it now, but my Fathers last Words methinks chills my Blood, how shall you like the Yoke without lining think you ha!

Fran. Don't wrong my Love *Lavinia,* or think that I can want any Thing when possest of thee.

Love shall make up what Fortune does deny,
And Love alone shall all our Wants supply. [Exeunt.

The SCENE *changes to the Street, Count* Pirro *and Lord* Gravello.

Grav. Now my Lord ſhe's your's again, *Palante* dies.

Pirro. So noble were the Carriage of the Youths that I could almoſt pity their hard Sentence.

Grav. I admire *Palante*'s Conſtancy, he ſeem'd regardleſs when the Jury pronounc'd his Sentence, as if he feared not Death, but when his Friends came on, I obſerved the Tears to fall.

Pirro. He begg'd very hard to ſave his Friend.———

Grav. And his Friend as eagerly to die with him, truly I think *Clerimont*'s Crime did not deſerveDeath, but our *Sicilian* Laws dooms all to Death that have but the leaſt Hand in ſtealing of an Heireſs, but ſee the Lord *Euphenes*, he ſtickled hard to ſave his Foſter Son, let's avoid him, for I know he'll rail. [*Exit.*

Enter Lord Euphenes.

Euph. Unhappy poor *Palante*, the Law has caſt thee in Spite of all that I could do to ſave thee, I'd give my whole Eſtate to reſcue thee from Death: In thee methought my loſt *Lyſander* liv'd, and in loſing thee I'm childleſs now indeed. I lov'd thee like my own Son, I reſcu'd thee from Pyrates, by which my Child was loſt.

Enter Alphonſo.

Alphon. Thus once again from twenty Years Exile.
(Toſt by the Storms of Fortune to and fro)
Has gracious Heav'n giv'n me Leave to tread
My native Earth of *Sicily*, and draw
That Air that fed me in my Infancy.

Euph. Ha! either my Eyes deceive me or 'tis my good old Friend *Alphonſo.*

Alph. My Lord *Euphenes?*

Euph. *Alphonſo*, welcome to *Sicily*, I thought thee dead with my unhappy Son, or what was worſe, in Slavery, where no Intelligence cou'd find thee, for I have us'd my utmoſt Diligence.

Alph. In Part you have gueſs'd aright, for I have been twenty tedious Years in gauling Slavery, for when the *Argives* ſurprized the Fort they hurried me on board, and becauſe I made a brave Reſiſtance, they ne'er wou'd give me Leave to offer at my Ranſom, ſo violent was their Hate, but now worn out with Age, unfitting for their Labour, they turn'd me Home, an uſeleſs Drone, your Son they

put

put on board another Ship, and by some I heard it rumoured, he being wondrous fair, that they design'd to breed him for the Sultan's Use, but some Years after I heard he was retaken on this Coast.

Euph. Ha!

Alph. I conceal'd his Name, least the many Conquests you have gain'd against them shou'd have wing'd their Revenge, and made 'em kill the lovely Child, I call'd him *Palante*, have you ever heard of such a one?

Euph. Oh all ye immortal Powers, the very same, I took, and is *Palante* then *Lysander*, and have I found thee once to lose thee ever?

Albp. Ha! what means all this?

Euph. 'Twas Nature then that work'd my Soul, and I by Instinct lov'd him. Oh my *Alphonso*, this Discovery comes too late, and instead of bringing Comfort to my Age, thou hast plung'd me down in deep Despair.

Alph. Alas, my Lord, how have I err'd? pray explain yourself.

Euph. Oh *Alphonso*! the Youth thou speak'st of I retook from *Argive* Pirates, I bred him, and tho' not sensible who he was, I lov'd him tenderly: He is this very Day condemn'd for stealing of an Heiress, now judge if my Grief falls not with Weight upon me.

Alph. Unfortunate Mischance, is there no Way to save him?

Euph. None I fear, but yet I'll try all Means, if my long Service to my Country, my Winter Camps, and Summer Heats, and all my stormy Fate at Sea can plead, I will expand my Deeds as *Rome*'s Consuls did of old, make bare my Breast, and shew my scar'd Bosom to move and raise their Pity.

I that ne'er mention'd aught my Arm has done,
Will now urge all to save my darling Son. [Exeunt.

ACT V. SCENE *a Prison*.

Palante *and* Clerimont *come forward*.

Pal. OH! *Clerimont*, I swear by my malignant Stars,
Death brings no Terrors with it but for thee;
The Thoughts of thine, and that I have involv'd
In my sad Fate, my best and only Friend,

Sits heavy on my Soul, and gives me double Death:
My Father's Tears, whom now too late I know,
Pierce not my Breast with half this killing Grief,
This gnaws me worse than my *Lucasia*'s Loss;
And, like a *Vulture*, preys upon my Heart.
I was rewarded, call'd *Lucasia* mine:
For such a Treasure who wou'd refuse to die?
But thou'rt condemn'd for only aiding me,
I am the Cause of thy sad Fate, my Friend;
Hurry'd by me to an untimely Grave:
Thou fall'st for him thou ever hast oblig'd.

Cler. No more *Palante*———
Why dost thou call me by the Name of Friend?
Yet think I cou'd descend from Friendship's Rules:
For so I must shou'd I repine at Death,
Or fear to suffer with so brave a Man.
To die is nothing to a Man resolv'd:
Why shou'd we wish to hold this mortal Frame,
By Nature subject to such various Ills,
Which first or last brings certain Death to all?
Were there no Hand, indeed, but human Laws
To cut the Thread of our Mortality,
Then we had Cause for Grief; but when we reflect
We only leap th' Abyss a little sooner,
Where all Mankind must follow by degrees,
The Apprehension moves not me.

Pal. Oh! Noble Constancy———
After Ages shall record the Story,
And rank thee with the bravest *Roman* Youths;
And melancholy Virgins when they read,
In moving Accents celebrate thy Name.

Cler. What baleful Planet rul'd when thou wer't born,
That mark'd for thee this Path of Sorrow out?
Oh! ye malicious Stars, when ye had stood
So long the rude Buffets of blind Fortune,
And now just as the pleasing Scene appear'd,
I' th' Moment when th' art found of noble Birth,
And wed to thy long wish'd for Bride *Lucasia*,
Then to snatch thee hence, is twice to kill thee.
Oh! it is the Mock'ry of spiteful Fates,
When we with Labour reach the aim'd at Wish,
Straight this unstable Fairy World removes.
We die, or are dash'd back again to what we were.

Enter

Enter Eugenio *and* Lucasia.

Luc. Faithful *Irus* how shall I reward thee?
Ha! see where stands *Palante* and his Friend!
Oh! lead me *Irus*, quickly, lead me back,
Else I shall grow a Statue at this Sight:
Not all the frightful Noise of Chains we've past,
And meagre Looks of Wretches in Despair,
Are half so terrible as this.

Pal. My *Lucasia!*
Art thou come to take thy last Adieu, and
Bless my Eyes before they close for ever?

Luc. Oh! *Palante!*

Pal. What! no more? Give thy labouring Sorrows vent,
That like Convulsions heaves thy snowy Breasts,
And struggles for a Passage to thy Tongue.

Luc. O! I had dy'd e'er seen this fatal Hour;
But this good Man pursu'd with Care my Steps,
And stop'd my Hand, which else had giv'n the Blow,
When first I heard the sad and dreadful News,
That thou, *Palante*, wer't condemn'd to die.

Eug. Still all I ask is, that you wou'd have Patience;
I'll to Court where Lord *Euphenes* is,
Now begging for his Son, in Hope to bring you Happiness.
[*Exit.* Eug.

Luc. Fly *Irus*, fly, and bring us instant Word.
Oh! my aking Brain is near Distraction;
For much I fear there is no Help for me.

Pal. Yet I rejoice in this, I'm found of Noble Birth——
That in succeeding Ages, when this Act,
With all its Circumstances shall be told,
No Blot may rest upon thy Virgin Fame;
No censuring Tongue reflect upon thy Choice;
And say thy Husband was a Wretch unknown,
And quite unworthy of *Lucasia*'s Arms.

Luc. What Comfort's in this late Discovery found?
Will the Greatness of thy Race protect thee?
Virtue and ev'ry Good was thine before;
Yet the cruel Pow'rs are deaf to all my Prayers:
Nor will thy Merit plead with angry Heav'n,
To ward the Stroke, and save thy precious Life.
Oh Greatness! thou vain and vap'rish Shew,
That, like a Mist, dazzles the Eyes of Men,
And as the Fogs destroy the Body's Health,

That poisons deep, and gangrenes in the Soul;
But seldom's found t' assist the virtuous Man.
Thou wert———
As dear to these desiring Eyes before,
And honour'd full as much in this poor Heart.
Oh! I cou'd curse the separating Cause,
And wish *Lucasia* never had been born.

Pal. Be calm, my Love, my everlasting Dear,
Cease to lament, and give thy Spirits ease.
Oh! hear me Heav'n, and grant my last Request;
May Health, long Life, and ev'ry Bliss beside,
Conduce to make *Lucasia* happy still.
Let nothing fall to interrupt her Joy,
But make it lasting as you make it great.
Grant this, and I to rigorous Destiny
Submit with Pleasure.

Luc. Long Life; no, rather wish me sudden Death,
To rid me of my Cares, and that Way give me Ease.
Ha! I'm seiz'd with an unusual Terror, Fear
And Horror swim in Shades of Night around,
How sad and dreadful are these Prison Walls!
Thy Voice seems hollow too, and Face looks pale.
Oh! my *Palante*, my Heart———
Throbs, as if the Strings of Life were breaking.
[*A Bell tolls within.*
Hark! hark! Oh! 'twas this that it foretold.
Ope' Earth, hide me in thy unfathom'd Womb,
To drown the Call of Fate——this dismal Bell.

Cler. Madam———
Be patient, add not to his Misery;
For whilst he sees you thus, his Soul's unfit
For aught but Earth; th' Approach of Death is near,
A little Time is necessary now,
To calm his Mind to suffer like a Man.

Luc. Oh! Heav'n help me. [*Faints.*

Pal. Oh! She's dying; do not thus rend my Soul with Grief.

Enter an Officer.

Officer. Gentlemen, this, Bell gives warning, that within Half an Hour you must prepare to die.

Pal. 'Tis very well, we shall be ready.
Canst thou conduct this Lady to her Father's House?

Luc.

Luc. Stand off, and touch me not: No, I will ſtay with thee. Do not puſh me from thee, my dear *Palante*; For I ſhall die apace, and go before.

Officers. The Officers all wait to conduct ye to the Place of Execution.

Cler. We come now, Friend, when ſhall we meet again.

Pal, The bleſs'd Pow'rs can tell, in Heav'n ſure.

Luc. *Oh! all ye Maids that now are crown'd above;*
Did any feel, like me, the Wrecks of Love?
By Tempeſts torn from my dear Huſband's Side,
And made a Widow, when I'm ſcarce a Bride.

SCENE *the Governor's Houſe*.

Enter Governor and Count Pirro, *and Lord* Gravello.

Govern. This is ſtrange *Palante* ſhould be found The Lord *Euphenes*'s Son; but fear not Nephew, the Law has paſs'd, and he ſhall ſuffer.

Pirro. I urge ſtill, my Lord, ſhe was my promiſed Wife; Her. Father ſo deſign'd her, had he then been known *Euphenes*'s Son. I urge that, ſpeak my good Father.

Grav. My Lord, I had; yet let me own, I rather wiſh the unknown *Palante*, had ſuffer'd for my Daughter, than the Son of one, who tho' my Foe, I muſt acknowlege great and brave.

Govern. So wou'd I my Lord, but there's no Fence for Accidents; I do expect to be beſet with Prayers and Tears, but all in vain; ſee where he comes.

Enter Euphenes *and* Alphonſo.

Euph. Behold! Lord Governor, my aged Knees, are bent to thee,
'Tis in thy Power to wreſt this heavy Judgment of the Law;
Suſpend it at leaſt, till the King ſhall hear the Cauſe,
And ſave my Son.

Gover. Riſe *Euphenes*, your Speech carries a double Meaning, you pray and threaten with the ſame Breath, we are not to be frighted Lord; the Laws of *Sicily* have had their Courſe, your Son falls by them.

Euph. Oh! miſtake me not, I am as humble as your Pride can wiſh me; but give me Leave to ſpeak, tho' 'tis my hard Fortune to offend; let me the Anguiſh of my Soul deliver to that injurious Lord, the Father of *Lyſander*'s, or by the more known Name, *Palante*'s Wife; hard-hearted Man! had'ſt

th-

[redacted]

Luc. Stand off, [illegible]
Do not push me from [illegible]
For I shall die [illegible]

Officers. The [illegible] Place of Execution.

Cler. We come now. [illegible]

Pal. The [illegible]

Luc. [illegible]

SCENE [illegible]

Enter [illegible]

Gov. [illegible] *Palante* [illegible]
The Lord [illegible] the Law has pass'd, and he shall suffer.

Pirro. I urge [illegible] Her Father [illegible] *Euphenes's* Son. I urge [illegible] my good Father.

Grac. My Lord, [illegible] the unknown *Palante*, [illegible] the Son of one, who [illegible] acknowledge great and brave.

Govern. So wou'd I my Lord, but [illegible] Accid[illegible] Tears, but all [illegible]

Enter [illegible]

E[illegible] My Lord Governor, my aged Knees, are

[illegible] Judgment of the Laws
[illegible] King [illegible] Cause,

[illegible] a double Mean-
[illegible] same Breath, we are not
[illegible] *Sicily* have had their

[illegible] humble as your Pride
[illegible]peak, tho' 'tis my hard
[illegible]h of my Soul deliver
[illegible]*sander*'s, or by the [illegible]
[illegible]d-hearted Man! [illegible]

thou no other Way to wreck thy canker'd and long foster'd Hate upon my Head, but this? Thus cruelly, by my Son's Suffering, and for such a Fault as thou shou'dst Love him, rather? Is thy Daughter injur'd by this Marriage? Is his Blood base? Or can his now rising Fortunes know an Ebb? This Law was made to restrain the Vile from wronging noble Persons, by Attempts of such a kind; but where Equality meets in the Match, there is no Crime; or if there is, forgive his Youth, and have Pity on him.

Gover. *Euphenes*, you wrong your Virtue when you'd save a Criminal, the Law condemns; tho' the righteous Judgment falls upon your Son, and your Appeal shall come too late.

Euph. Then you have set a Period to a loyal House and Family, that have been Props of the *Sicilian* Crown, and with their Blood in Wars, won many an honour'd Field. I can spend no more in Tears, I'll spend the sad Remnant of my childless Age, and only wish to rest i'th' Grave together.

Alph. Hear me thou Governor, not kneeling, but erect as old Age and Slavery has left me: This noble *Sicilian* Youth was lost in defending *Sicily* from the fam'd Fortress, which beat back a thousand Times, invading Foes, and sunk 'em in the working Seas, from thence the Child was ta'en, and must he 'scape the Hazards of the rowling Waves, Rocks, Tempests, Pirates, and ignominious Fate, to perish in his native Isle: Oh! barbarous Usage, stop yet at least his Judgment, and let this poor old Man see once again, his dear *Palante*; for that I'll bow my stubborn Knees, and ask the Blessings as I importune Heaven.

Euph. Oh! my Lord, let my unhappy Son appear before ye, e'er the cruel Sentence comes to Execution.

Grav. If you deny them this, it may be ill represented to the King.

Pirro. I fear, my Lord, you are staggering.

Gover. Nephew, be silent, and be safe; they shall have their Will, but to no Purpose, only a Moment's short Delay: for I have sworn, and he shall die——Guard bring here the Prisoner.

Euph. I thank the Governor.

Gov. Oh spare thy Thanks, till thou hast real Cause; the Law, the Statute's plain, and he must die for't, there is no Remedy.

Enter

Enter, brought in by the Guards, Palante, Clerimont, Lucasia *and* Eugenio.

Euph. Oh! Son!

Alph. Palante!

Pal. Pardon me, Sirs, I have too much of Tenderneſs upon my Soul already, too many Clogs that drag it downwards; oh! forgive me, if I beg ye wou'd not add more Weight to Death.

Gra. Madam, 'twere more becoming your Quality and Modeſty, to be at Home; thou doſt but ill return thy Father's Care.

Luc. I have no Father, nor ever had that I remember, but born and deſtin'd for an out-caſt Wretch, and curſt to ruin a moſt noble Huſband: Oh he was the Pride of the *Sicilian* Youths, and Glory of the World; but he is dead, or doom'd to die, and that's alike diſtracting.

Euph. Heav'n bleſs thee, thou Mirrour of thy Sex, that in the Sea of thy tranſcendant Virtues, drown'ſt all thy Father's Malice, and in my Thought, redeem'ſt more than thy Race can loſe.

Gov. Lord *Euphanes*, what End had you in this, in bringing here the Criminals?

Euph. To move your Mercy, was my End; but Wolves ·d Tygers know not what Pity means.

·v. Forbear Reproach, and hear me; I'll ſtand it ·King, and all the World; here is an Heireſs ſtole, the · Robberies; he is condemn'd by the Law, he fell ·dgment of the Law; I ſurrender him. Guards, · the Pris'ners.

· Oh! cruel Sentence! hear me, Sir.

·way with 'em.

·tay yet a little, thou moſt imperious Governor; ·e heard.

·hou! What art thou?

·y Name is *Irus*; Lord *Pirro* knows me.

·Ia!

·ou trembleſt, Lord, hear; you · ·ſe noble Friends, and hunt th· ·; ſentence to Death a Man for · ·; hear, a black Deed will ſtart · make you own the Crime befo·

Gov. What means the Fellow!

Eug. Nay, 'tis not a Frown can stop me, nor will my Fate be long; know then, this Lord gave out his Son *Eugenio* dy'd at *Rome*, but he was well, and in this City.

Palan. How say'st thou?

Luc. Proceed, dear *Irus*.

Eug. First stop Lord *Pirro*; for my Story will not please him: I say *Eugenio* lived; which when I discover'd to that trembling Lord, he brib'd me with a thousand Crowns to poison him: Here's the Agreement under his own Hand; and here's a Letter from *Eugenio* to his Father, which denotes that he was poison'd, and dying.

Gra. Let me see it: Oh! 'tis his Hand. Wretch that I am, is my dissembled Grief turn'd to true Sorrow? Were my acted Tears but Prophecies of my ensuing Woe? And is he dead? Oh! pardon me, dear Ghost of my *Eugenio!* 'twas my Crimes that call'd this hasty Vengeance from above, and shorten'd thus thy Life; for whilst with Fallacies I sought to fasten Wealth upon our House, I brought a Cannibal to be the Grave of me and mine; base, bloody, murdering Lord.

Pirro. Vile Cozener, Cheater and Dissembler, now indeed we both are caught.

Euph. Oh! cruel Man! now see the Justice of offended Heav'n; thou who pursu'st the poor *Palante*'s Life with so much Violence, thou now must feel the Weight of a Son's Loss.

Gov. This will prove a Tragedy indeed; away with the Prisoners. Your Trial's next, Lord *Pirro*.

Pirro. I do confess———

Eug. Hold, is there no Means left to save them? Wou'd not you now, Lord *Gravello*, give your Daughter freely to *Palante*?

Gra. More willingly than I wou'd live another Hour.

Euph. Oh! you are kind too late; had you been thus when Need required, you had sav'd yourself and me, and both our hapless Sons.

Gov. Oh Nephew, my Prompter still in Cruelty,
Now thou thyself must feel the Rigour of the Law.

Eug. Now ye behold the Good from Bad, which nought but this Extremity had shewn; yet all be safe, *Eugenio* lives, and fair *Lucasia* is no Heiress now.

Omnes.

Omnes. How ! lives !

Eug. Yes, lives to call thee Brother, worthy *Palante*, and thou, my dear *Lucasia*, Sister. [*Throws off his Disguise*.

Luc. Oh ! *Irus*, *Eugenio*, *Palante*, where am I ?

Palan. Oh ! *Lucasia*, *Clerimont* ; my Friend, my Love, my Wife.

Eug. Pardon me ye most afflicted Sufferers,
That I thus long have kept myself conceal'd;
My End was honest, to let my Father see
The Frailty, I will not call it by a harder Name,
Of Count *Pirro* ; the Son he coveted so eagerly,
To raise the Storms to their most dreadful Height,
That Calms, and Peace might be more pleasing.

Gra. I see it was *Eugenio*, and thou *Palante*.
Now, my Son, give me thy Hand, here take thy Wife,
And for the Wrong that I intended thee, thy Portion shall be double.

Pal. Oh! I am over-paid, *Lucasia* and my Friend secure.
This is the Work of Heav'n, and oh ye gracious Powers
I thank ye for it.

Cler. Joy rises from my Heart, and with unutterable Transports stops my Speech ; thus once again let me embrace thee.

Euph. And has a Father nothing from a Son ?

Alph. And old *Alphonso* too expects a Welcome.

Pal. Oh ! take me, Father, Brother, Friend, *Lucasia!*
There's the Sum of all.

Luc. Sure such Hours as these give us a Taste of Immortality.

Gra. My Lord *Euphanes*, I hope all Enmity is now forget betwixt our Houses.

Euph. Let it be ever so ; I do embrace your Love.
But speak *Eugenio*, what hast thou to ask ?
Whose timely Care prevented our undoing.

Eug. My Lord, you have a virtuous Niece, for whom
I long have sigh'd, I beg your leave to own my Flame.

Euph. She's yours; I've often heard her praise *Eugenio*.
And all things else within my Power command.
My Lord the Governor, you alone seem sad.

Gov. I am not so at your good Fortune, but that my Nephew whom I have found so base, urg'd me to such Cruelty :

Cruelty: Be gone, and hide thy ignominious Head, for I will never see thee more.

Pirro. No matter, I am free, and will enjoy myself in spight of all Mankind. [*Exit*

Gov. However this my Care shall do, I will solicit earnestly the King to mitigate this cruel Law, and make the Thefts of Love admit of Pardon.
Who have we here? they seem to rejoice too.

Enter Larich *singing*, Francisco, Lavinia, Sancho *and* Trist

Larich. Ha, hey, what, every body in Joy! Good News, Coz, *Palante* come off safe; my pretty Niece pleas'd here, and Son-in-law, *Francisco*, just receiv'd a certain Information of an Uncle's Death, that has left him, let me see, let me see; ay, ay, enough to please me.

Sancho. Nay, nay, hold, every body is not so well pleas'd neither; I am melancholy, I came hither to see the Execution; but I see no body has occasion to be hanged but myself, for I have lost my Mistress; faith I have,

Tristram. What Account shall I give my Father of this Match?

Tris. Fackins, Master, I cannot tell.

Larich. Then *Lavinia* is a pure Virgin still, for all the Tricks she play'd; faith she is: Was it not a sly one, ha, Brother?

Gra. I know nothing of the Matter.

Luc. Cousin, I wish you Joy, as large a Share as I possess, and Fate itself can give no more.

Lav. I am doubly bless'd to see you happy.

Fran And I have nothing left to wish.

Pal. Come, my *Lucasia*, now we are bless'd, let us retire, and give a loose to Raptures yet unknown.

Virtue survives thro' all the Turns of Fate,
Let not impatient Man think Mercy late;
For Heaven does still the justest Side regard,
And virtuous Lovers always meet Reward.

The End of the FIRST VOLUME.

9781332913497

BV - #0016 - 140323 - C0 - 229/152/21 - PB - 9781332913497 - Gloss Lamination